ANNALS OF
ENGLISH LITERATURE
1475–1925

ANNALS OF ENGLISH LITERATURE
1475–1925

THE PRINCIPAL PUBLICATIONS OF
EACH YEAR TOGETHER WITH AN
ALPHABETICAL INDEX OF AUTHORS
WITH THEIR WORKS

OXFORD
AT THE CLARENDON PRESS
1936

OXFORD
UNIVERSITY PRESS
AMEN HOUSE, E.C. 4
London Edinburgh Glasgow
New York Toronto Melbourne
Capetown Bombay Calcutta
Madras
HUMPHREY MILFORD
PUBLISHER TO THE
UNIVERSITY

First edition 1935
Reprinted with corrections 1936

PRINTED IN GREAT BRITAIN

PREFACE

THIS little book has its origin in an aspiration of Sir Walter Raleigh, who used to dream of *Annals of English Literature*. How many volumes such a work would comprise, if it listed every publication under its year, was never calculated; guesses might now be based on the bulk of the *Short-Title Catalogue, 1475–1640*.

The more modest purpose of the present compilation is to give the student, at a glance, the main literary output of any year or series of years; to show what books people were likely to be reading at any time, and with what rivals a candidate for literary fame had to reckon. Though the main object is to discover any book in its chronological setting, and so to serve the ends of a work of reference, it has been found in practice that these brief annals can be read continuously with profit, and even with pleasure.

The Index of Authors gives at once a conspectus of any literary career, and the means of studying it, by reference to the text, in its proper environment.

It has necessarily been assumed that the date of publication is that at which any work became public property and passed into the stream of national consciousness. This inference must, of course, be drawn with reserve in the earlier period. Before the invention of printing there was no datable publication; and after the invention of printing there are many famous examples of books which had profoundly influenced their age before they came to be printed.

The dates assumed are in general those on the title-page. It is well known that books published near the end of a year were often dated the year following; and there are other sources of confusion. But the error is not serious for the purposes of an elementary manual.

The principle of choice has been the inclusion of all the books (but not all the occasional writings, contributions to periodicals, and the like) of the major authors, and a selection of the more influential publications of the minors. It is not expected that the choice will meet with uniform approval; but the attempt has been made to keep the work in focus.

To economize space, and to avoid tedious iteration, Christian names have not as a rule been given in the main text, except to obscure or ambiguously named writers. The space so saved is used

v

for the birth-date (if known). Thus the author's age when he published a book is immediately apparent, and the reader is reminded that Pope was twenty-seven when he began to publish the *Iliad*, Dickens twenty-four when he began to publish *Pickwick*, and Hardy sixty-eight when he completed *The Dynasts*. If the Christian name is wanted, it will generally be found under the birth-year in the side column, and always in the Index. For posthumous works not the birth-date but the death-date is given, and the fact that publication was belated, and probably unauthorized, is at once apparent.

In the side-column are recorded the births and deaths of authors, the publication of newspapers, periodicals, translations, editions, and other compilations not to be classed as original literature; together with a selection of foreign events which had a bearing on the course of English literature.

The compilation of the Annals is the work of Mr. J. C. Ghosh, D.Phil.; the Annals 1901–25, and the Index, are the work of Miss E. G. Withycombe, B.A. The Index ends, in general, at 1925, but the opportunity has occasionally been taken to complete a literary career which has since been terminated by death, or to mention a recent edition of a classic. The publisher and compilers are indebted to a very large number of scholars who have read the work or parts of it in manuscript or in proof and have made valuable additions or removed serious errors.

Abbreviations:

P = Prose	T = Tragedy
V = Verse	C = Comedy
	D = Drama

Note on the Second Impression.

The rapid exhaustion of the first edition has made it necessary to reprint early. The opportunity has been taken to correct some errors and omissions; it is hoped that scholars will continue to report their discoveries.

1475

Gesta Romanorum, *c.* 1475.

Alexander Barclay b.?
Gavin Douglas b.?
Michelangelo b.
Caxton prints his first book
  'Recuyell of the His-
  tories of Troy' (trs.
  Raoul Le Fèvre) c. 1475
  at Bruges.

1476

Sir John Fortescue d.?
Caxton prints 'Game and
  Playe of the Chess' (trs.
  Jacobus de Cessolis) c.
  1476 at Bruges.
Caxton sets up press at
  Westminster.

1477

Caxton (1422?): History of Jason [n.d.]. P
Lydgate (d. 1450?): Temple of Glass [n.d.; prtd.
  Caxton; later edd. 1500 (?), 1530 (?)]. V
  Horse, Goose and Sheep [n.d.; prtd. Caxton;
  another ed. 1500(?)]. P
  Churl and the Bird [n.d.; prtd. Caxton; other
  edd. 1493 (?), 1520 (?)]. V
Wydeville, A., Earl Rivers: Trs. Dictes and Say-
  ings of Philosophers [first book printed by
  Caxton in England]. P

1478

Chaucer (d. 1400): Canterbury Tales [n.d.; prtd.
  Caxton; also 1484 (?); prtd. Pynson 1492 (?),
  1526; prtd. Wynkyn de Worde 1498; ed. Tyr-
  whitt 1775–8; Wright 1848–51; Furnivall
  1868 ff.; Skeat 1894–7]. P
  Trs. Consolation of Philosophy of Boethius
  [n.d.; prtd. Caxton]. P
  Parliament of Fowls [incl. Gentilesse, Truth,
  Fortune, Envoy to Scogan, Anelida and
  Arcite, Compleynte to his Purse; n.d.; prtd.
  Caxton]. V
Wydeville, A., Earl Rivers (1442?): Trs. Moral Pro-
  verbs of Christyne de Pise [prtd. Caxton]. P

Sir Thomas More b.
First book printed at Ox-
ford c. 1478.

1479

Caxton (1422?): Book of Courtesy [n.d.]. P
  Cordyale, or the Four Last Things [trs. attri-
  buted to A. Wydeville, Earl Rivers]. P
Lydgate (d. 1450?): Stans puer ad Mensam [n.d.].
  V

Caxton (1422?): Chronicles of England [called
    Caxton's Chronicle; really The Chronicle of
    Brute]. P
Lydgate (d. 1450?): Court of Sapience [n.d.]. V

1481

Caxton (1422?): Reynard the Fox [trs. Dutch]. P
    Mirror of the World [trs. Vincent de Beauvais].
    P
    Tully of Old Age [trs., through Fr., of Cicero]. P
    Godfrey of Boulogne [trs. Fr.]. P

*Pulci, 'Morgante Mag-
giore'.*

1482

Chaucer (d. 1400): Troylus and Creseyde [n.d.;
    prtd. Caxton; prtd. Wynkyn de Worde 1517,
    Pynson 1526]. V
Trevisa, John (d. 1402): Trs. Ranulph Higden's
    Polychronicon [another ed. 1495]. P

1483

Caxton (1422?): Golden Legend [n.d.; trs. Legenda
    Aurea of Jacobus de Voragine; other edd.
    1487 (?), 1493, 1498, 1512, 1527]. P
Gower, John (d. 1408): Confessio Amantis [other
    edd. 1493, 1532, 1534]. V
Lydgate (d. 1450?): Pilgrimage of the Soul [trs.
    Guillaume de Deguileville]. P

King Edward V.
King Richard III 1483–5.
Luther b.
Francesco Guicciardini b.

1484

Caxton (1422?): Trs. Æsop's Fables [Pynson's trs.
    1497 (?), 1500 (?); Middleton's 1550(?)]. P
    Order of Chivalry.
    Book of the Knight of the Tower [trs. Fr.].
Lydgate (d. 1450?): Life of our Lady [n.d.; also
    1531]. V

Ulrich Zwingli b.
Julius Caesar Scaliger b.
Pulci d.

1485

Caxton (1422?): Life of Charles the Great. P
Malory, Sir Thomas (d. 1471): Morte d'Arthur
    [trs. Fr.; prtd. Caxton; prtd. Wynkyn de
    Worde 1498, 1529; other edd. 1557, 1585
    (?), 1626]. P

Henry VII 1485–1509.

2

Berners, Dame Juliana (1388?): The Boke of St Albans [2nd ed. 1496]. P
Chaucer (d. 1400): House of Fame [n.d.; another ed. with other works 1526 (?)]. V
Medwall, Henry: Interlude of Nature [acted between 1486 and 1500; prtd. *c.* 1525].

Bartolomeo Diaz circumnavigates the Cape.
Paston Letters (of the family of Sir John Paston: written 1440–86) concluded (two vols. of Selections first pub. 1787; two more 1789; and a fifth 1825; the Letters ed. J. Gairdner 1901).

1487

Caxton (1422?): Book of Good Manners.

1488

Miles Coverdale b.
Duke Humphrey's Library opened at Oxford.

1489

Caxton (1422?): Doctrinal of Sapience [trs. Fr.]. P
Governal of Health [trs. Lat.]. P
Blanchardin and Eglantine [trs. Fr.]. P

Thomas Cranmer b.
Villon, 'Le Grand Testament', 'Le Petit Testament'.

1490

Caxton (1422?): Eneydon [n.d.; trs. Fr.].

Sir Thomas Elyot b.?
Sir David Lindsay b.

1491

Caxton (1422?): Art and Craft to know how well to die [trs. F.]. P

William Caxton d.

1492

Aretino b.
Columbus discovers the West Indies.

1493

1494

Hylton, Walter (d. 1396): Scala Perfectionis [also called Ladder of Perfection]. P
Devout Book to a Temporal Man. P
Lydgate (d. 1450?): Falls of Princes [trs. Boccaccio; also 1527–54–55(?)]. V

Boiardo d.
Angelo Poliziano d.
Sebastian Brandt, 'Narrenschiff'.
'Natura Brevium' in French (see 1532).

1495

Trevisa, John (d. 1412): Trs. De Proprietatibus Rerum of Bartholomew Anglicus [rev. by Stephen Batman as Batman upon Bartholome 1582].

John Bale b.
Rabelais probably b.
(1483 also suggested).
Boiardo, 'Orlando Inamorato'.

1496

'Mandeville, Sir John' (Jean d'Outremeuse?): Travels [n.d.; later edd. 1499, 1501–3–68–83(?)–1618–25–40–68 (ed. T. Este); all these from a defective MS.: the Cotton MS. first prtd. 1725, the Egerton MS. 1899].
Rolle, Richard, of Hampole (d. 1349?): Abbaye of the Holy Ghost [n.d.]. P
Skelton (1460?): Epitaffe of Jasper Duke of Beddeford [n.d.; doubtful if by S.]. V

1497

Trs. Æsop's Fables [prtd. Pynson; n.d.; another ed. 1500 (?): see 1484].

John Heywood b.?
Clément Marot b.
Cabot discovers American Mainland.

1498

Lydgate (d. 1450?): Assembly of the Gods [n.d.; also 1500 (?)]. V

Savonarola burned.
Vasco da Gama discovers sea-route to India.
Erasmus visits Oxford.

1499

1500

Chaucer (d. 1400): Mars and Venus [n.d.]. V
Lydgate (d. 1450?): Story of Thebes [n.d.]. V

Robert Henryson d.?
Erasmus, 'Adagia' (Eng. trs. 1539).

1501

Fernando de Roja, 'Celestina'.

1502

Arnold, Richard: Chronicle.

1503

Atkinson, William: Trs. De Imitatione Christi of Thomas à Kempis [first Eng. trs.].

Sir Thomas Wyatt b.?
Erasmus, 'Enchiridion' (Eng. trs. 1533).

Matthew Parker b.
Colet Dean of St. Paul's.
Sanazzaro, 'Arcadia'.

1505

Barclay (1475?): Castell of Laboure [n.d.; earliest ed. b. d. 1506; earlier Paris ed. *c.* 1503; trs. Gringoire]. V
Hawes (1474?): Temple of Glass [n.d.]. V

Nicholas Udall b.
John Knox b.

1506

Rolle, Richard, of Hampole (d. 1349?): Contemplations of the dread and love of God. P

John Leland b.?
Columbus d.

1507

1508

Anon.: Maying or Disport of Chaucer [attr. Chaucer]. V
Dunbar, William (1460?): Poems prtd. by Chapman and Myllar [n.d.; incl. Ballade of Lord Barnard Stewart, Flyting of Dunbar and Kennedy, Goldyn Targe, Twa Marrit Women and the Widow, Lament for Makaris, Dance of the Seven Deadly Sins, Thrissil and the Rois. D.'s Poems ed. David Laing 1824].
Fisher (1459): Treatise concerning the Fruitful Sayings of David.
Henry the Minstrel ('Blind Harry'): Wallace [n.d.; a fragment; trs. Lat. of J. Blair; ed. J. Moir 1884–9].
Rolle, Richard, of Hampole (d. 1349?): Remedy against the Troubles of Temptation. P

1509

Barclay (1475?): Ship of Fools [trs. Brandt's Narrenschiff]. V
Hawes (1474?): Pastime of Pleasure [also 1517, 1554–5]. V
Conversion of Swearers [also 1530 (?)]. V
Coronation of Henry VIII [n.d.]. V

Henry VIII 1509–47.
Calvin b.
Erasmus, 'Moriae Encomium'.

Anon.: Everyman: A Moral Play [n.d.; between 1510–30].
  Hyckescorner: an Interlude [n.d.].
  Cock Lorrell's Bote [n.d.]. V
Hawes (1474?): Example of Virtue [n.d.; also 1530]. V
Lydgate (d. 1450?): Treatise of a Gallant [n.d.; attrib. L.]. V
More (1478): Life of John Picus Earl of Mirandula [n.d.; trs. Giovanni Pico della Mirandola]. P

Colet founds St. Paul's School.

1511

Lydgate (d. 1450?): Governaunce of Kings and Princes.

Erasmus Greek Reader at Cambridge 1511–14.

1512

1513

Anon.: Flowers of Ovid [first Eng. trs. of Ars Amatoria].
Lydgate (d. 1450?): Troy Book [also 1553, 1555; trs. Guido delle Colonne]. V
Skelton (1460?): Ballade of the Scottish King [n.d.]. V

Battle of Flodden.
Machiavelli composes 'Il Principe'.

1514

Wolsey Archbishop of York.

1515

Barclay (1475?): Eclogues [i–iii only; n.d.; another ed. 1548 (?); Eclogues iv–v 1521 (?)]. V
Lydgate (d. 1450?): Testament of John Lydgate [n.d.]. V

Roger Ascham b.
Probable date of the John Asloan MS. of Scottish literature.

1516

Fabyan, Robert: Chronicles.
More (1478): A Merry Jest how a Sergeant would learn to be a Friar [n.d.]. V
  Utopia [in original Lat. and prtd. at Louvain; first Eng. trs. by R. Robinson 1551; trs. Gilbert Burnet 1684; trs. Arthur Cayley 1808].

John Foxe b.
Erasmus, 'Novum Instrumentum'.
Ariosto, 'Orlando Furioso' (in final form 1532).

1517

Henry Howard, Earl of Surrey b.
Luther's 'Theses' at Wittenberg.

Lydgate (d. 1450?): Lamentation of Our Lady [attr. L.; n.d.; before 1519].

1519

Medwall, Henry: Interlude of Fulgens, Cenatoure of Rome [n.d.; before 1520].

John Colet d.
Cortes in Mexico.
First Journey round the World (Magellan 1519–20).

1520

Scots New Testament [of Murdoch Nisbet] c. 1520.
Anon.: Interlude of Youth [n.d.; fragment only; other edd. c. 1557, 1562].
Trs. Terence's Andria [n.d.; earliest trs.]
Trs. Four Cardinal Virtues of Mancinus [n.d.; earliest trs.].
Barclay (1475?): Chronicle of the War which the Romans had against Jugurtha [trs. Sallust; n.d.]. P
Life of St. Thomas. P
Lydgate (d. 1450?): Damage and Destruction in Realms [n.d.; called Serpent of Division 1559]. P

Thomas Churchyard b.?
William Dunbar d.?

1521

Barclay (1475?): Introductory to write and pronounce French. P
Eclogues iv–v [n.d.; see 1515]. V
Fisher (1459): Sermon against the Doctrine of Luther [n.d.].

John Siberch prints books at Cambridge 1521–2.
Papal ban on Luther at the Diet of Worms.

1522

Anon.: Interlude of the World and the Child.

Gavin Douglas d.
William Lily d.
Luther's Bible 1522–34.

1523

Barclay (1475?): Mirror of Good Manners [n.d.; trs. Mancinus]. P
Bourchier, John, Lord Berners: Trs. Froissart's Chronicles, pt. i [ii 1525]. P
Fitzherbert, John: Book of Surveying [10th ed. 1587 (?)].
Book of Husbandry [11th ed. 1598: these two books have been wrongly attr. to Sir Anthony Fitzherbert].
Skelton (1460?): Goodly Garland or Chapelet of Laurell. V

Stephen Hawes d.?

Anon.: Trs. Gesta Romanorum [prtd. by Wynkyn
de Worde; n.d.; other translations of Gesta
1557, 1595].
Cox, Leonard: Arte or Crafte of Rhethoryke [n.d.].
P

Thomas Tusser b.?
Camoens d.
Ronsard b.
Luther, 'Geistliche Lieder'.

1525

Medwall, Henry: Interlude of Nature [n.d.].
Rastell, John: Interlude of Gentylness and No-
bylitie [n.d.; sometimes attr. John Heywood].
Interlude of the Four Elements [n.d.].
Interlude wherein is described as well the
beauty and good property of Women as their
vices [n.d.; commonly known as Calisto and
Melibea; adaptation of Celestina of Fernando de Rojas].
Tyndale, William: Trs. New Testament [pub.
abroad: see 1530, 1531].
Walton, John: Book of Comfort [trs. De Consola-
tione Philosophiae of Boethius].

John Stow b.?
George Gascoigne b.?
Sir Thomas Lyttleton,
'Tenures' in English
(n.d.).

1526

Anon.: A Hundred Merry Tales [n.d.].
Boece, Hector: Scotorum Historiae [pub. abroad;
for Eng. trs. see 1535].

1527

Colet (1467?): Æditio [incl. William Lily's Gram-
matices Rudimenta; developed with Eras-
mus's revisions into Eton Latin Grammar;
see 1549].

Machiavelli d.
Castiglione, 'Il Corte-
giano'.

1528

Copland, William: Jest of a Man called Howle-
glass [n.d.; trs. Tyl Eulenspiegel].
Fisher (1459): Sermon had at Paul's [on 11 Feb.
1525] concernynge certaine heretickes [n.d.].
Roy, William: Rede me and be nott wrothe [n.d.;
pub. abroad; first Eng. ed. 1546]. V
Tyndale, William: Obedience of a Christian Man
[pub. abroad]. P
Parable of Wicked Mammon [pub. abroad]. P

Execution of Patrick
Hamilton and begin-
ning of Reformation in
Scotland.

1529

Fish, Simon: Supplication of Beggars [anon.; n.d.].
P
More (1478): Supplication of Souls [against the
Supplication of Beggars above; n.d.]. P
Dialogue of Diverse Matters. P

John Skelton d.
Fall of Wolsey.

Anon.: Everyman: a moral play [n.d.; between 1510–30].

Colet (d. 1519): Sermon made to the Convocation at Paulis [n.d.].

Poyntz, Sir Francis (d. 1528): Trs. Tables of Cebes the Philosopher. P

Tyndale, William: Trs. Pentateuch [pub. abroad; n.d.: see 1525, 1531].
  Practice of Prelates [pub. abroad]. P

Cardinal Wolsey d.

1531

Golden Litany in English.

Elyot (1490?): The Boke named the Governour. P

Tyndale, William: Trs. Book of Jonah [pub. abroad: see 1525, 1530].
  Answer to Sir Thomas More's Dialogue [pub. abroad; n.d.: see More 1529].

Ulrich Zwingli d.

1532

Chaucer (d. 1400): Works ed. William Thynne [all genuine works hitherto pub. or unpub., and the following that are spurious: Testament of Cresseid (by Henryson); Flower of Courtesie and Complaint of the Black Knight (Lydgate); Testament of Love (Thomas Usk); Letter of Cupid (Occleve); Cuckoo and Nightingale (Sir Thomas Clanvowe?); La Belle Dame sans Mercie (Sir Richard Ross); Assembly of Ladies (unknown); Lamentation of Mary Magdalen (unknown), and others.
  Later edd. of Works with spurious poems added: ed. Thynne (Plowman's Tale) 1542, 1545 (?); ed. Stow (Court of Love and some short poems) 1561; ed. Speght (Flower and the Leaf, Jack Upland, Chaucer's A.B.C., and a new Chaucer's Dream) 1598, 1602, 1687; ed. Urry (Tale of Gamelyn, Pardoner and the Tapster, and Second Merchants Tale) 1721.
  Modern edd. of Works: ed. Singer 1822, Morris 1866, Skeat 1894–7, Pollard 1897].

Elyot (1490?): Pasquil the Plaine. P

Henryson (d. 1500): Testament of Cresseid [in Works of Chaucer above]. V

Hervet, Gentian: Trs. Xenophon's Treatise of Household. P

Lydgate (d. 1450): Flower of Courtesie, Complaint of the Black Knight [in Works of Chaucer above]. V

More (1478): Confutation of Tyndale's Answer [Second Part of Confutation 1533]. P

Henry VIII divorces Katherine of Aragon.
'Natura Brevium' in English.
Rabelais, 'Pantagruel', bk. i (bk. ii called Gargantua 1534, bk. iii 1545, bk. iv 1548–52, bk. v (of doubtful authenticity) 1562–4).
Ariosto, 'Orlando Furioso' (in final form: see 1516).
Machiavelli, 'Il Principe'.
Erasmus, 'Apophthegmata'.

Anon.: Trs. Erasmus's Enchiridion [prtd. Wynkyn de Worde].

Montaigne b.
Ariosto d.

Elyot (1490?): Of the Knowledge which maketh a
wise man. P

Grimald, Nicholas: Trs. Three Books of Duties of
Cicero. P

Heywood (1497?): Johan the husband, Tyb the
wife and Sir Johan the Priest. D interlude.
The Pardoner, the Frere, the Curate and Neigh-
bour Pratte. D interlude.
Play of the Wether. D interlude.

Lydgate (d. 1450?): Life of Albon and Amphabel. V

More (1478): Apology of Sir Thomas More. P

Skelton (d. 1529): Magnificence: a goodly Interlude [n.d.]. D

Tyndale, William: Treatise of the Sacraments. P
Supper of the Lord. P

Udall, Nicholas: Floures of Latin speaking,
gathered out of Terence, and translated into
English.

1534

Bourchier, John, Lord Berners: Trs. Huon of Bor-
deaux [3rd ed. 1601].

John Leland's antiqua-
rian tour through Eng-
land 1534–43 ('Itine-
rary' first pub. 1710;
'Collectanea' 1715. See
1549).
Rabelais, 'Pantagruel',
bk. ii (see 1532).

Colet (d. 1519): A Right Fruitful Admonition. P

Elyot (1490?): Sermon of Holy Saint Ciprian.
Rules of a Christian Life [trs. Mirandola]. P
Doctrine of Princes [trs. Isocrates]. P
Castel of Health [see 1539]. P

Heywood (1497?): A Play of Love. D interlude.

Lydgate (d. 1450?): Life of St. Alban.

Whytington, R.: Three Books of Tullyes Offices
[trs. Cicero]. P

1535

Bellenden, John: Chronicles of Scotland [trs.
Hector Boece: see 1526]. P

Sir Thomas North b.?
Sir Thomas More execu-
ted.
Act of Supremacy.
Suppression of religious
houses 1535–9.
Calvin, 'Institution of
Christian Religion' (last
corrected ed. 1559; Eng.
trs. 1561).

Bourchier, John, Lord Berners: Golden Book of
Marcus Aurelius [trs. Antonio de Guevara]. P

Coverdale (1488): Trs. Bible [pub. abroad: see
1537].

Fisher (1459): Spiritual Consolation to his Sister
[n.d.]. P

1536

Anon.: Remedy for Sedition [sometimes attrib.
Sir John Cheke]. P

William Tyndale burnt.
Erasmus d.

Copland, Robert: Hye Way to the Spyttel House
[n.d.]. V

Coverdale (1488): Trs. Bible [modified version of the trs. of 1535; first Bible prtd. in England].
Cranmer (1489) and others: Institution of a Christian Man. P
Fortescue (d. 1476?): De Laudibus Legum Angliae [in Latin]. P
Rogers, John: Matthews' Bible [so called because trs. under pseudonym of Thomas Matthews].

1538

Elyot (1490?): Dictionary [Latin-English; another ed. 1545; rev. by T. Cooper as Bibliotheca Eliotae 1548–52–59].
Lindsay (1490): Complaint of a Popinjay [earliest extant ed.]. V
Ockham, William of (d. 1349?): Dialogue betwene a knight & a clerke [Trs. from Latin: possibly not by Ockham].

1539

The Great Bible [also called Cranmer's Bible].   *John Fisher executed.*
Elyot (1490?): Banquet of Sapience. P
  Castel of Health [earliest extant, i.e. 2nd ed.; originally in 1534]. P
Taverner, Richard: Trs. Bible.
  Garden of Wisdom. P
  Proverbs & Adagies [trs. Adagia of Erasmus]. P

1540

Anon.: Jack Upland [n.d.; sometimes attrib. Chaucer]. V
  Schoolhouse of Women [n.d.]. V
Bourchier, John, Lord Berners: Castell of Love [trs. D. de San Pedro; n.d.]. P
Elyot (1490?): Image of Governance [trs. Eucolpius]. P
Lindsay (1490): Satyr of Three Estates [acted: prtd. 1602]. D

Barnabe Googe b.
George Turberville b.?
Barnabe Rich b.?
Guicciardini d.

1541

Paracelsus d.

1542

Anon.: Plowman's Tale [attrib. Chaucer in ed. below: separately 1545 (?)]. V

Sir Thomas Wyatt d.
Montemayor, 'Diana'.

Boorde, Andrew (1490?): Dietary of Health [n.d.].

Chaucer (d. 1400): Works, 2nd ed. by William Thynne [see 1532].

Halle, Edward: Union of the Families of Lancastre and Yorke [commonly known as 'Halle's Chronicle'; first ed. undated and a fragment; 2nd ed. 1548; 3rd the most complete 1550].

Lily, William (d. 1522): Introduction to the Eight Parts of Speech [final and approved form of L.'s Grammar].

Recorde, Robert: Ground of Arts, teaching Arithmetic.

Udall, Nicholas: Trs. Apophthegms of Erasmus. P

1543

Hardyng, John (d. 1465?): Chronicle of England [with the Continuation by Richard Grafton].

Thomas Deloney b.?
Copernicus (d. 1543), 'De Revolutionibus'.
English Litany separately printed.

More (d. 1535): History of Richard the Third [first pub. in Hardyng's Chronicle above; later in Halle's Chronicle 1548, and in M.'s English Works 1557; attribution to M. not certain]. P

1544

Bale (1495): Chronicle concerning Sir John Oldcastle [pub. abroad]. P

George Whetstone b.?
Tasso b.
Clément Marot d.

Leland (1506?): Assertio Inclytissimi Arturii Regis Britanniae [in original Latin; trs. R. Robinson as Assertion of the Life of Prince Arthur 1582]. P

1545

The King's Primer.

Sir Thomas Bodley b.
Nicholas Breton b.?
Council of Trent meets.
Rabelais, 'Pantagruel', bk. iii (see 1532).

Ascham (1515): Toxophilus. P

Elyot (1490?): Defence of Good Women. P
Preservative against Death. P

Heywood (1497?): The Four P.P. [n.d.]. D interlude.

Rhodes, Hugh: Book of Nurture for Men, Servants and Children [n.d.]. P

Skelton (d. 1529): Book of Phillip Sparrow [n.d.]. V

Colin Clout [n.d.]. V

Why come ye not to Court [n.d.]. V

Certain Books compiled by Master Skelton [n.d.; incl. Speak Parrot, Death of Edward IV, Treatise of the Scots, Tunning of Elinour Rumming, and other poems, enlarged 1565 (?)].

Bale (1495): Act of English Votaries. P
Heywood (1497?): Proverbs [enlarged 1555, 1560, 1562]. V
Wiclif (d. 1384): Wyclif's Wicket [attrib. Wiclif]. P

Sir Thomas Elyot d.
Luther d.

1547

Book of Homilies [promoted by Cranmer].
Baldwin, William: Treatise of Moral Philosophy [trs. Diogenes Laertius, and others; enlarg. 1555(?) ed. Paulfreyman with additions 1557, 1564, 1567, 1584, 1620 (?)]. P
Bale (1495): Interlude manifesting Chief Promises of God [n.d.; pub. abroad; first Eng. ed. 1577]. D
   Interlude concerning Temptation of our Lord [n.d.; pub. abroad; first Eng. ed. 1870]. D
Boorde, Andrew (1490?): Breviary of Health [also 1552].
   First Book of the Introduction of Knowledge [n.d.]. P
Ingelend, Thomas: Interlude of Disobedient Child [performed *c.* 1547; prtd. *c.* 1570].
Sternhold, Thomas, and Hopkins, John: Psalms [first instalment: see 1549, 1562].
Wilkinson, John: Ethiques of Aristotle [first Eng. trs.]. P

Edward VI 1547–53.
Henry Howard, Earl of Surrey, executed.
Cervantes b.

1548

Order of the Communion.
Bale (1495): Interlude concerning Three Laws of Nature [n.d.; prtd. abroad; first Eng. ed. 1562].
   Kynge Johan [acted *c.* 1548; prtd. 1838]. D interlude.
   Illustrium Majoris Britanniae Scriptorum Summarium [commonly called Catalogus; greatly enlarg. 1557–9].
Brinkelow, Henry: Complaynt of Roderyck Mors [n.d.]. P
Latimer (1485): A Notable Sermon preached at Paul's Church [Plough Sermon]. P
Lindsay (1490): Tragical Death of David Beaton [n.d.]. V
Udall, Nicholas: Trs. Erasmus's Paraphrase of the New Testament [vol. ii, 1549, but not by U.]. P

Rabelais, 'Pantagruel', bk. iv 1548–52 (see 1532).

Book of Common Prayer [mainly the work of Cranmer; called the First Prayer Book of Edward VI; Second Prayer Book of Edward VI 1552; rev. as Elizabethan Prayer Book 1559; Prayer Book in final form 1662].

Anon.: Complaynt of Scotland [n.d.; prtd. at Paris?]. P

Baldwin, William: Canticles of Solomon in Englyshe Metres.

Cheke, Sir John: Hurt of Sedition. P

Cooper, Thomas: Chronicle [completed from unfinished work of Thomas Lanquet; other edd. 1560, 1565].

Latimer (1485?): Seven Sermons preached before the King in 1549.

Leland (1506?): Journey and Search for England's Antiquities given as a New Year's Gift to King Henry VIII. P

Sternhold, Thomas, and Hopkins, John: Psalms [2nd instalment: see 1547, 1562]. V

Wyatt (d. 1542): Certaine Psalmes drawne into English meter.

Giles Fletcher, senr. b.?
William Lily and John Colet, 'Short Introduction of Grammar'.
La Pléiade (Ronsard, Jodelle, Belleau, Baïf, Daurat, Joachim du Bellay, and Pontus de Tyard).
Du Bellay, 'Défense de la langue française'.

1550

Bansley, Charles: Tract showing the Pride and Abuse of Women [n.d.]. V

Cranmer (1489): Defence of the Catholike Doctrine of the Sacrement. P

Crowley, Robert: One and Thirty Epigrams. V

Halle, Edward: Chronicle [see 1542]. P

Harington, John: Book of Friendship [trs. Cicero].

Hunnis, William: Certain Psalmes in English Metre. V

Langland (d. 1400?): Vision of Pierce the Plowman [what is known as the B-text; another ed. with Crede of Pierce the Plowman added 1561; ed. Wright 1842, 1856, 1895; ed. Skeat 1869, 1896; A-text ed. Skeat 1867; C-text ed. Whitaker 1813, Skeat 1873; the three texts ed. Skeat 1886]. V

Nicolls, Thomas: Trs. History of Thucydides [earliest trs.].

Wiclif (d. 1384): Prologue written in an old English Bible.

Ronsard, 'Odes' and 'Amours de Cassandre' between 1550 and 1554.
Vasari, 'Lives of Painters' (concl. 1578).

1551

Robynson, Raphe: Trs. More's Utopia [also 1556, 1597; corrected 1624; another ed. 1639: see 1516]. P

Turner, William: A New Herball [pt. ii 1562, pts. i and ii rev. and pt. iii added 1568]. P

Wilson, Thomas (1525?): Rule of Reason. P

William Camden b.

Second **Prayer Book of Edward VI** [mainly the work of Cranmer: see 1549].

Forty-two Articles [promulgated by Cranmer: see 1560].

Churchyard (1520?): A Mirror for Man [n.d.]. V

Edmund Spenser b.?
Walter Raleigh b.?
Richard Hakluyt b.?
John Speed b.?
John Leland d.
Alexander Barclay d.
Autobiography and Diary of Dr. Simon Forman from 1552 to 1602 (pub. J. O. Halliwell-Phillips 1849).
Jodelle, 'Cléopâtre'.

1553

Anon.: Interlude of Jacke Jugeler [performed between 1553 and 1558; prtd. between 1562 and 1569].

Douglas (d. 1522): Trs. Æneid. V

Palace of Honour [n.d.; also 1579]. V

More (d. 1535): Dialogue of Comfort [corrected 1573]. P

Wilson, Thomas (1525?): Arte of Rhetorique. P

Queen Mary 1553–8.
Anthony Munday b.
Rabelais d.
Sir Hugh Willoughby sails for Cathay.
Mendoza (?) 'Lazarillo de Tormes'.

1554

Lindsay (1490): Dialogue betwixt Experience and Ane Courtier [n.d.; later edd., mostly with other works added, 1558, 1566, 1575]. V

Lydgate (d. 1450): Dance of Death [in ed. of Falls of Princes: see 1494]. V

Sir Philip Sidney b.
John Lyly b. ?
Fulke Greville b.
Richard Hooker b.?
Meeting of John Knox and Calvin at Geneva.
Stationers' Registers 1554–1640 (ed. E. Arber 1875–94).
Bandello, 'Novelle', vol. i–iii (iv 1573).
Ronsard, 'Amours de Marie' and 'Hymnes' between 1554 and 1560.

1555

Anon.: Institution of a Gentleman. P

Baldwin, William (ed.): Memorial of such Princes as have been unfortunate in the realm of England [suppressed first ed. of Mirror for Magistrates; n.d.: see 1559]. V

Bourchier, John, Lord Berners: History of Arthur of Little Britain [trs. Fr.; n.d.; another ed. *c.* 1582]. P

Eden, Richard: Decades of the New World or West India [trs. Peter Martyr]. P

Heywood (1497?): Two Hundred Epigrams [see 1546, 1560, 1562]. V

Lancelot Andrewes b.
Malherbe b.
Latimer and Ridley burnt.
Sir David Lindsay d.

The Genevan Psalter [pub. abroad: chiefly work of William Whittingham].

Colville, George: Book called Comfort of Philosophy [trs. Boethius].

Heywood (1497?): Spider and the Fly. V

Recorde, Robert: Castle of Knowledge. P

Thomas Cranmer burnt.
Nicholas Udall d.
Pietro Aretino d.

1557

Anon.: Interlude of Youth [n.d.].

More (d. 1535): Works written in English [ed. William Rastell].

North (1535?): Diall of Princes. Famous Book of Marcus Aurelius [trs. Antonio de Guevara; rev. and enlarg. 1568]. P

Recorde, Robert: Whetstone of Wit [first book of Algebra].

Surrey (d. 1547): Trs. Certaine Books of Virgil's Æneis [bks. ii and iv]. V

Tottel, Richard, and Grimald, Nicholas (compilers): Songs and Sonnets [called Tottel's Miscellany; contributors: Surrey, Wyatt, Lord Vaux, John Heywood, Edward Somerset, and others. Later edd. 1559, 1565, 1567, 1574, 1585, 1587; ed. J. Nott 1812; R. Bell 1854; E. Arber 1870, 1903; H. Rollins 1928–9].

Tusser (1524?): Hundreth Good Pointes of Husbandrie [see 1573]. V

Thomas Kyd b.?
Stationers' Company incorporated.

1558

Anon.: Interlude of Wealth and Health [n.d.]. D

Bullein, William: Government of Health [n.d.].

Knox (1505): First Blast of the Trumpet against the Monstrous Regiment of Women. P

Morwyng, P.: History of the Jewes Commune Weale [trs. Joseph ben Gorion]. P

Phaer, Thomas: Trs. Æneid, bks. i–vii [i–ix 1562; completed in 13 bks. by Thomas Twyne 1584]. V

Queen Elizabeth 1558–1603.
Thomas Lodge b.?
George Peele b.?
William Warner b.?
Julius Caesar Scaliger d.
Marguerite de Navarre, 'Heptameron' (concl. 1559).

Elizabethan Prayer Book [see 1549].

Aylmer, John: Harbour against the late blown blast concerning Government of Women [reply to Knox: see 1558]. P

Baldwin, William (ed.): Mirror for Magistrates [later edd. with alterations and additions 1563, 1571, 1574 (ed. John Higgins), 1578 (ed. Thomas Blenerhasset), 1587 (ed. John Higgins), 1610 (ed. Richard Nicols); 1815 (ed. J. Haslewood); notable contributions: Induction and Complaint of Buckingham by Thomas Sackville, Shore's Wife by Thomas Churchyard, and Edward the Fourth by John Skelton: see 1555]. V

Heywood, Jasper: Trs. Troas of Seneca [see 1581]. T

Act of Uniformity.
George Chapman b.?
Isaac Casaubon b.
Jacques Amyot, trs. Plutarch.

1560

Geneva Bible [also called Breeches Bible; mainly the work of William Whittingham; pub. at Geneva].

Thirty-nine Articles.

Anon.: Interlude called the Nice Wanton [n.d.]. D
Interlude called Impatient Poverty [n.d.]. D
Interlude called Thersytes [n.d.; by Nicholas Udall?]. D
Proud Wives Paternoster. V

Barker, W.: Trs. Bookes of Xenophon containing Discipline and Education of Cyrus [n.d.]. P

C., T.: Pleasant History of Galesus [trs. Boccaccio; n.d.].

Fisher (d. 1535): Treatise declaring Benefits of Prayer. P

Googe (1540): Zodiake of Life, bks. i–iii [bks. i–vi 1561; complete in 12 bks. 1565; trs. Marcellus Palingenius]. V

Heywood, Jasper: Trs. Thyestes of Seneca [see 1581]. T

Heywood (1497?): A Fourth Hundred of Epigrams [see 1546, 1555, 1562]. V

Howell, Thomas: Fable of Narcissus [trs. Ovid].

Knox (1505): Treatise on Predestination. P

Whitehorne, Peter: Trs. Machiavelli's Art of War [concl. 1562]. P

Robert Greene b.?
The anon. comedies 'Misogonus' and 'The Bugbears' performed about this date.
Ronsard, 'Discours des Misères de ce temps' and Epic 'Franciade' between 1560 and 1574.

Anon.: Pierce the Ploughman's Creed [see Langland 1550. Ed. Skeat 1867, 1906]. V

Godly Queen Hester. D moral interlude.

Beware the Cat [n.d.]. P

Chaucer (d. 1400): Works, ed. Stow [see 1532].

Eden, Richard: Art of Navigation [trs. Cortes].

Gilby, Goddard: Trs. Cicero's Epistle to Quintus.

Heywood, Jasper: Trs. Hercules Furens of Seneca [see 1581]. T

Hoby (1530): The Courtyer [trs. Castiglione]. P

Norton, Thomas: Trs. Calvin's Institution of Christian Religion. P

Francis Bacon b.
Robert Southwell b.?
Sir John Harington b.
'Gorboduc' acted at Inner Temple (see 1565).

1562

Bale (1495): Interlude concerning Three Laws of Nature [see 1548]. D

Broke, Arthur: History of Romeus and Juliet. V

Bullein, William: Bulwark against all Sickness.

Grafton, Richard: Abridgement of the Chronicles of England [later edd. 1563–64–70–72].

Heywood (1497?): Works [i.e. Proverbs and Epigrams: see 1546, 1555, 1560].

Ballad against Slander and Detraction. V

Jewel, John: Apology for the Church of England [both Latin original, and Eng. trs. by Ann, Lady Bacon: see 1567]. P

Latimer (d. 1555): XXVII Sermons [see 1571].

Sternhold, Thomas, Hopkins, John, and others: Whole Book of Psalms [first complete ed., and known as the Old Version; sectionally 1547–49–61. For New Version see 1696]. V

Samuel Daniel b.
Lope de Vega b.
Sir John Hawkins's Voyages 1562–8.
Rabelais, 'Pantagruel', bk. v 1562–4 (see 1532).

1563

Foxe (1516): Actes and Monuments [commonly called Book of Martyrs; edd. during F.'s lifetime 1570–76–83; other edd. 1596, 1610–32–41–84; ed. Cattley 1837–41, Stoughton 1877].

Golding, Arthur: Trs. Histories of Justin. P

Googe (1540): Eclogs, Epitaphs and Sonnets. V

Nevyle, Alexander: Oedipus [trs. Seneca: see 1581]. T

Rainolde, Richard: Foundacion of Rhetorike. P

Plague in London.
Michael Drayton b.
Joshua Sylvester b.
John Bale d.
Index Librorum Prohibitorum.

1564

Scots Psalter.

Bullein, William: Dialogue against the Fever Pestilence.

William Shakespeare b.
Christopher Marlowe b.
Henry Chettle b.
Galileo b.
Calvin d.
Michelangelo d.
Queen Elizabeth visits Cambridge.

Anon.: Interlude of Kyng Darius. D
Contention between Liberalitie and Prodiga-
litie [acted: prtd. 1602]. D interlude.
Awdeley, John: Fraternity of Vagabonds.
Twenty-five Orders of Knaves. P
Golding, Arthur: Trs. Ovid's Metamorphoses, bks.
i–iv [complete: bks. i–xv 1567].
Trs. Caesar's Exploits in Gallia. P
Grafton, Richard: Manual of the Chronicles of
England [n.d.]. P
Norton, Thomas, and Sackville, Thomas: Tragedy
of Gorboduc [called Ferrex and Porrex 1570].
Peend, T.: Fable of Hermaphroditus and Sal-
macis [trs. Ovid].
Stow (1525?): Summarie of English Chronicles
[later edd., with additions up to date: 1566–
67–70–73–74–75–87–90–98–1604; continued
by Howes 1607–10; by Allde (?) 1618].
Underdowne, Thomas: Hermaphroditus and
Salmacis [trs. Ovid].
Weaver, R.: Interlude called Lusty Juventus
[n.d.]. D

*John Davies of Here-
ford b.?*
*Thomas Cooper, 'Thesau-
rus Linguae Romanae
et Britannicae'.*
Cinthio, 'Hecatommithi.'

1566

Anon.: Albion Knight [n.d.]. D moral interlude.
Adlington, William: Trs. Golden Ass of Apuleius. P
Drant, Thomas: A Medicinable Moral, that is, two
Books of Horace his Satyres.
Gascoigne (1542): Supposes [acted: see 1573;
adapted from Ariosto]. C
Jocasta [acted; see 1573; adapted from Euri-
pides]. T
Grantham, H.: A Pleasant Disport entitled Philo-
copo [n.d.; trs. Boccaccio]. P
Lindsay (d. 1555): Deploration of Death of Queen
Magdalen [in ed. of Dialogue between Ex-
perience and ane Courtier: see 1554]. V
Painter, William: Palace of Pleasure [vol. ii 1567;
corrected and enlarg. 1575; trs. tales chiefly
from Boccaccio and Bandello]. P
Studley, John: Trs. Agamemnon of Seneca [see
1581]. T
Trs. Medea of Seneca [see 1581]. T
Udall (d. 1556): Ralph Roister Doister [n.d.]. C
Wager, Lewis: Life and Repentance of Mary Mag-
dalene. D moral interlude.

Gowrie Conspiracy.
*Queen Elizabeth visits Ox-
ford.*
*Diary of James Melville,
minister of Kilrenny
1566–1601 (pub. Ban-
natyne Club 1829).*
*Martin Luther, 'Tisch-
reden'.*

Anon.: Interlude called Trial of Treasure. D
Drant, Thomas: Arte of Poetrie, Pistles and Satyrs [trs. Horace]. V
Fenton, Sir Geoffrey: Certaine Tragicall Discourses [trs. Bandello]. P
Hake, E.: Trs. De Imitatione Christi.
Harman, Thomas: Caveat or Warening for Common Cursetors Vulgarely called Vagabones [earliest extant, i.e. 2nd, ed.]. P
Jewel, John: Defence of the Apologie of the Church of Englande [see 1562]. P
Mulcaster, Richard: A Learned Commendation of the Laws of England [trs. De Laudibus Legum Angliae of Sir John Fortescue]. P
Paynell, Thomas: Trs. Amadis of France. P
Pickering, John: History of Horestes, a new Interlude. D
Rastell, John: Expositions of the Termes of the Lawes. P
Sandford, James: Trs. Manual of Epictetus.
Turberville (1540?): Epitaphs, Epigrams, Songs, and Sonnets.
  Trs. Heroical Epistles of Ovid. V
  Trs. Eclogues of Mantuan. V

Revolt of the Netherlands.
Sir William Alexander, Earl of Stirling b.?
Thomas Nash b.
Thomas Campion b.

1568

The Bishops' Bible [chiefly the work of Matthew Parker].
Anon.: History of Jacob and Esau. D interlude.
Baker, Humphrey: Well-Spring of Sciences [Book of Arithmetic].
Fulwell, Ulpian: Interlude entitled Like Will to Like.
Grafton, Richard: Chronicle at Large [2nd ed. 1569]. P
Howell, Thomas: Arbor of Amitie. V
  New Sonnets and Pretty Pamphlets [n.d.]. V
Lindsay (d. 1555): Works [incl. all works except Satire of Three Estates (pub. 1602), and History of Squire Meldrum pub. in 1582 ed. of Works. Works ed. Laing 1879].
Skelton (d. 1529): Pithy, Pleasant and Profitable Works, now Collected [works ed. A. Dyce 1843].
Tilney, Edmund: Discourse of Duties in Marriage. P
Turberville (1540?): Plain Path to Perfect Virtue [trs. Mancinus]. V

Mary Queen of Scots in England.
Sir Henry Wotton b.
Gervase Markham b.?
Miles Coverdale d.
Roger Ascham d.
Probable date of compilation of George Bannatyne MS. of Scottish literature (prtd. in entirety by Hunterian Club 1873–1902).
William Lambarde's 'Archaionomia'.

Hawkins, Sir John: True Declaration of his Voyage in 1567 and 1568 [his third voyage]. P

Newton, Thomas: Trs. Cicero's Paradoxa Stoicorum. P

Worthy Book of Old Age [trs. Cicero].

Sandford, J.: Trs. Cornelius Agrippa's Of the Vanitie of Artes and Sciences.

T., C.: Notable History of Nastagio [trs. Boccaccio].

Underdowne, Thomas: Trs. Æthiopian History of Heliodorus [n.d.]. P

Trs. Ovid his Invective against Ibis. V

Sir John Davies b.
Sir James Melville's 'Memorials of Transactions in Scotland' 1569–73 (first pub. 1683; prtd. Bannatyne Club 1827).

1570

Anon.: Marriage of Wit and Science [n.d.]. D interlude.

Ascham (d. 1568): The Schoolmaster. P

Barbour (d. 1395): Bruce [n.d.; also 1616, 1620]. V

Fenton, Sir Geoffrey: Discourse of Civil Wars of France [n.d.; trs. Fr.].

Foxe, John: Sermon of Christ Crucified. P

Googe (1540): The Popish Kingdom [trs. Thomas Kirchmayer].

Henryson (d. 1500?): Moral Fables of Æsop [also 1621] V

Ingelend, Thomas: Interlude called Disobedient Child [n.d.: see 1547].

North (1535?): Moral Philosophy of Doni [trs. Fables of Bidpai]. P

Phillips, John: Patient and Meek Grissil [n.d.]. D interlude.

Preston, Thomas: Cambises, King of Persia [n.d.]. D

Wilson, Thomas (1525?): Trs. Three Orations of Demosthenes.

Thomas Dekker b.?
Thomas Middleton b.?

1571

Edwards, Richard: Damon and Pithias. C

Grafton, Richard: Treatise containing many proper tables and rules [enlarg. 1611]. P

Latimer (d. 1555): Fruitful Sermons, pt. i [pts. ii and iii 1575; later collective edd. of Sermons 1578–84–94–1607–35].

Act for incorporation of the Universities of Oxford and Cambridge.
Kepler b.

Cartwright, Thomas: Second Admonition to
Parliament. P

Churchyard (1520?): Trs. First three books of
Ovid's Tristia [n.d.]. V

Fenton, Sir Geoffrey: Monophylo, or a philosophical discourse of love. V

Field, John, and Wilcox, Thomas: Admonition to
Parliament. P

Parker, Matthew: De Antiquitate Britanniae
Ecclesiae [supposed first privately printed
book in England].

'R. H.': Trs. Ludwig Lavater's Of Ghosts and
Spirits walking by Night.

Wilson, Thomas (1525?): Discourse upon Usury.

*Massacre of St. Bartholo-
mew.
Unattached companies of
actors declared rogues
and vagabonds.
Society of Antiquarians
founded by Matthew
Parker.
John Knox d.
Camoens, 'Os Lusiados'.*

1573

Anon.: New Custom. D moral interlude.

Gascoigne (1542): A Hundreth Sundry Flowers
[n.d.; anon and unauthorized; cont. Supposes, Jocasta (b. d. 1566), Master Ferdi-
nando Ieronimo, Devices of Sundry Gentlemen, Dan Bartholomew of Bath: see 1575].

Tusser (1524?): Five Hundreth Pointes of Good
Husbandrie [enlarged 1580: see 1557]. V

Tyndale (d. 1536): Whole Works of Tyndale, John
Frith and Doctor Barnes [cont. Lives of the
authors extracted from Foxe's Martyrs.].

*Ben Jonson b.?
John Donne b.
William Laud b.
Bandello, 'Novelle', vol. iv
(see 1554).
Tasso, 'Aminta'.*

1574

Hellowes, Edward: Trs. Familiar Letters of Antonio de Guevara.

Higgins, John: Ed. Mirror for Magistrates [see
1559].

Parker, Matthew: Lives of the Seventy Archbishops of Canterbury. P

Rich, Barnabe (1540?): Dialogue between Mercury and an English Souldier [n.d.].

Scot, Reginald: Perfit Platform of a hop garden. P

*Earl of Leicester's theatri-
cal company formed.
Joseph Hall b.
Richard Barnfield b.*

1575

Anon.: Gammer Gurtons Needle [William Stevenson now supposed author; formerly John
Still]. C

B., R.: Appius and Virginia. D tragi-comedy.

Breton (1545?): Small handful of fragrant flowers. V

Churchyard (1520?): First Part of Churchyards
Chippes. V

*John Marston b.?
Cyril Tourneur b.?
Samuel Purchas b.?
Thomas Heywood b.?
Jacob Boehme b.
Matthew Parker d.*

Fenton, Sir Geoffrey: Trs. Golden Epistles [trs. Spanish of Guevara; corrected 1577, 1582].

Gascoigne (1542): A Glasse of Government. D
  Posies of George Gascoigne [cont. enlarged version of works 1573; adds Notes of Instruction concerning Making of Verse: see 1587].

Rolland, John: Treatise callit the Court of Venus. V

Turberville (1540?): Book of Falconrie [rev. and enlarg. 1611]. P
  Noble Art of Venerie [n.d.].

1576

Edwards, Richard; Heywood, Jasper; Lord Vaux, and others: Paradise of Dainty Devices [later edd. 1578–80–85–96–98 (?)–1600–6]. V

Fleming, Abraham: Panoplie of Epistles [trs. Cicero, Pliny the Younger, and others].

Gascoigne (1542): Steele Glas. Complainte of Phylomene. V
  Droomme of Doomesday [trs. Lat. of Conti]. P
  Delicate Diet for Daintie mouthde Droonkardes. P
  Princelye Pleasures at Courte of Kenelworth [with G. Ferrers, H. Goldingham, and W. Hunnis]. D masque or entertainment.

Gilbert, Sir Humphrey: Discourse of a New Passage to Cataia. P

Lambarde, William: Perambulation of Kent. P

Pettie, George: Petite Pallace of Pettie his Pleasure [n.d.]. P

Whetstone (1544?): Rocke of Regard. V and P

Sack of Antwerp.
Martin Frobisher's Voyages, 1576–7.
Erection of The Theater (first theatre in London).

1577

Bale (d. 1563): Chief Promises of God [see 1547]. D interlude.

Breton (1545?): Works of a Young Wit. V
  Floorish upon Fancie. V

Eden, Richard (d. 1576): History of Travel in East and West Indies [completed by R. Willes]. P

Gascoigne (d. 1577): Spoyle of Antwerpe [n.d.]. P

Golding, Arthur: Tragedy of Abrahams Sacrifice [trs. Fr. of Theodore Beza]. D

Googe (1540): Four Books of Husbandry [trs. Conrad Heresbach]. V

Hellowes, Edward: Lives of Ten Emperors of Rome [trs. Spanish of Guevara]. P

Holinshed, Raphael: Chronicles [incl. Harrison's Description of England; enl. 1587]. P

Kendall, Timothy: Flowres of Epigrams. V

Peacham, Henry, senr.: Garden of Eloquence. P

Drake's voyage round the world, 1577–80.
The Curtain Theatre opened c. 1577.
Robert Burton b.
Thomas Coryate b.?
George Gascoigne d.
David Moysie's Memoirs of Affairs of Scotland, 1577–1603 (first pub. Bannatyne Club 1830).

Best, George: Discourse of the Voyages of Martin Frobisher. P

Churchyard (1520): Woful Wars in Flaunders. V
Discourse of the Queenes Entertainment in Suffolk and Norfolk. V

Day, Richard: Book of Christian Prayers.

Hellowes, Edward: Invention of the Art of Navigation [trs. Spanish of Guevara]. P

Lupton, Thomas: All for Money. D moral interlude.

Lyly (1554?): Euphues, the Anatomy of Wit [n.d.; corrected and augmented 1579; pt. ii Euphues and his England 1580; pts. i–ii combined 1617]. P

Proctor, Thomas: Gorgeous Gallery of Gallant Inventions [Verse collection].

Rich, Barnabe (1540?): Alarm to England. P

Whetstone (1544?): Promos and Cassandra. C
Remembrance of the Life of George Gascoigne [n.d.]. V

George Sandys b.
William Harvey b.
Thomas Blenerhasset ed. 'Mirror for Magistrates' (see 1559).
Du Bartas, 'La Semaine' ('La Seconde Semaine' 1584).

1579

Churchyard (1520?): General Rehearsal of Wars [n.d.]. V
Miserie of Flaunders. V

Day, Richard: Christ Jesus Triumphant. D

Fenton, Sir Geoffrey: History of the Wars of Italy [trs. Guicciardini]. P

Frampton, John: Trs. Travels of Marco Polo. P

Gosson, Stephen: School of Abuse. P
Ephemerides of Phialo [cont. Apologie for School of Abuse]. P

Lodge (1558?): Defence of Stage Plays [reply to Gosson; known copies want title and date; about 1579–80]. P

Munday (1553): Mirror of Mutabilitie. V

North (1535?): Trs. Plutarch's Lives [Lives of Epaminondas and Philip of Macedon added 1602; trs. through Fr. of Amyot]. P

Spenser (1552?): Shepheards Calender. V

Puritan Attack on the Stage: Gosson's *School of Abuse* (1579) and *Apologie for School of Abuse* (1579); Lodge's Reply to Gosson (1579); Gosson's *Plays Confuted* (1582) and Lodge's rejoinder in Preface to *Alarum against Usurers* (1584); Stubbes's *Anatomie of Abuses* (1583) and Nash's attack on Stubbes in *Anatomie of Absurditie* (1589).

John Fletcher b.

Bullokar, William: Book for the amendment of English Orthographie. P

Churchyard (1520?): Churchyardes Charge. V

Gifford, Humfrey: Posie of Gilloflowers. V

Lyly (1554?): Euphues and his England [see 1578]. P

Munday (1553): Zelauto, the Fountain of Fame. P
Pain of Pleasure. P

Roger, J.: Trs. De Imitatione Christi. P

Spenser and Harvey, Gabriel (1552?): Three Letters and two other Letters passed between two university men. P

Stow (1525?): Chronicles of England [n.d.; see 1592]. P

John Webster b.?
Raphael Holinshed d.?
John Heywood d.?
Thomas Tusser d.
Probable date of the MS. of the Collection of ancient Scottish Literature made by Sir Richard Maitland (1496–1586).
Camoens d.
Quevedo b.
Montaigne, 'Essais', bks. i, ii (bk. iii 1588; 'Essais' in final form 1595).
Belleforest, 'Histoires Tragiques' (concl. 1582).

1581

Hall, Arthur: Ten Books of Homer's Iliades. V

Heywood, Newton, Studley, Nevyle, and Nuce: Seneca his Ten Tragedies [collected; separately 1559–60–61–63–66].

Howell, Thomas: Howell his Devises. V

Lambarde, William: Eirenarchia. P

Mulcaster, Richard: Positions. P

Pettie, George: Trs. Civil Conversations of Stefano Guazzo, bks. i–iii [completed in 4 bks. by Bartholomew Young 1586]. P

Rich, Barnabe (1540?): Rich his Farewell to the Military Profession [enlarg. 1606]. P
Adventures of Don Simonides [vol. ii 1584]. P

Woodes, Nathaniel: Conflict of Conscience. D

James Ussher b.
Sir Thomas Overbury b.
Tasso, 'Gerusalemme Liberata'.

1582

The Rheims and Douay Bible [N.T. pub. at Rheims 1582; O.T. pub. at Douay 1609–10].

Gosson, Stephen: Plays Confuted in five actions [n.d.]. P

Hakluyt (1552?): Diverse Voyages touching Discovery of America. P

Lindsay (d. 1555): History of Squire Meldrum [see 1568]. V

Mulcaster, Richard: Elementarie. P

Munday (1553): Discovery of Edward Campion. P
English Roman Life. P

Parsons, Robert: Book of Christian Exercise [later called Christian Directory]. P

Stanyhurst, Richard: Trs. Æneid [bks. i–iv only]. V

Watson, Thomas: Ecatompathia, or a Passionate Century of Love [n.d.]. V

Whetstone, George (1544?): Heptameron of Civil Discourses [trs. Cinthio; as Aurelia 1593]. P

Plague in London, 1582–3.
Edinburgh University founded.
Phineas Fletcher b.
Shakespeare's marriage to Anne Hathaway.
George Buchanan, 'Rerum Scoticarum Historiae'.
R. Robinson Trs. Leland's 'Life of Prince Arthur' (see 1544).

Greene (1560?): Mamillia, pt. i [ii 1593]. P
Melbancke, Brian: Philotimus. P
Smith, Sir Thomas (d. 1577): De Republica Anglorum: the manner of Government of England. P
Stubbes, Philip: Anatomy of Abuses [enlarg. 1584-5, 1595]. P

Queen's Company of Players formed.
Edward Herbert, Lord Herbert of Cherbury b.
Philip Massinger b.
Grotius b.

1584

Greene (1560?): Myrror of Modestie. P
Gwydonius. P
Arbasto. P
Morando. P
James VI of Scotland, I of England: Essays of a Prentice in the Art of Poesie.
Lodge (1558?): Alarum against Usurers. P
Lyly (1554?): Campaspe. C
Sapho and Phao. C
Munday (1553): Watchword to England. P
Norden, John: Pensive Man's Practice. P
Peele (1558?): Arraignment of Paris. D pastoral.
Phaer, Thomas: Trs. Æneid [completed by Thomas Twyne: see 1558]. V
R., B.: Trs. History of Herodotus [translator sometimes supposed to be Barnabe Rich]. P
Robinson, Clement, and others: Handful of Pleasant Delites [earliest extant ed.; originally *c.* 1566]. V
Scot, Reginald: Discoverie of Witchcraft. P
Warner (1558?): Pan his Syrinx [n.d.; corrected 1597]. P
Whetstone (1544?): Mirrour for Magistrates of Cities. P
Wilson, Robert: Three Ladies of London. D moral Interlude.

William of Orange assassinated.
Raleigh's Charter of Colonization.
John Selden b.
John Hales b.
Francis Beaumont b.

1585

Bullokar, William: Trs. Æsop's Fables.
Munday (1553): Fedele and Fortunio [trs. Italian of Luigi Pasqualigo]. C
Watson, Thomas: Amynta [in Latin: based on Tasso's Aminta].

Leicester's Expedition to the Netherlands.
William Drummond of Hawthornden b.
William Rowley b.?
Shakespeare leaves Stratford.
Ronsard d.

Bowes, T.: Trs. Pierre de la Primaudaye's French Academy.

Camden (1551): Britannia [in Latin: other edd., corrected, 1587–90–94, 1600, 1607; Abridgement 1626; Eng. trs. by Philemon Holland 1610, 1637; ed. by Edmund Gibson 1695, 1722; by Richard Gough 1789].

Day, Angell: English Secretorie. P

Rowland, David: Trs. Lazarillo de Tormes [earliest extant, i.e. 2nd, ed.; originally *c.* 1576]. P

Warner (1558?): Albions England, bks. i–iv [rev. and enlarg. into 6 bks., 1589; into 9 bks., 1592; into 12 bks., 1596; into 13 bks., 1602; into 16 bks., 1606]. V

Webbe, William: Discourse of English Poetrie [reprinted 1815; Arber 1870]. P

Whetstone (1544?): English Mirror. P

John Ford b.
Sir Philip Sidney d.
With the object of checking the flow of Puritan pamphlets the decree is passed (under instigation of John Whitgift, Archbishop of Canterbury) by the Star Chamber forbidding all publications unless previously approved of by ecclesiastical authorities. This intensifies the episcopal controversy and leads on to the Martin Marprelate Tracts, 1588.

1587

Churchyard (1520?): Worthiness of Wales. V

Day, Angell: Daphnis and Chloe [trs. Amyot's version of Longus]. P

Fraunce, Abraham: Lamentations of Amyntas [trs. Thomas Watson's Latin version of Tasso: see 1585]. V

Gascoigne (d. 1577): Whole Works of George Gascoigne [see 1575; Works ed. W. C. Hazlitt 1868–9; ed. J. W. Cunliffe 1907–8].

Gifford, George: Discourse of Subtill Practices of Devils. P

Greene (1560?): Penelope's Web. P

Euphues his Censure to Philautus. P

Grove, Matthew: History of Pelops and Hippodamia. Epigrams, Songs, and Sonnets. V

Hakluyt (1552?): Voyages made into Florida. P

Hughes, Thomas: Misfortunes of Arthur [in Certain Devices and Shows presented to her Majesty]. D

Knox (d. 1572): History of the Reformation in Scotland. P

Mascall, Leonard: Book of Cattle. P

Penry, John: Treatise containing the Aequity of an Humble Supplication. P

Rankins, William: Mirrour of Monsters [anti-stage pamphlet]. P

Turberville (1540?): Tragical Tales [chiefly from Boccaccio]. V

Whetstone (d. 1587?): Sir Philip Sidney, his Honourable Life [n.d.]. V

Young, Bartholomew: Amorous Fiametta [trs. Boccaccio]. P

Execution of Mary Queen of Scots.
Nathaniel Field b.
George Whetstone d.?

Anon.: Trs. Six Idillia of Theocritus. V

Bigges, Walter: A summarie and true discourse of Sir Francis Drake's West Indian Voyage P

Byrd (1538?): Psalmes, sonets, and songs. V

Fraunce, Abraham: Arcadian Rhetorick. P

Greene (1560?): Perimides the Blacke Smith. P
Pandosto [called Dorastus and Fawnia 1636]. P

Munday (1553): Banquet of Dainty Conceits. V
Trs. Palmerin de Oliva [pt. ii 1597]. P
Palladins of England [trs. Fr.]. P

Udall, John: State of Church of England [commonly called Diotrephes]. P

Martin Marprelate Tracts 1588–9: (1) *The Epistle*; (2) *The Epitome*; (3) *The Minerall Schoolpoints*; (4) *Hay any work for Cooper*; (5) *Theses Martinianae or Martin Junior*; (6) *Just Censure and Reproof or Martin Senior*; and (7) *The Protestation*. Suspected authors: John Udall, John Penry, and Job Throckmorton.

Some Anti-Martin tracts: *Pappe with a Hatchet* by John Lyly; *Whip for an Ape* by John Lyly (?); *Pasquil's Apology* (anon.); *Return of Pasquil* (anon.); *Almond for a Parrat* by Thomas Nash (?); *Plaine Percivall* (anon.; Richard Harvey?); *Lamb of God* by Richard Harvey; *Martin's Months Mind* (anon.); *Admonition to People of England* by Thomas Cooper.

Defeat of Spanish Armada
Thomas Hobbes b.
George Wither b.
Martin Marprelate Controversy, 1588–90.
Thomas Kyd trs. 'Householder's Philosophy' of Tasso.
Maurice Kyffin trs. 'Andria' of Terence.
Montaigne, 'Essais', bk. iii (see 1580).

1589

Anon.: Rare Triumphs of Love and Fortune. D
A Copie of a Letter sent from sea by a Gentleman. P

Byrd (1538?): Songs of sundrie natures. V

Cooper, Thomas: Admonition to People of England. P

Devereux, Robert, 2nd Earl of Essex (1566): A True Coppie of a Discourse. P

Greene (1560?): Spanish Masquerado. P
Ciceronis Amor, Tullies Love. P
Menaphon [called Greene's Arcadia, or Menaphon 1599]. P

Hakluyt (1552?): Principall Navigations, Voyages and Discoveries [see 1598]. P

Lodge (1558?): Scillaes Metamorphoses [called Glaucus and Scilla 1610]. V

Nashe (1567): Anatomy of Absurditie. P

Peele (1558?): Farewell to Sir John Norris. A Tale of Troy. V

Puttenham, George: Art of English Poesy [Lord Lumley also supposed to be author]. P

Davies (1569): Epigrammes [n.d.; cont. Marlowe's trs. of Elegies from Ovid]. V

Greene (1560?): Royal Exchange. P
Greene's Mourning Garment. P
Greene's Never Too Late. P

Holland, Henry: Treatise against Witchcraft. P

Lodge (1558?): Rosalynde. P

Marlowe (1564): Tamburlaine the Great, pts. i, ii. T
Trs. Ovid's Elegies [see Davies above]. V

Munday (1553): Amadis de Gaul, pt. i [trs. Fr.; n.d.; pt. ii 1595; iii, iv 1618]. P

Nashe (1567): First Part of Pasquil's Apology. P

Sidney (d. 1586): Countess of Pembroke's Arcadia [augmented 1593, 1598]. P

Spenser (1552?): Faerie Queene, bks. i–iii [see 1596]. V
Muiopotmos or Fate of the Butterfly. V

Sylvester, Joshua (1563): Canticle of the Victory of Henry the Fourth [trs. Du Bartas]. V

Vallans, William: Tale of Two Swans. V

Watson, Thomas: Eglogue upon the Death of Sir Francis Walsingham. V

Webbe, Edward: Rare and Most Wonderful Things E. W. has seen. P

Wilson, Robert: Three Lords and Three Ladies of London. D morality.

1591

Anon.: Troublesome Raigne of John King of England [first pub. anon. 1591; attrib. Shakespeare 1611 and 1622 edd.]. D

Robert Herrick b.
William Browne b.

Breton (1545?): Briton's Bower of Delights. V

Drayton (1563): Harmonie of the Church. V

Fletcher (1549?): Of the Russe Commonwealth. P

Fraunce, Abraham: Countess of Pembroke's Yvychurch, pts. i, ii [iii 1593]. V
Countess of Pembroke's Emanuel. V

Greene (1560?): Greene's Farewell to Folly. P
Notable Discovery of Coosenage [i.e. pt. i of Conny Catching]. P
Second Part of Conny Catching. P

Harington (1561): Orlando Furioso in English heroical verse [rev. 1607, 1634]. V

Lodge (1558?): Robert Duke of Normandy. P
Catharos. P

Lyly (1554?): Endymion, the Man in the Moon. C

Raleigh (1552?): The Fight about the Azores. P

Savile, Sir Henry: Trs. Histories of Tacitus. P

Sidney (d. 1586): Astrophel and Stella [first authorized ed. in 1598 ed. of Arcadia]. V

Southwell (1561?): Mary Magdalens Funeral Tears. P

Spenser (1552?): Complaints. V
Daphnaida. V

Wilmot, Robert: Tancred and Gismund. T

Anon.: Arden of Feversham [pseudo-Shakespeare]. T

Hypneromachia, The Strife of Love in a Dream. V

Breton (1545?): Pilgrimage to Paradise. Countess of Pembroke's Love. V

Churchyard (1520?): Handful of Gladsome Verses given to the Queen's Majesty.

Constable, Henry: Diana [enlarg. 1594]. V

Daniel (1562): Delia [27 sonnets were published unauthorized in 1591 ed. of Sidney's Astrophel]. V

Complaint of Rosamond [in 2nd ed. of Delia; Delia and Rosamond augmented 1594, 1595, 1598]. V

Greene (d. 1592): Third Part of Conny Catching [see 1591]. P

Disputation between a hee Conny Catcher and a shee Conny Catcher. P

Black Bookes Messenger. P

Philomela. P

Quip for an Upstart Courtier. P

Groatsworth of Wit. P

Greene's Vision. P

Repentance of Greene.

Harvey, Gabriel: Four Letters and Certain Sonnets especially touching Robert Greene.

Kyd (1557?): Spanish Tragedy [n.d.]. T

Lodge (1558?): Euphues Shadow. P

Lyly (1554?): Gallathea. C

Midas. C

Nashe (1567): Pierce Penniless his Supplication to the Devil. P

Strange News of the Intercepting Certain Letters [called Apology of Pierce Penniless 1593]. P

Rich, Barnabe: Adventures of Brusanus. P

Sidney, Mary (Countess of Pembroke): A Discourse of Death; Antonius [both trs. Fr.]. D

Smith, Henry (d. 1591): Sermons [ed. Thomas Fuller 1657].

Stow (1525?): Annals of England [begun *c.* 1580 as Chronicles of England; re-issued by S. under present name and with additions up to date 1592, 1600, 1601, 1605; continued by Edward Howes 1615, 1618, 1631–2]. P

Sylvester, Joshua (1563): Trs. La Semaine of Du Bartas [completed in four instalments 1592–3–8–9; for collective ed. see 1605]. V

Plague revives in London.

Rose Theatre opened c. 1592.

Francis Quarles b.

Robert Greene d.

Philip Henslowe's Diary begins (see 1603).

Beginning of the quarrel between Greene, Nashe, and Gabriel Harvey (concl. 1597).

Montaigne d.

Greene-Nashe-Harvey Quarrel: Greene's *Quip for
an Upstart Courtier* (1592) attacks Gabriel
Harvey and his brother Richard; Nashe's
Pierce Penniless (1592) attacks the Harveys;
G. Harvey's *Four Letters Intercepted* (1592)
attacks Greene; Nashe replies in *Strange News
of the Intercepting Certain Letters* (1592; called
Apology of Pierce Penniless in 1593); Nashe's
Christ's Tears over Jerusalem with concilia-
tory preface (about Sept. 1593); G. Harvey's
Pierce's Supererogation and *New Letter of
Notable Contents* (written before he had seen
Christ's Tears) issued in autumn of 1593;
Nashe re-issues *Christ's Tears* with new Pre-
face renewing attack in 1594; further attack
by Nashe in *Have with you to Saffron Walden*
(1596).

1593

Anon.: Phoenix Nest [verse collection].
Life and Death of Jack Straw [attrib. Peele]. T
Barnes, Barnabe (1569?): Parthenophil and
Parthenophe. V
Chettle, Henry: Kind Heart's Dream [n.d.]. P
Churchyard (1520?): Churchyard's Challenge. V
Drayton (1563): Idea, the Shepherds Garland
[rev. as Eglogs in Poems 1606 (?); as Pastorals
in Poems 1619]. V
Fletcher (1549?): Licia, or Poems of Love [n.d.]. V
Gifford, George: Dialogue concerning Witches and
Witchcraft. P
Harvey, Gabriel: Pierce's Supererogation. P
New Letter of Notable Contents. P
Henryson (d. 1500?): Testament of Cressid [first
separate ed.; originally in Chaucer's Works
1532]. V
Lodge (1558?): Phillis. V
Life of William Longbeard. P
Markham (1568?): Discourse of Horsemanship. P
Marlowe (d. 1593): Trs. bk. i of Lucan's Pharsalia. V
Morley, Thomas (1557): Canzonets. V
Nashe (1567): Christ's Tears over Jerusalem. P
Norden, John: Speculum Britanniae [pt. i De-
scription of Middlesex; pt. ii Description of
Hertfordshire 1598].
Peele (1558?): Chronicle of Edward the First. D
Honour of the Garter [n.d.]. V
Shakespeare (1564): Venus and Adonis. V
Watson, Thomas (d. 1592): Tears of Fancie. V
Whetstone, George (d. 1587?): Aurelia [see 1582]. P

*Sir Richard Hawkins's
Voyage.
Izaak Walton b.
George Herbert b.
Christopher Marlowe d.
Theatres closed in London
between February and
end of the year on ac-
count of the Plague.*

31

Anon.: First Part of the Contention betwixt the Houses of York and Lancaster [see 1595; now regarded as a bad Quarto of Shakespeare's 2 Henry VI]. D

Tragical Raigne of Selimus [attrib. Greene]. D

True Tragedy of Richard the Third. D

Wars of Cyrus King of Persia. D

Taming of a Shrew. C

Knacke to Know a Knave. C

Zepheria. V

Bacon, Richard: Solon his Follie. P

Barnfield (1574): Affectionate Shepherd. V

Carew, Richard (1555): Godfrey of Bulloigne [trs. Cantos I–V of Tasso's Jerusalem Delivered]. V

Chapman (1559?): Shadow of Night. V

Daniel (1562): Cleopatra [in augmented ed. of Delia and Rosamond: see 1592]. T

Davys, John: Seaman's Secrets. P

Drayton (1563): Piers Gaveston [n.d.]. V

Matilda. V

Ideas Mirror [sonnets, rev. and enlarg. 1599, 1602, 1605; final ed. 1619]. V

Greene (d. 1592): Historie of Orlando Furioso. D

Looking Glass for London and England [with Lodge]. D

Friar Bacon and Friar Bongay. C

Hooker (1554?): Of the Laws of Ecclesiastical Polity, bks. i–iv [n.d.; v 1597; vi and viii 1648 (also 1651); vii in Gauden's ed. of H.'s Works 1662. Authenticity of bks. vi–viii doubtful]. P

Kyd (1557?): Cornelia [trs. Fr. of Robert Garnier]. T

Lodge (1558?): Wounds of Civil War. T

Looking Glass for London and England [with Greene]. D

Lyly (1554?): Mother Bombie. C

Marlowe (d. 1593): Edward the Second. T

Tragedie of Dido [with Nashe]. T

Morley, Thomas (1567): Madrigalls to Four Voices. V

Munday (1553): John a Kent and John a Cumber [acted *c.* 1594; prtd. J. P. Collier 1851].

Nashe (1567): Terrors of the Night. P

Unfortunate Traveller or Life of Jack Wilton. P

Peele (1558?): Battle of Alcazar. T

Percy, William: Sonnets to Fairest Celia. V

Shakespeare (1564): Lucrece [called Rape of Lucrece 1616]. V

Titus Andronicus. T

Sylvester (1563): Monodia [n.d.]. V

Willoby, Henry: Willobie his Avisa [corrected and enlarg. 1605, 1611]. V

James Howell b.?
Barnabe Googe d.
Erection of the Swan Theatre between 1594 and 1600.

Anon.: Alcilia. Philoparthens Loving Folly. V

  Tragedy of Locrine [attrib. Shakespeare on title-page]. D

  True Tragedy of Richard Duke of York [now regarded as a bad Quarto of Shakespeare's 3 Henry VI; combined with First Part of Contention betwixt Houses of York and Lancaster (see 1594) as Whole Contention between Houses of York and Lancaster, 1619]. D

Barnes, Barnabe: Divine Century of Spiritual Sonnets.

Barnfield (1574): Cynthia, with Certain Sonnets, and Legend of Cassandra. V

Beddingfield, Thomas: Trs. Florentine History of Macchiavelli [first Eng. trs.]. P

Breton (1545?): Marie Magdalen's Love. V

Chapman (1559?): Ovid's Banquet of Sence. A Coronet for Mistress Philosophy and other poems. V

Chettle, Henry: Piers Plainnes Seven Years Prenticeship. P

Churchyard (1520?): A Praise of Poetrie. V

  Consort of Heavenly Harmonie called Churchyard's Charitie. V

Copley, Anthony: Wits, Fittes and Fancies. Love's Owle. V and P

Daniel (1562): Civil Wars between Houses of Lancaster and York, bks. i–iv [bk. v added in 2nd ed. same year; bk. vi 1601, complete in bks. i–viii 1609]. V

Davys, John: World's Hydrographical Description. P

Drayton (1563): Endimion and Phoebe [n.d.]. V

Edwards, Thomas: Cephalus and Procris. V

Forde, Emanuel: Ornatus and Artesia [n.d.]. P

Lodge (1558?): Fig for Momus. V

Markham (1568?): Tragedy of Sir Richard Grenville. D

Morley, Thomas (1559): First Book of Ballets. V

Peele (1558?): Old Wives' Tale. C

Sidney (d. 1586): Apologie for Poetrie [another ed. same year called Defence of Poesy]. P

Southwell (d. 1595): Saint Peter's Complaint. V

  Moeoniae, or Certain Poems.

  Triumphs over Death. P

Spenser (1552?): Amoretti. Epithalamion. V

  Colin Clouts come home again [cont. Astrophel, and Mourning Muse, two poems on death of Sir Philip Sidney]. V

W. W.: Trs. of Plautus' Menaechmi. C

Sir Walter Raleigh's Voyage to Guiana.
Thomas Carew b.?
Thomas May b.
Robert Southwell executed.
Thomas Kyd d.?
Andrew Maunsell, 'Catalogue of English Books'.
Tasso d.
Montaigne, 'Essais' (in final form: see 1580).

Anon.: Delightful History of Celestina the Fair [trs. by W. Barley?]. P

Raigne of King Edward the Third [pseudo-Shakespeare]. D

Knacke to Know an Honest Man. C

The Goode Housewife's Jewell (cookery book).

Copley, Anthony: A Fig for a Fortune. V

Dannett, Thomas: Trs. History of Philip de Commines [another trs. by 'R. B.' 1639]. P

Davies (1569): Orchestra. V

Dickenson, John: Shepherd's Complaint [n.d.]. V

Drayton (1563): Tragical Legend of Robert, Duke of Normandy. V

Mortemeriados [rev. as Barons' Wars 1603]. V

Griffin, Bartholomew: Fidessa more Chaste than Kind. V

Harington (1561): Metamorphosis of Ajax. P

Anatomy of the metamorphosed Ajax. P

Ulysses upon Ajax. P

An Apology or rather a Recantation [n.d.]. P

Lodge (1558?): Margarite of America. P

Wits Miserie. P

Devil Conjured. P

Prosopopeia [doubtful if by L.].

Lynche, Richard: Diella, certain sonnets. V

Markham (1568?): Poem of Poems, or Sion's Muse [n.d.]. V

Middleton (1580): Wisdom of Solomon Paraphrased. V

Munday (1553): Trs. Palmerin of England. P

Nashe (1567): Have with you to Saffron Walden. P

Raleigh (1552?): Discovery of the Empire of Guiana. P

Smith, William: Chloris or Complaint of Passionate Shepherd. V

Spenser (1552?): Faerie Queene [bks. i–iii revised, with addition of bks. iv–vi; also 1609, 1611: see 1590]. V

Prothalamion. V

Fowre Hymns. V

Blackfriars Theatre opened.

James Shirley b.

Shakespeare's son Hamnet dies.

Descartes b.

Bacon (1561): Essays. Meditationes Sacrae. Colours of Good and Evil [Ten Essays only; Essays enlarged 1612, 1625]. P

Beard, Thomas: Theatre of God's Judgements. P

Breton (1595?): Arbour of Amorous Devices [with others]. V

Auspicante Jehoua, Maries Exercise. V

Wits Trenchamour. P

Will of Wit or Wit's Will or Will's Wit [corrected 1606]. P

Dowland, John (1563?): First Book of Songs. V

Drayton (1563): England's Heroical Epistles. V

Gerard, John: Herball. P

Hall (1574): Virgidemiae, bks. i–iii [see 1598]. V

Hooker (1554?): Laws of Ecclesiastical Polity, bk. v [see 1594]. P

James VI, King of Scotland: Demonologie. P

Ling, Nicholas (ed.): Politeuphuia or Wits Commonwealth [John Bodenham also supposed to be editor; 12th ed. 1630 (?)].

Lok, Henry: Ecclesiasticus, with Sundrie Sonnets.

Lyly (1554?): Woman in the Moon. C

Montgomery, Alexander: The Cherrie and the Slae. V

Rowley (1585?): Birth of Merlin [acted between 1597–1607; prtd. 1662; alleged collaboration of Shakespeare]. D

S., E.: Discovery of the Knights of the Post [Edward Sharpham author?]. P

Shakespeare (1564): King Richard the Second. T
Romeo and Juliet. Q 1 [Q 2 1599]. T
Richard the Third. T

Tofte, Robert: Laura. V

George Peele d.?

Shakespeare buys New Place in Stratford.

Nashe's play ' Isle of Dogs' suppressed and author imprisoned.

Isaac Casaubon's diary 'Ephemerides' begins (ends with his death 1614; pub. 1850).

Elizabeth]

1598

Anon.: Comedy of Mucedorus [enlarg. 1610; pseudo-Shakespeare]. D

Famous Victories of Henry V. D

Pilgrimage to Parnassus. Return from Parnassus, pts. i, ii [acted *c.* 1598, *c.* 1601, *c.* 1602 at St. John's, Cambridge; pt. ii of Return prtd. 1606; the trilogy prtd. W. D. Macray 1886]. C

Sir Thomas More [written before this date; prtd. A. Dyce 1844; partly by Shakespeare?]. D

Barnfield (1574): Encomion of Lady Pecunia. Complaint of Poetry for Death of Liberality. Combat between Conscience and Covetousness. Poems in Divers Humours. V

Bastard, Thomas: Chrestoleros: seven books of Epigrams. V

Bernard, Richard: Terence in English [trs. Adelphi, Andria, Eunuchus, Heautontimoroumenos, Hecyra, Phormio]. D

Breton (1545?): Solemn Passion of the Soul's Love. V

Chapman (1559?): Blind Beggar of Alexandria. C

Seven Bookes of the Illiades [1st instalment of trs. Iliad]. V

Achilles Shield: other seven books of Homer [2nd instalment of trs. Iliad: see 1610,1611]. V

Chaucer (d. 1400): Works, ed. Thomas Speght [see 1532].

Forde, Emanuel: Parismus [pt. ii Parismenos 1599]. P

Greene (d. 1592): Scottish History of James the Fourth. D tragi-comedy.

Guilpin, Edward: Skialethia, or a Shadow of Truth in Certain Epigrams and Satires. V

Hakluyt (1552?): Principall Navigations, Voyages and Discoveries [concl. 1600; enlarg. from work of 1589]. P

Hall (1574): Virgidemiae, bks. iv–vi [see 1597]. V

Marlowe (d. 1593): Hero and Leander [completed by Chapman]. V

Marston (1575?): Metamorphosis of Pigmalion's Image, and Certain Satires. V

Scourge of Villainie [enlarg. 1599]. V

Meres, Francis: Palladis Tamia. P

Rankins, William: Seven Satires applied to the Week. V

Rowlands, Samuel: Betraying of Christ, with other Poems.

Shakespeare (1564): Henry IV, pt. i. D

Love's Labour's Lost. C

Southwell (d. 1595): A Short Rule of Good Life [n.d.]. P

Edict of Nantes.
Death of Burghley.
First quarrel between Ben Jonson and Marston (see 1601).
Giovanni Florio, 'World of Wordes' (Italian and English Dictionary; rev. 1611).
First Eng. trs. of Aristotle's 'Politics' by J. D.
Voiture b.

Stow (1525?): Survay of London [another ed.
1603; contd. and enlarg., by Anthony
Munday 1618; Munday and Dyson 1633; ed.
J. Strype 1720, W. J. Thoms 1876, C. L.
Kingsford 1908].

Tofte, Robert: Trs. Orlando Inamorato of Boiardo
[bks. i–iii only]. V

Young, Bartholomew: Trs. Diana of George Montemayor. P and V

1599

Anon.: Passionate Pilgrim [cont. two sonnets by
Shakespeare and poems by Barnfield and
others].

Edmund Spenser d.
Globe Theatre opened.

Warning for Fair Women. T

Sir Clyomon and Sir Clamydes [sometimes
attrib. Peele]. D

Tragedy of Solimon and Perseda [attrib. Kyd]. D

Comedy of George a Greene [attrib. Greene]. D

Allott, Robert (ed.): Wit's Theatre of the Little
World [verse miscellany].

Chapman (1559?): An Humorous Days Mirth. C

Cutwode, Thomas: Caltha Poetarum, or the
Bumble Bee. V

Daniel (1562): Musophilus. Letter from Octavia
to Marcus Antonius. V

Poetical Essays [collection of previously pub.
poems: see 1601].

Davies (1569): Nosce Teipsum [corrected 1602]. V
Hymnes of Astraea. V

Greene (d. 1592): Alphonsus King of Arragon. C
Orpharion. V

Hakluyt (1522?): Principall Navigations, Voyages
and Discoveries [completed: see 1598]. P

Hayward, Sir John: Life and Raigne of King
Henry IV. P

Heywood (1575?): King Edward the Fourth, pts.
i, ii. D chronicle.

James VI, King of Scotland: Basilikon Doron. P

M.,T.: Micro-cynicon, six snarling satires
[Thomas Middleton or Thomas Moffat?].

Nashe (1567): Nashes Lenten Stuffe. P

Peele (d. 1597?): Love of King David and Fair
Bethsabe. D

Porter, Henry: Two Angry Women of Abington.
D

Shakespeare (1564): Julius Cæsar [acted *c.* 1599;
printed 1623]. T

Weever, John: Epigrams in the Oldest Cut. V

1600

Anon.: Book of Merry Riddles [earliest known ed.].

Wisdom of Dr. Dodypoll. D

Weakest goeth to the Wall. D

Look about you. C

Maid's Metamorphosis [attrib. Lyly]. D

First Part of the Life of Sir John Oldcastle [now attrib. Munday, Drayton, and others. Another issue, dated 1600 but really prtd. 1619, attributes the play to Shakespeare]. D

True and Credible Report of a great and very dangerous fight at Sea. P

Allott, Robert (ed.): England's Parnassus [collection of verse by various hands].

Bodenham, John (ed.): England's Helicon [collection of verse by various hands; another ed. 1614].

Belvedere [collection of verse by various hands; another ed. 1610].

Breton (1545?): Pasquil's Fooles Cap. V

Pasquil's Mistresse. V

Pasquil's passe and passeth not. V

Melancholike Humours. V

Pasquil's Mad-Cap and Mad-Cappe's Message. V

Second Part of Pasquil's Mad Cap, entitled Fooles Cap. V

Strange Fortune of two Excellent Princes. P

Cornwallis, Sir William: Essayes [enlarg. 1610; Essays or Encomions 1616; Essays of Paradoxes 1616; Essays Corrected 1632].

Dekker (1570?): Shoemaker's Holiday. C

Comedy of Old Fortunatus. D

Dowland, John (1563?): Second Book of Songs. V

Fairfax, Edward: Godfrey of Bulloigne [trs. Jerusalem Delivered of Tasso]. V

Haughton, William: Grim the Collier of Croyden [acted *c.* 1600; prtd. 1662].

Heywood (1575?): Ovid's Art of Love [trs. by H., appropriated by H. Austin; n.d.; 1600–10(?)]. V

Holland, Philemon: Trs. Livy's Roman History. P

Jonson (1573?): Everyman out of His Humour. C

Kemp, William: Kemp's Nine Daies Wonder. P

Markham (1568?): Tears of the Beloved. V

Marlowe (d. 1593): Massacre at Paris [n.d.]. T

Trs. bk. i of Lucan's Pharsalia. V

Nashe (1567): Summers Last Will and Testament. C

Rowlands, Samuel: Letting of Humours Blood in the Head Vaine. V

East India Company founded.

Fortune Theatre opened.

Peter Heylyn b.

William Prynne b.

Richard Hooker d.

Thomas Deloney d.?

William Gilbert, 'De Magnete'.

Sir Edward Coke's 'Reports' (of law suits) in French 1600–15 (in English 1658).

Calderon b.

Shakespeare (1564): Henry IV, pt. ii. D
   Henry V. D
   Merchant of Venice. D
   Midsummer-Night's Dream. C
   Much Ado about Nothing. C
   As You Like It [acted *c.* 1600; prtd. 1623]. C
Thynne, Francis: Emblems and Epigrams. V
Tourneur (1575?): Transformed Metamorphosis. V
Vaughan, William (1577): Golden Grove [enlarg.
    1608]. P
   Natural and Artificial Directions for Health. P

1601

Anon.: Jack Drum's Entertainment. C
Breton (1545?): A Divine Poem in two parts. V
   Upon the Longing of a Blessed Heart. V
Chester, Robert (ed.): Love's Martyr [cont. poems
   by Jonson, Chapman, Marston, and others,
   and The Phoenix and Turtle attrib. Shake-
   speare]. V
Cornwallis, Sir William: Discourses on Seneca. P
Daniel (1562): Works, newly augmented [cont.,
   among unpub. works, bk. vi of Civil Wars
   (see 1595) and Pastoral to the Delia Sonnets.
   Later edd. of Works, mostly rev. and enlarg.
   1605-7-11-23; ed. Grosart 1885].
Holland, Philemon: Trs. Pliny's Natural History. P
Jones, Robert (fl. 1616): First Booke of Songs &
   Aires. V
   Second Booke of Songs & Aires. V
Jonson (1573?): Everyman in his Humour. C
   Cynthia's Revels. C
Lyly (1554?): Love's Metamorphosis. C
Markham (1568?): Marie Magdalen's Lamenta-
   tions. V
Morley, Thomas (1557): The Triumphs of Oriana. V
Munday (1553): Death of Robert Earl of Hunting-
   ton [with Henry Chettle]. T
   Downfall of Robert Earl of Huntington [pt. ii
   of above]. T
Shakespeare (1564): Twelfth Night [acted *c.* 1601;
   prtd. 1623]. C

*Queen Elizabeth's Poor
  Law.
Execution of Essex.
John Earle b.
Thomas Nashe d.
Sir Thomas North d.?
Ben Jonson's quarrel with
  Dekker and Marston.*

Anon.: Liberalitie and Prodigalitie. D
 Chronicle History of Thomas Lord Cromwell
  [attrib. Shakespeare on title-page]. D
 A Larum for London. D
 How a Man may chuse a Good Wife from a Bad. D
Basse, William: Sword and Buckler. V
 Three pastoral Elegies. V
Beaumont (1584): Salmacis and Hermaphroditus
  [trs. Ovid: see 1640]. V
Beaumont, Sir John: Metamorphosis of Tobacco. V
Breton (1545?) Soule's Harmony. V
 Old Madcap's New Gallimawfry. V
 Mother's Blessing. V
 True Description of Unthankfulness. V
 Wonders worth the Hearing. P
 Poste with a mad Packet of Letters [enlarg.
  1603; pt. ii 1606; many edd. to 1637]. P
Campion (1567): Art of English Poesie. P
Carew, Richard (1555): Survey of Cornwall. P
Davies (1565?): Mirum in Modum. V
Davison, Francis: Poetical Rapsody [by various
  hands: enlarg. 1608, 1611, 1621]. V
Dekker (1570?): Satiro-mastix. C
Jonson (1573?): Poetaster, or the Arraignment. C
Lindsay (d. 1555): Satyr of the Three Estates
  [see 1540, 1568]. D
Lodge (1558?): Paradoxes.
 Trs. Works of Flavius Josephus.
Mansell, Sir Robert (1573): A True Report of the
  Service done upon certaine Gallies. P
Patricke, Simon: Means of Well Governing against
  Niccolo Macchiavel [trs. Gentillet]. P
Marston (1575?): Antonio and Mellida. T
 Antonio's Revenge [pt. ii of above]. T
Middleton (1580)?: Blurt Master-Constable. C
Rowlands, Samuel: Greenes Ghost haunting
  Conie Catchers. P
 Tis Merry when Gossips meet. V
Shakespeare (1564): Merry Wives of Windsor. C

*William Chillingworth b.
Bodleian Library opens.
First Eng. trs. of Guari-
ni's 'Il Pastor Fido' by
Edward Dymock.
The anon. play 'Narcissus'
acted at St. John's, Ox-
ford, c. 1602–3 (prtd.
1893).*

1603

Anon.: Bachelor's Banquet [trs. Quinze Joyes de
  Marriage]. P
Bacon (1561): Union of England and Scotland. P
Breton (1545?): Dialogue full of Pith and Pleasure
  between Three Philosophers. P
 A Mad World my Masters [also 1635]. P
Chettle, Henry: England's Mourning Garment. V
Daniel (1562): Panegyricke Congratulatorie to
  the King's Majestie. V Poetical Epistles. V
 Defence of Rhyme. P

*Death of Queen Elizabeth.
Accession of James I.
Plague in London.
Sir Kenelm Digby b.
Shakerley Marmion b.
Philip Henslowe's 'Diary'
ends (began 1592; pub.
1845).
John Barclay 'Euphor-
mionis Satyricon'
(concl. 1607).*

Davies (1565?): Microcosmos. V
Dekker (1570?): The Wonderful Year 1603. P
 Patient Grissel [with Chettle & Haughton]. C
Dowland, John (1563?): Third Book of Songs. V
Drayton (1563): Barrons Wars [see 1596]. V
Florio, John: Trs. Montaigne's Essays. P
Fowldes, W.: Trs. Batrachomyomachia. V
Hall (1574): The King's Prophecie. V
Holland, Philemon: Trs. Plutarch's Morals. P
James I: True Law of Free Monarchies. P
Knolles, Richard (1550?): History of the Turks
 [enlarg. 1610–21–31–38]. P
Lodge (1558?): Treatise on the Plague. P
Norden, John: A Pensive Soul's Delight. P
Shakespeare (1564): Hamlet Q 1. T
 Troilus and Cressida [acted *c.* 1603; prtd. 1609].

1604

Anon.: Palladis Palatium [anthology].
Alexander (1567?): Aurora. V
 A Paraenesis to the Prince. V
 Monarchick Tragedies [Croesus, Darius: see
 1607]. T
Bacon (1561): His Apology. P
 Considerations touching better Pacification of
 the Church of England. P
Breton (1545?): Passionate Shepherd. V
 Grimello's Fortune. P
Churchyard (d. 1604): Churchyard's Goodwill. V
Daniel (1563): Vision of the Twelve Goddesses. D
Dekker (1570?): Honest Whore [pt. i; with
 Middleton? See 1630]. D
 Entertainment given to King James. D
Drayton (1563): The Owle. V
 Moyses in a Map of his Miracles. V
 Paean Triumphall for the Societie of Goldsmiths
 of London. V
Hayward, Sir John: Sanctuarie of a troubled
 Soul [pt. ii 1607; two pts. together 1616]. P
James I: Counterblast to Tobacco. P
Marlowe (d. 1593): Tragical History of Dr. Faus-
 tus. T
Marston (1575?): The Malcontent [another ed.
 same year enlarg. by Webster]. D
Middleton (1580): Father Hubbard's Tales. P
 The Blacke Booke. P
Rowlands: Look to it, for I will stab ye. V
Rich, Barnabe (1540?): A Souldier's Wish to
 Briton's Welfare. P
 Fruits of Long Experience [pt. ii of above]. P
Shakespeare (1564): Hamlet Q 2 [see 1603].
 Measure for Measure [acted *c.* 1604; prtd. 1623].
 Othello [acted; prtd. 1622].

Fall of Ostend.
Hampton Court Confer-
 ence.
Abolition of private pat-
 ronage of players.
English players at Fon-
 tainebleau.
Jasper Mayne b.
Thomas Churchyard d.

Anon.: London Prodigall [attrib. Shakespeare on
title-page]. C
First Part of Ieronimo [doubtfully attrib. Kyd]. T
Chronicle History of King Leir. D
Life and Death of Captain Thomas Stukeley. T
Trial of Chivalry. D
Fair Maid of Bristow. D
History of the Triall of Chevalry, with Life of
Cavaliero Dicke Bowyer. D
School of Slovenrie [trs. Grobianus of Dede-
kind].

Bacon (1561): Advancement of Learning. P
Breton (1545?): Soul's Immortal Crown. V
Honour of Valour. V
Camden (1551): Remains of a Greater Work con-
cerning Britain [see 1586]. P
Carew, Richard (1555): Excellency of the English
Tongue [in Camden's Remains above]. P
Chapman (1559?): All Fooles, a comedy.
Eastward Ho [with Ben Jonson and Marston]. C
Daniel (1562): Certaine Small Poems [Ulysses and
the Siren and others]. Philotas. T
Davies, John (1565?): Humours Heaven on Earth
[Civil Wars of Death and Fortune. Triumph
of Death]. V
Wits Pilgrimage [n.d.]. V
Drayton (1563): Poems [earliest collection; later
collections mostly rev. and enlarg. 1606(?)
8–10–13–19–20–30–7; Poems ed. J. P. Collier
1856; ed. R. Hooper 1876; W. Hebel 1931].
Hall (1574): Meditations and Vows (enlarg. 1609,
1621]. P
Heywood (1575?): If you know not me, you know
Nobody [see 1606]. D
Jonson (1573?): Sejanus his Fall. T
The Masque of Blackness. D
Marston (1575?): Dutch Courtezan. C
Montgomery, Alexander: Mind's Melody. V
Rowlands, Samuel: Hell's broke loose. V
Rowley, Samuel: When you see me you know me
or Chronicle History of King Henry VIII. D
Shakespeare (1564): Macbeth [acted *c.* 1605; prtd.
1623]. T
Sylvester, Joshua (1563): Du Bartas his Divine
Weekes and Works [collective ed. of trs. of
La Semaine and other works of Du Bartas;
concl. 1606; later edd. 1608–11–13; with other
works of Sylvester 1633–41: see 1592]. V
Wodehouse, Peter: Democritus his Dream; or the
Contention betweene the Elephant and the
Flea. V

Gunpowder Plot.
James I visits Oxford.
Sir Thomas Browne b.
Bulstrode Whitelocke b.
Thomas Randolph b.
Sir William Dugdale b.
William Habington b.
John Stow d.
Imprisonment of the au-
thors of 'Eastward Ho'
for references to the
Scotch.
'Don Quixote', pt. i (com-
plete 1615).

Anon.: Return from Parnassus, pt. ii [see 1598]. C
Wily Beguiled. C
Sir Gyles Goosecap. C
Burton, William: Seven Dialogues [trs. Colloquia of Erasmus].
Chapman (1559?): Monsieur D'Olive. C
Gentleman Usher. C
Daniel (1562): The Queen's Arcadia, a Pastoral tragi-comedy.
Day, John: Ile of Guls. C
Dekker (1570?): Seven Deadly Sins of London. P
News from Hell [enlarg. as A Knight's Conjuring 1607]. P
The Double P.P. V
Drayton (1563): Poems Lyrick and Pastoral [n.d.; among new poems: Ballad of Agincourt, Man in the Moon, To His Coy Love, To Cupid, The Virginian Voyage].
Hall (1574): Art of Divine Meditation. P
Heaven upon Earth. P
Heywood (1575?): If you know not me you know Nobody, pt. ii [see 1605]. D
Holland, Philemon: Trs. History of Twelve Caesars by Suetonius. P
Jonson (1573?): Hymenaei. D masque.
Marston (1575?): Parasitaster or the Fawne. C
Wonder of Women, or Tragedy of Sophonisba. T
Peacham, Henry, jnr.: Art of Drawing [called Graphice 1612]. P
Rich, Barnabe (1540?): Faults, Faults, and Nothing Else but Faults [called My Ladies Looking Glass 1616]. P
Rowlands, Samuel: Terrible Battle between the Consumers of the World. P and V
Southwell (d. 1595): Fourefold Meditation of Foure Last Things [? by Philip, Earl of Arundel]. V
Warner (1558?): Albions England [see 1586]. V
West, Richard: News from Bartholomew Fair. V

Sir William D'Avenant b.
Edmund Waller b.
Pierre Corneille b.
John Lyly d.

Anon.: Tragedy of Caesar and Pompey. T
  Tragedy of Claudius Tiberius Nero [not to be
  confused with Tragedy of Nero 1624]. T
  The Puritaine or Widow of Watling Street
  [pseudo-Shakespeare]. D
Alexander (1567?): Monarchick Tragedies [adds
  Alexandraean and Julius Caesar to those of
  1604]. T
Barnes, Barnabe: The Devil's Charter. D
Beaumont (1584) **and Fletcher** (1579): The
  Woman Hater. D
Campion (1567): Masque presented in Honour of
  Lord Hayes.
Chapman (1559?): Bussy D'Ambois: a Tragedie.
Davies, John (1565?): Summa Totalis. V
Day, John: Travailes of Three English Brothers
  [with Rowley and George Wilkins]. D
Dekker (1570?): Whore of Babylon. D allegory.
  History of Sir Thomas Wyatt [with Webster]. T
  Westward Ho [with Webster]. C
  Northward Ho [with Webster]. C
  Jests to Make you Merry [with George Wilkins]. P
  Knights Conjuring. P
Drayton (1563): Legend of Great Cromwell
  [altered as History of Life and Death of Lord
  Cromwell 1609]. V
Grimestone, Edward: Admirable and Memorable
  Histories. P
Hall (1574): Holy Observations. P
Heywood (1575?): A Woman kilde with Kind-
  ness. T
  Fair Maid of the Exchange. C
  Fortune by Land and Sea [acted; prtd. 1655;
  with Rowley]. D
Jones, Robert (fl. 1616): First set of Madrigals. V
Jonson (1573?): Volpone or the Fox. C
Markham (1568?): Cavelarice or the English
  Horseman. P
  English Arcadia [pt. ii 1613]. P
Marston (1575?): What you will. C
Middleton (1580): Michaelmas Term. C
  The Phoenix. C
Niccols, Richard: The Cuckow. V
Norden, John: The Surveyor's Dialogue. P
Rowlands, Samuel: Diogenes Lanthorne. V & P
  Democritus, or Dr. Merriman his Medicines. V
Shakespeare (1564): Timon of Athens [acted;
  prtd. 1623].
Sharpham, Edward: Cupid's Whirligig. C
  The Fleire. C
Tomkis, Thomas: Lingua, or Combat of the
  Tongue and the Five Senses. C

John Owen, 'Epigrams'
  (Eng. trs. 1619).
Final ed. of Camden's
  'Britannia' (see 1586).
Scudéry b.
D'Urfé, 'Astrée', 1607–27.
Malherbe, 'Odes' between
  1607 and 1628.

Topsell, Edward: History of Fourefooted Beasts
[trs. Conrad Gesner]. P
Tourneur (1575?) (?): Revenger's Tragedy. T
Walkington, Thomas: Optick Glass of Humours. P
West, Richard: Court of Conscience or Dick
Whippers Sessions. V
Wilkins, George: Miseries of Inforst Marriage. D

1608

Anon.: Merry Devil of Edmonton. C
A Yorkshire Tragedy [attrib. Shakespeare on
title-page]. T
Armin, Robert: A Nest of Ninnies. D
Breton (1545): Divine Considerations of the Soul. P
Chapman (1559?): Conspiracy of Charles Duke of
Byron [two parts]. T
Day, John: Humour out of Breath. C
Law Tricks, or Who would have thought it. C
Dekker (1570?): Belman of London. P
Lanthorne and Candlelight [pt. ii of above; rev.
in 1609; (O per se O); 1616 (Villanies Dis-
covered); 1632 (English Villanies)]. P
The Dead Term or Westminster's Complaint. P
Grimestone, Edward: General History of the
Netherlands. P
Hall (1574): Characters of Virtues and Vices. P
Six Decades of Epistles. P
Heywood (1575?): Rape of Lucrece. T
Two Most Worthy Histories [trs. Catiline Con-
spiracy and Jugurthan War of Sallust]. P
Jones, Robert (fl. 1616): Ultimum Vale. V
Jonson (1573?): Two Royall Masques [Of Black-
ness, Of Beauty].
Markham (1568?): Dumb Knight [with Lewis
Machin]. C
Middleton (1580): Family of Love. C
A Mad World, my Masters. C
A Trick to Catch the Old One. C
Your Five Gallants [n.d.]. C
Perkins, William: Discourse of the Art of Witch-
craft. P
Rowlands, Samuel: Humours Looking Glass
[attrib. R.]. V
Shakespeare (1564): King Lear. T
Coriolanus [acted *c.* 1608; prtd. 1623]. T
West, Richard: Century of Epigrams.
Wiclif (d. 1384): Two Treatises against the Order
of Begging Friars. P

John Milton b.
Thomas Fuller b.
*Opening of the salon of
the Hôtel de Rambouillet
by Catherine de Vivonne,
Marquise de Rambouil-
let.*

Anon.: Every Woman in her Humour. C
Armin, Robert: Two Maids of More-clacke. D
 Italian Taylor and his Boy. D
Burton, Charles: Feminine Monarchie [3rd edition in phonetic spelling 1634].
Daniel (1562): Civil Wars between Houses of Lancaster and York [completed: see 1595]. V
Davies (1565?): Holy Roode. V
Dekker (1570?): Guls Hornbooke. P
 Ravens Almanack. P
 Four Birds of Noahs Ark. P
 Work for Armourers. P
Drayton (1563): Life and Death of Lord Cromwell [see 1607]. V
Greville (1554): Tragedy of Mustapha [improved version 1633]. D
Hall (1574): Discovery of a New World [Mundus alter et idem trs. by John Healy; n.d.]. P
 Solomon's Divine Arts. P
Heywood (1575?): Troia Britannica. V
Holland, Philemon (1552): Trs. Ammianus.
Jewel, John (d. 1571): Works ed. Fuller. P
Jones, Robert (fl. 1616): A Musicall Dream. V
Jonson (1573?): Case is Alter'd. C
 Masque of Queens.
 Epicoene. C.
'M., W.': Man in the Moon telling strange Fortunes. P
Rich, Barnabe (1540?): Roome for a Gentleman [pt. ii of Faults, Faults, 1606]. P
Rowlands, Samuel: Knave of Clubs [originally Tis Merry when Knaves Meet *c*. 1600]. V
 Whole Crew of Kind Gossips. V
Rowley (1585?): A Search for Money. C
Shakespeare (1564): Sonnets.
 Troilus and Cressida. D
 Pericles [with George Wilkins and William Rowley?]. D
Spenser (d. 1599): Two Cantos of Mutabilitie in new ed. of Fairie Queene [see 1590]. V

Edward Hyde (Earl of Clarendon) b.
Benjamin Whichcote b.
Sir John Suckling b.
Sir Matthew Hale b.
William Warner d.
Bacon, 'De Sapientia Veterum Liber' (for Eng. trs. see 1619).

1610

Anon.: Histriomastix [partly by Marston?]. C
Campion (1567): Two Books of Airs [n.d.: see 1612]. V
Chapman (1559?): Homer Prince of Poets [3rd instalment of Iliad; n.d.: see 1598, 1611]. V
Daniel (1562): Tethys Festival. D masque.
Dent, Arthur (d. 1607): The Plain Man's Pathway to Heaven. P

George Turberville d.?
Richard Niccols ed. 'Mirror for Magistrates'(final ed.; see 1559).
Scarron b.
Hardy, 'Mariamne'.

Donne (1573): Pseudo-Martyr. P
Fletcher, Giles, jnr. (1588?): Christ's Victory and
Triumph, 2 pts. V
Fletcher (1579): Faithful Shepherdess [n.d.; 2nd
ed. corrected 1629; 3rd ed. enlarg. 1634]. D
Heath, John: Two Centuries of Epigrams. V
Holland, Philemon (1552): Trs. Camden's Britan-
nia [another ed. 1637: see 1586]. P
Jones, Robert (fl. 1616): The Muses' Garden of
Delights. V
Markham (1568?): Markham's Masterpiece. P
Rich (1540?): New Description of Ireland [called
New Irish Prognostication 1624]. P
Rich, Richard: News from Virginia. V
Scot, Thomas: Philomythie or Philomythologie
[enlarg. 1616, 1622; pt. ii 1625]. V
Selden (1584): England's Epinomis. P
Duello, or Single Combat. P
Shakespeare (1564): The Tempest, Cymbeline,
A Winter's Tale; acted between 1610 and
1612 [printed 1623].
Sharpe, Roger: More Fools Yet [epigrams]. V

1611

Authorized Version of the Bible.
Byrd (1538?): Psalmes, Songs, & Sonnets. V
Chapman (1559?): May Day, a comedy.
Trs. Iliad [complete: see 1598, 1610]. V
Coryate (1577?): Coryats Crudities. P
Coryats Crambe. P
Odcombian Banquet. P
Davies (1565?): Scourge of Folly [n.d.]. V
Donne (1573): Anatomy of the World [The First
Anniversary and A Funeral Elegy; 2nd ed.
with The Second Anniversary added 1612]. V
Ignatius his Conclave. P
Fenton, Roger: Treatise of Usury. P
Heywood (1575?): The Golden Age. D
Jonson (1597?): Catiline his Conspiracy. T
Middleton (1580): The Roaring Girl or Moll Cut-
purse [with Dekker]. C
Speed (1552?): History of Great Britain [rev.
1623, 1627; enlarg. 1632; originally com-
menced as Theatre of the Empire of Great
Britain 1611]. P
Genealogies recorded in Sacred Scriptures. P
Tourneur (1575?): Atheist's Tragedy. T

James Harrington b.
Sir Thomas Urquhart b.
Robert Leighton b.
Giles Fletcher senr. d.
*Shakespeare's retirement
to Stratford about this
date.*
*Randle Cotgrave, 'Dic-
tionary of French and
English Tongues' (ed.
with Eng.-Fr. Diction-
ary by R. Sherwood
1632; ed. J. Howell
1650-60-73).*

Alexander (1567?): Elegy on Death of Prince Henry. V

Breton (1545?): Wit's Private Wealth. P
Cornucopiae. Pasquil's Night Cap. V

Campion (1567): Third and Fourth Book of Airs [n.d.: see 1610]. V

Chapman (1559?): Widow's Tears, a comedy.
Trs. Petrarch's Penitential Psalms. V
An Epicede, or Funeral Song on Death of Prince Henry. V

Daniel (1562): History of England, pt. i [to end of Stephen; pt. ii, continued to Edward III, 1618]. P

Davies (1569): Discovery of Causes why Ireland was never subdued. P

Davies (1565?): Muse's Sacrifice, or Divine Meditations. V

Dekker (1570?): If it be not good, the Devil is in it. C
Troia Nova Triumphans.

Deloney (d. 1607?): Thomas of Reading [earliest extant ed.; first pub. probably before 1600]. P

Dowland, John (1563?): A Pilgrim's Solace. V

Drayton (1563): Polyolbion pt. i [n.d.: see 1622]. V

Field, Nathaniel: A Woman is a Weathercock. C

Hall (1574): Contemplations, vol. i [ii 1614, iii 1615, iv 1618, v 1620, vi 1622, vii 1623, viii 1626]. P

Heywood (1575?): Apology for Actors [altered by William Cartwright as Actor's Vindication 1658]. P

Hooker (d. 1600): Learned Discourse of Justification. P
Sermon of the Nature of Pride. P
Answer to the Supplication of Mr. Travers. P
Remedy against Sorrow and Fear. P
Sermon of the Certainty and Perpetuity of Faith. P

Jonson (1597?): The Alchemist. C

Purchas (1575?): Purchas his Pilgrimage, or Relation of the World. P

Rowlands, Samuel: Knave of Hearts. V

Sylvester (1563): Lachrimae Lachrimarum [enlarg. 1613]. V

Webster (1580?): The White Devil. T

Wither (1588): Prince Henry's Obsequies. V
Epithalamia, or Nuptial Poems. V

Death of Henry, Prince of Wales.
Samuel Butler b.
Thomas Killigrew senr. b.
Sir John Harington d.
First Eng. trs. of 'Don Quixote', pt. i by Thomas Shelton (see 1620).

Bayly, Lewis, Bishop of Bangor: Practice of Piety [earliest extant, i.e. 3rd, ed.; first pub. earlier in the century]. P

Beaumont (1584): Masque of the Inner Temple [n.d.].
Knight of the Burning Pestle [with Fletcher]. D burlesque.

Browne (1591): Britannia's Pastorals, pt. i [n.d.; pt. ii 1616; iii prtd. T. C. Croker 1852]. V

Campion (1567): Songs bewailing the Death of Prince Henry. V
Entertainment given by Lord Knowles. D masque.

Chapman (1559?): Revenge of Bussy D'Ambois. T
Masque of Middle Temple [n.d.].

Dekker (1570?): Strange Horse Race. P

Drummond (1585): Tears on Death of Meliades. V
Mausoleum [elegies by D., Chapman, Wither, Rowley, and others]. V

Hayward, Sir John: Lives of the Three Norman Kings of England. P

Heywood (1575?): The Brazen Age. D
The Silver Age. D

Markham (1568?): The English Husbandman [bk. ii 1614; rev. 1635]. P

Marston (1575?): Insatiate Countess. T

Rich (1540?): Opinion Defied. P
Excellency of Good Women. P

Rowlands, Samuel: More Knaves Yet. V

Scoggin, John: Scoggin his Jests [earliest extant collection; originally *c.* 1565; Jests gathered by Andrew Boord 1626].

Shakespeare (1564): Henry VIII [acted; prtd 1623]. D

Wither (1588): Abuses stript and whipt [includes The Scourge and Epigrams]. V

Globe Theatre burnt.
Jeremy Taylor b.
Richard Crashaw b.?
John Cleveland b.
La Rochefoucauld b.
Sir Thomas Overbury d.
Sir Thomas Bodley d.

Alexander (1567?): Doomesday. V
Bacon (1561): Charge touching Duels. P
Brathwaite, Richard: The Scholar's Medley.
Browne (1591): Shepherd's Pipe [with poems by
    Wither, Christopher Brooke, and John
    Davies of Hereford]. V
Campion (1567): A Masque presented at Marriage
    of Earl of Somerset.
Chapman (1559?): Trs. Odyssey, bks. i–xii [n.d.:
    see 1615]. V
Cooke, John: Greene's Tu Quoque, or the City
    Gallant. C
Fletcher (1579): Bonduca [acted *c.* 1614; prtd.
    1647]. T
Gentleman, Tobias: England's Way to win
    Wealth. P
Gorges, Sir Arthur: Trs. Lucan's Pharsalia. V
Heywood (1575?): Life and Death of Hector
    [modernization of Lydgate's Troy Book]. V
Jonson (1597?): Sad Shepherd [acted; prtd.
    1641]. D
    Bartholomew Fair [acted; prtd. 1631]. C
Lodge (1558?): Trs. Works of Seneca both Moral
    and Natural (enlarg. 1620]. P
Overbury (d. 1613): Characters [with A Wife now
    the Widow of Sir Thomas Overbury; enlarg.
    1614, 1615, 1616, &c.; 16th ed. 1638]. P
Raleigh (1552?): History of the World [ed. with
    Life by William Oldys 1736]. P
Rich (1540?): Honesty of this Age. P
Selden (1584): Titles of Honour. P
Sylvester (1563): Parliament of Virtues Royal
    [n.d.; Second Session of the Parliament *c.*
    1615; trs. Jean Bertaut; cont. other pieces by
    S.]. V
Tailor, Robert: The Hogge hath lost his Pearl. C

Henry More b.
John Barclay, 'Icon Ani-
    marum' (trs. Thomas
    May 1631).
John Napier's 'Mirifici
    Logarithmorum Cano-
    nis Descriptio'.
Isaac Casaubon d.
La Calprenède b.

1615

Anon.: Valiant Welshman. D
Andrews, John: Anatomie of Baseness. V
Beaumont (1584) and Fletcher (1579): Cupid's
    Revenge. D
Brathwaite, Richard: Strappado for the Devil. V
Breton (1545?): Characters upon Essays Moral
    and Divine. P
Chapman (1559?): Trs. Odyssey [complete in
    24 bks.; n.d.: see 1614]. V
Daniel (1562): Hymen's Triumph. D masque.
Harington (d. 1612): Epigrams [enlarg. 1618]. V
Heywood (1575?): Four Prentices of London. D
Jonson (1573): Mercurie Vindicated. D masque.
Rowlands, Samuel: Melancholy Knight. V

King James visits Cam-
    bridge.
The Cockpit Theatre
    erected c. 1615.
Richard Baxter b.
Sir John Denham b.
William Camden, 'An-
    nales', pt. i (pt. ii 1627;
    Eng. trs. of pt. i by
    Abraham Darcie 1627;
    of pt. ii by Thomas
    Browne 1629; of whole
    by Richard Norton
    1630).
'Don Quixote' (completed,
    see 1605).

Sandys (1578): Relation of a Journey begun in 1610. P
Stephens, John: Satyrical Essays, characters. P
Tomkis, Thomas: Albumazar, a comedy.
Wither (1588): Shepherds Hunting. V
  Fidelia [corrected and enlarg. 1619]. V

1616

Beaumont (d. 1616) and Fletcher (1579): Scornful Lady. C
Breton (1545?): Crossing of Proverbs. P
Browne (1591): Britannia's Pastorals, pt. ii [see 1613]. V
Bullokar, John: English Expositor, teaching interpretation of hardest Words. P
Chapman (1559?): Whole Works of Homer [collective ed. of Iliad and Odyssey; n.d.: see 1611, 1615, 1624]. V
Coryate (1577?): Greeting from the Court of the Great Mogul. P
Cotta, John: Trial of Witchcraft. P
Davies (1565?): A Select Husband for Sir Thomas Overburie's Wife. V
Drummond (1585): Poems [see 1656].
Haughton, William: Englishmen for my Money, or A Woman will have her Will. C
James I, King of England: Works. P
Jonson (1597?): Works of Benjamin Jonson [1st vol. of the First Folio; cont. all plays pub. (1600–12) except Case is Altered, and adding Epicoene, Epigrams, The Forest, and eighteen masques and entertainments: see 1631, 1640, 1692].
Markham (1568?): Markham's Method or Epitome. P
Niccols, Richard: Sir Thomas Overburie's Vision. V

Joseph Beaumont b.
Roger L'Estrange b.
William Shakespeare d.
Francis Beaumont d.
Richard Hakluyt d.
William Harvey expounds theory of circulation of the blood to College of Surgeons (see 1628, 1651).
John Selden, ed. of Sir John Fortescue's 'De Laudibus Legum Angliae'.
Cervantes d.
D'Aubigné, 'Les Tragiques', 'Histoire Universelle' (concl. 1620).

1617

Davies (1565?): Wit's Bedlam. V
Drummond (1585): Forth Feasting. V
Greene (d. 1592): Alcida. P
Hall (1574): Quo Vadis? A just Censure of Travel. P
Lyly (d. 1606): Euphues [complete: see 1578]. P
Middleton (1580): A Faire Quarrell [with Rowley]. D
Moryson, Fynes (1566): Itinerary. P
Rich (d. 1617): The Irish Hubub, or the English Hue and Cry. P
Sylvester (1563): Tobacco Battered and the Pipes Shattered. V

Ralph Cudworth b.
Elias Ashmole b.
Barnabe Rich d.
Thomas Coryate d.
John Selden, 'De Diis Syris Syntagmata'.
D'Aubigné, 'Faeneste' (concl. 1630).
Théophile, 'Pyrame et Thisbé', c. 1617

Breton (1545?): The Court and the Country. P
Chapman (1559?): Trs. Georgics of Hesiod. V
Coryate (1577?): To his Friends in England: from Agra. P
Field, Nathaniel: Amends for Ladies. C
Harington (d. 1612): Epigrams [complete in 4 bks.: see 1615]. V
Holyday, Barten: Technogamia, or Marriage of the Arts. C
Mynshul, Geoffray: Essays and Characters of a Prison and Prisoners. P
Selden (1584): History of Tithes. P
Stow (d. 1605): Summary of English Chronicles [final ed., embodying all additions and continuations by S. and others: see 1565]. P

Synod of Dort.
Thirty Years War 1618–48.
Richard Lovelace b.
Abraham Cowley b.
Sir John Denham b.
Sir Walter Raleigh executed.
John Davies of Hereford d.
Joshua Sylvester d.
Meeting of Ben Jonson and Drummond of Hawthornden (see 1711, 1827).
J. Brinsley trs. Ovid's 'Metamorphoses'

1619

Anon.: Whole Contention between Houses of York and Lancaster [see 1594, 1595]. D
Beaumont (d. 1616) and Fletcher (1579): Maid's Tragedy. T
　A King and No King. T
Deloney (d. 1607?): History of John Winchcomb [earliest extant, i.e. 8th, ed.; first pub. probably before 1600]. P
Fletcher (1579): Humorous Lieutenant [acted; prtd. 1647]. C
　Little French Lawyer [acted *c.* 1619; prtd. 1647; written with Massinger]. C
Hutton, Henry: Folly's Anatomy. V
Middleton (1580): Inner Temple Masque.
　Triumphs of Love and Antiquity. D pageant.
Purchas (1575?): Purchas his Pilgrim. Microcosmus. P
Shakespeare (d. 1616): Quartos of Henry VI, Pericles, A Yorkshire Tragedy (ascribed to S.), Merry Wives of Windsor, Merchant of Venice, Lear, Henry V, Sir John Oldcastle (ascribed to S.), Midsummer-Night's Dream, printed by W. Jaggard, some with false dates.
Wither (1588): Preparation to the Psalter.

William Chamberlayne b.
Samuel Daniel d.
Webster's 'Appius and Virginia' acted before 1619 (prtd. 1654).
Sir A. Gorges, 'Wisdom of the Ancients' (trs. of Bacon; see 1609).
John Vicars trs. John Owen's 'Epigrams' (see 1607).

Anon.: Horae Subsecivae [Essays: attrib. Grey Brydges, Lord Chandos; or Gilbert Cavendish]. P

Trs. Boccaccio's Decameron [first complete trs., prtd. Isaac Jaggard]. P

Bloody Banquet, a tragedy.

Swetnam, the Woman Hater. C

Two Merry Milkmaids. C

Beaumont (d. 1616) and Fletcher (1579): Philaster. T

Brathwaite, Richard: Essays upon the Five Senses. P

Dekker (1570?): Dekker his Dreame. V

Middleton (1580): World Tost at Tennis [with Rowley]. D masque.

Peacham, Henry, jnr.: Thalia's Banquet. V

Quarles (1592): Feast for Worms [also Hymne to God, Eleven Meditations, Pentelogia]. V

Rowlands, Samuel: The Night Raven. V

Sylvester (d. 1618): Sacred Works, gathered into one volume. V

Woodman's Bear. V

Pilgrim Fathers emigrate to America.
John Evelyn b.
Thomas Campion d.
Bacon, 'Instauratio Magna'.
'Don Quixote', pt. ii translated (see 1612).
Sir Thomas Overbury trs. Ovid's 'Remedy of Love'.
J. Webbe trs. 'Familiar Epistles of Cicero' (anon.; n.d.).

1621

Burton (1577): Anatomy of Melancholy [later edd. 1624–8–32–8–51–2–60–76]. P

Culpeper, Sir Thomas: Tract against Usury. P

Fletcher (1579): Wild Goose Chase [acted: prtd. 1652]. C

The Pilgrim [acted: prtd. 1647]. D

Thierry and Theodoret. T

Hall (1574): Works [later collections, with additions, during H.'s life-time 1625–28–34: see 1660, 1662].

Heylyn (1600): Microcosmus [see 1652]. P

Mason, William: Handful of Essays. P

Middleton (1580): Sun in Aries. D pageant.

Entertainments Composed for the City. D

Mun, Thomas: Discourse of Trade unto the East Indies. P

Quarles (1592): Hadassa. V

Rowley (1585?) with Middleton and Dekker: Witch of Edmonton [acted *c.* 1621; prtd. 1658]. D tragi-comedy.

Wither (1588): Wither's Motto. V

Songs of Old Testament. V

Wroth, Lady Mary: Countess of Montgomerie's Urania. P

Trial and Condemnation of Bacon.
Andrew Marvell b.
Roger Boyle, Earl of Orrery, b.
John Barclay, 'Argenis' (trs. K. Long 1625).
La Fontaine b.

Bacon (1561): History of the Reign of Henry VII. P
Historia Naturalis et Experimentalis [Latin]. P
Breton (1545?): Strange News out of Diverse
Countries. P
Drayton (1563): Second Part of Polyolbion [see
1612]. V
Hannay, Patrick: The Nightingale. V
Hawkins, Sir Richard: Observations in his Voyage
into the South Sea. P
Mabbe (1572): The Rogue. P
Markham (1568?): Herod and Antipater [with
William Sampson]. T
Massinger (1583): Virgin Martyr [with Dekker]. T
May (1595): The Heir. C
Peacham, Henry, jnr.: Compleat Gentleman. P
Shakespeare (d. 1616): Othello. T
Wither (1588): Fair Virtue. V
Juvenilia. V

Henry Vaughan b.
Thomas Vaughan b.
The Weekly News-pamphlets, 'The Corantos', begin (concl. 1641; interrupted 1632–8).
Molière b.

1623

Daniel (d. 1619): Whole Works. V
Drummond (1585): Flowers of Sion. V
Cypress Grove. P
Feltham, Owen: Resolves [n.d.: see 1628]. P
Fletcher (d. 1623): Reward of the Faithful. P
Jonson (1573?): Pan's Anniversarie (masque).
Neptune's Triumph (masque).
Massinger (1583): Duke of Milan. T
Shakespeare (d. 1616): First Folio, ed. J. Heminge and H. Condell [cont. 36 plays of which
the following had not appeared before: Tempest, Two Gentlemen of Verona, Measure for
Measure, Comedy of Errors, As You Like It,
Taming of the Shrew, All's Well that Ends
Well, Twelfth Night, Winter's Tale, King
John, 1 Henry VI, 2 Henry VI, 3 Henry VI,
Henry VIII, Coriolanus, Timon of Athens,
Julius Caesar, Antony and Cleopatra, Macbeth, Cymbeline. Pericles (see 1609) is
omitted. See 1632, 1663, 1685].
Webster (1580?): Duchess of Malfi. T
Devil's Law Case. C
Wither (1588): Hymns and Songs for the Church.

Massacre at Amboyna.
Sir William Petty b.
William Camden d.
Giles Fletcher jnr. d.
Bacon, 'De Augmentis'.
'The Spanish Gipsy' and 'The Changeling' by Middleton and Rowley acted about this date (prtd. 1653).
J. Bingham trs. 'History' of Xenophon.
Pascal b.
Charles Sorel, 'Francion'.

Anon.: Tragedy of Nero. D
Love's Garland [verse miscellany].
Chapman (1559?): Trs. Batrachomyomachia or Homer's Battle of Frogs and Mice [n.d.: see 1616]. V
Donne (1573): Devotions upon Emergent Occasions. P
Massinger: The Bondman. D
Parliament of Love [acted; prtd. 1805]. C
Quarles (1592): Job Militant. V
Sion's Elegies. V
Smith, Captain John: General Historie of Virginia. P
Wotton (1568): Elements of Architecture. P

War declared against Spain.
George Fox b.
Margaret Cavendish (Duchess of Newcastle) b.?
Thomas Heywood's 'Captives' written before this date (first prtd. 1885).
Lord Herbert of Cherbury's 'De Veritate' in Paris (first Eng. ed. 1645): his Autobiography ends (pub. 1764).
Jacob Boehme d.

1625

Bacon (1561): Essays [in final form: see 1597]. P
Apophthegms New and Old. P
Trs. Certain Psalmes. V
Dekker (1570?): Rod for Runaways. P
Markham (1568?): The Souldier's Accidence. P
Middleton (1580): Game at Chess [n.d.]. C
Purchas, Samuel: Hakluytes Posthumus, or Purchas his Pilgrims. P
Quarles (1592): Sion's Sonnets sung by Solomon. V
Alphabet of Elegies. V
Wither (1588): Scholar's Purgatory [n.d.]. P

Accession of Charles I.
Plague in London.
Thomas Lodge d.
John Fletcher d.
John Webster d.?
Abraham Darcie trs. Camden's 'Annales', pt. i (see 1615).
K. Long trs. John Barclay's 'Argenis'.
Grotius, 'De Jure belli et pacis'.
Racan, 'Les Bergeries'.

1626

Breton (d. 1626?): Pasquils Mad-Cappe. V
Fantasticks. P
Donne (1573): Five Sermons [collected: separately 1622-3-5-6].
Drake, Sir Francis, jnr.: Sir Francis Drake revived [relation of D.'s voyage to West Indies]. P
Hall (1574): Contemplations [completed: see 1612]. P
Parrot, Henry: VIII Cures for the Itch: Characters, Epigrams, Epitaphs. V
Roper, William (d. 1578): Life of Sir John More. P
Sandys (1578): Trs. Ovid's Metamorphoses. V
Smith, Captain John: Accidence for Young Seamen [amplified into Seaman's Grammar 1653].
Vaughan, William (1577): Golden Fleece. P and V

Francis Bacon d.
Sir John Davies d.
Cyril Tourneur d.
Samuel Purchas d.
Nicholas Breton d.?
William Rowley d.
Sir Henry Spelman, 'Glossarium Archaiologicum'.
Abridgement of Camden's 'Britannia'.
Mme de Sévigné b.

Bacon (d. 1626): Sylva Sylvarum [cont. New Atlantis]. P
Bernard, Richard (1568): The Isle of Man. P
Drayton (1563): Battaile of Agincourt, Miseries of Queen Margarite, Nimphidia, Quest of Cynthia, Shepherd's Sirene, The Moon Calfe. V
Fletcher, Phineas (1582): Locustæ [The Locusts; in 2 pts.; Eng. and Latin]. V
May (1595): Trs. Lucan's Pharsalia [concl. 1630]. V
Niccols, Richard: The Beggers Ape. V

Robert Boyle b.
John Hall b.
Dorothy Osborne b.
Richard Barnfield d.
Thomas Middleton d.
Camden, 'Annales' pt. ii (see 1615).
Bossuet b.
Honoré D'Urfé, 'Astrée' (final ed.: earliest prt. 1610).

1628

Anon.: Britain's Idea [Phineas Fletcher now supposed to be author; sometimes wrongly attrib. Spenser]. V
Anon.: Robin Good Fellow [earliest extant ed.].
Clavell, John: Recantation of an ill-spent Life.
Coke, Sir Edward: Institutes of the Laws of England [pt. ii 1642; iii and iv 1644].
Earle (1601): Microcosmographie [enlarg. 1629 –30–3–8]. P
Feltham, Owen: Resolves [complete; first instalment *c.* 1623]. P
Fletcher, Francis: The World Encompassed by Sir Francis Drake. P
Gomersall, Robert: Tragedy of Lodovick Sforza. D
Raleigh (d. 1618): Prerogative of Parliaments. P
Reynolds, Henry: Tasso's Aminta Englisht. D pastoral.
Wither (1588): Britain's Remembrancer. P

George Villiers, Duke of Buckingham, b.
John Bunyan b.
Fulke Greville d.
Sir William Temple b.
William Harvey's system of blood circulation set forth in 'Exercitatio Anatomica de Motu Cordis et Sanguinis in Animalibus' (see 1616, 1651).
Perrault b.
Malherbe d.
Charles Sorel, 'Le Berger Extravagant'.

1629

Adams, Thomas: Works, being the Summe of his Sermons.
Andrewes, Lancelot (d. 1626): XCVI Sermons [also 1631, 1635].
Bacon (d. 1626): Certain Miscellany Works, ed. Rawley. P
  Advertisement touching a Holy War. P
Beaumont, Sir John (d. 1627): Bosworth Field. V
Carlell, Lodowick: The Deserving Favourite. D
Chapman (1559?): Justification of a Strange Action of Nero. Trs. Fifth Satire of Juvenal. V

Whitefriars Playhouse.
John Speed d.?
Thomas Browne trs. Camden's 'Annals', pt. ii (see 1615).
W. Cross trs. Works of Sallust.
Pierre Corneille, 'Mélite'.

D'Avenant (1606): Tragedy of Albovine. D
Ford (1586): Lover's Melancholy. C
Hobbes (1588): Trs. Peloponnesian War of Thucydides. P
Lightfoot, John: Erubhim, or Miscellanies Christian and Judaicall. P
Markham (1568?): Markham's Faithful Farrier. P
Massinger (1583): Roman Actor. T
Parkinson, John: Paradisi in sole, Paradisus Terrestris. P
Quarles (1592): Argalus and Parthenia. V
Shirley (1596): The Wedding. D

1630

Anon.: Pathomachia, or Battle of Affections. D
'B., A.': Merry Tales of the Mad Men of Gotham [sometimes attrib. Andrew Boorde].
Bacon (d. 1626). Maxims of the Law. P
Brathwaite, Richard: The English Gentleman. P
D'Avenant (1606): The Cruel Brother. T
  The Just Italian. D
Dekker (1570?): Second Part of the Honest Whore [pt. i 1604]. D
Drayton (1563): Muses Elizium [Noah's Flood; Moses his Birth and Miracles (see 1604); David and Goliah]. V
Hall (1574): Occasional Meditations. P
Hayward, Sir John (d. 1627): Life and Reign of King Edward VI. P
Higgeson, Francis (d. 1630). New England's Plantation. P
Massinger (1583): The Picture. D tragi-comedy.
  The Renegado. D tragi-comedy.
Middleton (d. 1627): A Chaste Mayd in Cheapside. C
Randolph (1605): Aristippus. The Conceited Pedler. C
Shirley (1596): Grateful Servant. C
Taylor, John (1580): All the Works of John Taylor the Water Poet [reprtd. Spenser Society 1868–9; other works not in this collection reprtd. same Society 1870–8].

Isaac Barrow b.
John Tillotson b.
Charles Cotton b.
Gabriel Harvey d.
Richard Norton trs. 'Annals' of Camden (both parts: see 1615).
Kepler d.
Balzac, 'Dissertations', 1630–40.
Pierre Corneille, 'Clitandre'.

1631

Anon.: Comedie of Fair Em. D

Brathwaite, Richard: The English Gentlewoman. P

Whimzies, or a new cast of characters. P

Chapman (1559?): Wars of Pompey and Caesar [also called Caesar and Pompey]. T

Chettle, Henry: Tragedy of Hoffman, or Revenge for a Father [acted 1602]. D

Dekker (1570?): Match me in London, a tragi-comedy.

Penny wise pound foolish. P

Fletcher (1582): Sicelides, a Piscatory. D pastoral.

Fuller (1608): David's Heinous Sinne. V

Heywood (1575?): Fair Maid of the West, pts. i, ii. C

England's Elizabeth, her Life and Troubles. P

Jonson (1597?): Bartholomew Fair. Devil is an Ass. Staple of News [see 1640]. C

New Inne, or The Light Heart [see 1692]. C

Love's Triumph (masque).

Chloridia (masque).

Lenton, Francis (fl. 1630–40): Characterismi. P

Lloyd, David: Legend of Captain Jones [enlarg. 1648; another ed. 1656]. V

Mabbe, James ('Don Diego Puede-Ser'): Spanish Bawd, represented in Celestina; or the tragick comedy of Calisto and Melibea [trs. Fernando de Rojas].

Markham (1568?): Way to get Wealth. P

Massinger (1583): Believe as You List [acted; prtd. 1849]. C

May (1595): Tragedy of Antigone. D

Mirror of Minds [trs. John Barclay's Icon Animarum, 1614].

Powell, Thomas: Tom of all Trades. P

Quarles (1592): Historie of Samson. V

Shirley (1596): School of Compliment [called Love Tricks 1667].

Stow (d. 1605): Annals of England [final ed. embodying all additions by S. and continuations by E. Howes; Appendix, &c. 1632: see 1592]. P

Charles I visits Cambridge.
John Dryden b.
John Phillips b.
Catherine Philips
  ('Matchless Orinda') b.
John Donne d.
Michael Drayton d.
John Selden, 'De Successionibus'.

1632

Brome, Richard: Northern Lass. C

Donne (d. 1631): Death's Duell [his last sermon]. P

Heywood (1575?): The Iron Age, pts. i, ii. D

Holland, Philemon: Trs. Cyropaedia of Xenophon. P

Lupton, Donald: London and the Countrey carbonadoed and quartred (characters). P

Marmion (1603): Holland's Leaguer. C

John Locke b.
Anthony à Wood b.
Thomas Dekker d.
Spinoza b.

Massinger (1583): Emperor of the East. D tragi-comedy.
  Fatal Dowry [with Nathaniel Field]. T
  Maid of Honour. D
  City Madam [acted; prtd. 1658]. C
Quarles (1592): Divine Fancies. V
Raleigh (d. 1618): Instructions to his Son. P
Randolph (1605): Jealous Lovers. C
Reynolds, Henry: Mythomystes, wherein a Short Survey is taken of true poesy [n.d.]. P
Rowley (d. 1626): A New Wonder, A Woman never Vext. C
Shakespeare (d. 1616): Second Folio [contents same as First Folio: see 1623].
Shirley (1596): Changes, or Love in a Maze. C
Wither (1588): Psalms of David translated. V

1633

Anon.: The Costlie Whore. C
Cowley (1618): Poetical Blossoms [enlarg. 1636, 1637]. V
Donne (d. 1631): Poems [later edd., mostly with additions, 1635-9-49-50-4-69; ed. Grosart 1872, Chambers 1896, Grierson 1912].
  Juvenilia, or Paradoxes and Problems. P
Fletcher (1582): Purple Island [with Piscatory Eclogues and other poetical miscellanies]. V
Ford (1586): The Broken Heart. T
  Love's Sacrifice. T   Tis Pity She's a Whore. T
Forde, Emanuel: Famous History of Montelyon. P
Greville (d. 1628): Certain Learned and Elegant Works [Humane Learning, Fame and Honour, Treatise of Wars, Cœlica, Tragedy of Alaham, Tragedy of Mustapha (see 1609)].
Herbert (d. 1633): The Temple. V
Heywood (1575?): The English Traveller. D
Marlowe (d. 1593): Jew of Malta. T
Marmion (1603): A Fine Companion. D
Massinger (1583): New Way to pay old Debts. C
  The Guardian [acted; prtd. 1655].
May (1595): Reigne of King Henry the Second. V
Prynne (1600): Histrio-mastix. P
Quarles (1552): Divine Poems [collection of all biblical paraphrases pub. hitherto, and Alphabet of Elegies, 1625].
Rowley (d. 1626): All's Lost by Lust. T
  A Match at Midnight. C
Shirley (1596): Bird in a Cage. C
  Witty Fair One. C
  Contention for Honour and Riches. D masque.
  Triumph of Peace, a masque.
Spenser (d. 1599): View of the Present State of Ireland [i.e. in 1596; pub. in Sir James Ware's Two Histories of Ireland]. P

George Savile (Marquis of Halifax) b.
Samuel Pepys b.
Wentworth Dillon (Earl of Roscommon) b.?
George Herbert d.
Anthony Munday d.
Prynne pilloried for 'Histriomastix'.
W. Saltonstall trs. Ovid's 'Tristia'.

Carew (1595?): Coelum Britannicum, a masque.
D'Avenant (1606): Temple of Love, a masque.
Fletcher (d. 1625): Two Noble Kinsmen [with Shakespeare]. T
Ford (1586): Chronicle History of Perkin Warbeck. D
Habington (1605): Castara [enlarg. 1635, 1640]. V
Heywood (1575?): Late Lancashire Witches [with Richard Brome]. C
    A Maidenhead Well Lost. C
Rowley (d. 1626): The Noble Soldier. T

Robert South b.
John Marston d.
George Chapman d.
Sir John Reresby d.
Meric Casaubon trs. 'Meditations of Marcus Aurelius'.
Pierre Corneille, 'La Veuve', 'La Suivante'.

1635

D'Avenant (1606): Triumphs of Prince d'Amour. D masque.
Heywood (1575?): Hierarchie of Blessed Angels. V
    Philocothonista, or the Drunkard. V
May (1595): Victorious Reigne of Edward the Third. V
Quarles (1592): Emblems. V
Rutter, Joseph: The Shepherd's Holiday. D pastoral.
Shirley (1596): The Traitor. T
Swan, John: Speculum Mundi. P
Wither (1588): Collection of Emblems. V

Sir George Etherege b.?
Edward Stillingfleet b.
Thomas Sprat b.
Thomas Randolph d.
John Selden, 'Mare Clausum' (Eng. trs. by M. N. 1652).
Académie Française founded.
Pierre Corneille, 'Medée'
Lope de Vega d.

1636

D'Avenant (1606): The Wits, a comedy.
    The Platonick Lovers. D tragi-comedy.
Davies (d. 1618): Writing Schoolmaster [16th ed.; no earlier copy extant]. P
Dekker (d. 1632): Wonder of a Kingdom. D tragi-comedy.
Heylyn (1600): History of the Sabbath. P
Heywood (1575?): Love's Mistress, or the Queen's Masque.
    Challenge for Beauty. D
    Discourse of two Upstart Prophets. V
Massinger (1583): Great Duke of Florence. C
    Bashful Lover [acted; prtd. 1655]. C
Sandys (1578): Paraphrase upon Psalms of David [called Paraphrase upon Divine Poems 1638]. V
Wither (1588): Nature of Man [trs. Nemesius]. P

Charles I visits Oxford.
Joseph Glanvill b.
J. Carpenter trs. Ovid's 'Remedy of Love'.
W. Saltonstall trs. Ovid's 'Epistles'.
William Prynne, 'News from Ipswich' (attack on Bishop of Norwich).
Annalia Dubrensia (on Dover's Cotswold Games).
Boileau b.
Pierre Corneille, 'Le Cid'.

Alexander (1567?): Recreations with the Muses. V
Deloney (d. 1607?): The Gentle Craft [earliest extant ed.; first pub. probably *c.* 1600]. P
Fletcher (d. 1625): The Elder Brother. C
Heywood (1575?): Royal King and the Loyal Subject. D
Pleasant Dialogues and Dramas [trs. Lucian]. P
Hobbes (1588): Art of Rhetorique [trs. Aristotle; n.d.]. P
Jordan (1612?): Poeticall Varieties. V
Marmion (1603): Cupid and Psyche. V
Milton (1608): A Masque presented at Ludlow Castle [Comus: acted 1634].
Nabbes, Thomas: Hannibal and Scipio. T
Microcosmus, a moral masque.
Shirley (1596): The Example. D
The Gamester. D
Hide Park. C
Lady of Pleasure. C
Young Admiral. D

Thomas Traherne b.?
Ben Jonson d.
Gervase Markham d.
Joseph Rutter trs. 'Le Cid' of Corneille (pt. ii 1640).
Descartes, 'Discours de la Méthode'.
Gomberville, 'Polexandre.'
Desmarets, 'Les Visionaires'.

1638

Brathwaite, Richard: Barnabae Itinerarium. V
Chillingworth (1602): Religion of Protestants a safe way to Salvation. P
Cowley (1618): Love's Riddle, a pastoral comedy.
D'Avenant (1606): Madagascar and other Poems.
Ford (1586): Fancies, Chaste and Noble. C
Heywood (1575?): Wise Woman of Hogsdon. C
Killigrew, Henry: The Conspiracy [called Pallantus and Eudora 1653]. T
Milton (1608): Lycidas [in Obsequies to the memorie of Mr. Edward King]. V
Nabbes, Thomas: Covent Garden. C
Tottenham Court. C
Quarles (1592): Hieroglyphikes of Life of Man. V
Randolph (d.1635): Poems. Muses Looking Glass. D
Amyntas. D
Rowley (d. 1626): A Shoemaker a Gentleman. C
Shirley, Henry: The Martyr'd Souldier. T
Shirley (1596): The Royal Master. D
The Duke's Mistress. D
Suckling (1609): Aglaura. D tragi-comedy.

Thomas Shelton, 'Tachygraphy'.
Henry Peacham, jnr., 'Truth of our Times'.

Beaumont (d. 1616) and Fletcher (d. 1625): Bloody
  Brother [Rollo, Duke of Normandy 1640]. T
  Wit without Money. C
Carlell, Lodowick: Arviragus and Philicia. pts. i,
  ii. D
Cartwright, William: The Royal Slave. D
Chapman (d. 1634) and Shirley (1596): The Ball. C
  Chabot, Admiral of France. T
D'Avenant (1606): Salmacida Spolia, a masque.
Davenport, Robert: New Trick to Cheat the Devil. C
  A Crowne for a Conqueror. V
Fletcher (d. 1625): Monsieur Thomas. C
Ford (1586): The Ladies Trial. D
Fuller (1608): History of the Holy War. P
Glapthorne, Henry: Argalus and Parthenia. D
  Tragedy of Albertus Wallenstein. D
Massinger (1583): The Unnatural Combat. T
May (1595): Tragedy of Cleopatra. D
  Tragedy of Julia Agrippina. D
Mayne (1604): The City Match, a comedy.
Shirley (1596): The Maid's Revenge. T

Sir Charles Sedley b.?
Sir Henry Wotton d.
Thomas Carew d.?
Shakerley Marmion d.
W. Page trs. 'De Imitatione Christi'.
J. Sherburne trs. Ovid's 'Heroical Epistles'.
Sir Henry Spelman, 'Concilia Decreta Leges Constitutiones' (concl. 1664).
Z. Catlin trs. Ovid's 'Tristia'.
Racine b.
Pierre Corneille, 'Horace', 'Cinna'.

1640

Beaumont (d. 1616): Poems [see 1602].
Brome, Richard: The Antipodes, a comedy.
  Sparagus Garden, a comedy.
Carew (d. 1639?): Poems [Collected; also 1642,
  51-71-2; ed. Maitland 1824, W. C. Hazlitt
  1870, Ebsworth 1893, Vincent 1899].
Donne (d. 1631): LXXX Sermons, with Life by
  Izaak Walton [i.e. vol. i of collective ed. of
  Sermons pub. by D.'s son; vol. ii L Sermons
  1649; vol. iii XXVI Sermons 1660].
Fletcher (d. 1625): The Nightwalker. C
  Rule a Wife and Have a Wife. C
Fuller (1608): Joseph's Party-Coloured Coat. P
Glapthorne, Henry: The Hollander, a comedy.
  The Ladies Privilege, a comedy.
  Wit in a Constable, a comedy.
Greville, Robert, Baron Brooke: Nature of Truth. P
Habington (1605): Queen of Arragon. D
  History of Edward the Fourth of England. P
Hall (1574): Episcopacy by Divine Right. P
  Christian Moderation. P
Harvey, Christopher: The Synagogue, or Shadow
  of the Temple. V
Herbert (d. 1633): Wit's Recreations with a thou-
  sand outlandish Proverbs [anthology of
  verse by various hands].
Heywood (1575?): Exemplary Lives and Memor-
  able Acts of Nine Most Worthy Women.
Howell (1594): Dendrologie, Dodona's Grove. P

Long Parliament.
John Crowne b.
William Wycherley b.?
Aphra Behn b.
Philip Massinger d.
Sir William Alexander, Earl of Stirling, d.
John Ford d.?
Robert Burton d.
John Selden, 'De Jure Naturali'.
First Eng. trs. of Macchiavelli's 'Prince' by Edward Dacres.
J. Gower, 'Ovid's Festivals' (trs. 'Fasti').
John Parkinson, 'Theatrum Botanicum'.
Bay Psalm Book.
Mme de Maintenon's first series of letters about this time.
Pierre Corneille, 'Polyeucte'.

Jonson (d. 1637): Works of Benjamin Johnson [2nd vol. of First Folio (see 1616); cont. Bartholomew Fair, Devil is an Ass, Staple of News (all dated 1631); Magnetic Lady, Tale of a Tub, Sad Shepherd (dated 1641), Mortimer his Fall, Underwoods, Horace his Art of Poetry, English Grammar, Timber, or Discoveries (dated 1641), Masques: see 1616, '92].

Mabbe (1572): trs. Cervantes' Exemplary Novels. P

Milton (1608): Of Reformation touching Church Discipline. P

Nabbes, Thomas: Unfortunate Mother. T
The Bride, a comedy.

Quarles (1592): Enchyridion. P

Rawlins, Thomas: The Rebellion. T

Richards: Messalina the Roman Empress. T

Sandys (1578): Christ's Passion. V

Selden (1584): Discourse concerning the Power of Peers and Commons of Parliament. P

Shirley (1596): A Pastoral called the Arcadia. D
Constant Maid. C
Humorous Courtier. C; Love's Cruelty. T
The Opportunity. C; St. Patrick for Ireland. D
The Coronation [prtd. as by Fletcher]. C

Suckling (1609): Discontented Colonel [n.d.]. T

Walton (1593): Life of Donne [see Donne above; rev. and separate ed. 1658]. P

1641

Cavendish, George: Negotiations of Thomas Woolsey [2nd rev. ed. 1667]. P

Day, John: Parliament of Bees. D masque.

Habington (1605): Observations upon Historie. P

Hartlib, Samuel: Description of Macaria. P

Jonson (d. 1637): Sad Shepherd [see 1640]. C
Timber, or Discoveries [see 1640]. P

Killigrew (1612): The Prisoners. Claracilla [see 1664]. D tragi-comedy.

Marmion (d. 1639): The Antiquary, a comedy.

Sandys (1578): Paraphrase upon the Song of Solomon. V

Sylvester (d. 1618): Collected Works.

Whiting, Nathaniel: Albino and Bellama. V

Wither (1588): Hallelujah [hymns].

Execution of Strafford.
Irish Rebellion.
Thomas Rymer b.
Thomas Heywood d.
The Episcopacy Controversy.
Evelyn's Diary begins (ends 1706; pub. 1818).
George Thomason Collection of Tracts, 1641–62 (catalogued Fortescue 1908).
Pierre Corneille, 'La Mort de Pompée'.
Scudéry, 'Ibrahim'.

The Episcopacy Controversy: Joseph Hall, *An Humble Remonstrance in Favour of Episcopacy* (1641); 'Smectymnuus' (Stephen Marshall, Edmund Calamy, Thomas Young, Matthew Newcomen, and William Spurstow) *Answer to An Humble Remonstrance* (1641); Hall's *Defence of the Remonstrance* (1641) and *Vindication of the Answer* (1641) by 'Smectymnuus'; Milton's *Reformation touching Church Discipline, Of Prelatical Episcopacy* and *Animadversions upon the Remonstrant's Defence* in 1641, and *Reason of Church Government urged against Prelaty* and *Apology for Smectymnuus* in 1642; James Ussher's *Original of Bishops and Metropolitans* (1641).

Bacon (d. 1626): Reading on the Statute of Uses. P
Baron, Robert: Mirza. D
Denham (1615): The Sophy. T
   Cooper's Hill [final version 1655]. V
Fuller (1608): Holy State and Profane State. P
Hartlib, Samuel: Reformation of Schools [trs. Comenius]. P
Howell (1594?): Instructions for Foreign Travel [enlarg. 1650]. P
Kynaston, Sir Francis: Leoline and Sydanis. V
Milton (1608): Reason of Church Government urged against Prelaty. P
   Apology for Smectymnuus. P
More (1614): Psychozoia Platonica, a Platonical Song of the Soul [see 1647]. V
Raleigh (d.1618): The Prince, or Maxims of State. P
Selden (1584): Privileges of Baronage. P
Taylor (1613): Sacred Order and Offices of Episcopacy. P

Civil War.
Theatres closed.
Isaac Newton b.
Thomas Shadwell b.?
Sir John Suckling d.
Milton's first marriage (with Mary Powell).
Hobbes, 'De Cive' (see 1651).
Jeremiah Rich and William Cartwright, 'Semigraphy'.
Henry Peacham, jnr., 'Art of Living in London'.
Galileo d.
Pierre Corneille, 'Le Menteur'.
La Calprenède, 'Cassandre' (concl. 1645).

1643

Baker, Sir Richard: Chronicle of the Kings of England [contd. to 1660 by Edward Phillips 1660; 9th ed. with successive continuations 1696; contd. to end of George I's reign 1730]. P
Browne (1605): Religio Medici [first authorized ed.: unauthorized 1642]. P
D'Avenant (1606): Unfortunate Lovers. T
Digby (1603): Observations upon Religio Medici. P
Milton (1608): Doctrine and Discipline of Divorce [enlarg. 1644]. P
Prynne (1600): Sovereign Power of Parliaments. P
   Opening of the Great Seal of England. P

Gilbert Burnet b.
John Strype b.
William Browne d.?
Mercurius Aulicus, 1643–5.
Mercurius Britannicus, 1643–6.
Mercurius Civicus, 1643–6.

1644

Hammond, Henry (1605): Practical Catechism [enlarg. 1648]. P
Milton (1608): Of Education: to Mr Hartlib. P
   (Trs.) Judgement of Martin Bucer concerning Divorce. P
   Areopagitica. P
Quarles (d. 1644): Barnabas and Boanerges. P
Raleigh (d. 1618): To-day a Man, To-morrow None [cont. Letter to his Wife]. P
Williams, Roger (1604?): The Bloudy Tenent of Persecution for the Cause of Conscience. P

William Penn b.
George Sandys d.
Francis Quarles d.
William Chillingworth d.
Sir Henry Manwayring, 'Seaman's Dictionary'.
First Letters of Mme de Sévigné about this time.

Digby (1603): Treatise of Bodies and of Man's Soul. P

Fuller (1608): Good Thoughts in Bad Times. P

Howell (1594?): Epistolae Ho-elianae vol. i [ii 1647, iii 1650, iv 1655; ed. J. Jacobs 1890]. P

Milton (1608): Tetrachordon. P
Colasterion. P
Poems [Christ's Nativity; L'Allegro; Il Penseroso; Sonnets; reprts. of Comus (see 1637) and Lycidas (see 1638); Arcades; and juvenile poems in Latin, Greek, and Italian: see 1673, 1694].

Quarles (d. 1644): Solomon's Recantation. V

Ussher (1581): A Body of Divinitie.

Waller (1606): Poems [also 1664 (supposed first authorized ed.) and 1668; Second Part of Poems 1690; a collected ed. 1711; ed. Elijah Fenton 1729; ed. Thorn Drury 1893].

Wither (1588): Vox Pacifica. V

Execution of William Laud.
Battle of Naseby.
Earliest Eng. trs. of Jacob Boehme's Works by John Sparrow and others (concl. 1662).
Pierre Corneille, 'Théodore'.
Scarron, 'Jodelet'.
Grotius d.
Quevedo d.

1646

Browne (1605): Pseudodoxia Epidemica [or Vulgar Errors]. P

Crashaw (1613?): Steps to the Temple [enlarg. 1648; ed. Martin 1927]. V

Edwards, Thomas: Gangraena. P

Fuller (1608): Andronicus, or the Unfortunate Politician. P

Hall (1627): Horae Vacivae, or Essays.

Quarles (d. 1644): Shepherds Oracles. V.
Judgment and Mercy for Afflicted Souls [partly pub. as Barnabas and Boanerges, 1644]. P

Shirley (1596): Poems [cont. Triumph of Beauty, a masque].

Suckling (d. 1642): Fragmenta Aurea [cont., among unpub. works, Session of the Poets, The Goblins, Letters, Account of Religion by Reason: see 1659, 1696].

Taylor (1613): Discourse Concerning Prayer. P

Vaughan, Henry (1622): Poems.

Selden, 'Uxor Ebraica'.
Jeremiah Rich and William Cartwright, 'Charactery' (see 1642).
Pierre Corneille, 'Rodogune'.
Rotrou, 'Saint Genest'.
Leibnitz b.

Bacon, Nathaniel (1593): Uniformity of Government of England from Edward III to Elizabeth [completed 1651]. P

Beaumont (d. 1616) and Fletcher (d. 1625): Comedies and Tragedies, ed. James Shirley [cont. thirty-four unpub. plays: see 1652, 1679].

Cleveland (1613): Character of a London Diurnall and other Poems. V

Corbet, Richard (d. 1635): Certain Elegant Poems [enlarg. 1672, 1807].

Cowley (1618): The Mistress. V

Fanshawe, Sir Richard: Trs. Pastor Fido of Guarini.

Fuller (1608): Cause and Cure of a Wounded Conscience. P

Good Thoughts in Worse Times. P

Hall, John (1627): Poems.

Hall, Joseph (1574): Hard Measures. P

May (1595): History of the Long Parliament. P

More (1614): Philosophical Poems [cont. enlarg. version of Song of the Soul, 1642].

Peacham, Henry, jnr.: Worth of a Penny [date probably misprint for 1641]. P

John Wilmot (Earl of Rochester) b.

Trs. Gomberville's 'Polexandre' by W. Browne (not the poet William Browne d. 1643?).

John Selden ed. 'Fleta' (written c. 1290).

Voiture d.

Scarron, 'Virgile Travesti'.

Mercurius Melancholicus, 1647–9.

Rotrou, 'Venceslas'.

La Calprenède, 'Cléopâtre'.

1648

Beaumont, Joseph (1616): Psyche. V

Denham (1615): Cato Major [trs. Cicero]. V

Hall (1627): Satire against Presbytery. V

Emblems. V

Herrick (1591): Hesperides [incl. Noble Numbers; ed. Moorman 1915]. V

Hooker (d. 1600): Ecclesiastical Politie, bks. vi and viii [see 1594]. P

Raleigh (d. 1618): Arraignment and Conviction of ——, with a few letters. P

Stearne, John: Confirmation and Discovery of Witchcraft. P

Taylor (1613): Liberty of Prophesying. P

Wither (1588): Prosopopoeia Britannica. V

Elkanah Settle b.

Robert Barclay b.

Edward Herbert, Lord Herbert of Cherbury, d.

Society of Friends founded by George Fox between 1648 and 1650.

Cavendish, William, Duke of Newcastle: The Country Captain. The Varieties. C

D'Avenant (1606): Love and Honour. D

Donne (d. 1631): Fifty Sermons [see 1640]. P

Dryden (1631): Upon the Death of the Lord Hastings. V

Gauden, John (?): Eikon Basilike. P

Herbert, Edward, Lord Herbert of Cherbury (d. 1648): Life of Henry VIII. P

Howell (1594?): Description of the Country of Scotland. P

Lovelace (1618): Lucasta. V

Milton (1608): Tenure of Kings and Magistrates. P
Eikonoklastes. P

Prynne (1600): Historical Collection of the Ancient Parliaments of England. P

R. B. (ed.): Lachrymae Musarum [poems on death of Lord Hastings by Dryden, Marvell, Herrick, and Denham].

Taylor (1613): The Great Exemplar. P

Execution of Charles I.
The Commonwealth.
William Drummond of Hawthornden d.
Richard Crashaw d.
John Ogilby trs. 'Virgil'.
Descartes, 'Traité des Passions'.
Scudéry,'Le Grand Cyrus' (concl. 1653).

1650

Baron, Robert: Pocula Castalia. V

Baxter (1615): Saints' Everlasting Rest. P

Bradstreet, Anne (c. 1612): The Tenth Muse. V

Cowley (1618): The Guardian [see 1663]. C

Fuller (1608): Pisgah Sight of Palestine. P

Hall (1627): Paradoxes.

Heath, Robert: Clarastella. V

Hobbes (1588): Human Nature. P
De Corpore Politico, or Elements of Law, Moral and Politic. P

Raleigh (d. 1618): Judicious and Select Essays and Observations.

Satterstall,Wye: Picturæ Loquentes (characters). P

Taylor (1613): Rule and Exercises of Holy Living. P

Vaughan, Henry (1622): Silex Scintillans, [with pt. ii 1655]. V

Vaughan, Thomas (1622): Anthroposophia Theomagica. V

Weldon, Sir Anthony (d. 1649?): The Court & Character of King James I. P

Jeremy Collier b.
Phineas Fletcher d.
Thomas May d.
James Ussher, 'Annales Veteris Testamenti' (concl. 1654).
Mercurius Politicus, 1650–60.
Probable date of the MS. of Percy Folio: see 1765 (ed.Hales and Furnivall 1867).
Descartes d.
Pierre Corneille, 'Andromède'.

Cartwright, William (d. 1643): Comedies, Tragicomedies, with other Poems [cont. Lady Errant, Royal Slave, The Ordinary, The Siege].

Cleveland (1613): Poems.

D'Avenant (1606): Gondibert [cont. D.'s Preface to Gondibert and Hobbes's Answer to it]. V

Denham (1615): Anatomy of Play. P

Donne (d. 1631): Essays in Divinity. P
Letters to Several Persons of Honour. P

Hobbes (1588): Leviathan. P
Philosophical Rudiments Concerning Government and Society [trs. De Cive, 1642]. P
Epistle to D'Avenant on Gondibert.

Laud (d. 1645): Sermons [see 1695].

Sherburne, Sir Edward: Salmacis. V

Stanley, Thomas: Collected Poems [original poems and translations, first pub. 1647–9–50: ed. Brydges 1814–15; ed. Guiney 1907].

Taylor (1613): Rule and Exercises of Holy Dying. P

Vaughan, Henry (1622): Olor Iscanus [collection of poems and translations]. P and V

Walton (1593): Life of Sir Henry Wotton [see below]. P

Wotton (d. 1639): Reliquiae Wottonianae, with Life of Wotton by Izaak Walton [3rd ed. enlarg. 1672; 4th ed. with further additions 1685].

Charles II crowned at Scone.
Battle of Worcester.
Nathanael Culverwel d.
William Harvey 'Exercitationes de generatione animalium' (see 1616, 1628).
John Ogilby trs. Aesop (pt. ii 1665).
Fénelon b.
Scarron, 'Roman Comique'.
Racan, 'Psaumes'.

1652

Ashmole, Elias: Theatrum Chemicum. P

Beaumont (d. 1616) **and Fletcher** (d. 1625): Wild Goose Chase. C

Benlowes, Edward: Theophila. V

Brome (d. 1652?): A Jovial Crew, or Merry Beggars. C

Culverwel (d. 1651): Of the Light of Nature. P

Donne (d. 1631): Paradoxes, Problems, Essays, Characters. P

Fanshawe, Sir Richard: Trs. Select Parts of Horace.

Greville (d. 1628): Life of Sir Philip Sidney. P

Hall (1627): Trs. Longinus on the Height of Eloquence. P

Herbert (d. 1633): Remains, ed. with Life by B. Oley [cont. A Priest to the Temple].

Heylyn (1600): Cosmographie [enlarg. through many edd. from Microcosmus, 1621].

Middleton (d. 1627): The Widow [with Jonson and Fletcher]. C

Tatham, John: The Scots Figgaries. C

Vaughan, Henry (1622): Mount of Olives. P and V

Thomas Otway b.
Nahum Tate b.
Richard Brome d.?
Dorothy Osborne's Letters, 1652–4 (first pub. 1888).
Pierre Corneille, 'Nicomède'.

Basse, William (d. 1653?): Pastorals and other Poems [ed. J. P. Collier 1870; Works ed. R. W. Bond 1893].

Brome (d. 1652?): Five New Plays [Mad Couple Well Matcht, Novella, Court Beggar, City Wit, Damoiselle].

Cleveland (1613): Poems [later important collections with additions 1659-77-87].

Hammond, Henry: Paraphrase and Annotations upon the New Testament.

Hookes, Nicholas (1628): Amanda. V

Middleton (d. 1627): Spanish Gipsie [with Rowley]. D tragi-comedy.

The Changeling [with Rowley]. T

More (1614): Antidote against Atheism. P

Conjectura Cabbalistica. P

Newcastle (1624?): Poems and Fancies [Select Poems, ed. Brydges 1813]. V

Philosophical Fancies. P

Shirley (1596): Six New Plays [the Brothers, Sisters, Doubtful Heir, Imposture, Cardinall, Court Secret].

Cupid and Death, a masque.

Taylor (1613): Two Discourses [Of Baptism, Of Prayer]. P

Eniautos . . . Sermons for all the Sundays in the Year [concl. 1656; enlarg. 1667-8]. P

Urquhart (1611): Trs. Rabelais, bks. i, ii [bk. iii 1693; 2nd ed. of bks. i, ii with introductory matter by P. A. Motteux 1694; complete version by Urquhart, Motteux, and others 1708]. P

Walton (1593): Compleat Angler [2nd ed., largely re-written, 1655; also 1661, 1668; pt. ii, being a treatise on fly-fishing by Charles Cotton 1676]. P

Cromwell Protector.
Nathaniel Lee b.?
John Oldham b.
Thomas D'Urfey b.
Roger North b.
Eng. trs. of Scudéry's 'Le Grand Cyrus' (1653-5).
Molière, 'L'Étourdi'.
Scarron, 'Don Japhet'.

1654

Chapman (d. 1634): Revenge for Honour. T

Alphonsus Emperor of Germany. T

Hobbes (1588): Of Liberty and Necessity [surreptitious]. P

Johnson, Edward (1589): History of New England. P

Orrery (1621): Parthenissa, pt. i [complete 1665]. P

Vaughan, Henry (1622): Flores Solitudinis [trs. religious tracts from Latin]. P

Walton, Brian (ed.): Polyglot Bible [concl. 1657].

Webster (d. 1625?): Appius and Virginia. T

John Selden d.
William Habington d.
Molière, 'Le Dépit Amoureux'.
Scudéry, 'Alaric', 'Clélie' (concl. 1660).
Cyrano, 'Le Pédant Joué'.

Cotgrave, John: English Treasury of Literature and Language [miscellany].
Wit's Interpreter: the English Parnassus [miscellany].

Davenport, Robert: King John and Matilda. T

Drummond (d. 1649): History of Scotland, 1423–1524 [with Memorials of State, and other prose works: see 1711]. P

Dugdale (1605): Monasticon Anglicanum [with Roger Dodsworth; concl. 1673].

Fuller (1608): Church History of Britain. P
History of Cambridge University. P
History of Waltham Abbey. P

Hammond, William: Poems.

Heywood (d. 1641): Fortune by Land and Sea [with Rowley]. D tragi-comedy.

Marvell (1621): First Anniversary of the Government under the Lord Protector. V

Massinger (d. 1640): Three New Plays [Bashful Lover, Guardian, The Very Woman].

Newcastle (1624?): Philosophical and Physical Opinions [see 1668]. P

Phillips (1631): Satyr against Hypocrites [called Religion of the Hypocritical Presbyterians, 1661]. V

Shirley (1596): Gentleman of Venice. D tragi-comedy.
The Polititian. T

Spottiswood, John (d. 1639): History of the Church and State of Scotland. P

Stanley, Thomas: History of Philosophy, vol. i [ii 1656, iii 1660, iv 1662, collected 1687]. P

Strode, William (d. 1645): The Floating Island. D tragi-comedy.

Taylor (1613): Golden Grove [enlarged as Choice Manual 1677]. P

Vaughan, Henry (1622): Hermetical Physics [trs. of Latin Tracts]. P
Silex Scintillans, pts. i, ii [see 1650]. V

Waller (1606): Panegyric to my Lord Protector. V

Richard Blackmore b.?
Walter Charleton trs. Epicurus's 'Morals'.
Sir Richard Fanshawe trs. 'Lusiad' of Camoens.
John Davies of Kidwelly trs. Letters of Voiture.
Francis Junius's ed. of Caedmon pub. at Amsterdam.
Sir William Lower trs. 'Polyeucte' of Pierre Corneille.
John Wallis, 'Arithmetica Infinitorum'.
Hobbes, 'Elementorum Philosophiae Sectio prima de Corpore' (Eng. trs. 1656: see 1658).

1656

Bunyan (1628): Some Gospel Truths opened. P

Collop, John: Poesis Rediviva. V

Cowley (1618): Poems [cont. Miscellaneous Poems, Mistress (see 1647), Davideis, Pindarique Odes; the last two now first pub.]

D'Avenant (1606): Siege of Rhodes made a representation by the art of perspective in scenes [see 1663].

Denham (1615): Destruction of Troy [trs. Virgil: with prefatory essay on Translation]. V

Gerard Langbaine b.
Joseph Hall d.
John Hall d.
John Hales d.
James Ussher d.
Milton's second marriage (with Catharine Woodcock).
'Parnassus Biceps'.
'Choyce Drollery'.
'Wit and Drollery'.

Drummond (d. 1649): Poems, ed. Edward Phillips [incl. many unpub. pieces: see 1711].
Dugdale (1605): Antiquities of Warwickshire. P
Ford (d. 1640?): The Sun's Darling [with Thomas Dekker]. D masque.
Harington (1611): Commonwealth of Oceana. P
Hobbes (1588): Questions concerning Liberty, Necessity and Chance. P
  Eng. trs. of Elementorum Philosophiae: De Corpore [original Latin 1655].
Massinger (d. 1640): Old Law [with Middleton and Rowley]. C
More (1614): Enthusiasmus Triumphatus. P
Newcastle (1624?): Nature's Pictures drawn by Fancy's Pencil [cont. Autobiography, reprtd. 1814: see 1667]. V
Osborne, Francis (1593): Advice to a Son [pt. ii 1658]. P

John Davies of Kidwelly trs. ' Clélie' of Scudéry.
Pascal, 'Lettres Provinciales'.
Chapelain, 'La Pucelle'.

1657

Baker, Augustine (d. 1641): Sancta Sophia [compiled out of B.'s treatises by S. Cressy]. P
Baxter (1615): Call to the Unconverted. P
Brome (d. 1652?): The Queen's Exchange. C
Carlell, Lodowick: The Fool would be a Favourite. D
  Osmond, the Great Turk. D
D'Avenant (1606): First Day's Entertainment at Rutland House. D show.
Hall, John (d. 1656): Hierocles upon the Golden Verses of Pythagoras, ed. with Life by John Davies of Kidwelly. V
Heylyn (1600): Ecclesia Vindicata. P
Howell (1594?): Londinopolis. P
King, Henry (1592): Poems [enlarg. 1664; Sacred Poems ed. Hannah 1843; Selected Poems ed. Tutin 1904, ed. Sparrow 1925].
Marlowe (d. 1593): Lust's Dominion [attrib. M. on the title-page; probably by Dekker, John Day, and William Haughton]. T
Middleton (d. 1627): No Wit, no Help like a Woman's. C
  Two New Plays [Women Beware Women, More Dissemblers besides Women]. C
Raleigh (d. 1618): Remains [enlarg. from collection of tracts pub. 1651, 1656].
Taylor, (1613): Discourse of Friendship. P
  Polemical and Moral Discourses. P

John Dennis b.
Matthew Tindal b.
John Norris b.
Richard Lovelace d.
William Harvey d.
Edward Sexby's tract, 'Killing no Murder'.
Joshua Poole, 'England's Parnassus'.
George Thornley trs. 'Daphnis and Chloe'.

Anon.: Whole Duty of Man [Lady Dorothy Pakington or Richard Allestree?]. P
Brathwaite (1558?): The Honest Ghost. V
Browne (1605): Hydriotaphia, or Urne-Buriall. Garden of Cyrus. P
Chamberlayne (1619): Love's Victory [called Wits led by the Nose 1678]. D tragi-comedy.
D'Avenant (1606): Cruelty of Spaniards in Peru [afterwards formed part of Playhouse to be Let, 1673]. D opera.
Dugdale (1605): History of St. Paul's Cathedral. P
Flecknoe, Richard: Enigmaticall Characters. P
Harrington (1611): Prerogative of Popular Government. P
Massinger (d. 1640): City Madam. C
May (d. 1650): The Old Couple, a comedy. D
Raleigh (d. 1618): Cabinet Council [pub. by Milton]. P
Rowley (d. 1642?): Witch of Edmonton [with Dekker and Ford]. D tragi-comedy.
Ussher (d. 1656): Annals of the World [trs. of Latin Works first pub. 1650, 1654]. P
Waller (1606): Passion of Dido for Æneas [with Sidney Godolphin]. V

Richard Cromwell Protector.
Oliver Cromwell d.
John Cleveland d.
William London, 'Catalogue of most vendible books in England' (supplement 1660).
Edward Phillips, 'New World of Words' (enlarg. ed. Kersey 1700, 1706, 1720).
Hobbes, 'Elementorum Philosophiae, sectio secunda de Homine' (see 1655).
'Wit Restor'd' (anthology).

1659

Baxter (1615): Holy Commonwealth. P
Brome (d. 1652?): Five New Plays [English Moor, Lovesick Court, Covent Garden Weeded, New Academy, Queen and Concubine].
Chamberlayne (1619): Pharonnida. V
Cleveland (d. 1658): John Cleveland revived [poems, orations, epistles, &c.]. V
D'Avenant (1606): History of Sir Francis Drake, expressed by instrumental and vocal music [afterwards formed part of Playhouse to be Let, 1673]. D opera.
Day, John: Blind Beggar of Bednal Green. C
Dryden (1631): Poem upon the Death of his late Highness Oliver Lord Protector. V
Evelyn (1620): Character of England. P
  Trs. Golden Book of St. Chrysostom. P
Fuller (1608): Appeal of Injured Innocence. P
Hales (d. 1656): Golden Remains [enlarg. 1673].
Harrington (1611): Aphorisms Political [n.d.]. P
  Art of Lawgiving [abridgement of Oceana]. P
Lovelace (d. 1657): Posthume Poems.

James Harrington's club, the Rota, meets in Miles's Coffee-house in Palace Yard, London, 1659–60.
John Rushworth, 'Collection of State Papers, 1618–48' (concl. 1701; 2nd ed. 1721).
William Somner's 'Dictionarium Saxonico-Latino-Anglicum'.
Molière, 'Les Précieuses ridicules'.
Pierre Corneille, 'Oedipe'.

Mayne (1604): The Amorous War. D tragi-
comedy.
Milton (1608): Treatise of Civil Power in Ecclesi-
astical Causes. P
  Likeliest Means to remove Hirelings out of the
  Church. P
More (1614): Immortality of the Soul. P
Pearson, John: Exposition of the Creed. P
Shirley (1596): Honoria and Mammon. D
  Contention of Ajax and Achilles [contains The
  glories of our blood and state]. D
Stillingfleet (1635): Irenicum. P
Suckling (d. 1642): Last Remains [cont. unpub.
  poems, letters, and the unfinished tragedy
  The Sad One: see 1646, 1696].
Waller (1606): Upon the late Storm and Death of
  His Highness. V

1660

Boyle (1627): New Experiments Physico-Mech-
anical. P
Cary, Lucius, Viscount Falkland (d. 1643): Dis-
course of Infallibility. P
Donne (d. 1631): XXVI Sermons [see 1640]. P
Dryden (1631): Astraea Redux. V
Fuller (1608): Alarum to the Counties of England
and Wales. P
  Mixt Contemplations in Better Times. P
Hall, Joseph (d. 1656): Shaking of the Olive Tree
  [collection of posthumous pieces: see 1621,
  1662].
Harrington (1611): Political Discourses. P
Howard, Sir Robert (1626): Poems.
Milton (1608): Ready and Easy Way to establish
  a Free Commonwealth. P
  Present Means and Brief Delineation of a Free
  Commonwealth. P
More (1614): Grand Mystery of Godliness. P
Phillips (1631): Montelion, 1660; or the Propheti-
cal Almanack. V
Pordage, Samuel (1633): Poems. V
Smith, John (d. 1652): Select Discourses. P
Tatham, John: The Rump. C
Taylor (1613): Ductor Dubitantium. P
  Worthy Communicant. P
Ussher (d. 1656): Chronologia Sacra. P
Winstanley, William: England's Worthies [rev.
1684]. P

*The Restoration: Charles
II King.
Thomas Southerne b.
Peter Anthony Motteux b.
Sir Thomas Urquhart d.
Patents for re-opening
  theatres granted to
  Thomas Killigrew (sr.)
  and Sir William D'Ave-
  nant: the King's and the
  Duke of York's com-
  panies formed.
Establishment of the Royal
  Society (charter granted
  1662).
Pepys (b. 1633) begins
  Diary on 1 Jan. (ends
  31 May 1669; first pub.
  1825).
Imprisonment of Bunyan,
  1660–72.
Hobbes, 'Examinatio et
  Emendatio'.
John Ogilby trs. 'Iliad'.
Scarron d.
Molière, 'Sganarelle'.
Corneille, 'La Toison
  d'or'.
Scudéry, 'Almahide'.*

Anon.: Tom Tyler and his Wife [performed *c.* 1540]. D interlude.

Boyle (1627): The Sceptical Chymist. P

Davenport, Robert: The City Night Cap. D

Dryden (1631): To His Sacred Majesty. V

Evelyn (1620): Fumifugium. P

Flecknoe, Richard: Erminia. D tragi-comedy.

Glanvill (1636): Vanity of Dogmatising [recast as Scepsis Scientifica 1665]. P

Graunt, John: Natural and Political Observations on the Bills of Mortality. P

Heylyn (1600): Ecclesia Restaurata. P

Mackenzie, Sir George (1636): Aretina. P

Middleton (d. 1627): Mayor of Quinborough [acted *c.* 1596]. C

Waller (1606): St. James's Park. V

To my Lady Morton. V

Webster (d. 1625?) **and Rowley** (d. 1626): Two New Plays [Cure for a Cuckold, The Thracian Wonder]. C

Daniel Defoe b.?
Anne Finch (Countess of Winchilsea) b.
Sir Samuel Garth b.
Thomas Fuller d.
Boyle's Law of Compressibility.
Hobbes, 'Dialogus Physicus'.
'Wit and Drollery'.
'Merry Drollery'.
La Calprenède, 'Pharamond'.
Molière, 'Don Garcie du Navarre', 'L'École des maris', 'Les Fâcheux'.

1662

The Prayer Book [final version: see 1549].

Baker, Sir Richard (d. 1645): Theatrum Redivivum [reply to Prynne's Histrio-Mastix]. P

Butler (1612): Hudibras, pt. i [bears date 1663; really end of 1662: see 1663, 1678].

Dryden (1631): To My Lord Chancellor. V

Dugdale (1605): History of Imbanking and Draining of Fens and Marshes. P

Evelyn (1620): Sculptura. P

Fuller (d. 1661): Worthies of England. P

Glanvill (1636): Lux Orientalis. P

Hall (d. 1656): Works [fuller collection ed. J. Pratt 1808; Peter Hall 1837; P. Wynter 1863: see 1621].

Haughton, William: Grim the Collier of Croyden [performed *c.* 1600]. C

Hobbes (1588): Considerations upon the Reputations, Loyalty, Manners and Religion of —. P

Hooker (d. 1600): Works, ed. with Life by Gauden [re-issued with Life by Izaak Walton 1666; with corrections by Strype 1705; ed. Randolph 1793; Dobson 1825; Hanbury 1831; Keble 1836; R. W. Church 1888: see 1594].

Middleton (d. 1627): Anything for a Quiet Life. C

Newcastle (1624?): Plays [21 plays: see 1668].

Petty (1623): Treatise of Taxes and Contributions. P

Rowley (d. 1626): Birth of Merlin [alleged contribution by Shakespeare: see 1597]. C

Stillingfleet (1635): Origines Sacrae. P

Winstanley, William: Loyal Martyrology. P

Act of Uniformity.
Royal Society's First Charter.
Richard Bentley b.
Francis Atterbury b.
Peter Heylyn d.
Milton's third marriage (with Elizabeth Minshull).
The series of anon. verse almanacks and chapbooks, 'Poor Robin's Almanack or Complaint', begins to appear (originator probably William Winstanley; continued by various hands to 1776).
Pascal d.
Molière, 'L'École des femmes'.

Boyle (1627): Considerations concerning the Usefulness of Experimental Philosophy. P

Butler (1612): Hudibras, pt. ii [bears date 1664; really end of 1663: see 1662, 1678]. V

Cowley (1618): Cutter of Coleman Street [new version of The Guardian 1650]. C

Verses upon several occasions.

Davenant (1606): Siege of Rhodes, pt. i, ii [see 1656]. D opera.

Philips (1631): Pompey [trs. Corneille]. D

Shakespeare (d. 1616): Third Folio [two issues, the 2nd dated 1664: cont. Pericles (first pub. 1609) and the following spurious plays not in First Folio:—London Prodigal (first pub. 1605), Chronicle History of Thomas Lord Cromwell (1602), Sir John Oldcastle (1600), The Puritan (1607), Yorkshire Tragedy (1608), Tragedy of Locrine (1595): see 1623].

Stapylton, Sir Robert: Slighted Maid. C

Tuke, Sir Samuel: Adventures of Five Hours. C

Thomas Brown of Shifnal b.
Roger L'Estrange starts 'The Intelligencer' (concl. 1666).
Edward Somerset, Marquis of Worcester, 'Century of Inventions'.
La Calprenède d.

1664

Boyle (1627): Experiments concerning Colour. P

Cary, Henry, Viscount Falkland (d. 1633): The Marriage Night. C

Cotton (1630): Scarronides, or first Book of Virgil Travestie [enlarg. 1670]. V

Dryden (1631): Rival Ladies [with prefatory defence of rhyme in tragedy]. D tragi-comedy.

Etherege (1635?): Comical Revenge. C

Evelyn (1620): Sylva [enlarg. 1670, 1679, 1706; with other works on gardening 1729]. P

Flecknoe, Richard: Love's Kingdom, a tragi-comedy [cont. Short Discourse on the English Stage]. P

Jordan (1612?): A Royall Arbour of Loyall Poesie. V

Killigrew (1612): Comedies and Tragedies [cont., besides those of 1641: the Princess, The Parson's Wedding, The Pilgrim, Cicilia and Clorinda, Thomaso, Bellamira].

Killigrew, Sir William (1606?): Three Plays [Selindra, Pandora, Ormasdes; Four Plays, adding Siege of Urbin, 1666].

More (1614): Mystery of Iniquity. P

Mun, Thomas (d. 1641): England's Treasure by foreign trade [written *c*. 1630].

Patrick, Simon: Parable of the Pilgrim. P

Stapylton, Sir Robert: The Stepmother. D

Tillotson (1630): Wisdom of being religious. P

Wilson, John (1626): The Cheats. C

Waller (1606): Poems [supposed first authorized collection: see 1645].

Sir John Vanbrugh b.
Matthew Prior b.
Katherine Philips ('Matchless Orinda') d.
Francis Junius, 'Gothicum Glossarium'.
Racine, 'La Thébaide'.

1665

Burnet (1643): Discourse on Sir Robert Fletcher of Saltoun. P
Crowne, John: Pandion and Amphigenia. P
Head, Richard (?): The English Rogue. P
Herbert of Cherbury (d. 1648): Poems [ed. G. C. Moore-Smith 1923].
Howard, Sir Robert: Four Plays [the Surprisal, The Committee, The Vestal Virgin, and The Indian Queen, written with Dryden: cont. Preface starting controversy on dramatic poetry with Dryden].
Jordan (1612?): Pictures of Passions, Fancies, and Affections. V
Lloyd, David (1635): Statesmen and Favourites of England [ed. with additions by Charles Whitworth and called State Worthies 1766]. P
Marvell (1621): Character of Holland. V
Sprat (1635): Observations on Monsieur de Sorbier's Voyage into England [Sorbière's book was pub. in 1664]. P
Stevenson, Matthew (1627): Poems. V
Waller (1606): Upon Her Majesty's new Building at Somerset House. V
Walton (1593): Life of Richard Hooker. P
Wilson, John (1626): The Projectors. C

Charles Gildon b.
Sir Kenelm Digby d.
John Earle d.
The Great Plague.
Henry Muddiman starts 'The London Gazette' (nos. 1–23 called Oxford Gazette).
John Phillips trs. Scarron's 'Typhon'.
Robert Hooke, 'Micrographia'.
John Ogilby trs. 'Odyssey'.
Molière, 'Don Juan'.
La Rochefoucauld, 'Maximes'.
Francis Junius, ed. of the Moeso-Gothic Text of Ulphilas.

1666

Boyle (1627): Origin of Forms and Qualities. P
Hydrostatical Paradoxes. P
Bunyan (1628): Grace Abounding. P
The Holy City. P
Glanvill (1636): Philosophical Considerations concerning Witches and Witchcraft (4th ed. Blow at Modern Sadducism 1668; 5th ed. Sadducismus Triumphatus 1681]. P
Tillotson (1630): Rule of Faith. P
Waller (1606): Instructions to a Painter. V

James Shirley d.
James Howell d.
Thomas Vaughan d.
Fire of London.
Boileau, 'Satires'.
Molière,' Le Misanthrope', 'Le Médecin malgré lui'.
Furetière, 'Roman bourgeois'.

1667

Cavendish, George: Life and Death of Thomas Woolsey [see 1641]. P
Davies, John, of Kidwelly: Trs. Novels of Scarron [collected: separately 1657, 1662]. P
Denham (1615): Instructions to a Painter. V
Dryden (1631): Annus Mirabilis. V
Indian Emperor [sequel to Indian Queen: see Howard 1665]. T
Flecknoe, Richard: Damoiselles a la Mode. C
Laud (d. 1645): Sum of Devotions [complete: parts in 1650, 1663]. P

Jonathan Swift b.
John Arbuthnot b.
Susannah Centlivre b.?
George Granville b.
William Whiston b.
Jeremy Taylor d.
George Wither d.
Abraham Cowley d.
Racine, 'Andromaque'.
Molière 'Tartuffe'.

Marvell (1621): Clarendon's House-Warming [in Denham's Instructions above].

Milton (1608): Paradise Lost [in 10 books; 5th issue of 1st ed., cont. the paragraph 'Verse' defending absence of rhyme, 1668 (?); 2nd ed., rev. and rearranged in 12 books, 1674]. V

More (1614): Enchiridion Ethicum. P

Newcastle (1624?): Life of William Cavendish, Duke of Newcastle [ed. with Autobiography of the Duchess (see 1656) by M. A. Lower 1872; ed. C. H. Firth 1886]. P

Philips (d. 1664): Collected Works. V

Sprat (1635): History of the Royal Society. P

1668

Child, Sir Josiah: A New Discourse of Trade. P

Cowley (d. 1667): Works, ed. Thomas Sprat [cont. Poems of 1656 and Verses upon Several Occasions of 1663, Essays in Prose and Verse now first pub.; pt. ii of Works added 1681; 7th ed. of Works incorporating additions in successive edd. up to date 1707; Works ed. Grosart 1876–9; ed. Waller 1905–6].

D'Avenant (d. 1668): The Rivals, a comedy.

Denham (1615): Collected Poems [later edd.: 1671–6–84–1709].

Dryden (1631): Sir Martin Mar-all. C
Secret Love. D tragi-comedy.
Essay of Dramatick Poesie. P
Defence of Essay of Dramatick Poesie [in 2nd ed. of Indian Emperor: see 1667]. P

Etherege (1635?): She wou'd if she cou'd. C

Glanvill (1636): Plus Ultra, or Progress of Knowledge since Aristotle. P
Blow at Modern Sadducism [see 1666, 1681]. P

Heylyn (d. 1662): Cyprianus Anglicanus [Life of Archbishop Laud]. P

Howard, Sir Robert: The Great Favourite. D

Jordan, Thomas: Money is an Asse. C

More (1614): Divine Dialogues [best ed. 1713]. P

Newcastle (1624?): Plays never before printed [cont. five plays: see 1662].
Grounds of Natural Philosophy [altered ed. of Philosophical and Physical Opinions 1655]. P

Orrery (1621): History of Henry V. D
Tragedy of Mustapha. D

Penn (1644): Sandy Foundation Shaken. P
Truth Exalted. P

Sedley (1639?): Mulberry Garden. C

Shadwell (1642?): Sullen Lovers. C

Wilkins, John: Essay towards a Real Character and a Philosophical Language. P

Sir William D'Avenant d.
Dryden poet-laureate.
William Penn committed to the Tower (released 1669).
Term Catalogues Commence (concl. 1709; ed. Arber 1903–6).
First instalment of Robert Clavell's Catalogue of Books published from 1666 to 1700 (series completed 1700).
Roger L'Estrange trs. 'Visions' of Quevedo.
Lesage b.
La Fontaine, 'Fables', pt. i.
Molière, 'Amphitryon', 'L'Avare'.
Racine, 'Les Plaideurs'.

1669

Burnet (1643): Conference between a Conformist and a Nonconformist. P
Chamberlayne, Edward: Angliae Notitiae, or Present State of England. P (Frequent editions until 1755.)
D'Avenant (d. 1668): The Man's the Master. C
Dryden (1631): The Wild Gallant. C
Orrery (1621): The Black Prince. Tryphon. T
Penn (1644): No Cross No Crown. P
  Innocency with her Open Face. P
Shadwell (1642?): Royal Shepherdess. D

Sir John Denham d.
William Prynne d.
Pepys's Diary ends on 31 May (see 1660).
University Press at Oxford housed in the Sheldonian Theatre: moved to new habitation and called Clarendon Press 1713.
Milton, 'Latin Grammar'.
John Wallis, 'Mechanica' (concl. 1671).
Racine, 'Britannicus'.
Molière, 'Monsieur de Pourceaugnac'.
Bossuet, 'Oraison funèbre de la reine d'Angleterre'.

1670

Baxter (1615): Life of Faith. P
Dryden (1631): The Tempest [altered from Shakespeare: with D'Avenant]. C
  Tyrannick Love. T
Greville, Sir Fulke (Lord Brooke) (d. 1628): Remains [complete works ed. Grosart 1870].
Milton (1608): History of Britain. P
Heylyn (d. 1662): Aerius Redivivus, or History of Presbyterianism. P
Parker, Samuel: Discourse of Ecclesiastical Polity [Defence and Continuation of same 1671]. P
Walton (1593): Life of George Herbert. P
  Lives of Donne, Wotton, Hooker, and Herbert [collected].

William Congreve b.
John Toland b.
Bernard Mandeville b.?
Laurence Echard b.?
Pascal, 'Pensées'.
Molière, 'Le Bourgeois gentilhomme', 'Les Amants magnifiques'.
Racine, 'Bérénice'.
Corneille, 'Tite et Bérénice'.
Mme de la Fayette, 'Zayde'.

1671

Behn (1640): Forc'd Marriage. D tragi-comedy.
Bunyan (1628): Confession of my Faith. P
Collins, Samuel: Present State of Russia in a Letter to a Friend in London. P
Crowne, John: Juliana. T
Dryden (1631): An Evening's Love. C
Howard, Edward: Women's Conquest. D
  Six Days' Adventure. D
Milton (1608): Paradise Regained. Samson Agonistes. V
Settle (1648): Cambyses King of Persia. T
Shadwell (1642?): The Humorists. C

Anthony Ashley Cooper, third Earl of Shaftesbury b.
Colley Cibber b.
'Westminster Drollery'.
'Windsor Drollery'.
'Oxford Drollery'.
Molière, 'Psyché', 'Les Fourberies de Scapin'.
Corneille, 'Psyché'.
Bossuet, 'Exposition de la Foi catholique'.
Mme de Sévigné, first series of letters to Mme de Grignan.

Ashmole (1617): Institution, Laws, Ceremonies of the Order of the Garter [with Continuation by T. Walker as History of the Order of the Garter 1715]. P

Buckingham (1628) **and others**: The Rehearsal [with a 'Key' 1709]. D burlesque.

Cave, William: Primitive Christianity. P

Dryden (1631): Conquest of Granada; pt. i, ii [pt. ii called Almanzor and Almahide: cont. Essay on Heroic Plays and Essay on Dramatic Poetry of the Last Age]. T

Josselyn, John: New England's Rarities Discovered. P

Lacy, John: The Old Troop, or Monsieur Ragout. C
The Dumb Lady. C

Marvell (1621): The Rehearsal Transpros'd [pt. ii 1673]. P

Phillips (1631): Maronides, or Virgil Travesty [an enlarged 2nd ed. 1673]. V

Ravenscroft, Edward: Citizen turned Gentleman [called Mamamouchi 1675]. C

Shadwell (1642): The Miser. C

Temple (1628): Observations upon the United Provinces of the Netherlands. P

Wycherley (1640?): Love in a Wood. C

Joseph Addison b.
Richard Steele b.
Jasper Mayne d.
'Covent Garden Drollery'.
Hobbes, 'Lux Mathematica'.
Cumberland's ' De Legibus Naturae Disquisitio Philosophica'.
Racine, 'Bajazet'.
Molière, 'Les Femmes Savantes'.

1673

Behn (1640): The Dutch Lover. C

Burnet (1643): Mystery of Iniquity Unveiled. P

D'Avenant (d. 1668): Collected Works [incl. unpub. poems and following unpub. plays; News from Plymouth, Fair Favourite, Distresses, The Siege, Law against Lovers, and Playhouse to be let].

Dryden (1631): Marriage à la mode. C
The Assignation. C
Amboyna. T

Milton (1608): Poems upon various occasions [a revision, with additions, of 1645; all the minor poems except those of 1694: see 1645].

Pordage, Samuel: Herod and Mariamne. T

Ravenscroft, Edward: Careless Lovers. D

Settle (1648): Empress of Morocco. T

Shadwell (1642?): Epsom Wells. C

Wycherley (1640?): Gentleman Dancing Master. C

John Oldmixon b.
'Holborn Drollery'.
'Norfolk Drollery'.
'London Drollery'.
Molière d.
Molière, 'Malade Imaginaire'.
Racine, 'Mithridate'.

Cotton (1630): Complete Gamester. P

D'Avenant (d. 1668): Macbeth [made into opera].

Flatman, Thomas: Poems and Songs [enlarged ed. 1686].

Hammond, Henry (d. 1660): Collected Works, ed. W. Fulman [concl. 1684; ed. Pocock 1847–50].

Hobbes (1588): Trs. Odyssey [with Iliad 1675; cont. Essay on Vertues of an Heroique Poem]. V

Howard, James: English Mounsieur. C

Josselyn, John: Two Voyages to New England. P

Milton (1608): Paradise Lost [2nd ed., in 12 books; see 1667]. V

Epistolarum Familiarium Liber unus. P

Rymer (1641): Reflections on Aristotle's Treatise of Poesie [trs. of Rapin]. P

Shadwell (1642): The Tempest [made into opera].

Isaac Watts b.
Nicholas Rowe b.
John Milton d.
Robert Herrick d.
Thomas Traherne d.
Edward Hyde, first Earl of Clarendon d.
Margaret Cavendish, Duchess of Newcastle, d.
Dryden, Shadwell, and Crowne attack Settle in 'Notes and Observations on the Empress of Morocco'.
Settle replies in 'Notes and Observations on the Empress of Morocco revised'.
Anthony à Wood, 'Historia et Antiquitatis Universitatis Oxoniensis' (Eng. trs. by Wood 1791–6).
Boileau, 'Lutrin', 'Art Poétique'.
Racine, 'Iphigénie'.
Malebranche, 'Recherche de la verité'.
Giambattista Basile, 'Il Pentamerone'.

1675

Barnes, Joshua: Gerania, or the Discovery of a little sort of people called Pygmies. P

Cotton (1630): Planter's Manual. P

Burlesque upon Burlesque. V

Crowne, John: The Country Wits. C

Calisto. D opera. Andromache. T

Lee (1653?): Tragedy of Nero. T

Leigh, Richard (1649): Poems. V

Marvell (1621): Dialogue between Two Horses. V

Otway (1652): Alcibiades. T

Phillips, Edward: Theatrum Poetarum. P

Settle (1648): Love and Revenge. T

Shadwell (1642?): Psyche. D opera.

Traherne (d. 1674): Christian Ethics. P

Wycherley (1640?): Country Wife. C

William Somerville b.
Ambrose Philips b. ?
Bulstrode Whitelocke d.
Sir William Dugdale, 'Baronage of England' (concl. 1676).
William Higford (?), 'The Courtier's Calling'.
'The City Mercury' started by Roger L'Estrange (?).
John Ogilby, 'Book of Roads'.
Saint-Simon b.

Barclay, Robert (1648): Apology. P
Cotton (1630): Part II of Walton's Compleat Angler [see 1653]. P
Dryden (1631): Aureng-Zebe. T
Etherege (1635?): Man of Mode. C
Glanvill (1636): Essays on Several Important Subjects. P
Lee (1653?): Sophonisba. T
  Gloriana. T
Otway (1652): Don Carlos. T
Settle (1648): Conquest of China. T
Shadwell (1642?): The Libertine. C
  The Virtuoso. C

John Philips b.
Benjamin Hoadly b.
Sir Matthew Hale d.

1677

Banks, John: Rival Kings. T
Behn (1640): The Rover [see 1681]. C
  The Debauchee. C
  The Town-Fopp. C. Abdelazer. T
Cavendish, William, Duke of Newcastle (d. 1676): Triumphant Widow. C
  Humorous Lovers. C
Cleveland (d. 1658): Clevelandi Vindiciae. V
Crowne, John: Destruction of Jerusalem. T
Davenant, Charles: Circe. D
Dryden (1631): State of Innocence. D opera.
D'Urfey (1653): Madam Fickle. C
  Fond Husband, or The Plotting Sisters. C
Hales (d. 1656): Several Tracts. P
  Sermons preached at Eton. P
Hubbard, William (c. 1621): Troubles with the Indians. P
Lee (1653?): Rival Queens. T
Mather, Increase (1639): The Troubles that have happened in New England. P
Otway (1652): Titus and Berenice. Cheats of Scapin [adapt. Racine and Molière]. D
Plot, Robert (1640): Natural History of Oxfordshire. P
Ravenscroft, Edward: Scaramouch. C
  King Edgar and Alfreda. D tragi-comedy.
  Wrangling Lovers. C
Sedley (1639?): Antony and Cleopatra. T
Settle (1648): Ibrahim, the Illustrious Bassa. T
  Pastor Fido. D pastoral.
Tate, Nahum (1652): Poems. V
Waller (1606): Of the Lady Mary. V
Webster, John (1610): Displaying of Supposed Witchcraft. P
Wycherley (1640?): The Plain Dealer. C

James Harrington d.
Isaac Barrow d.
William Cave, 'Apostolici or History of Martyrdoms'.
John Phillips's trs. of La Calprenède's 'Pharamond', Scudéry's 'Almahide', and Six Voyages of Tavernier's 'Voyages'.
Mme de Lafayette, 'Princesse de Clèves'.
Racine, 'Phèdre'.
Spinoza d.
Spinoza, 'Ethics'.

Barclay (1648): Apology for the True Christian Divinity. P

Barrow (d. 1677): Sermons on Various Occasions.

Behn (1640): Sir Patient Fancy. C

Bunyan (1628): Pilgrim's Progress, pt. i [ii 1684]. P

Butler (1612): Hudibras, pt. iii [see 1662, 1663]. V

Calderwood, David (d. 1650): History of the Church of Scotland. P

Cudworth (1617): True Intellectual System of the Universe. P

Dryden (1631): All for Love. T

D'Urfey (1653): Fool turn'd Critick. C

Trick for Trick. C

Hobbes (1588): Decameron Physiologicum. P

Lee (1653?): Mithridates. T

Marvell (d. 1678): Advice to a Painter [n.d.]. V

Otway (1652): Friendship in Fashion. C

Pordage, Samuel: Siege of Babylon. T

Ravenscroft, Edward: English Lawyer. C

Rymer (1641): Tragedies of the Last Age Considered. P

Edgar, an Heroick Tragedy. T

Shadwell (1642?): Timon of Athens [adapt. Shakespeare]. T

Spelman, Sir John (d. 1643): Life of Alfred the Great [Latin trans. ed., with additions, Hearne 1709]. P

Tate, Nahum: Brutus of Alba. T

Vaughan, Henry (1622): Thalia Rediviva. V

Walton (1593): Life of Dr. Sanderson. P

The Popish Plot.
Henry St. John (Viscount Bolingbroke) b.
George Farquhar b.
Andrew Marvell d.
Henry Cave starts 'The Pacquet of Advice from Rome' (weekly 1678–83).
Narcissus Luttrell's 'Brief Historical Relations' begun (concl. 1714; pub. 1857).
Bossuet, 'Politique', c. 1678.
La Fontaine, 'Fables', pt. ii 1678–9.

1679

Bancroft, John: Tragedy of Sertorius. T

Banks, John: Destruction of Troy. T

Beaumont (d. 1616) and Fletcher (d. 1625): Fifty Comedies and Tragedies [cont. all plays and masques pub. in 1647 and 1652 and others previously pub. but not collected. Works, ed. Theobald, Seward, and Sympson 1750; Colman 1778; Weber 1812 (The Faithful Friend first appears here); Darley 1840; Dyce 1843–6; A. H. Bullen and others 1904 ff. (variorum ed.); Glover and Waller 1905 ff.].

Behn (1640): The Feign'd Courtezans. C

Burnet (1643): History of the Reformation, pt. i [ii 1681; iii 1714; ed. Pococke 1865]. P

Crowne, John: Ambitious Statesman. D

Dryden (1631): Oedipus [with Nat. Lee]. T

Troilus and Cressida [adapt. Shakespeare; with Preface concerning grounds of criticism in Tragedy]. T

Thomas Parnell b.
Charles Johnson b.
Thomas Hobbes d.
Roger Boyle, Earl of Orrery, d.
On 18 Dec. Dryden assaulted by hired men in Rose Alley, Covent Garden (D. wrongly supposed to have been author of Mulgrave's Essay on Satyr in which Rochester had been satirized).
Collected ed. of the 'Year Books'.
Benjamin Harris starts 'The Domestic Intelligencer'.
Licensing Act expires.

D'Urfey (1653): Squire Oldsapp. C
Oldham (1653): Garnet's Ghost. V
Shadwell (1642?): A True Widow. C
South (1634): Sermons [concl. in six volumes,
    1715; another vol. with memoirs and account
    of Travel in Poland with Rochester 1717;
    five more in 1744]. P

1680

Barrow (d. 1677): Treatise of the Pope's Suprem-
    acy, ed. John Tillotson. P
Blount, Charles: Two First Books of Apollonius
    Tyaneus. P
    Great is Diana of the Ephesians. P
Bunyan (1628): Life and Death of Mr. Badman. P
Burnet (1643): Passages of the Life and Death of
    the Earl of Rochester. P
Dillon, Wentworth, Earl of Roscommon (1633?):
    trs. Horace's Art of Poetry. V
Dryden (1631): The Kind Keeper. C
    Trs. Ovid's Epistles [with others]. V
D'Urfey (1653): The Virtuous Wife. C
Filmer, Sir Robert (d. 1653): Patriarcha, or the
    Power of Kings [cont. other treatises]. P
Hobbes (d. 1679): Historical Narrative concern-
    ing Heresy. P
Lee (1653?): Caesar Borgia. T
    Theodosius. T
L'Estrange (1616): Trs. Select Colloquies of Eras-
    mus [enlarg. 1689]. P
Otway (1652): History and Fall of Caius Marius. T
    The Orphan. T
    Poet's Complaint of his Muse. V
Radcliffe, Alexander: Ovid Travestie. V
    Bacchinalia Caelestia. V
Rochester (d. 1680): Poems by the E—— of
    R—— [surreptitious].
Settle (1648): Female Prelate. T
    Fatal Love. T
Shadwell (1642?): Woman Captain. C
Tate, Nahum: Loyal General. T
Temple (1628): Miscellanea, pt. i [cont., among
    others, Essay on Government, Survey of the
    Constitution: see 1692, 1701]. P

Samuel Butler d.
*John Wilmot, Earl of
    Rochester, d.*
Joseph Glanvill d.
La Rochefoucauld d.
*Fénelon, 'Dialogues sur
    l'Eloquence'   (concl.
    1690).*
*'A compleat catalogue of
    all the slitch'd books and
    single sheets printed
    since the first discovery
    of the Popish Plot.'*

Behn (1640): The Rover, pt. ii [see 1677]. C
Cotton (1630): Wonders of the Peak. V
Cowley (d. 1667): Collected Works, pt. ii [see 1668].
Crowne, John: Henry the Sixth, pt. i. T
  Thyestes. T
Dryden (1631): Absalom and Achitophel, pt. i
  [see 1682]. V.   Spanish Friar. C
D'Urfey (1653): Sir Barnaby Whigg. C
Glanvill (d. 1680): Sadducismus Triumphatus [see
  1666, 1668]. P
Heylyn (d. 1662): Historical and Miscellaneous
  Tracts. P
Hobbes (d. 1679): Behemoth [first authoritative
  ed.; surreptitious ed. 1679]. P
  Dialogue between a Philosopher and a Student
  of Common Law. P
  Art of Rhetoric. P
Lee (1653?): Lucius Junius Brutus. T
Marvell (d. 1678): Miscellaneous Poems [later edd:
  Cooke 1726; with unpub. letters, prose
  tracts, and poems 1776 (ed. Thompson);
  Works ed. Grosart 1872–5; Poems and Satires
  ed. Aitken 1892; Poems and Letters ed. Mar-
  goliouth 1927].
Oldham (1653): Satyrs upon the Jesuits. Satire
  against Virtue. V [unauthorized edd. of parts
  of it 1679, 1680].
  Horace's Art of Poetry imitated. V
Otway (1652): The Souldiers Fortune. C
Tate, (1652): History of King Richard the
  Second. T
  King Lear [adapt. Shakespeare]. T

*Roger L'Estrange starts
'The Observator' (13
Apr. 1681 to 9 March
1687).*
*Bossuet, 'Histoire Uni-
verselle'.*
Calderon d.
*Thomas Burnet, 'Telluris
Theoria Sacra' (Eng-
lish Version, 1684–89).*
*Stair, 'Institutions of the
Law of Scotland'.*

1682

Banks, John: Unhappy Favourite. T
  Virtue Betray'd. T
Behn (1640): The Roundheads. C
  The City-Heiress. C.   The False Count. C
Bunyan (1628): The Holy War. P
Burnet (1643): Life and Death of Sir Matthew
  Hale. P
Coppinger, Matthew: Poems.
Dryden (1631): The Medall. V
  Religio Laici. V.   Mac Flecknoe. V
  Absalom and Achitophel, pt. ii [with Nahum
  Tate: see 1681]. V
D'Urfey (1653): The Injur'd Princess. T
  The Royalist. D tragi-comedy.
  Butler's Ghost, or Hudibras, the fourth part. V
  Wit and Mirth, or Pills to purge Melancholy [an-
  thology of poems and songs; other volumes
  1699, 1700, 1706, 1710; final ed. 1719–20].

Sir Thomas Browne d.
*William Cave, 'Eccle-
siastici' (writings and
Lives of Fathers of the
Church).*
'Wit and Drollery.'
*Thomas Creech trs. Lu-
cretius.*
*Nehemiah Grew, 'Ana-
tomy of Plants'.*
*John Ray, 'Methodus
Plantarum Nova'.*
*John Nalson, 'Impartial
Collection of the Great
Affairs of State'.*
*Sir Simonds D'Ewes,
'Journal of all the Par-
liaments during the reign
of Queen Elizabeth'.*

Hobbes (d. 1679): Seven Philosophical Problems [trs. Problemata Physica, 1662]. P
Milton (d. 1674): Brief History of Muscovia. P
Otway (1652): Venice Preserv'd. T
Petty (1623): Essay concerning multiplication of Mankind; together with an Essay on Political Arithmetick [see 1690]. P
Pordage, Samuel: Azaria and Hushai. V
  Medal Revers'd. V
Radcliffe, Alexander: The Ramble. V
Ravenscroft, Edward: London Cuckolds. C
Settle (1648): Absalom Senior, or Achitophel Transpros'd. V
  Heir of Morocco. D
Shadwell (1642?): Lancashire Witches, with First part of Tegue O Divelly [see 1690]. C
  (?) Medall of John Bayes. V
Sheffield, John, Earl of Mulgrave: An Essay on Poetry. V
Southerne (1660): The Loyal Brother. T
Tate, Nahum: Ingratitude of a Commonwealth, or Fall of Coriolanus. T
Whitelocke (d. 1675): Memorials of English Affairs from the beginning of the Reign of Charles I to the Restoration [enlarg. 1732; this reprtd. Oxford, 1853].

1683

Ayres, Philip (1638): Emblemata Amatoria. Emblems of Love. V
Barrow (d. 1677): Works, ed. John Tillotson [concl. 1687; ed. Napier 1859].
Chalkhill, John: Thealma and Clearchus [cont. Preface by Izaak Walton dated 1678]. V
Crowne, John: City Politiques. C
Dryden (1631): Duke of Guise [with Nat. Lee]. T
  Vindication of the Duke of Guise. P
  Trs. Plutarch [with others]. P
Mason, John (1646): Songs of Praise. V
Oldham (d. 1683): Poems and Translations [Remains in Verse and Prose 1684; Works ed. E. Thompson 1770; Bell 1854].
Shipman, Thomas (1632): Carolina. V

Siege of Vienna by the Turks.
Rye House Plot.
Algernon Sidney and Lord Russell executed.
Conyers Middleton b.
Edward Young b.
Izaak Walton d.
John Oldham d.
Thomas Killigrew senr. d.
Benjamin Whichcote d.
Pepys's Narrative of Voyage to Tangiers written (called The Second Diary: first published 1840).

Banks, John: IslandQueens[laterAlbionQueens].T
Browne (d. 1682): Miscellany Tracts, ed. Tenison.
Bunyan (1628): Pilgrim's Progress, pt. ii [see 1678]. P
Burnet (1643): Trs. More's Utopia. P
Creech, Thomas: Trs. Horace. V
  Trs. Theocritus. V
Dillon, Wentworth, Earl of Roscommon (1633?): Essay on Translated Verse. V
Dryden (1631): Miscellany Poems [by various writers: pub. by Jacob Tonson]. See 1709. V
  Trs. History of the League. P
Lacy, John (d. 1681): Sir Hercules Buffoon. C
Lee (1653?): Constantine the Great. T
Mather, Increase (1639): Illustrious Providences. P
Otway (1652): The Atheist. C
Southerne (1660): The Disappointment. C

Robert Leighton d.
'The Turkish Spy' begins (trs. from Italian of Marana by William Bradshaw or R. Midgeley?).
Corneille d.
Esquemeling, 'History of the Bucaniers of America' (trs. 2nd volume by Basil Ringrose, 1683).

1685

Cotton (1630): Trs. Montaigne's Essays. P
Crowne, John: Sir Courtly Nice. C
Dryden (1631): Albion and Albanius. D opera.
  Threnodia Augustalis. V
  Ed. Sylvae, or the second part of Poetical Miscellanies [see 1684].
Otway (d. 1685): Windsor Castle. V
Rochester (d. 1680): Valentinian. T
Shakespeare (d. 1616): Fourth Folio [contents same as second issue of Folio III, 1663–4].
Sprat (1635): A true Declaration of the Horrid Conspiracy. P
Stillingfleet (1635): Origines Britannicae. P
Tate, Nahum: A Duke and no Duke. D
Waller (1606): Divine Poems. V
Wesley, Samuel (1662): Maggots. V

Accession of James II.
Edict of Nantes revoked.
Insurrection of Monmouth.
John Gay b.
George Berkeley b.
Aaron Hill b.
New Licensing Act (for 10 years).
Thomas Otway d.
Wentworth Dillon, Earl of Roscommon, d.
Fontenelle, 'Dialogues des Morts' and 'Discours sur la Pluralité des Mondes'.

1686

Browne (d. 1682): Works (folio). P
Bunyan (1628): Book for Boys and Girls [abridged 1701 as Divine Emblems]. V
Burnet (1643): Some Letters containing an Account of Switzerland and Italy. P
Compton, Henry (1632): Episcopalia. P
Dryden (1631): To the Memory of Mrs. Anne Killigrew. V
D'Urfey (1653): Commonwealth of Women. D
  Banditti. D
Halifax (1633): Letter to a Dissenter. P
Killigrew, Anne (d. 1685): Poems.
Parr, Richard: Life of James Ussher. P
Plot, Robert (1640): Natural History of Staffordshire. P

William Law b.
Allan Ramsay b.
Thomas Tickell b.
Sir William Dugdale d.
John Ray, 'Historia Plantarum' (concl. 1704).

Ayres, Philip (1638): Lyric Poems made in imitation of the Italians. V

Behn (1640): Lucky Chance. C

Emperor of the Moon. C

Cleveland (d. 1658): Works [ed. Berdan 1903].

Clifford, Martin (d. 1677): Notes upon Mr. Dryden's Poems in Four Letters [with Reflections on Hind and Panther by Thomas Brown of Shifnal].

Dryden (1631): Song for St. Cecilia's Day. V

Hind and the Panther. V

Langbaine, Gerard (1656): Momus Triumphans [2nd ed. 1687 entitled A New Catalogue of English Plays]. P

Norris (1657): Miscellanies. P

Phillips (1631): History of Don Quixote. P

Prior (1664) and Montague, Charles: Hind and the Panther Transvers'd to the Story of the Country Mouse and the City Mouse. V

Sedley (1639?): Bellamira. C

Tate, Nahum: The Island Princess. D

Winstanley, William: Lives of the English Poets. P

Declaration of Indulgence.
George Villiers, Duke of Buckingham, d.
Henry More d.
Edmund Waller d.
Sir William Petty d.
Newton, 'Principia' (3rd ed. rev. 1726; see 1727).
John Wallis, 'Institutio Logicae'.
Bossuet, 'Oraison funèbre de Condé'.
Fénelon, 'Education des Filles'.

1688

Barnes, Joshua: Life of Edward III. P

Boyle (1627): Disquisition Concerning Causes of Natural Things. P

Crowne, John: Darius, King of Persia. T

Dryden (1631): Britannia Rediviva. V

D'Urfey (1653): A Fool's Preferment. C

Halifax (1633): Character of a Trimmer [circulated in MS. in 1685]. P

A Lady's New Year Gift, or Advice to a Daughter. P

Anatomy of an Equivalent. P

Peacock (d. 1460?): Book of Faith. P

Shadwell (1642?): Squire of Alsatia. C

The Revolution.
Alexander Pope b.
Lewis Theobald b.
John Bunyan d.
Ralph Cudworth d.
Shadwell poet-laureate.
William Cave, 'Scriptorum Ecclesiasticorum Historia Literaria'.
La Bruyère, 'Caractères'.
Bossuet, 'Variations des Eglises protestantes'.
Perrault, 'Parallèles des anciens et des modernes' (concl. 1697).

1689

Cotton (d. 1687): Collected Poems [another ed. called Genuine Works 1715].

Lee (1653?): Princess of Cleve. T

Locke (1632): First Letter on Toleration [see 1690, 1692]. P

Selden (d. 1654): Table Talk [ed. Singer 1847; David 1854; Reynolds 1892; Gollancz 1899].

Shadwell (1642?): Bury Fair. C

Sherlock, William: Practical Discourse Concerning Death. P

Accession of William and Mary.
Toleration Act.
Advocates' Library founded.
Samuel Richardson b.
Lady Mary Wortley Montagu b.
Aphra Behn d.
William Chamberlayne d.
Sir John Reresby d.
Hickes, 'Anglo - Saxon Moeso-Gothic Grammar'.
Montesquieu b.
Racine, 'Esther'.

Behn (d. 1689): Widow Ranter. C
Browne (d. 1682): Letter to a Friend upon the Death of his Intimate Friend. P
Crowne, John: English Friar. C
Dryden (1631): Don Sebastian. T
    Amphitryon. C
Lee (1653?): Massacre of Paris. T
Locke (1632): Two Treatises on Government. P
    Essay concerning Human Understanding [enlarg. 1694-5-1700]. P
    Second Letter on Toleration [see 1689, 1692]. P
Norris (1657): Christian Blessedness. P
Orrery (d. 1679): Mr. Anthony. C
Petty (d. 1687): Political Arithmetick. P
Shadwell (1642?): Amorous Bigotte, with Second Part of Tegue O Divelly [see 1682]. C
Waller (d. 1687): Poems, pt. ii [see 1645, 1664].

Robert Barclay d.
John Phillips starts journal 'Present State of Europe' (concl. 1706: a retrospective vol. entitled 'General History of Europe', added 1692)
John Dunton starts 'The Athenian Gazette' (concl. 1696).
Sir Thomas Pope Blount's 'Censura Celebriorum Authorum'.
Boursault, 'Fables d'Æsope'.
Furetière, 'Dictionnaire'.

1691

Congreve (1670): Incognita. P
Dryden (1631): King Arthur. D opera.
D'Urfey (1653): Love for Money. C
Langbaine (1656): Account of the English Dramatick Poets [ed. Gildon under title Lives and Characters of English Dramatic Poets, 1699]. P
Settle (1648): Distress'd Innocence. T
Shadwell (1642?): The Scowrers. C
Southerne (1660): Sir Anthony Love. C
Wharton, Henry: Anglia Sacra [lives of Archbishops]. P
Wilson, John (1626): Belphegor. D
Wood (1632): Athenae Oxonienses [with the Fasti; vol. ii 1692; enlarged ed. 1721; ed. Bliss 1813-20]. P

Thomas Amory b.?
Sir George Etherege d.
George Fox d.
Richard Baxter d.
Robert Boyle d.
Boyle Lectures founded.
Racine, 'Athalie'.
Perrault, 'Contes' (concl. 1697).

1692

Bentley (1662): Boyle Lectures [on Folly of Atheism; delivered and pub. 1692-3].
Blount, Sir Thomas Pope (1649): Essays on Several Subjects. P
Bunyan (d. 1688): Works, ed. C. Doe [incomplete; first complete ed., Wilson, 1736; ed. Whitefield 1767; Hogg 1780; Stebbing 1859].
Burnet (1643): Discourse of Pastoral Care. P
Dryden (1631): Eleonora. V
    Cleomenes. T
    ? Trs. Miscellaneous Essays of Saint-Évremond, with character of Saint-Évremond.
Jonson (d. 1637): Second Folio [see 1616, 1640; adds New Inn (see 1631) to Folio I].

Joseph Butler b.
Thomas Shadwell d.
Nathaniel Lee d.
Elias Ashmole d.
Nahum Tate poet-laureate.
Edmund Gibson edits 'Anglo-Saxon Chronicle'.

Leighton, Robert (d. 1684): Works, ed. Fall [concl. 1708; ed. Pearson 1825; Aikman 1835; West 1875].

L'Estrange (1616): Fables of Æsop and other Mythologists [pt. ii 1699]. P

Locke (1632): Third Letter on Toleration [see 1689, 1690]. P

Considerations of the Consequences of Lowering the Interest and Raising the Value of Money [see 1695]. P

Motteux (1660): ed. Gentleman's Journal, or the Monthly Miscellany [concl. 1693; contained poems, essays, short stories, &c., by various writers].

Settle (1648): The Fairy Queen. D opera.

Southerne (1660): The Wives' Excuse. C

Temple (1628): Miscellanea, pt. ii [cont., among other essays, Ancient and Modern Learning, which started the Phalaris Controversy].

Walsh, William (1663): Poems.

Phalaris Controversy: Temple in above essay draws attention to Phalaris; Wotton refutes him in *Reflections of Ancient and Modern Learning* (1694); Boyle edits Epistles of Phalaris (1695) with animadversions on Bentley; Bentley refutes Temple and reviews Boyle's *Phalaris* in *A Dissertation on the Epistles of Phalaris* in 2nd ed. of Wotton's *Reflections* (1697); Boyle, Atterbury, and others reply in *Bentley's Dissertation Examined* (1698); Bentley's *Dissertation upon Epistles of Phalaris* (1699).

1693

Congreve (1670): Old Bachelor. C

Dennis (1657): Impartial Critic [reply to Rymer].P

Dryden (1631): Examen Poeticum, being the third part of Miscellany Poems [see 1684]. V

Trs. Juvenal (assisted by others) and Persius [prefaced by D.'s Discourse on Satire]. V

D'Urfey (1653): Richmond Heiress. C

Hacket, John (d. 1670): Scrinia Reserata. P

Locke (1632): Thoughts concerning Education. P

Mather, Cotton (1663): Wonders of the Invisible World. P

Orrery (d. 1679): Guzman. C

Penn (1644): Some Fruits of Solitude [pt. ii, More Fruits of Solitude, 1782]. P

Rymer, Thomas (1641): A Short View of Tragedy. P

Shadwell (d. 1692): The Volunteers. C

Southerne (1660): Maid's Last Prayer. C

Urquhart (d. 1660), **Motteux** (1660), and others: Trs. Rabelais, bk. iii [see 1653]. P

George Lillo b.

John Ray, 'Methodus Animalium'.

La Fontaine, 'Fables', pt. iii, 1693–4.

Addison (1672): Trs. Fourth Georgic; Account of the Greatest English Poets; Song for St. Cecilia's Day; trs. Ovid's Salmacis [in Annual Miscellany, ed. Dryden]. V

Banks, John: Innocent Usurper. T

Blount, Sir Thomas Pope (1649): De Re Poetica. P

Burnaby, William: Trs. Satyricon of Petronius. P

Burnet (1643): Four Discourses. P

Burthogge, Richard (d. 1694?): Essay upon Reason and the Nature of Spirits. P

Congreve (1670): Double Dealer. C

Crowne, John: Married Beau. C
  Regulus. T

Dryden (1631): Love Triumphant. D
  Annual Miscellany, being the fourth part of Miscellany Poems [see 1684].
  To Congreve. V

D'Urfey (1653): Comical History of Don Quixote, pts. i, ii [pt. iii, 1696]. C

Echard, Laurence (1670?), and others: Trs. Plautus and Terence. V

Fox (d. 1691): Journal, ed. Ellwood, Preface by Penn [original MS. pub. 1911]. P

Milton (d. 1674): Letters of State written to Princes and Republics of Europe, 1649–59, trs. with Life by E. Phillips [cont. unpub. Sonnets to Cromwell, Fairfax, Vane, Skinner].

Settle (1648): Ambitious Slave. T

Southerne (1660): Fatal Marriage. T

Strype (1643): Memorials of Thomas Cranmer. P

Wotton, William: Reflections on Ancient and Modern Learning. P

Wright, James (1643): Country Conversations. P

Death of Queen Mary; William III reigns alone.
Bank of England founded.
Philip Dormer Stanhope, fourth Earl of Chesterfield, b.
Francis Hutcheson b.
John Tillotson d.
Voltaire b.
Racine, 'Cantiques'.
Bossuet, 'Réflexions sur la Comedie'.
Boileau, 'Réflexions sur Longin'.
Dictionary of the French Academy.

1695

Addison (1672): A Poem to his Majesty.

Blackmore (c. 1655): Prince Arthur [enlarg. 1697]. V

Blount, Charles (d. 1693): Miscellaneous Works, ed. Charles Gildon.

Burnet (1643): Essay on Memory of Queen Mary. P

Congreve (1670): Love for Love. C

Dryden (1631): Trs. Du Fresnoy's De Arte Graphica [with Preface on the Parallel between Painting and Poetry]. P

Henry Vaughan d.
George Savile, Marquis of Halifax, d.
Anthony à Wood d.
Dorothy Osborne, Lady Temple, d.
Licensing Act lapses.
George Ridpath starts 'The Flying Post' (tri-weekly; concl. 1714).
Abel Roper starts 'The Post Boy' (tri-weekly; concl. 1710).

Laud (d. 1645): Collected Works, ed. Henry Wharton [concl. 1700; ed. Scott and Bliss 1847–60].

Locke (1632): Reasonableness of Christianity. P
Vindication of the Reasonableness of Christianity. P
Further Considerations concerning Raising the Value of Money [see 1692]. P

Milton (d. 1674): Poetical Works ed. Patrick Hume [1st annotated ed.: later edd.: Bentley 1732, Newton 1749–50, Todd 1801, '08, '26, Masson 1877, '90, Beeching 1900].

Tanner, Thomas: Notitia Monastica [enlarged ed. by John Tanner 1744; reprtd. with additions by Nasmith 1787].

Temple (1628): Introduction to the History of England. P

Tillotson (d. 1694): Works, ed. R. Barker [concl. 1704; ed. Birch 1752].

Charles Boyle ed. of 'Epistles of Phalaris' (see 1692 note).
Edmund Gibson trs. Camden's 'Britannia'.
La Fontaine d.

1696

Aubrey, John: Miscellanies. P
Banks, John: Cyrus the Great. T
Baxter (d. 1691): Reliquiae Baxterianae, ed. from B.'s MSS. by Matthew Sylvester.
Behn (d. 1689): Younger Brother. C
Brady, Nicholas, and Tate, Nahum: Trs. Psalms [called the New Version; see 1562]. V
Cibber, Colley (1671): Love's Last Shift. C
Dennis (1657): Letters written between Dryden, Wycherley, Congreve, and Dennis; with Select Letters of Voiture. P
Dryden (1631): Ode on Henry Purcell. V
Granville, George, Lord Lansdowne (1667): The She-gallants. C
Leslie, Charles: Snake in the Grass. P
Motteux (1660): Love's a Jest. C
Oldmixon, John (1673): Poems on Several Occasions. V
Penn (1644): Primitive Christianity Revived. P
Rowe, Mrs. Elizabeth (1674): Poems on Several Occasions by Philomela. P
Southerne (1660): Oroonoko. T
Suckling (d. 1642): Works, first collected [ed. W. C. Hazlitt 1874; Thompson 1910].
Toland (1670): Christianity not Mysterious. P
Whiston, William (1667): New Theory of Earth. P

Henry Home(Lord Kames) b.
William Oldys b.
John Wilson d.
Edward Phillips d.?
Mme de Sévigné d.
Regnard, 'Le Joueur'.
Bayle, 'Dictionnaire historique et critique'.

Bentley (1662): Dissertation upon Epistles of Phalaris [in 2nd ed. of William Wotton's Reflections upon Ancient and Modern Learning:
refutes Temple and reviews Boyle's Phalaris.
See 1692, 95].

Cibber, Colley (1671): Woman's Wit. C

Collier (1650): Essays. P

Congreve (1670): Mourning Bride. T

Dampier, William (1652): Voyages [concl. 1709].
P

Defoe (1661 ?): Essay upon Projects. P

Dryden (1631): Alexander's Feast. V

Trs. Virgil. V

Evelyn (1620): Numismata. P

Norris (1657): Account of Reason and Faith in
Relation to Mysteries of Christianity. P

Prideaux, Humphrey (1648): Life of Mahomet. P

Ravenscroft (d. 1697): The Anatomist. C

Vanbrugh (1664): Relapse. C

Provok'd Wife. C

Æsop. C

Charles Macklin b. ?
William Hogarth b.
Edward Ravenscroft d.
Bossuet, 'États d'oraison'.
Fénelon, 'Maximes des
Saints'.

1698

Behn (d. 1689): Histories and Novels [collected].
Poetical Remains, ed. Charles Gildon.

Boyle, Charles, Atterbury, Francis, and others:
Dr. Bentley's Dissertations upon the Epistles
of Phalaris Examined [see 1697]. P

Collier (1650): Short View of the Immorality and
Profaneness of the English Stage [see below]. P

Crowne, John: Caligula. T

Defoe (1661): Occasional Conformity of Dissenters. P

Fletcher, Andrew (1655): Discourse of Government relating to Militias. P

Two Discourses concerning Scotland. P

Granville (1667): Heroick Love. T

Lacy, John (d. 1681): Sauny the Scott. C

Leslie, Charles (1650): Short and Easy Method
with the Deists. P

Ludlow, Edmund (d. 1692): Memoirs [concl. 1699;
ed. Firth 1894].

Milton (d. 1674): Collected Prose Works, English
and Latin, ed. with Life by John Toland [an
anon. ed. of Eng. prose works in 1697].

Motteux (1660): Beauty in Distress. T

Sidney, Algernon (d. 1683): Discourses concerning
Government. P

William Warburton b.
Edward Ward's 'London
Spy' (monthly from
Nov.; collected 1703).
'Society for Promoting
Christian Knowledge'
founded.
Metastasio b.

Whichcote (d. 1683): Select Sermons, ed. with Preface by Shaftesbury.

Jeremy Collier Controversy: John Dennis's *Usefulness of the Stage* and Filmer's *Defence of Dramatic Poetry* and *Further Defence of Dramatic Poetry*, 1698; Congreve's *Amendments of Mr. Collier's False Citations* and Vanbrugh's *Vindication of the Relapse and Provok'd Wife*, 1699; Collier's reply to Congreve and Vanbrugh, *A Defence of the Short View*, 1699; John Drake's *Ancient and Modern Stages Surveyed*, 1699, and Collier's reply to it, *A Second Defence of the Short View*, 1700; Dryden's reply to Collier in Preface to *Fables* and in Epilogue to Vanbrugh's *Pilgrim*, 1700; Filmer's *Defence of Plays*, 1707, and Collier's reply to it, *A Further Defence of the Short View*, 1708.

1699

Bentley (1662): Dissertation upon the Epistles of Phalaris [concludes the controversy: see 1692]. P

Brown, Thomas (1663): Collection of Miscellany Poems, Letters, etc.

Burnet (1643): Exposition of the Thirty-nine Articles. P

Cibber, Colley (1671): Xerxes. T

Dennis (1657): Rinaldo and Armida. T

Evelyn (1620): Acetaria. P

Fairfax, Thomas, Lord Fairfax (d. 1671): Memorials, written by himself, ed. B. Fairfax [incomplete: complete, ed. Lodge, 1808].

Farquhar (1678): Love and a Bottle. C
Constant Couple. C

Garth (1661): Dispensary. V

King, William (1663): A Journey to London in 1698. P
Dialogues of the Dead. P

Toland (1670): Amyntor. P

Traherne (d. 1674): Serious and Patheticall Contemplation of the Mercies of God. P

Robert Blair b.
Joseph Spence b.
Edward Stillingfleet d.
Sir William Temple d.
Joseph Beaumont d.
'History of the Works of the Learned', 1699–1711.
Racine d.
Fénelon, 'Télémaque'.

Blackmore (*c.* 1655): Satyr against Wit. V
Brown (1663): Amusements Serious and Comical. P and V
Congreve (1670): Way of the World. C
Dennis (1657): Iphigenia. T
Dryden (d. 1700): Fables. V
　A Secular Masque. V
Halifax (d. 1695): Miscellanies [Advice to a Daughter, Character of a Trimmer, Anatomy of an Equivalent, Letter to a Dissenter, Maxims of State, etc.].
Harington (d. 1677): Collected Works, ed. with Life by John Toland [enlarged ed. Millar 1737].
Motteux (1660): Trs. Don Quixote, vol. i (vol. ii, 1701, vol. iii, 1703).
Pomfret, John (1667): The Choice. V
Southerne (1660): Fate of Capua. T
Tate, Nahum (1652): Panacea; a Poem on Tea.
Temple (d. 1699): Letters, ed. Swift, vols. i–ii [iii, 1703].
Vanbrugh (1664): Pilgrim [altered from Fletcher]. C

James Thomson b.
John Dyer b.?
John Dryden d.
Fénelon, 'Dialogues des morts'.

1701

Cibber, Colley (1671): Love makes a Man. C
Congreve (1670): Judgement of Paris. D masque.
Defoe (1661?): True-born Englishman. V
Dennis (1657): Advancement of Modern Poetry. P
Dryden (d. 1700): Collected Plays [later edd.: Congreve 1717, Scott 1808, Saintsbury 1882].
　Collected Poems [later edd.: Brougham 1743, Derrick 1760, Warton 1811, Christie 1870, Sargeaunt 1910].
Farquhar (1678): Sir Harry Wildair. C
Gildon (1665): Examen Miscellaneum. P
　A New Miscellany of Poems [incl. works by Dorset, Sedley, Fleetwood, Sheppard, &c.].
Norris, John (1657): Ideal and Intelligible World, pt. i (ii, 1704). P
Philips, John (1676): The Splendid Shilling. V
Rowe (1674): Ambitious Stepmother. T
　Tamerlane. T
Settle (1648): Virgin Prophetess. T
Steele (1672): Christian Hero. P
　The Funeral. C
Swift (1667): Contests in Athens and Rome. P
Temple (d. 1699): Miscellanea, pt. iii ed. Swift [see 1680, 1692].
Whichcote (d. 1683): Several Discourses. P

Act of Settlement.
James II d.
Sir Charles Sedley d.
Jeremy Collier, 'Historical, Geographical, Genealogical, and Poetical Dictionary' (concl. 1721).

Bacon (d. 1626): Letters written during the reign of James II, ed. R. Stephens [see 1734].

Brown, Thomas (1663): Letters from the Dead to the Living. P

Bysshe, Edward: Art of English Poetry [pts. ii–iii pub. as British Parnassus, 1734]. P

Clarendon (d. 1674): History of the Rebellion [concl. 1704; later edd.: Bandinel 1826, Macray 1888: see 1759]. P

Defoe (1661 ?): Shortest Way with Dissenters. P

Echard (1670 ?): General Ecclesiastical History. P

Farquhar (1678): The Inconstant. C

Gildon (1665): Comparison between the Two Stages. P

King, William (1650): De Origine Mali. P

Mather, Cotton (1663): Magnalia Christi Americana. P

Pomfret, John (d. 1702): Collected Poems.

Raleigh (d. 1618): Three Discourses, pub. by Philip Raleigh. P

Shaftesbury (1671): Paradoxes of State. P

Vanbrugh (1664): False Friend. D

Accession of Queen Anne.
Philip Doddridge b.
'*The Daily Courant*' (*first daily paper*) *in March* (*concl. 1735*).
'*Observator*', *1702–12.*
'*Poems on Affairs of State*', *1702–7* (*one of the principal edd.*).

1703

Addison (1672): Letter from Italy to Lord Halifax. V

Boyer, Abel (1667): History of the Reign of Queen Anne [concl. 1720]. P

Cibber, Colley (1671): She would and She would not. C

Defoe (1661 ?): Hymn to the Pillory. V

Farquhar (1678): Twin-Rivals. C

Rowe (1674): Fair Penitent. T

Whichcote (d. 1683): Moral and Religious Aphorisms, ed. Jeffrey (enlarg. 1753).

John Wesley b.
Henry Brooke b.?
Robert Dodsley b.
Gilbert West b.
Samuel Pepys d.
George Hickes, '*Thesaurus*'.
Edward Ward, '*London Spy*' (*collected: see 1698*).
Thomas Hearne, '*Reliquiae Bodleianae*'.
Perrault d.

1704

Brown, Thomas (d. 1704): Dialogues [collected]. P

Burnet (1643): Tracts and Discourses [collected]. P

Defoe (1661 ?): The Review [1704–12]. P
The Consolidator.

Fletcher, Andrew (1655): Account of a Conversation concerning a Right Regulation of Governments. P

Steele (1672): Lying Lover. C

Swift (1667): Tale of a Tub, Battle of the Books. P

Tonson, Jacob (pub.): Poetical Miscellanies [5th pt. of Miscellanies, begun by Dryden, 1684].

Wycherley (1640 ?): Miscellany Poems.

Battle of Blenheim.
Roger L'Estrange d.
John Locke d.
Thomas Brown of Shifna d.
Robert Nelson, '*Companion for Festivals and Fasts*'.
First Eng. trs. of Newton's '*Optics*'.
Thomas Rymer and Robert Sanderson (*ed.*), '*Foedera*' (*concl. 1735: see also 1725*).

Addison (1672): The Campaign. V
Remarks on Italy. P
Blackmore (*c.* 1655): Eliza. V
Centlivre, Susannah (1667?): The Gamester. C
Cibber, Colley (1671): Careless Husband. C
Clarke (1675): Being and Attributes of God. P
Coppinger, Matthew: A Session of the Poets. V
Dunton, John (1659): Life and Errors. P
King, William (1663): Miscellanies (n.d.).
Farquhar (1678): Stage-Coach [with Motteux]. C
Locke (d. 1704): On the Epistles of St. Paul. P
Mandeville (1670?): Grumbling Hive [repub. as
Fable of the Bees, 1714, 1723]. V
Philips, John (1676): Blenheim. V
Steele (1672): Tender Husband. C
Vanbrugh (1664): The Confederacy. C
Ward, Edward (1667): Hudibras Redivivus. V

Abraham Tucker b.
David Mallet b.?

1706

Centlivre, Susannah (1667?): Love at a Venture. C
Basset Table. C
Defoe (1661?): Apparition of Mrs. Veal. P
Jure Divino. V
Dennis (1657): On the Operas after Italian
Manner. P
Farquhar (1678): Recruiting Officer. C
Hughes, John (1677): History of England. P
Kennett, White (1660): History of England. P
Locke (d. 1704): Posthumous Works [cont.
Conduct of the Understanding, Discourse of
Miracles, Fourth Letter on Toleration].
Philips, John (1676): Cerealia. V
Rowe (1674): Ulysses. T
Tindal (1657): Rights of the Christian Church. P
Vanbrugh (1664): The Mistake. C
Watts (1674): Horæ Lyricæ. V

Union with Scotland.
Act of Succession.
Benjamin Franklin b.
John Evelyn d.
John Phillips d.
James Watson, '*Choice*
Collection of Scottish
Poems'.

1707

Addison (1672): Fair Rosamond. D opera.
Brown, Thomas (d. 1704): Works [concl. 1708.
Remains 1721: complete ed. 1760].
Echard (1670?): History of England, vol. i [ii–iii
1718]. P
Farquhar (1678): Beaux' Stratagem. C
Philips, John (1676): Ode to Bolingbroke. V
Prior (1664): Poems on Several Occasions [un-
authorized, see 1709].
Rowe (1674): Royal Convert. T
Sedley (d. 1701): Poetical works and Speeches
[collected; another ed. enlarg. 1776].
Tickell (1686): Oxford. V
Watts (1674): Hymns.

Henry Fielding b.
Charles Wesley b.
George Farquhar d.
Newton, '*Arithmetica*
Universalis'.
'*The Muses Mercury*',
1707–8.
Lesage, '*Diable boiteux*'.

Bingham, Joseph (1668): Origines Ecclesiasticae [concl. 1722]. P

Cibber, Colley (1671): Lady's Last Stake [n.d.]. C

Collier (1650): Ecclesiastical History of Great Britain, vol. i (ii 1714; ed. Barham 1840, Lathbury 1852). P

Downes, John (*fl.* 1662–1710): Roscius Anglicanus. P

Henry, Matthew (1662): Exposition of the Testaments (concl. 1710). P

King, William (1663): Art of Cookery [n.d.]. V

Locke (d. 1704): Letters [ed. Forster 1830].

Ockley, Simon (1678): History of the Saracens, vol. i (ii 1718, iii 1757). P

Motteux, Urquhart, and others: Trs. of Rabelais [complete: see 1653, 1693]. P

Philips, John (1676): Cyder. V

Shaftesbury, Anthony Ashley Cooper, First Earl of (d. 1683): Letter concerning Enthusiasm. P

Swift (1667): Predictions for 1708. P

Elegy upon Partridge. V

John Hughes trs. of Fontenelle's 'Dialogues of the Dead'.

1709

Berkeley (1685): New Theory of Vision. P

Centlivre, Susannah (1667 ?): The Busybody. C

Defoe (1661 ?): History of the Union of Great Britain. P

Dennis (1657): Appius and Virginia. T

King, William (1663): The Art of Love. V

Manley, Mary (1663): New Atlantis. P

Philips, Ambrose (1675 ?): Pastorals [in Poeticall Miscellanies, the sixth part]. V

Epistle to Earl of Dorset. V

Pope (1688): Pastorals [in Poetical Miscellanies, the sixth part]. V

Prior (1664): Poems on Several Occasions [see 1707; enlarg. 1718].

Steele (1672): The Tatler [April 1709–Jan. 1711].

Strype (1643): Annals of the Reformation [concl. 1731]. P

Swift (1667): Project for the Advancement of Religion. P

Letter concerning Sacramental Test. P

Baucis and Philemon. V

Temple (d. 1699): Memoirs, pt. iii ed. Swift.

Tonson, Jacob (pub.): Poetical Miscellanies [6th pt. of Miscellanies begun by Dryden, 1684].

Whitelocke (d. 1675): Memorials of English Affairs. P

First Copyright Act imposes penalties for infringement and fixes term of copyright at 14 years, renewable, if the author is still alive, for another 14 years. See 1774, 1842.

Samuel Johnson b.

George Lyttelton b.

John Armstrong b.

Arthur Collins, 'Peerage of England' (with add. 1710–11, 1717; first complete ed. 1735; standard ed. Brydges 1812).

Thomas Hearne's ed. of Spelman's 'Life of Alfred' with additions (see 1678).

A. Hall's ed. of Leland's 'De Scriptoribus Britannicis'.

Nicholas Rowe's ed. of Shakespeare (concl. 1710; stage ed. 1714).

Lesage, 'Turcaret'.

Berkeley (1685): Principles of Human Knowledge. P

Burnet (1643): Exposition of Church Catechism. P

Centlivre, Susannah (1667 ?): The Man's bewitched [n.d.]. D

Congreve (1670): Collected Works [ed. Leigh Hunt 1840].

Gildon (1665): Life of Betterton. P

Granville (1667): The British Enchanters [an opera].

Hill (1685): Elfrid [rewritten as Athelwold, 1732]. T

Manley, Mary (1663): Memoirs of Europe [afterwards printed as vols. 3 and 4 of New Atlantis: see 1709]. P

King, William (1663): Historical Account of Heathen Gods and Heroes. P

Stillingfleet (d. 1699): Works, with Life by Richard Bentley.

Swift (1667): Meditation upon a Broomstick. P

Thomas Reid b.
Addison starts 'The Whig Examiner' (Sept. and Oct.).
'The Examiner' (1710–12) started by Bolingbroke, Swift, Prior, and others.
Thomas Hearne's ed. of Leland's 'Itinerary' (concl. 1712).
Bayle's Historical and Critical Dict.; first ed. in English.
Leibnitz, 'Théodicée'.

1711

Addison (1672): The Spectator [1 Mar. 1711–6 Dec. 1712; coll. 1714, ed. G. Smith 1907].

Alexander (d. 1640): Anacrisis: or a censure of some poets [in Works of Drummond below]. P

Atterbury (1662): Representation of the State of Religion. P

Blackmore (*c.* 1655): Nature of Man. V

Centlivre, Susannah (1667?): Mar-plot. C

Dennis (1657): On the Genius and Writings of Shakespeare. P
Essay upon Public Spirit. P

Drummond (d. 1649): Collected Works, ed. Sage and Ruddiman [cont. imperfect version of D.'s Conversations with Ben Jonson. See 1842].

Pope (1688): Essay on Criticism. V

Shaftesbury (1671): Characteristics of Men and Manners [collection of treatises pub. from 1708 onwards: 2nd ed. enlarg. 1714; Baskerville ed. 1773]. P

Swift (1667): Miscellanies [cont. An Argument against abolishing Christianity].
Conduct of the Allies. P

Waller (d. 1687): Collected Works [later edd.: Elijah Fenton 1729; Thorn Drury 1893].

Whiston (1667): Primitive Christianity Revived [concl. 1712]. P

David Hume b.
John Norris d.
Abel Boyer, 'Political State of Great Britain' (monthly: completed 1729).
Richard Bentley's ed. of Horace.
Joseph Trapp, 'Praelectiones Poeticae' (vol. ii, 1715).
Boileau d.
Crébillon, 'Rhadamiste et Zénobie'.

Arbuthnot (1667): Art of Political Lying. P
  History of John Bull. P
Berkeley (1685): Passive Obedience. P
Blackmore (c. 1655): Creation. V
Browne (d. 1682): Posthumous Works [see 1716].
Clarke, Samuel (1675): Scripture Doctrine of
  Trinity. P
Gay (1685): The Mohocks. D
Granville (1667): Poems upon Several Occasions.
  V
Hughes, John (1677): Calypso and Telemachus. D
Motteux (1660): Trs. of Don Quixote. P
Oldmixon (1673): Secret History of Europe. P
Philips, Ambrose (1675?): Distressed Mother. T
Pope (1688): Rape of the Lock [in Miscellaneous
  Poems and Translations: rev. 1714, 1717]. V
  To a Young Lady, with the Works of Voiture
  [in Miscellaneous Poems as above: enlarged
  ed. 1714]. V
  Messiah [in Spectator, 14 May]. V
Swift (1667): Advice to Members of the October
  Club. P
  Some Remarks on the Barrier Treaty. P
  Proposal for Correcting the English Language.
  P
Tickell (1686): To the Lord Privy Seal [1713]. V

The Stamp Act.
Richard Glover b.
Edward Moore b.
Woodes Rogers, 'A Cruis-
  ing Voyage round the
  World'.
Rousseau b.
Fénelon, 'Existence de
  Dieu'.
Fontenelle, 'Éloge des
  Académiciens'.

1713

Addison (1672): Cato. T
Bentley (1662): Remarks upon a Discourse of
  Free-thinking [see Collins below]. P
Berkeley (1685): Dialogues between Hylas and
  Philonous. P
Carey, Henry: Poems on Several Occasions [see
  1729].
Collier, Arthur (1680): Clavis Universalis. P
Collins, Anthony (1676): Discourse of Free-
  thinking. P
Dennis (1657): Remarks upon Cato. P
Gay (1685): Rural Sports. V
  Wife of Bath [revised 1730]. C
Parnell (1679): Essay on different Styles of
  Poetry. V
Pope (1688): Windsor Forest. V
  Ode for Musick [Ode on St. Cecilia's Day]. V
Steele (1672): The Guardian [12 Mar.–1 Oct.].
  The Englishman [6 Oct. 1713–11 Feb. 1714].
Swift (1667): Importance of the Guardian con-
  sidered. P
Winchilsea, Countess of: Miscellany Poems
  [enlarg. ed. M. Reynolds 1903].

Treaty of Utrecht.
Laurence Sterne b.
Anthony Cooper, third
  Earl of Shaftesbury, d.
Thomas Rymer d.
Thomas Sprat d.
In this year Pope, Swift,
  Arbuthnot, Gay, Parnell,
  Congreve, Lord Oxford,
  and Atterbury form the
  Scriblerus Club (see
  1741).
Anthony Hamilton, 'Mém-
  oires du comte de Gram-
  mont' (see 1714).

Centlivre, Susannah (1667?): The Wonder! A Woman Keeps a Secret. C
Ellwood, Thomas (d. 1713): History of the Life of Thomas Ellwood, written by his own hand [with a Supplement by Joseph Wyeth]. P
Gay (1685): The Fan. V
The Shepherd's Week. V
Locke (d. 1704): Collected Works [later edd.: 1768–91–1801–12–23].
Mandeville (1670?): Fable of the Bees [with An Inquiry into the Origin of Moral Virtue: see 1705, 1723]. P and V
Rowe (1674): Jane Shore. T
Steele (1672): The Ladies' Library. P
Swift (1667): Public Spirit of the Whigs. P
Young (1683): Force of Religion. V

Accession of George I.
William Shenstone b.
George Whitefield b.
James Hervey b.
James Burnett (Lord Monboddo) b.
Abel Boyer's trs. of 'Memoirs of Count Grammont' (see 1713).
Narcissus Luttrell's 'Brief Relation' ends (see 1678, 1857).
La Motte, 'Iliade'.
Leibnitz, 'Monadologie'.

1715

Bullock, Christopher (1690?): Woman's Revenge. C
Cibber, Colley (1671): Hob, or the Country Wake. C
Cotton (d. 1687): Collected Works.
Defoe (1661?): Appeal to Honour and Justice. P
Garth (1661): Claremont. V
Gay (1685): What d'ye call it [n.d.]. D burlesque.
Johnson, Charles (1679): Country Lasses. C
Pope (1688): Iliad vol. i, with prefatory essay by Thomas Parnell [ii 1716, iii 1717, iv 1718, v–vi 1720]. V Key to the Lock. V Temple of Fame. V
Rowe (1674): Lady Jane Grey. T
Tickell (1686): Iliad [bk. i only]. V
Watts (1674): Divine Songs for Children. V

First Jacobite Rebellion.
Richard Graves b.
Richard Jago b.
William Whitehead b.
John Brown b.
Gilbert Burnet d.
Nahum Tate d.
Nicholas Rowe poet-laureate.
John Hughes's ed. of Spenser.
Thomas Hearne's ed. of Leland's 'Collectanea'.
Society of Antiquaries revived.
Louis XIV d.
Lesage, 'Gil Blas' (concl. 1735).

1716

Addison (1672): The Drummer. C
The Freeholder [23 Dec. 1715–9 June 1716].
Blackmore (c. 1655): Essays. P
Poems on Various Subjects.
Browne (d. 1682): Christian Morals, ed. J. Jeffrey. P
Gay (1685): Trivia [n.d.]. V
Hill (1685): Fatal Vision. T
Gideon, bk. i, ii [iii–iv 1749]. V
Pope (1688): Epistle to Jervas [in ed. of Du Fresnoy's Art of Painting]. V
Horrid and Barbarous Revenge . . . on Curll. P
Pope, Gay, and Wortley Montagu: Court Poems [see 1747]. V
Prideaux, Humphrey (1648): Old and New Testament connected in the History of Jews. P
Shaftesbury (d. 1713): Letters to a Student at the University. P

Septennial Act.
Thomas Gray b.
William Wycherley d.
Thomas Hearne's ed. of 'Old English Chronicles' between 1716 and 1735.
'Historical Register', 1716–38.
Daniel Defoe, 'Mercurius Politicus', 1716–20.
Leibnitz d.
Fénelon, 'Lettre à l'Académie'.

Ashmole, Elias (d. 1698): Memoirs, drawn up by himself. P

Duke, Richard (d. 1711): Poems upon Several Subjects [in Roscommon's Poetical Works].

Fenton, Elijah (1683): Poems on Several Occasions.

Garth, Samuel (1661): Ed. Ovid's Metamorphoses, trs. by eminent hands [Dryden, Addison, Tate, Croxall, Gay, Garth]. V

Gay, Pope, and Arbuthnot: Three Hours after Marriage. C

Hoadly (1676): Nature of the Kingdom of Christ. P

Law (1686): Letters I and II to the Bishop of Bangor [i.e. Hoadly above. Letter III 1719]. P

Parnell (1679): Homer's Battle of the Frogs and the Mice. V

Pope (1688): Collected Works [cont. the unpub. Elegy to the Memory of an Unfortunate Lady, and Eloisa to Abelard. Continued 1735-36-42. Later edd.: Warburton 1751, Wakefield 1794, Warton 1797, Bowles 1806, Carruthers 1858, Ward 1869, Elwin and Courthope 1871-89].

Tickell (1686): Epistle from a Lady in England. V

Horace Walpole b.
David Garrick b.
Richard Owen Cambridge b.
Congreve's ed. of Dryden.
The Bangorian Controversy, 1717-20.

1718

Centlivre, Susannah (1667?): Bold Stroke for a Wife. C

Cibber, Colley (1671): The Non-juror. C

Gildon (1665): Complete Art of Poetry. P

Prior (1664): Poems [cont., among unpub. works, Alma, and Solomon on the Vanity of the World: see 1709].

Ramsay (1686): Christ's Kirk on the Green. V

Rowe (d. 1718): Trs. of Lucan. V.

Nicholas Rowe d.
Thomas Parnell d.
William Penn d.
Peter Anthony Motteux d.
Eusden poet-laureate.
Joseph Trapp, trs. of Æneid, vol. i (vol. ii, 1720; complete, with notes, 1731, 1735).
Society of Antiquaries refounded.
Voltaire, 'Œdipe'.
Massillon, 'Petit Carême'.

1719

Addison (d. 1719): The Old Whig. P

Defoe (1661?): Robinson Crusoe. P
   Further Adventures of Robinson Crusoe. P

Jacob, Giles (1686): Poetical Register [2nd vol. 1720]. P

Southerne (1660): Spartan Dame. T

Watts (1674): Psalms of David. V

Young (1683): Busiris. T
   Letter to Mr. Tickell [on Addison's death]. V

Giuseppe Baretti b.
Joseph Addison d.
Samuel Garth d.
'Daily Post' (ran till 1746).
La Motte, 'Fables'.
Voltaire, 'Lettres sur Œdipe'.

Clarendon (d. 1674): History of the Rebellion in Ireland. P
Croxall, Samuel: Fair Circassian. V
    Select Collection of Novels [concl. 1722; enlarg. 1729]. P
Defoe (1661?): Memoirs of a Cavalier. P
    Captain Singleton. P
    Duncan Campbell. P
Gay (1685): Collected Poems.
Hill (1685): The Creation. V
Hughes (d. 1720): Siege of Damascus. T
Pope (1688) and others: New Miscellany of Original Poems ['Hammond's Miscellany', incl. P.'s Verses to Lady M. W. Montagu].
Prior (1664): The Conversation. V
Ramsay, (1686): Poems [8vo, see 1721].
Swift, (1667): Proposal for the Universal use of Irish Manufactures. P

South Sea Bubble.
Gilbert White b.
Richard Hurd b.
Samuel Foote b.
Charlotte Lennox b.
Mrs. Elizabeth Montagu b.
John Hughes d.
Countess of Winchilsea d.
Arthur Collins, 'Baronetage of England' (final ed. Wotton 1741).
Stow's 'Survey of London' ed. and enlarged by Strype.
Marivaux, 'Arlequin poli par l'amour'.

1721

Addison (d. 1719): Works, ed. with prefatory elegy by Thomas Tickell [cont. unpub. essays on Ancient Medals and Evidences of Christian Religion. Later edd.: Baskerville 1761, Hurd 1811, Greene 1856].
Gildon (1665): Laws of Poetry. P
Pope (1688): To Mr. Addison [in A.'s Works above]. V
    To Robert, Earl of Oxford. V
Ramsay (1686): Poems [4to, see 1720; vol. ii 1727].
Shaftesbury (d. 1713): Letters to Robert Molesworth. P
Strype (1643): Ecclesiastical Memorials. P
Swift (1667): Letter to a Young Gentleman lately entered into Holy Orders. P
    Letter of Advice to a Young Poet. P
Young (1683): The Revenge. T

William Collins b.
Tobias Smollett b.
Thomas Francklin b.
Mark Akenside b.
William Robertson b.
Matthew Prior d.
Nathan Bailey, 'Universal Etymological English Dictionary' (Suppl. vol. 1727; enlarged as 'Dictionarium Britannicum', 1730).
John Urry's ed. of Chaucer.
Montesquieu, 'Lettres persanes'.

1722

Bolton, Edmund (d. 1633?): Hypercritica [in Anthony Hall's Nicolai Triveti Annalium Continuatio]. P
Buckingham, Duke of (John Sheffield: d. 1721): Works, ed. Pope.
Croxall, Samuel: Fables of Æsop and others. P

John Burgoyne b.
John Home b.
Thomas Leland b.
Christopher Smart b.
Joseph Warton b.
John Toland d.

Defoe (1661 ?): Journal of the Plague Year. P
  Moll Flanders. P
  Colonel Jacque. P
  History of Peter the Great. P
Parnell (d. 1718): Poems, ed. with Epistle to
    Lord Oxford by Pope [later edd.: Goldsmith
    1770, Mitford 1833, Aitken 1894: see 1758].
Philips, Ambrose (1675 ?): The Briton. T
Tickell (1686): To Sir Godfrey Kneller. V
  Kensington Gardens. V

1723

Blackmore (*c.* 1655): Alfred. V
Burnet (d. 1715): History of my own time, vol. i
    [ii 1734; whole work 1735; ed. Routh 1823,
    1833; (reign of Charles II only) Airy 1897–
    1900; Supplement to the History, from
    unpub. memoirs, letters, etc., ed. Foxcroft
    1902]. P
Centlivre, Susannah (d. 1723): The Artifice. C
Fenton, Elijah (1683): Mariamne. T
Law (1686): Remarks on the Fable of the Bees. P
Mandeville (1670 ?): Fable of the Bees, 2nd ed.
    with Essay on Charity, and Search into the
    Nature of Society [see 1705, 1714]. P and V
Philips, Ambrose (1675 ?): Humphrey, Duke of
    Gloucester. T
Prior (d. 1721): Down Hall. V
Steele (1672): Conscious Lovers. C

Adam Smith b.
Sir William Blackstone b.
Sir Joshua Reynolds b.
Richard Price b.
Thomas D'Urfey d.
Susannah Centlivre d.
*David Mallet, 'William
  and Margaret' (repub.
  in Ramsay's 'Tea Table
  Miscellany', 1724, and
  Percy's 'Reliques',
  1765).*
Voltaire, 'Henriade'.

1724

Boyle (d. 1679): State Letters.
Collins, Anthony (1676): Grounds of the Christian
    Religion. P
Defoe (1661 ?): Roxana. P
  Tour through Great Britain (concl. 1726). P
Johnson, Charles (fl. 1724–34): General History
    of the Robberies & Murders of the most
    Notorious Pyrates. P
Oldmixon (1673): Critical History of England
    [with Essay on Criticism prefixed; concl.
    1726]. P
Ramsay (1686): Ever Green. V
  Tea-table Miscellany, vol. i [ii 1726, iii
    1727(?)]. V
Savage, Richard: Sir Thomas Overbury. T
Swift (1667): Drapier's Letters. P

William Gilpin b.
Frances Brooke b.
Elkanah Settle d.
Charles Gildon d.
*Thomas Cooke's trs. of
  Bion and Moschus.*
*William Stukeley's 'Itine-
  rarium Curiosum'.*
Kant b.
Klopstock b.

Cooke, Thomas (1703): Battle of the Poets [enlarg. as Tales, Epistles, Odes, 1729]. V

Defoe (1661?): Complete English Tradesman [concl. 1727]. P

A New Voyage round the World. P

Account of Jonathan Wild. P

Hutcheson, Francis (1694): Original of our ideas of Beauty and Virtue. P

Mandeville, Sir John: Travels [first Eng. version from the Cottonian MS.: see 1499, 1889]. P

Pope (1688): Ed. of Shakespeare [2nd ed. accepting some of Theobald's corrections 1728: see 1726].

Odyssey, vols. i–iii [iv–v 1726; with William Broome and Elijah Fenton]. V

Ramsay (1686): Gentle Shepherd. D

Tindal, Nicholas (1688): Trs. of Rapin's History of England [concl. 1731; continuation of same 1744–5; continued by Smollett 1785–9].

Watts (1674): Logic. P

Young (1683): Universal Passion [seven Satires collected as Love of Fame 1728]. V

William Kenrick b.?
William Mason b.
Stephen Whatley, 'Acta Regia' (from Rapin's abridgement of Rymer's 'Foedera'; concl. 1727).

1726

Atterbury (1662): Sermons, 2 vols. P

Bolingbroke (1678): The Craftsman [concl. 1736: collected reprint 1731–7; editor Nicholas Amhurst as 'Caleb d'Anvers'].

Butler (1692): Fifteen Sermons.

Dennis (1657): The Stage defended [reply to Law below]. P

Hill (1685): Fatal Extravagance. T

Law (1686): Treatise upon Christian Perfection. P

Unlawfulness of Stage Entertainments. P

Penn (d. 1718): Works, ed. J. Besse.

Pope (1688) and others: Miscellanea, in 2 vols. ['Curll's Miscellany', incl. P.'s Letters to Henry Cromwell].

Shelvocke, George (fl. 1690–1728): A Voyage round the World. P

Swift (1667): Cadenus and Vanessa. V

Gulliver's Travels [pt. i Lilliput; ii Brobdingnag; iii Laputa; iv Houyhnhnms]. P

Theobald (1688): Shakespeare Restored (criticism of Pope's Shakespeare). P

Thomson (1700): Winter. V

Charles Burney b.
Maurice Morgann b.
Thomas Pennant b.
Sir John Vanbrugh d.
Jeremy Collier d.
'The Craftsman', 1726–47 (?).
Voltaire begins his three years' stay in England.

Bolingbroke (1672): The Occasional Writer [in
The Craftsman]. P
Defoe (1661?): History and Reality of Appari-
tions. P
Dorrington, Edward (?): The Hermit, or Adven-
tures of Philip Quarll. P
Dyer (1700?): Grongar Hill [early version as
An Irregular Ode in Miscellaneous Poems,
1726; rev. version in D. Lewis's Miscellaneous
Poems, 1726]. V
Gay (1685): Fables, series i (ii 1738; complete
1750). V
Harte, Walter (1709): Poems on Several Occa-
sions.
Pope (1688), **Swift, Arbuthnot,** and others:
Miscellanies i, ii [vol. i by Swift; vol. ii cont.
Pope's Imitation of English Poets; vol. iii
cont. Pope's Treatise on Bathos 1728; vol.
iv 1732; vol. v 1735; 'Motte's Miscellanies'].
Somerville (1675): Poems, Translations, Fables
and Tales. V
Thomson (1700): Summer. V
Warburton (1698): Inquiry into Prodigies,
Miracles. P

Accession of George II.
Arthur Murphy b.
John Wilkes b.
John Hoole b.
Sir Isaac Newton d.
*First Eng. trs. of Newton's
'Principia' (see 1687)
by Motte.*
*Thomas Wotton, 'English
Baronetage' (enlarged
1741; ed. Johnson and
Kimber 1771).*
*Destouches, 'Le Philo-
sophe marié'.*

1728

Carleton, Captain George: Memoirs (? by Defoe).
Cibber, **Colley** (1671): Provok'd Husband [from
Vanbrugh's Journey to London]. C
Fielding (1707): Love in Several Masques. C
Gay (1685): Beggar's Opera. D opera.
Hutcheson, Francis (1694): Nature and Conduct
of the Passions and Affections. P
Law (1686): Serious Call to Devout and Holy
Life. P
Pope (1688): Dunciad i–iii [rev. ed. as Dunciad
Variorum 1729; bk. iv entitled New Dunciad
1742; bks. i–iv in final form 1743; another ed.
with add. 1749]. V
Ramsay (1686): Poems [incl. Gentle Shepherd
and Nuptials of Duke of Hamilton: see 1721].
Rowe, Mrs. Elizabeth (1674): Friendship in
Death. P
Savage, Richard: Nature in Perfection. V
The Bastard. V
Swift (1667): Short View of the State of Ireland. P
Thomson (1700): Spring. V
Wycherley (d. 1716): Posthumous Works in Prose
and Verse, ed. Theobald.
Young (1683): Ocean: an ode. V
Vindication of Providence. P

Thomas Warton, jnr., b.
Robert Bage b.
*Thomas Cooke, trs. of
Hesiod.*
*Ephraim Chambers, 'Cy-
clopaedia'.*
*'Intelligencer' (Swift, &c.),
1728–9.*

Carey, Henry: Poems on Several Occasions [3rd ed., enlarg.; cont. Namby-Pamby and Sally in Our Alley: see 1713].

Cibber, Colley (1671): Damon and Phillida. D opera.

Gay (1685): Polly, an opera.

Johnson, Charles (1679): Village Opera. D

Oldmixon (1673): History of England [concl. 1739].

Savage, Richard: The Wanderer. V

Swift (1667): Modest Proposal for preventing the Children of the Poor People from being a Burthen to their Parents. P

Thomson (1700): Britannia. V
Poem to the Memory of Congreve. V

Edmund Burke b.
Thomas Percy b.
Clara Reeve b.
Richard Steele d.
William Congreve d.
Sir Richard Blackmore d.
Anthony Collins d.
First Eng. trs. of Perrault's 'Contes' by Robert Samber.
Elijah Fenton's ed. of Waller's Works.
Lessing b.
Moses Mendelssohn b.

1730

Bacon (d. 1626): Works, ed. Blackbourne [first collected ed.; cont. some unpub. legal tracts: see 1740, 1765].

Bolingbroke (1678): Remarks upon the History of England [in The Craftsman 1730–1]. P

Fielding (1707): Temple Beau. C
Author's Farce, Pleasures of the Town. C
Rape upon Rape, Coffee House Politician. C
Tom Thumb [enlarg. 1731]. Burlesque.

Thomson (1700): The Seasons. A hymn on the seasons and other poems [Autumn first appears in this vol.].
Sophonisba. T

Tindal, Matthew (1657): Christianity as old as the Creation. P

Watts (1674): Catechisms. P

Oliver Goldsmith b.
Laurence Echard d.
Colley Cibber poet-laureate.
John Martyn and Richard Russell start 'The Grub Street Journal' (1730–7; Pope probably contributed to it).
Voltaire, 'Brutus' and 'Préface de Brutus'.
Marivaux, 'Le jeu de l'amour et du hasard'.

1731

Cudworth (d. 1688): Eternal and Immutable Morality. P

Johnson (1709): Latin Trs. of Pope's Messiah [in J. Husbands' Miscellany of Poems].

Law (1686): The Case of Reason [reply to Tindal: see 1730]. P

Lillo (1693): The London Merchant. T

Mallet (1705): Eurydice. T

Pope (1688): Of Taste: an Epistle to the Earl of Burlington [later called Of False Taste: fourth moral essay: see 1732]. V

William Cowper b.
Erasmus Darwin b.
Charles Churchill b.
Daniel Defoe d.
Edward Cave starts 'The Gentleman's Magazine' (monthly to 1907).
'Daily Advertiser' started.
Marivaux, 'Marianne' (concl. 1742).

Berkeley (1685): Alciphron. P
Dodsley (1703): Muse in Livery. V
Fielding (1707): Covent Garden Tragedy. D
  Modern Husband. C
  Mock Doctor. C
Hill (1685): Athelwold [see 1710]. T
King, William (1685): The Toast. V
Lyttelton (1709): Progress of Love. V
Neal, Daniel (1678): History of the Puritans, vol.
  i [ii 1733, iii 1736, iv 1738]. P
Pope (1688): Of the Use of Riches; an epistle to
  Lord Bathurst [third moral essay]. V
Watts (1674): Scripture History. P

George Colman, senr., b.
William Falconer b.
Richard Cumberland b.
John Gay d.
Francis Atterbury d.
Richard Bentley's ed. of
  'Paradise Lost'.
'The London Magazine'
  or 'Gentleman's Monthly
  Intelligencer' appears.
'Poor Richard's Almanac'
  (ed. B. Franklin), 1732–
  57.
Voltaire, 'Zaïre'.
Destouches, 'Le Glorieux'.

1733

Bolingbroke (1678): Dissertation upon Parties [in
  The Craftsman: reprtd. 1735]. P
Fielding (1707): The Miser. C
Gay (1685): Achilles, an opera.
Johnson, Charles (1679): Caelia, or the perjured
  lover. D
Pope (1688): Essay on Man [The Universal
  Prayer added, and also pub. separately,
  1738]. V
  Of the Knowledge and Characters of Men:
  an epistle to Viscount Cobham [first moral
  essay]. V
  First Satire of bk. ii of Horace imitated. V
  The Impertinent. V
Swift (1667): Life and genuine Character of Dr.
  Swift. P
  On Poetry: a Rapsody.

Joseph Priestley b.
Matthew Tindal d.
Wieland b.
'The Bee', Feb. 1733–
  June 1735.
Voltaire, 'English Letters'.

1734

Atterbury (d. 1732): Sermons, 2 vols. P
Bacon (d. 1626): Letters and Remains, collected
  by R. Stephens [see 1702].
Carey, Henry: Chrononhotonthologos [n.d.]. D
  burlesque.
Fielding (1707): Don Quixote in England. C
Johnson, Charles (fl. 1724–34): General History
  of the Lives & Adventures of the most
  Famous Highwaymen.
Pope (1688): Second Satire of bk. ii of Horace. V
Reresby, Sir John (d. 1689): Memoirs [ed. Cart-
  wright 1875, Ivatt 1904: see 1813].
Sale, George (1697?): Trs. of the Koran.
Theobald, Lewis: Ed. of Shakespeare.

Roger North d.
John Dennis d.
First Eng. trs. (anon.) of
  La Fontaine's Fables.
'General Advertiser'
  started (from 1752 as
  'Public Advertiser').
Montesquieu, 'Grandeur
  et Decadence des Ro-
  mains'.
Thomas Cooke, trs. of
  Terence.

Berkeley (1685): The Querist, pt. i (ii 1736, iii 1737). P

Brooke, Henry (1703 ?): Universal Beauty. V

Dodsley (1703): The Toy Shop. D

    Beauty, or The Art of Charming. V

Hughes (d. 1720): Collected Poems, with Select Essays in Prose.

Johnson (1709): Voyage to Abyssinia [trs. Jerome Lobo]. P

Lillo (1693): Christian Hero. T

Lyttelton (1709): Letters from a Persian in England. P

Pope (1688): Characters of Women [second moral essay]. V

    Epistle to Arbuthnot. V

    Satires of Donne versified.

    Correspondence [pub. Curll; unacknowledged, though really manipulated by Pope: see 1726, 1737].

    Collected Works, vol. ii, see 1717.

Savage, Richard: Progress of a Divine. V

Somerville (1675): The Chace. V

Swift (1667): Collected Works, ed. Faulkner [4 vols., 6 vols. 1738, 8 vols. 1746].

Thomson (1700): Italy [Liberty, pt. i]. V

    Greece [Liberty, pt. ii]. V

    Rome [Liberty, pt. iii]. V

James Beattie b.
John Arbuthnot d.
John Wesley, 'Journals'
    (concl. 1790).
'Daily Gazetteer', 1735–
    48.
La Chausée, 'Préjugé à la
    mode'.
L'abbé Prévost, 'Manon
    Lescaut'.
Marivaux, 'Paysan par-
    venu'.

1736

Armstrong (1709): Œconomy of Love. V

Browne, Isaac Hawkins (1705): A Pipe of Tobacco. V

Butler (1692): Analogy of Religion. P

Carey, Henry: The Honest Yorkshireman. D ballad-farce.

Carte, Thomas: Life of James, Duke of Ormond. P

Duck, Stephen: Poems on Several Occasions.

Fielding (1707): Pasquin. D farce.

    Historical Register for 1736. D farce.

Hill (1685): Zara [from Voltaire]. D

    Alzira [from Voltaire]. D

Oldys (1696): Life of Sir Walter Raleigh [in ed. of R.'s History of the World]. P

Pope (1688): Bounce to Fop. V

Thomson (1700): Britain [Liberty, pt. iv]. V

    The Prospect [Liberty, pt. v]. V

    Liberty, a poem [composed of pts. pub. 1735–6].

Warburton (1698): Alliance between Church and State. P

Robert Jephson b.
James Macpherson b.
George Steevens b.
Newton, 'Method of Flux-
    ions'.
Voltaire, 'Le Mondain'
    and 'Enfant prodigue'.

Carey, Henry: Dragon of Wantley. D burlesque opera.

Dodsley (1703): King and Miller of Mansfield. D

Edwards, Jonathan (1703): The Surprising Work of God in the Conversion of Many Hundred Souls. P

Fletcher, Andrew (d. 1716): Political Works. P

Glover (1712): Leonidas. V

Green, Matthew (d. 1737): The Spleen. V

Hill (1685): Tears of the Muses. V

Lillo (1693): Fatal Curiosity. T

Oldys (1696): British Librarian. P

Pope (1688): Epistle VI of bk. i of Horace imitated. V

Epistle I of bk. i of Horace imitated. V

Epistles I and II of bk. ii of Horace imitated. V

Ode to Venus. V

Letters [Works in Prose; first acknowledged and authenticated ed.: see 1726, 1735].

Shenstone (1714): Poems on Various Occasions [cont. first draft of The Schoolmistress].

Thomson (1700): Poem to memory of Lord Talbot.

Warburton (1698): Divine Legation of Moses [concl. 1741]. P

Wesley, John (1703): Psalms and Hymns.

Edward Gibbon b.

Thomas Paine b.

John Strype d.

Alexander Cruden, 'Biblical Concordance'.

David Wilkins, 'Concilia'.

Thomas Cooke's trs. of Cicero's 'De Natura Deorum'.

William Oldys, 'British Librarian' (Jan.–June).

1738

Akenside (1721): A British Philippic. V

Edwards, Jonathan (1703): Discourses on Various Important Subjects. P

Gay (1685): Fables, ii [i 1727; complete 1750]. V

Hooke, Nathaniel: Roman History [concl. 1771]. P

Johnson (1709): London [in imitation of Juvenal, Sat. iii]. V

Pope (1688): Universal Prayer. V

One Thousand Seven Hundred and Thirty-Eight [two dialogues]. V

Swift (1667): Collection of Genteel Conversation. P

Thomson (1700): Agamemnon. T

Watts (1674): World to Come. P

John Wolcot ('Peter Pindar') b.

George Whitefield, 'Journals' (concl. 1741).

Thomas Birch's ed. of Milton's Prose Works (also 1753).

Voltaire, 'Discours sur l'homme'.

Piron, 'La Métromanie'.

Addison (d. 1719): Ancient and Modern Learning [doubtful if by A.]. P

Boyse, Samuel (1708): The Deity. V

Brooke, Henry (1703 ?): Gustavus Vasa [sometimes called The Patriot]. T

Carey, Henry: Nancy [called The Pressgang 1755, The True Blue 1787]. D musical interlude.

Glover (1712): London, or the Progress of Commerce. V

Admiral Hosier's Ghost. V

Hume (1711): Treatise of Human Nature [concl. 1740]. P

Johnson (1709): Marmor Norfolciense. P

Compleat Vindication of Licensers of the Stage [an attack on the censorship provoked by the prohibition of Brooke's Gustavus Vasa]. P

Mallet (1705 ?): Mustapha. T

Smith, William: Trs. of Longinus on the Sublime. P

Swift (1667): Verses on the Death of Dr. Swift.

Thomson (1700): Edward and Leonora. D T

West (1703): A Canto of the Faery Queen [imitation of Spenser].

Hugh Kelly b.
George Lillo d.
'Scots Magazine' started.
William Warburton, 'Commentary on Pope's Essay on Man' (remodelled 1741).
Henry Fielding and James Ralph start 'The Champion'.
The Letters and Despatches, 1611–40, of Thomas Wentworth, Earl of Strafford, ed. W. Knowler.

1740

Bacon (d. 1626): Works, ed. with Life by D. Mallet [see 1730, 1765].

Cibber, Colley (1671): Apology for his Life. P

Dyer (1700 ?): Ruins of Rome. V

Law (1686): Appeal to all that doubt. P

Lillo (1693): Elmerick. T

North, Roger (d. 1734): Examen, or An Enquiry into the Credit & Veracity of a pretended complete History. P

Pitt, Christopher (1699): Trs. of Æneid. V

Prior (d. 1721): Miscellaneous Works, ed. Adrian Drift [Poems ed. Evans 1779, Mitford 1835, 1892. Complete Works, incl. for the first time Dialogues of the Dead, ed. A. R. Waller 1905–7].

Richardson (1689): Pamela or Virtue Rewarded. P

Somerville (1675): Hobbinol. V

Thomson (1700) **and Mallet** (1705): Alfred [new version by Mallet 1751; cont. Rule Britannia]. D masque.

Whitefield, George: Short Account of God's dealings with George Whitefield [see 1747]. P

Christian History [concl. 1747]. P

James Boswell b.
Thomas Tickell d.
William Stukeley's 'Stonehenge'.
Saint-Simon, 'Mémoires', 1740 ff.

Arbuthnot, Pope, Gay, Parnell, and others: Memoirs of Scriblerus [in the 4to ed. of Pope's Works: mostly by Arbuthnot].

Betterton, Thomas (d. 1710): History of the English Stage [doubtful if by B.]. P

Dodsley (1703): Blind Beggar of Bethnal Green. D

Public Register [3 Jan.–13 June].

Fielding (1707): Shamela. P

Francklin (1721): Of the Nature of the Gods [trs. Cicero].

Hume (1711): Essays Moral and Political [concl. 1742].

Middleton (1683): Life of Cicero. P

Ogle, George (1704): Tales of Chaucer modernized by several hands [Dryden, Pope, and others].

Pope (1688): Works in Prose, vol. ii.

Richardson (1689): Familiar Letters. P

Shenstone (1714): Judgment of Hercules. V

Watts (1674): Improvement of the Mind. P

William Combe b.
Arthur Young b.
Sarah Trimmer b.
Edmond Malone b.
La Chaussée, 'Mélanide'.

1742

Campbell, John (1708): Lives of the Admirals, vol. i, ii [iii and iv 1744]. P

Cibber (1671): Letters to Mr. Pope. P

Collins (1721): Persian Eclogues [repub. as Oriental Eclogues 1757]. V

Cooke (1703): Boys' Battle [including revised ed. of Battle of the Books]. V

Fielding (1707): Joseph Andrews. P

North (d. 1734): Life of Francis North [see 1744]. P

Pope (1688): New Dunciad [bk. iv of Dunciad: see 1728]. V

Blast upon Bays. P

Shenstone (1714): Schoolmistress [revised; see 1737]. V

Somerville (d. 1742): Field Sports. V

Thurloe, John (d. 1668): Collection of State Papers, ed. Birch, 7 vols. P

West (1703): Order of the Garter [altered by Garrick 1771]. D

Young (1683): The Complaint, or Night Thoughts i–iv [v 1743, vi–vii 1744, viii–ix 1745]. V

William Somerville d.
Richard Bentley d.
John Oldmixon d.
Memorials of Sarah, Duchess of Marlborough, ed. Nathaniel Hooke.
Voltaire, 'Mahomet'.

Blair (1699): The Grave. V
Collins (1721): Verses on Hanmer's Shakespeare.
Fielding (1707): Miscellanies [cont. Jonathan Wild P, Journey from this World to the Next P, Eurydice D, The Wedding Day D, Essay on Nothing P, and other works].
Francis, Philip (1708?): Trs. Odes, Epodes, and Carmen Seculare of Horace [see 1746]. V
Gay (d. 1732): The Distress'd Wife. C
Hammond, James (d. 1742): Love Elegies. V
Hanmer (1677): Ed. of Shakespeare.
Hill (1685): Fancid. V
Milton (d. 1674): Letters and Papers of State addressed to Oliver Cromwell, ed. John Nickolls, jnr. [see 1694].
Pococke, Richard (1704): Description of the East and some other Countries [concl. 1745]. P
Pope (1688): The Dunciad [final form]. V

Anna Barbauld (née Aikin) b.
Hannah Cowley b.
William Paley b.
Henry Carey d.
Richard Savage d.
'Old England', 1743–53.
William Oldys, 'Catalogus bibliothecae Harleianae' (with contribution by Samuel Johnson; concl. 1744).
Cooke's trs. of Amphitruo of Plautus.

1744

Akenside (1721): Epistle to Curio. V
   Pleasures of Imagination (rev. ed. 1772). V
Armstrong (1709): Art of Preserving Health. V
Berkeley (1685): Philosophical Reflections concerning Tar-water [later called Siris]. P
Collins (1721): Dirge in Cymbeline. V
Denham (d. 1669): Psalms of David [with an essay on earlier metrical versions]. V
Dodsley (1709): Collection of Old Plays [ed. Reed 1780, Collier 1825–8, W. C. Hazlitt 1874–6].
Fielding, Sarah (1710): David Simple. P
Johnson (1709): Life of John Philip Barretier. P
   Life of Richard Savage. P
Moore, Edward (1712), and Brooke (1703?): Fables for the Female Sex.
North (d. 1734): Lives of Dudley North and John North [see 1742, 1890].
Warton, Joseph (1722): The Enthusiast. V

Alexander Pope d.
Lewis Theobald d.
William Oldys, 'Harleian Miscellany' (with Introduction by Samuel Johnson; concl. 1746).
Zachary Grey's ed. of 'Hudibras' (Supplement, cont. critical, historical, and explanatory notes, 1752).

1745

Akenside (1721): Odes on Several Subjects.
Carew, Bampfylde-Moore (1690): Life & Adventures. P
Doddridge (1702): Rise and Progress of Religion in the Soul. P
Johnson (1709): Observations on Macbeth [with Proposals for a new edition of Shakespeare]. P
Swift (1667): Directions to Servants. P
Thomson (1700): Tancred and Sigismunda. T

Second Jacobite Rebellion.
William Hayley b.
Henry Mackenzie b.
Hannah More b.
Thomas Holcroft b.
Henry James Pye b.
Jonathan Swift d.
Fielding starts 'The True Patriot' (concl. 1746).
Voltaire, 'Mérope'.
Gresset, 'Le Méchant'.

Blacklock, Thomas (1721, the blind poet): Poems.
Collier, John ('Tim Bobbin'): View of Lancashire
　　Dialect. V
Collins (1721): Odes [To Evening, How Sleep the
　　Brave, On Death of Colonel Ross, &c.].
Edwards, Jonathan (1703): A Treatise concerning
　　Religious Affections. P
Francis, Philip: Trs. Satires, Epistles, and Art of
　　Poetry of Horace [see 1743]. V
Hervey, James (1714): Meditations and Contem-
　　plations, vol. i (ii 1747). P
Pope (d. 1744): Verses on the Duchess of Marl-
　　borough. V
　　Character of the Duchess of Buckinghamshire. V
Upton, John (1707): Critical Observations on
　　Shakespeare [2nd ed. with attack on War-
　　burton 1748].
Walpole (1717): The Beauties. V
Warton, Joseph (1722): Odes.

Thomas Southerne d.
Robert Blair d.
Francis Hutcheson d.
Robert Dodsley starts ' The
　Museum' (concl. 1747).

1747

Birch, Thomas (1705): Lives [in Heads of Illus-
　　trious Persons engraved by Houbraken and
　　Vertue; concl. 1752]. P
Carte, Thomas: History of England [concl. 1755].
Garrick (1717): Miss in her Teens. D farce.
Glasse, Hannah (fl. 1747): The Art of Cookery
　　made Plain & Easy. P
Gray (1716): Ode on Eton College. V
Hoadly, Benjamin (1706): Suspicious Husband. C
Johnson (1709): Prologue [and Epilogue] at the
　　Opening of the Theatre in Drury Lane. V
　　Plan of a Dictionary of the English Language. P
Lyttelton (1709): Monody to the Memory of a
　　Lady [his wife]. V
Mallet (1705?): Amyntor and Theodora. V
Mason (1725): Musaeus (elegy on Pope). V
Montagu, Lady Mary Wortley (1689): Town
　　Eclogues [unauthorized ed. as Court Poems
　　1715]. V
Pococke, Richard (1704): Tours in Scotland. P
Sterne (1713): The Case of Elijah. P
Warburton, William: Ed. of Shakespeare.
Warton, Thomas (1728): Pleasures of Melan-
　　choly. V
West (1703): Observations on the Resurrection. P
Whitefield (1714): Full Account of God's Dealings
　　with George Whitefield. P

Uvedale Price b.
Anna Seward b.
Fielding starts ' The Jaco-
　bite's Journal' (concl.
　1748).
'Biographia Britannica'
　(concl. 1766; 2nd ed.
　1778–93).
Spence, 'Polymetis'.
Lesage d.

Akenside (1721): Ode to the Earl of Huntingdon. V
Anson, George (1697): Voyage Round the World. P
Bower, Archibald (1686): History of the Popes [concl. 1758]. P
Collins (1721): Odes (revised) in Dodsley's Collection [see 1746].
Dodsley (1703): Collection of Poems, vols. i–iii (iv 1755, v–vi 1758).
    The Preceptor. P
Edwards, Thomas (1699): Canons of Criticism [attack on Warburton's Shakespeare]. P
Gray (1716): Ode to Spring. On Death of a Favourite Cat [in vol. ii of Dodsley's Collection above]. V
Hume (1711): Philosophical Essays concerning Human Understanding [cont., among others, Essay upon Miracles]. P
Richardson (1689): Clarissa Harlowe. P
Smollett (1721): Roderick Random. P
Thomson (1700): Castle of Indolence. V
Whalley, Peter (1722): Enquiry into the Learning of Shakespeare. P

Jeremy Bentham b.
James Thomson d.
Isaac Watts d.
Somers Tracts (so called after Sir John Somers, 1651–1716) first published (concl. 1752; ed. Scott 1809).
Thomas Tanner, 'Bibliotheca Britannico-Hibernica'.
Montesquieu, 'Esprit des Lois'.
Voltaire, 'Zadig'.

1749

Ames, Joseph (1689): Typographical Antiquities [ed. Herbert 1785, Dibdin 1805]. P
Bolingbroke (1678): On the Spirit of Patriotism. P
    Idea of a Patriot King. P
    State of Parties at the Accession of George I. P
Chetwood, William: General History of the Stage. P
Collins (1721): On the Death of Thomson. V
Fielding (1707): Tom Jones. P
    The Case of Bosavern Penlez. P
    A Charge to the Grand Jury. P
Hartley, David (1705): Observations on Man. P
Hill (1685): Mérope [from Voltaire]. T
Johnson (1709): Vanity of Human Wishes [in imitation of Satire x of Juvenal]. V
    Irene: a tragedy.
Law (1686): Spirit of Prayer, pt. i (ii. 1750). P
Middleton (1683): Free Inquiry into Miraculous Powers. P
Smollett (1721): Trs. of Gil Blas. P
Thomson (d. 1748): Coriolanus. T
Warton, Thomas (1728): Triumph of Isis. V
West (1703): Trs. of Odes of Pindar. V

Charlotte Smith b.
Ambrose Philips d.
'The Monthly Review, or the Literary Journal' (concl. 1845).
Thomas Francklin's trs. of Epistles of Phalaris.
T. Newton's ed. of Milton's Poetical Works (concl. 1750).
Johann Wolfgang von Goethe b.
Buffon, 'Histoire Naturelle'.
Voltaire, 'Nanine'.
Diderot, 'Essai sur les aveugles'.

Campbell, John (1708): Political State of Europe. P
Dodsley (1703): Œconomy of Human Life. P
Fielding (1707): Intriguing Chambermaid. D
Halifax (d. 1695): Character of Charles II. P
Hobbes (d. 1679): Works, ed. J. Campbell [ed. Molesworth 1839–45].
Johnson (1709): Prologue at Representation of Comus. V
   The Rambler [bi-weekly from 20 Mar. 1750 to 14 Mar. 1752]. P
   Preface and Postscript to An Essay on Milton's Use and Imitation of Moderns by William Lauder. P
Smart (1722): Eternity of Supreme Being. V
Sterne (1713): Abuses of Conscience. P
Thomson (d. 1748): Poems on Several Occasions. P
Whitehead (1715): Roman Father. T

Richard Payne Knight b.
Sophia Lee b.
Aaron Hill d.
Elijah Fenton d.
The Blue-stocking parties begin.
Moses Browne's ed. of Walton's 'Compleat Angler' with alterations 'to suit the taste of the age'.
'The Student', 1750–1.
Rousseau, 'Discours sur les lettres'.

1751

Arbuthnot (d. 1735): Miscellaneous Works [collected; enlarg. ed. 1770].
Cambridge (1717): Scribleriad. V
Fielding (1707): Late Increase of Robbers. P
   Amelia. P
Gray (1716): Elegy wrote in a Country Churchyard [3rd ed. 1751 contains Redbreast stanza, omitted again in 1753]. V
Hume (1711): Enquiry concerning Principles of Morals. P
Kames (1696): Principles of Morality and Natural Religion. P
Paltock (1697): Peter Wilkins. P
Raleigh (d. 1618): Works, ed. with Life by Thomas Birch [Oxford ed. 1829].
Smollett (1721): Peregrine Pickle. P
West (1703): Education, a poem.

Richard Brinsley Sheridan b.
Henry St. John, Viscount Bolingbroke, d.
Philip Doddridge d.
'L'Encyclopédie' (1751–80).
D'Alembert,' Discours préliminaire de l'encyclopédie'.
Voltaire, 'Siècle de Louis XIV'.

1752

Birch, Thomas (1705): Life of Archbishop Tillotson. P
Bolingbroke (d. 1751): Study and Uses of History. P
   Reflections concerning Moral Principles. P
Hume (1711): Political Discourses. P
Law (1686): Way to Divine Knowledge. P
Lennox (1720): Female Quixote. P
Mason (1725): Elfrida. D
Smart (1722): Poems [incl. Hop Garden].

The calendar changed.
Thomas Chatterton b.
Frances Burney b.
Joseph Butler d.
Samuel Croxall d.
William Whitson d.
Fielding starts 'The Covent Garden Journal' (Jan.–Nov.).
William Dodd, 'Beauties of Shakespeare'.

Bolingbroke (d. 1751): Letter to Sir William Wyndham, Reflections on the State of the Nation, Introductory Letter to Pope. P

Cibber, Theophilus (1703): Lives of the Poets [really by Robert Shiels]. P

Lives of Actors and Actresses. P

Dodsley (1703): Public Virtue. V

Foote (1720): Englishman in Paris. C

Glover (1712): Boadicea. T

Gray (1716): Hymn to Adversity, &c. [in Designs by Bentley for Six Poems by Gray].

Hill (d. 1750): Works [correspondence and poems: see 1760].

Jones, Henry (1721): Earl of Essex. T

Law (1686): Collected Works.

Lennox (1720): Shakespear Illustrated. P

Moore (1712): The Gamester [with David Garrick]. T

Smart (1722): Hilliad. V

Smollett (1721): Ferdinand Count Fathom. P

Warton, Joseph (1722), and Pitt, Christopher: Ed. of Virgil with Eng. trs. in verse.

Young (1683): The Brothers. T

Elizabeth Inchbald b.
Dugald Stewart b.
William Roscoe b.
George Berkeley d.
Dodsley starts 'The World' (*concl. 1757*).
Hawkesworth, Johnson, Joseph Warton, and others start 'The Adventurer' (concl. 1754).
The Union, or Select Scots and English Poems.
Construction of Horace Walpole's house at Strawberry Hill started.
Charter of the British Museum.
Voltaire, 'Essai sur les mœurs' (1753–5).
William Smith, trs. Thucydides' Peloponnesian War.

1754

Birch, Thomas (1705): Memoirs of Reign of Queen Elizabeth. P

Bolingbroke (d. 1751): Collected Works, ed. David Mallet.

Butler (d. 1680): Genuine Remains. P and V

Edwards, Jonathan (1703): Freedom of Will. P

Gay (d. 1732): Rehearsal at Goatham. D farce.

Grey, Zachary: Notes on Shakespeare.

Hume (1711): History of England [The Stuarts, concl. 1757; Tudors 1759; Early History 1762].

Richardson (1689): Sir Charles Grandison (dated 1754; but vols. 1–4 appeared before Sep. 1753). P.

Warton, Thomas (1728): Observations on the Fairie Queene [2nd ed. corrected 1762]. P

Whitehead (1715): Creusa, Queen of Athens. T

Young (1683): Centaur not fabulous. P

George Crabbe b.
Henry Fielding d.
George Colman and Bonnell Thornton, 'The Connoisseur', Jan. 1754–Sept. 1756.
Chesterfield's Papers in 'The World' on Johnson's 'Dictionary'.
Erskine, 'Principles of the Law of Scotland'.
Diderot, 'L'Interprétation de la nature'.
Condillac, 'Traité des sensations'.

1755

Amory, Thomas (1691?): Memoirs of Several Ladies of Great Britain. P

Brown, John (1715): Barbarossa. T

Doddridge (d. 1751): Hymns.

Dodsley (1703): Collection of Poems, vol. iv [see 1748].

'The Monitor' started (concl. 1763).
Mary Barber's anthology, 'Poems by Eminent Ladies'.
'Edinburgh Review', 1755–6.

Fielding (d. 1754): Voyage to Lisbon. P
Grainger, James (1721 ?): Ode on Solitude. V
Hervey, James (1714): Theron and Aspasio. P
Hutcheson (d. 1746): System of Moral Philosophy. P
Johnson (1709): English Dictionary [abridged 1756; revised 1773].
Smollett (1721): Trs. of Don Quixote. P
Swift (d. 1745): Collected Works, ed. Hawkesworth.

Montesquieu d.
Voltaire, 'Orpheline de la Chine'.
Rousseau, 'Discours sur Inégalité'.

1756

Amory, Thomas (1691 ?): Life of John Buncle, vol. i (ii 1766). P
Brown, John (1715): Athelstane. T
Burke (1729): Vindication of Natural Society. P
Origin of our Ideas of the Sublime and Beautiful [2nd ed. cont. Discourse concerning Taste 1757]. P
Butler, Alban (1711): Lives of the Saints, vol. i [later vols. 1757–8–9].
Foote (1720): Englishman returned from Paris. D
Johnson (1709): Life of Sir Thomas Browne [in ed. of Christian Morals: see 1716]. P
Proposals for the Dramatick Works of Shakespeare. P
Mason (1725): Odes.
Moore (1712): Poems, Fables, and Plays [collected].
Smollett (1721): Compendium of Authentic Voyages. P
Warton, Joseph (1722): Genius and Writings of Pope, vol. i [ii 1782]. P

William Godwin b.
William Gifford b.
Robert and James Dodsley, 'Theatrical Records'.
John Shebbeare's 'Letters on the English Nation' begin to appear.
Smollett's 'Critical Review'.
Christopher Smart's trs. of Horace.
'Literary Magazine', 1756–8.
Mirabeau, 'Ami des hommes'.
Voltaire, 'Loi naturelle', 'Désastre de Lisbonne'.

1757

Brown, John (1715): Estimate of Manners and Principles of the Times. P
Burke (1729): An Account of the European Settlements in America [probably written by William Burke, revised and added to by Edmund Burke]. P
Collins (1721): Oriental Eclogues [see 1742].
Dyer (1700 ?): The Fleece. V
Gray (1716): Odes [Progress of Poesy, The Bard]. V
Home (1722): Douglas. T
Hume (1711): Four Dissertations [Natural History of Religion, Of the Passions, Of Tragedy, Of Standard of Taste]. P
Price (1723): Principal Questions in Morals. P
Smollett (1721): History of England [concl. 1758: see 1763]. P
Wilkie (1721): Epigoniad. V

William Blake b.
Colley Cibber d.
Edward Moore d.
William Whitehead poet-laureate.
Horace Walpole sets up Strawberry Hill Press.
'London Chronicle' started.
Diderot, 'Fils Naturel'.
Klopstock, 'Der Tod Adams'.

Akenside (1721): Ode to the Country Gentlemen of England. V
Armstrong (1709): Sketches. P
Dodsley (1703): Cleone. T
  Collection of Poems, vols. v–vi [see 1748].
Gibbon (1737): Essai sur l'étude de la littérature [at Lausanne, Eng. ed. 1764]. P
Goldsmith (1730): Memoirs of a Protestant [trs. Jean Marteilhe of Bergerac]. P
Johnson (1709): The Idler [in the Universal Chronicle, 15 Ap. 1758 to 5 Ap. 1760; collected 1761].
Lowth (1710): Life of William of Wykeham. P
Murphy (1727): The Upholsterer. D
Parnell (d. 1718): Posthumous Works [cont. unpub. poems: see 1722].
Swift (d. 1745): Four Last Years of the Queen. P
Walpole (1717): Catalogue of Royal and Noble Authors [rev. 1759]. P

John Dyer d.
Allan Ramsay d.
James Hervey d.
Elizabeth Carter's trs. of Epictetus.
John Upton's ed. of 'Faerie Queene'.
Diderot, 'Père de famille'.
Voltaire, 'Pauvre Diable'.
Helvétius, 'De l'esprit'.

1759

Butler (d. 1680): Remains in Verse and Prose, ed. R. Thyer [incl. Elephant in the Moon V, Characters P].
Clarendon (d. 1674): Life, being a Continuation of the History of the Rebellion [see 1702]. P
Gerard, Alexander (1723): Essay on Taste. P
Goldsmith (1730): Present State of Polite Learning [rev. 1774]. P
  The Bee [6 Oct.–24 Nov.]. P
Hurd (1720): Moral and Political Dialogues [enlarg. 1763]. P
Johnson (1709): Rasselas. P
Mason (1725): Caractacus. D
Murphy (1727): Orphan of China [from Voltaire]. T
Robertson (1721): History of Scotland. P
Smith, Adam (1723): Theory of Moral Sentiments. P
Townley (1714): High Life below Stairs. C
Wilkes, Thomas: General View of the Stage. P
Young (1683): Conjectures on Original Composition. P

Robert Burns b.
Mary Wollstonecraft b.
William Beckford b.
William Collins d.
British Museum opens.
Annual Register, vol. i (pub. Dodsley. Burke in charge till 1788).
'The Public Ledger' (daily) started.
Thomas Francklin's trs. of Sophocles.
Thomas Coxeter's ed. of Massinger.
Voltaire, 'Candide'.
Schiller b.
Lessing, 'Philotus'.
Lessing and others, 'Die Litteraturbriefe'.

Colman, senr. (1732): Polly Honeycombe. D
Foote (1720): The Minor. C
Goldsmith (1730): Citizen of the World [in The
　Public Ledger, 24 Jan. 1760 to 14 Aug. 1761 ;
　collected 1762].
Hamilton, William, of Bangour (d. 1754): Poems
　[first authoritative collection].
Hill (d. 1750): Collected Works [see 1753]. D
Johnstone, Charles (1719 ?): Chrysal, or Adven-
　tures of a Guinea. P
Lloyd (1733): The Actor. V
Lyttelton (1709): Dialogues of the Dead [see
　1765]. P
Macpherson (1736): Fragments of Ancient Poetry
　[first publication of Ossian: see 1762–3].
Murphy (1727): The Way to Keep Him. C
Sterne (1713): Tristram Shandy, vols. i–ii [iii–vi
　1761–2; vii–viii 1765; ix 1767; collected
　1767]. P
　Sermons of Yorick [concl. 1769]. P

Accession of George III.
Smollett, ‘British Maga-
　zine’.
Newbery’s ‘Public Ledger’.
Baretti, ‘Italian and Eng-
　lish Dictionary’.
Francis Fawkes’s trs. of
　Anacreon,　　Sappho,
　Bion, and others.
Capell, ‘Prolusions, or
　Select Pieces of English
　Poetry’.
Voltaire, ‘Tancrède’.
Rousseau, ‘Nouvelle Hé-
　loïse’.
Diderot, ‘La Religieuse’.
Palissot,　‘Les　Philo-
　sophes’.

1761

Armstrong (1709): Day: an Epistle to John
　Wilkes. V
Ascham (d. 1568): English Works, ed. J. Bennet
　[really S. Johnson; ed. Aldis Wright, 1904].
Brooke (1703 ?): Earl of Essex. T
Churchill (1731): Rosciad. V
　The Apology. V
Colman, senr. (1732): Jealous Wife. C
Dodsley (1703): Fugitive Pieces by Several
　Authors [ed. Joseph Spence]. P
Glover (1712): Medea. T
Johnson (1709): Life of Roger Ascham [in English
　Works of Ascham, nominally ed. J. Bennet].
Murphy (1727): All in the Wrong. C
　The Old Maid. C
Sheridan, Frances (1724): Memoirs of Miss Sidney
　Bidulph. P
Victor, Benjamin: History of the Theatres of
　London and Dublin. P

Samuel Richardson d.
William Law d.
Meeting of Johnson and
　Goldsmith.
‘St. James’s Chronicle’
　started.
Thomas　Percy,　‘Hau
　Kiou Choaan’　(from
　Portuguese trs. of a
　Chinese romance).
Francklin, Smollett, and
　others, trs. of Works of
　Voltaire (concl. 1774).
Kotzebue b.

Campbell (1719) : Dissertation on Miracles. P
Carter, Elizabeth (1717) : Poems.
Churchill (1731) : Night. V
    The Ghost, bks. i–iii (iv 1763). V
Falconer, William (1732) : The Shipwreck. V
Fielding (d. 1764) : Works, ed. with Life by
    Arthur Murphy.
Goldsmith (1730) : Citizen of the World [see 1760]. P
    Life of Richard Nash. P
    Mystery Revealed. P.   Art of Poetry. P
Hurd (1720) : Letters on Chivalry and Romance.
Kames (1696) : Elements of Criticism. P
Macpherson (1736) : Fingal, and Other Poems by
    'Ossian' [see 1760, 1763]. V
Smollett (1721) : Sir Lancelot Greaves. P
Stevenson, John Hall- (1718) : Crazy Tales. V
Walpole (1717) : Anecdotes of Painting [concl.
    1780].
Whitehead (1715) : School for Lovers. C
    A Charge to the Poets. V
Young (1683) : Resignation. V

George Colman jnr. b.
William Lisle Bowles b.
Helen Maria Williams b.
William Cobbett b.
Joanna Baillie b.
Lady Mary Wortley Mon-
    tagu d.
Johnson granted a pension.
'The Briton' (ed. Smollett),
    1762–3.
'The North Briton' (ed.
    Wilkes and Churchill),
    1762–3.
'The Auditor' (ed. Mur-
    phy), 1762–3.
John Parkhurst, 'Hebrew
    and English Lexicon'.
Robert Lowth, 'Introduc-
    tion to English Gram-
    mar'.
André Chénier b.
Rousseau,'Contrat Social'.
Fichte b.

1763

Bickerstaffe, Isaac : Love in a Village. D
Blair, Hugh (1718) : On the Poems of Ossian. P
Brooke, Frances (1724) : Lady Julia Mandeville. P
Brown (1715) : Dissertation on Poetry and Music. P
Burke (1729) : History of the Late War [repub.
    from The Annual Register, 1759–63]. P
Churchill (1731) : Prophecy of Famine; Epistle to
    Hogarth, The Conference, The Duellist,
    The Author. V
    Collected Poems [vol. ii 1766].
Colman, senr. (1732) : The Deuce is in him. D
Foote (1720) : The Mayor of Garratt. C
Goldsmith (1730) : Brookes's Natural History. P
Hoole (1727) : Trs. Jerusalem Delivered. V
Johnson (1709) : On Life and Writings of Collins
    [in The Poetical Calendar]. P
Keate, George (1729) : The Alps. V
Macpherson (1736) : Temora, with Other Poems
    by 'Ossian' [see 1760, 1762]. V
Mallet (1705 ?) : Elvira. T
Mason (1725) : Elegies. V
Montagu (d. 1762) : Letters [unauthorized ed. ;
    a fourth vol. 1767 : see 1803].
Murphy (1727) : The Citizen. D
Orme, Robert (1728) : History of Military Trans-
    actions of the British in Indostan. P
Percy (1729) : Five Pieces of Runic Poetry.
Shebbeare (1709) : History of the Sumatrans. P
Smart (1722) : Song to David. V
Smollett (1721) : Continuation of History of Eng-
    land [concl. 1765 : see 1757]. P

Samuel Rogers b.
William Shenstone d.
Prosecution of John
    Wilkes for having at-
    tacked the government in
    No. 45 of 'The North
    Briton'.
Meeting of Johnson and
    Boswell.
Fawkes and Woty, 'The
    Poetical Calendar', 12
    vols.
Voltaire, 'Traité sur la
    Tolérance'.
Jean-Paul Richter b.

Baker, David Erskine (1730): Companion to the Play-house [ed. Reed as Biographia Dramatica 1782; ed. Stephen Jones 1812]. P

'**Candor**' [**Sir Philip Francis**?]: A Letter to the Public Advertiser. P

Letter concerning Libels, Warrants [in Public Advertiser] P

Churchill (1731): Gotham, The Candidate, Independence, The Times, The Farewell. V

Falconer, William (1732): The Demagogue. V

Goldsmith (1730): History of England in a series of Letters (2 vols.; see 1771). P

The Traveller [1765]. V

Grainger, James (1721?): Sugar-cane. V

Herbert, Edward, Lord Herbert of Cherbury (d. 1648): Autobiography [ed. S. Lee 1886]. P

Murphy (1727): What we must all come to [as Three Weeks after Marriage, 1776]. C

No one's enemy but his own [from Voltaire]. D

Reid (1710): Enquiry into the Human Mind. P

Shenstone (d. 1763): Works in Verse and Prose [Letters added 1769].

Smollett (1721): Present State of all Nations. P

Wilson, John (1720): Earl Douglas. D

The Clyde. V

Thomas Morton b.?
Ann Radcliffe b.
Charles Churchill d.
Robert Dodsley d.
Thomas Warton jnr., '*Oxford Sausage*' *(anthology).*
Evan Evans, '*Specimens of the Poetry of the Ancient Welsh Bards*'.
George Ward and Thomas Langcake, trs. of Works of Jacob Boehme (concl. 1781).
Frances Brooke, trs. of Riccombini's '*Lady Juliet Catesby*'.
John Entick, '*Spelling Dictionary*'.
Rousseau, '*Émile*'.
Voltaire, '*Dictionnaire philosophique*'.
Sedaine, '*Le Philosophe sans le savoir*'.

1765

Bacon (d. 1626): Works, with unpub. Letters and Speeches, ed. Birch [later edd.: Montagu 1825; Ellis, Spedding, & Heath 1857–74].

Beattie (1735): Judgment of Paris. V

Bickerstaffe, Isaac: Maid of the Mill. D

Blackstone (1723): Commentaries on Laws of England [concl. 1769].

Bunyan (d. 1688): Relation of his Imprisonment. P

Collins (d. 1759): Poetical Works (collected).

Colman, senr. (1732): Trs. of Terence. V

Dulany, Daniel (1721): Taxes on Colonies. P

Goldsmith (1730): Essays [collected].

Edwin and Angelina [privately printed: included in Vicar of Wakefield 1766]. V

Heath (1704): Revisal of Shakespeare's Text. P

Johnson (1709): Ed. of Shakespeare [new ed. Steevens 1773, Reed 1785].

Lyttelton (1709): Four New Dialogues of the Dead [see 1760]. P

Percy (1729): Reliques of Ancient English Poetry [later edd.: 1767–75–94–1812; ed. Wheatley 1876–7, Schröer, 1893].

Smart (1722): Translation of Psalms of David. V

Walpole (1717): Castle of Otranto. P

Wesley, John (1703): Journal (publication continued until 1790; in 4 vols. 1827). P

Sir James Mackintosh b.
Edward Young d.
David Mallet d.
William Cole of Bletchley, Diary, 1765–7 (pub. 1932).

Anstey, Christopher (1724): New Bath Guide. V
Brooke, Henry (1703 ?): Fool of Quality. P
Burke (1729): Short Account of a Short Administration. P
Colman, senr. (1732): Clandestine Marriage [with Garrick]. C
Francklin (1721): Earl of Warwick. T
Goldsmith (1730): Vicar of Wakefield. P
Graves (1715): The Festoon. V
Griffith, Elizabeth (1720 ?): A Double Mistake. C
Johnson (1709): Miscellaneous Pieces [in Anna Williams's Miscellanies].
Smollett (1721): Travels through France and Italy. P
Steevens (1736): Shakespeare Quartos [see 1773].
Swift (d. 1745): Letters, ed. Hawkesworth [cont. Letters 1, 41–65 of Journal to Stella: see 1768].
Tyrwhitt (1730): Observations on Passages of Shakespeare. P

Thomas Robert Malthus b.
Isaac D'Israeli b.
Robert Bloomfield b.
The Old Pretender d.
Letters to 'The Public Advertiser' signed 'Anti-Sejanus' (James Scott).
Smollett, 'The British Magazine' (concl. 1767).
Rousseau in England.
Lessing, 'Laokoon'.
Wieland, 'Agathon'.

1767

Clarendon (d. 1674): State Papers, ed. Scrope and Monkhouse [selection only: see 1872].
Colman, senr. (1732): English Merchant [from Voltaire]. C
Farmer (1735): Essay on the Learning of Shakespeare. P
Ferguson, Adam (1723): History of Civil Society. P
Goldsmith (1730): Poems for Young Ladies. Beauties of English Poesy.
Hoole (1727): Trs. of Dramas of Metastasio. V
Jago (1715): Edge Hill. V
Kelly (1739): Memoirs of a Magdalen. P
Lyttelton (1709): History of Henry II. P
Mickle (1735): The Concubine [reissued as Sir Martin 1778]. V
Murphy (1727): School for Guardians. C
Sheridan, Frances (1724): History of Nourjahad. P
Thornton, Bonnell (1724): The Battle of the Whigs. V
 Trs. Plautus. V

Maria Edgeworth b.
John Byrom, 'Universal English Shorthand'.
Beaumarchais, 'Eugénie'.
Lessing, 'Minna von Barnhelm. Hamburgische Dramaturgie' (1767–8).
Herder, 'Fragmente' (which begins the Sturm und Drang period, ending with Schiller's 'Don Carlos', 1787).

Adams, John (1735): Canon and Feudal Law. P
Baretti (1719): Account of Italy. P
Bickerstaffe, Isaac: The Padlock. D
  Lionel and Clarissa [School for Fathers 1773]. D
Boswell (1740): Account of Corsica. P
Browne, Isaac Hawkins (d. 1760): Coll. Poems.
Capell (1713): Ed. of Shakespeare.
Foote (1720): Devil upon two Sticks. C
Goldsmith (1730): Good-natur'd Man. C
Gray (1716): Poems [cont. unpub. Fatal Sisters,
  Descent of Odin, Triumphs of Owen].
Hoole (1727): Cyrus. T
Kelly (1739): False Delicacy [with Garrick]. C
Montagu, Lady Mary Wortley (d. 1762): Poetical
  Works, ed. Reed.
Murphy (1727): Zenobia. T
Percy (1729): Ed. of Household Book of the Earl
  of Northumberland in 1512.
Priestley (1733): First Principles of Government. P
Ross, Alexander (1699): Fortunate Shepherdess. V
Sterne (d. 1768): Sentimental Journey through
  France and Italy. P
Swift (d. 1745): Letters, ed. Deane Swift [cont.
  Letters 2–40 of Journal to Stella: see 1766].
Tucker (1705): Light of Nature pursued, vols.
  i–iv [v–vii 1778]. P
Walpole (1717): Mysterious Mother. T
  Historic Doubts on Richard III. P

Sharon Turner b.
Laurence Sterne d.
Joseph Spence d.
Royal Academy founded.
The Letters of 'Junius'
  appear in 'The Public
  Advertiser', 1768–71.
'Encyclopaedia Britan-
  nica', 1st ed. (concl.
  1771; ed. William Smel-
  lie).
Chateaubriand b.

1769

Burke (1729): Observations on 'The Present
  State of the Nation'. P
Chatterton (1752): Elinoure and Juga [in Town
  and Country Magazine for May]. V
Colman, senr. (1732): Oxonian in Town. C
Goldsmith (1730): Roman History. P
Granger (1723): Biographical History of England
  [supplement 1774; continued by Noble 1806].
Gray (1716): Installation Ode. V
Griffith, Elizabeth (1720?): School for Rakes
  [from Beaumarchais's Eugénie]. C
Lennox (1720): The Sister. C
Montagu (1720): Essay on Shakespeare. P
Reynolds (1723): Discourses to the Royal
  Academy [see 1797].
Robertson (1721): History of Charles V. P
Smollett (1721): Adventures of an Atom [1749]. P
Sterne (1713): Political Romance addressed to
  —— Esq. of York [History of a Warm
  Watch Coat]. P

Amelia Opie b.
John Hookham Frere b.
William Falconer d.
Shakespeare Jubilee at
  Stratford-on-Avon (con-
  ducted by Garrick).
'The Morning Chronicle'.
'Town and Country
  Magazine'.
John Parkhurst, 'Greek
  and English Lexicon to
  the New Testament' (ed.
  H. J. Rose 1829).
David Herd, 'Ancient and
  Modern Scottish Songs'
  (enlarg. 1776).
William Falconer, 'Mar-
  ine Dictionary'.
Voltaire, 'Les Guèbres'.
Klopstock, 'Hermans-
  schlacht'.

Armstrong (1709): Miscellanies. P and V

Baretti (1719): Journey from London to Genoa. P

Beattie (1735): Essay on Truth. P

Bruce, Michael (d. 1767): Poems, ed. John Logan.

Burke (1729): Thoughts on the Present Discontents. P

Cumberland (1732): The Brothers. C

Dalrymple, Sir David (1726): Ed. of Ancient Scottish Poems from the MS. of George Bannatyne, 1568.

Goldsmith (1730): Deserted Village. V
  Life of Thomas Parnell. P
  Life of Viscount Bolingbroke. P

Hoole (1727): Timanthes. T

Johnson (1709): False Alarm. P

Kelly (1739): A Word to the Wise. C

Mickle (1735): Voltaire in the Shades. V

Percy (1729): Northern Antiquities [trs. of M. Mallet's Introduction to L'Histoire de Dannemarc]. P

Young (1741): A Six Months' Tour through the North of England. P

William Wordsworth b.
James Hogg b.
Mark Akenside d.
George Whitefield d.
Thomas Chatterton d.
The popular children's book 'London Cries' (anon.).
John and William Langhorne, trs. of Plutarch.
'Archaeologia' first pub.

1771

Beattie (1735): Minstrel, bk. i [ii 1774]. V

Burney, Charles (1726): Present State of Music in France and Italy. P

Cumberland (1732): West Indian. C

Dalrymple, Sir John (1726): Memoirs of Great Britain. P

Fletcher, John William (1729): Checks to Antinomianism. P

Goldsmith (1730): History of England [4 vols., distinct from History, 1764]. P

Griffith, Elizabeth (1720?): History of Lady Barton. P

Henry, Robert (1718): History of England [concl. 1793]. P

Hull, Thomas (1728): History of Sir William Harrington. P

Johnson (1709): Thoughts on Falkland's Islands. P

Mackenzie (1745): Man of Feeling. P

Pennant (1726): Tour in Scotland [supplement 1772]. P

Smollett (1721): Humphry Clinker. P

Wesley, John (1703): Collected Prose Works [concl. 1774].

Walter Scott b.
John Lingard b.
James Montgomery b.
Robert Owen b.
Thomas Gray d.
Tobias Smollett d.
Christopher Smart d.
Richard Price's pamphlet, 'Appeal to the Public on National Debt'.
Klopstock, 'Oden'.

Akenside (d. 1770): Poems (collected).
Brooke, Henry (1703 ?): Redemption. V
Chatterton (d. 1770): Execution of Sir Charles Bawdin. V
Cumberland (1732): Fashionable Lover. C
Ferguson, Adam (1723): Institutes of Moral Philosophy. P
Goldsmith (1730): Threnodia Augustalis. V
Graves (1715): Spiritual Quixote. P
Hurd (1720): Study of Prophecies. P
Jones, Sir William (1746): Poems consisting chiefly of Translations from the Asiatick Languages. V
'**Junius**': Letters [first auth. collection: see 1768; later edd.: Good 1812, Wade 1850].
Mason (1725): English Garden, bk. i [ii 1777, iii 1779, iv 1782]. V
Murphy (1727): Grecian Daughter. T
Trumbull, John (1750): The Progress of Dulness. V

Samuel Taylor Coleridge b.
Henry Francis Cary b.
Pierce Egan b.
David Ricardo b.
'The Morning Post' *(daily) started.*
Swedenborg d.
Hardenberg ('Novalis') b.
Lessing, 'Emilia Galotti', 'Miss Sara Sampson'.
Edward Lye, 'Dict. Saxonico-Latinum'.

1773

Barbauld (1743): Poems.
Barbauld and Aikin, John: Miscellaneous Pieces in Prose.
Byrom (d. 1763): Collected Poems.
Chapone, Hester (1727): Letters on the Improvement of the Mind. P
Cook (1728): Voyage round the World in the Years 1768–71 [in Hawkesworth below: see 1777, 1784].
Fergusson, Robert (1750): Poems [Part II '79].
Goldsmith (1730): She Stoops to Conquer. C
Hawkesworth (1715 ?): Voyages in the Southern Hemisphere. P
Hoole (1727): Trs. Orlando Furioso [concl. 1783]. V
Leland (1722): History of Ireland. P
Mackenzie (1745): Man of the World. P
Prince of Tunis. T
Macpherson (1736): Trs. Iliad. P
Mason (1725): Epistle to Chambers [and other anon. poems, concl. 1782].
Monboddo (1714): Origin and Progress of Language. P
More (1745): Search after Happiness. D pastoral.
Steevens (1736): Ed. of Shakespeare [with Johnson, and embodying contributions by Malone and Farmer: see 1766].
Strutt (1749): Regal and Ecclesiastical Antiquities of England. P

Francis Jeffrey b.
James Mill b.
Charles Apperley ('Nimrod') b.
Philip Dormer Stanhope, Earl of Chesterfield, d.
George Lyttelton d.
'The Newgate Calendar' about this date.
'Edinburgh Review', 1773–99.
Grose, 'Antiquities of England and Wales'.
Erskine, 'Institutes of the Law of Scotland'.
Tieck b.
Herder, 'Deutscher Art und Kunst'.
Bürger, 'Lenore'.
Goethe, 'Götz von Berlichingen'.

Barbauld (1743): Early Lessons for Children.
Brooke, Henry (1703 ?): Juliet Grenville. P
Burgoyne (1722): Maid of the Oaks. D
Burke (1729): Speech on American Taxation. P
Campbell, John (1708): Political Survey of England. P
Chesterfield (d. 1773): Letters to his Natural Son [ed. Mahon 1845, Dobrée 1932: see 1890]. P
Colman, senr. (1732): Man of Business. C
Goldsmith (d. 1774): Retaliation. V
   Grecian History. P
   History of Earth and Animated Nature. P
Hull, Thomas (1728): Henry II. T
Johnson (1709): The Patriot. P
Kames (1696): Sketches of the History of Man. P
Kelly (1739): School for Wives. C
More (1745): Inflexible Captive [from Metastasio]. D
Pennant, Thomas (1726): Tour in Scotland and Voyage to the Hebrides. P
Priestley (1733): Experiments on Different Kinds of Air [vol. ii 1775, vol. iii 1777, vol. iv 1779, vol. v 1780, vol. vi 1786].
Richardson, William (1743): A Philosophical Analysis of some of Shakespeare's Remarkable Characters. P
Strutt, Joseph (1749): Manners, Customs, etc. of People of England [concl. 1776]. P
Walpole (1717): Description of Strawberry Hill [enlarg. 1784]. P
Warton, Thomas (1728): History of English Poetry, vol. i [ii 1778, iii 1781; ed. R. Price 1824; W. C. Hazlitt 1874]. P

Decision of the House of Lords in the case of Donaldson v. Becket destroys the doctrine of perpetual copyright. See 1709.
Robert Southey b.
Oliver Goldsmith d.
Abraham Tucker d.
Goethe, 'Werther'.
Wieland, 'Abderiten'.

1775

Burke (1729): Speech on Conciliation with America. P
Crabbe (1754): Inebriety. V
Cumberland (1732): Choleric Man. D
De Lolme, John Louis: Constitution of England [trs. Fr.] P
Fletcher, John William (1729): Lelotus and Honestus. P
Francklin (1721): Matilda. T
Garrick (1717): Bon Ton. C
Gray (d. 1771): Poems ed. W. Mason, with Letters & Memoir [Works ed. Mathias 1814; ed. Mitford 1814–16 and 1835–53; Letters ed. Tovey 1900–12, ed. Toynbee and Whibley 1935].

War of American Independence.
Jane Austen b.
Charles Lamb b.
Walter Savage Landor b.
Matthew Gregory Lewis b.
Thomas Tyrwhitt, ed. of Canterbury Tales (concl. 1778).
Beaumarchais, 'Barbier de Seville'.
Goethe, 'Clavigo'.

Griffith, Elizabeth (1720?): Morality of Shake-
speare's Drama. P
Jephson (1736): Braganza. T
Johnson (1709): Journey to Western Islands of
Scotland [in 1773; see Boswell 1785]. P
Taxation no Tyranny. P
Luxborough, Lady (d. 1756): Letters to William
Shenstone [see 1778].
Macpherson (1736): History of Great Britain. P
Original Papers containing the Secret History
of Great Britain. P
Savage (d. 1743): Collected Works, with Life by
Johnson.
Sheridan (1751): The Rivals. C
Sterne (d. 1768): Letters from Yorick to Eliza. P
Twelve Letters to his Friends [with History
of a Watch Coat].
Letters to his Friends, ed. with Memoir by
L. Sterne de Medalle (ed. Curtis 1935).
Woolman, John (d. 1772): Journal. P

1776

Beattie (1735): Essays [on Poetry and Music,
&c.]. P
Bentham (1748): Fragment on Government. P
Burney, Charles (1726): History of Music, vol. i
(ii 1782, iii–iv 1789). P
Campbell, George (1719): Philosophy of Rhetoric. P
Cowley, Hannah (1743): The Runaway. C
Dalrymple, Sir David (1726): Annals of Scotland
[concl. 1779]. P
Gibbon (1737): Decline and Fall of the Roman
Empire, vol. i [ii–iii 1781, iv–vi 1788; ed.
Milman 1838–9, Bury 1896–1900]. P
Goldsmith (d. 1774): Haunch of Venison. V
Experimental Philosophy. V
Graves (1715): Euphrosyne. V
Griffith, Elizabeth (1720?): Lady Juliana Harley. P
Trs. of Beaumarchais's Barbier de Séville.
Hawkins (1719): History of Music. P
Mickle, William (1735): Trs. Lusiad of Camoens. V
More (1745): Sir Eldred of the Bower. V
Murphy (1727): Three Weeks after Marriage [see
1764]. C
Paine (1737): Common Sense. P
The Crisis [completed 1783]. P
Price (1723): Nature of Civil Liberty. P
Smith, Adam (1723): Wealth of Nations [3rd ed.
enlarged and corrected 1784]. P
Smollett (d. 1771): Trs. Télémaque of Fénelon.
Trumbull, John (1750): M'Fingal [completed
1782]. V

*Declaration of American
Independence.*
*Stamp Duty increased to
three halfpence.*
David Hume d.
*John Bell's 'British
Theatre' (1776–8; sup-
plement 1784; another
ed. 1791–7).*
*Condorcet, 'Pensées de
Pascal'.*
*Voltaire, 'Lettre à l'Aca-
démie sur Shakespeare'.*
Lessing, 'Laokoon'.
Goethe, 'Stella'.

Blair, Hugh (1718): Sermons [concl. 1801].
Burke (1729): Letter to the Sheriffs of Bristol. P
Chatterton (d. 1770): Poems, supposed to have
  been written by Thomas Rowley in the
  fifteenth cent., ed. T. Tyrwhitt [3rd ed., with
  Appendix, 1778; vindication of Appendix
  1782; ed. Sharpe 1794, Skeat 1898, Hare
  1911].
Chesterfield (d. 1773): Miscellaneous Works, with
  Life by M. Maty [Supplement 1778: see
  1817, 1890].
Combe (1741): Diaboliad, Diabolady, Anti-
  Diabolady. V
Cook (1728): Voyage Towards the South Pole and
  Round the World in the Years 1772-5 [see
  1773, 1784].
Hume (d. 1776): Two Essays [Suicide, Immor-
  tality of the Soul]. P
  His Own Life [prefixed to the History]. P
Johnson (1709): The Convict's Address to his
  Unhappy Brethren [nominally by William
  Dodd]. P
Mackenzie (1745): Julia de Roubigné. P
More (1745): Percy, a Tragedy. P
Morgann (1726): Essay on the Character of
  Falstaff. P
Reeve, Clara (1729): Champion of Virtue [called
  Old English Baron, 1778]. P
Robertson (1721): History of America. P
Roscoe (1753): Mount Pleasant. V
Strutt, Joseph (1749): Chronicle of England
  [concl. 1778].
Warton, Thomas (1728): Poems [later edd. 1791,
  Mant 1802].
Watson (1730?): History of Philip II of Spain. P

Henry Hallam b.
Thomas Campbell b.
Samuel Foote d.
Hugh Kelly d.
'Encyclopaedia   Britan-
nica', 2nd ed. (concl.
1783).

1778

Burke (1729): Letters to Two Gentlemen in
  Bristol. P
Burney, Frances (1752): Evelina. P
Carver, Jonathan (1732): Travels. P
Chatterton (d. 1770): Miscellanies in Prose and
  Verse, ed. Broughton [Supplement 1784].
Ellis, George (1753): Poetical Tales by Gregory
  Gander. V
Fielding (d. 1754): The Fathers. C

William Hazlitt b.
John Brown, 'Self-Inter-
preting Bible'.
Voltaire d.
Rousseau d.
Herder, 'Volkslieder'.
Wieland, 'Rosamund'.

Foote (1720): Trip to Calais. C
  The Nabob. C
Lowth, Robert: Trs. of Isaiah. P
More (1745): Essays on Various Subjects for
  Young Ladies.
Pennant (1726): Tour in Wales [concl. 1781]. P
Shenstone and others: Select Letters between
  Lady Luxborough (see 1775), Shenstone,
  Dodsley, and others, ed. T. Hull.
Tickell, Richard (1751): Anticipation. D
Warton, Thomas (1728): History of English
  Poetry, vol. ii [see 1774, 1781].

1779

Cowley, Hannah (1743): Albina. T
  Who's the Dupe? D farce.
Cowper (1731): Olney Hymns [with John New-
  ton].
Gibbon (1737): Vindication of Some Passages in
  the 15th and 16th chapters of the Decline
  and Fall.
Graves (1715): Columella. P
Hume (d. 1776): Dialogues concerning Natural
  Religion. P
Johnson (1709): Prefaces, Biographical and
  Critical, to Works of the English Poets
  [concl. 1781; the Prefaces issued as Lives of
  the Poets, 1781, new ed. 1783; ed. Peter
  Cunningham 1854; Birkbeck Hill 1905].
Knox (1752): Essays Moral and Literary. P
Monboddo (1714): Ancient Metaphysics. P
More (1745): Fatal Falsehood. T
Russell, William (1741): History of Modern Eur-
  ope [concl. 1786]. P

Thomas Moore b.
'Horace' Smith b.
John Galt b.
David Garrick d.
William Warburton d.
John Armstrong d.
*'The Mirror' (Henry
  Mackenzie and others),
  1779–80.*
*Lessing, 'Nathan der
  Weise'.*

1780

Burke (1729): Speech on Economic Reform and
  Independence of Parliament. P
  Speeches at the Guildhall in Bristol. P
Crabbe (1754): The Candidate. V
Davies, Thomas (1712 ?): Memoirs of Garrick. P
Lee, Sophia (1750): Chapter of Accidents. C
Madan, Martin (1726): Thelyphthora [see Cowper
  1781]. P
Paine (1737): Public Good. P
Young, Arthur (1741): Tour in Ireland. P

*Beginning of Sunday
  Schools.*
Gordon Riots in June.
Sir William Blackstone d.
*'Sunday Monitor' (first
  Sunday paper).*
*'The Morning Herald'
  (daily) started.*
*Nichols, 'Select Collection
  of Poems' (concl. 1782).*
Franklin's trs. of Lucian.
Wieland, 'Oberon'.

Bage (1728): Mount Henneth. P
Barbauld (1743): Hymns in Prose for Children.
Beckford, Peter (1740): Thoughts on Hunting. P
Brooke, Frances (1724): Siege of Sinope. T
Burgoyne (1722): Lord of the Manor. D opera.
Cowper (1731): Anti-Thelyphthora [see Madan 1780]. V
Crabbe (1754): Library. V
Gibbon (1737): Decline and Fall, ii–iii [see 1776]. P
Hayley (1745): Triumphs of Temper. V
   Essay on Painting. P
Holcroft (1745): Duplicity. C
Jefferson, Thomas (1743): The Rights of British America. P
Jephson (1736): Count of Narbonne. T
Johnson (1709): Beauties of Johnson.
Knox (1752): Liberal Education. P
Logan, John (1748): Poems.
Sheridan (1751): The Critic. C
   Trip to Scarborough. C
Tickell (1751): Carnival of Venice. D opera.
Walker, John (1732): Elements of Elocution. P
Warton, Thomas (1728): History of English Poetry, iii [see 1774, 1778]. P
Watson, Richard: Chemical Essays [concl. 1787]. P

Ebenezer Elliott b.
Lucy Aikin b.
Richard Jago d.
Rousseau, 'Confessions' (concl. 1788).
Lessing d.
Schiller, 'Die Räuber'.
Kant, 'Kritik der reinen Vernunft'.

1782

Burke (1729): Letter to a Peer of Ireland on Penal Laws. P
Burney, Frances (1752): Cecilia. P
Cowley (1743): Belle's Stratagem. C
Cowper (1731): Poems [Table Talk, Progress of Error, Expostulation, Charity, Consolation, &c.: see 1785].
   John Gilpin [in Public Advertiser, 14 Nov.].
Gilpin (1724): Observations on the Wye and South Wales. P
Hayley (1745): Essay on Epic Poetry in Five Epistles to Mason. V
More (1745): Sacred Dramas. V
Nichols, John (1745): Biographical and Literary Anecdotes of William Bowyer [see 1812, 1817, 1831]. P
Pennant (1726): Journey from Chester to London. P
Priestley (1733): Corruptions of Christianity. P
Scott, John (1730): Poetical Works.
Trimmer (1741): Easy Introduction to the Knowledge of Nature. P
Warton, Joseph (1722): Genius and Writings of Pope, vol. ii [see 1756]. P
Wolcot (1738): Lyric Odes to Royal Academicians.

Charles Robert Maturin b.
Susan Ferrier b.
Henry Home, Lord Kames, d.
John Bell, 'British Poets'.
'Biographia Dramatica', ed. Isaac Reed (see 1764, 1812).
Michel-Guillaume Jean de Crèvecœur, 'Letters of an American Farmer'.
'European Magazine' started.
Delille, 'Les Jardins'.

Beattie (1735): Dissertations Moral and Critical. P

Beckford, William (1759): Dreams, Waking Thoughts and Incidents, in a Series of Letters from Various Parts of Europe [suppressed: see 1834]. P

Blair, Hugh (1718): Lectures on Rhetoric. P

Blake (1757): Poetical Sketches. V

Brooke (1724): Rosina. D opera.

Capell, Edward (1713): Notes on Shakespeare. P

Cowley (1743): Bold Stroke for a Husband. C

Crabbe (1754): The Village. V

Davies, Thomas (1712?): Dramatic Miscellanies. P

Day, Thomas (1748): Sandford and Merton [concl. 1789]. P

James I of Scotland (d. 1437): The Kingis Quair, ed. Lord Woodhouselee. V

Logan, John (1748): Runnamede. T

Reeve, Clara (1729): The Two Mentors. P

Richardson, William (1743): Essays on Shakespeare's Dramatic Characters. P

Sheridan (1751): School for Scandal [first Eng. ed.: earlier Dublin edd.: 1777, 1781, 1782]. C
Duenna [songs, duets, &c. first pub. 1775]. D

Webster, Noah (1758): Spelling Book.

Williams, Helen Maria (1762): Ode on the Peace. V

Peace of Versailles.
Pitt's first ministry 1783–1802.
Fox's India Bill.
Washington Irving b.
Reginald Heber b.
Henry Brooke d.
Joseph Ritson, 'Collection of English Songs'.
Vicesimus Knox, 'Elegant Extracts' (prose: see 1789).
Schiller, 'Fiesco'.

1784

Astle, Thomas (1735): Origin and Progress of Writing. P

Bage (1728): Barham Downs. P

Berkeley (d. 1753): Collected Works [cont. unpub. Commonplace Book: ed. Campbell Fraser 1871, 1901]. P

Burke (1729): Speech on Fox's India Bill. P
Representation to His Majesty. P

Colman, jnr. (1762): Two to One. C

Cook (d. 1779): Voyage to the Pacific Ocean in the Years 1776–80 [with Capt. James King: see 1773, 1777].

Cowley (1743): More Ways than One. C

Dodington, Bubb, Lord Melcombe (d. 1762): Diary, 1748–61, ed. H. P. Wyndham.

Jago (d. 1781): Collected Poems.

Jefferson, Thomas (1743): Notes on the State of Virginia. P

Macklin (1697?): Love à la mode. C

Mitford, William (1744): History of Greece, vol. i (ii 1790; complete 1810). P

Swift (d. 1745): Works, ed. Thomas Sheridan [ed. Nichols 1801, Scott 1814, 1824].

Williams, Helen Maria (1762): Peru, a poem.

Leigh Hunt b.
James Sheridan Knowles b.
Bernard Barton b.
Samuel Johnson d.
Thomas Francklin d.
Arthur Young starts 'The Annals of Agriculture'.
Thomas Evans's 'Old Ballads'.
Diderot d.
Beaumarchais, 'Mariage de Figaro'.
Bernardin de Saint Pierre, 'Études de la nature'.
Ducis, 'Macbeth'.
Schiller, 'Kabale und Liebe'.
Herder, 'Ideen zur Philosophie'.
Klopstock, 'Hermann und die Fürsten'.

Boswell (1740): Tour to the Hebrides (with Johnson, 1773: see 1775). P

Burke (1729): Speech on Nabob of Arcot's Debts. P

Cowper (1731): Poems [vol. ii, see 1782; Task, Tirocinium, Epistle to Joseph Hill, John Gilpin].

Crabbe (1754): The Newspaper. V

Dwight, Timothy (1752): The Conquest of Canaan. V

Graves (1715): Eugenius. P

Hayley (1745): Essay on Old Maids. V

Holcroft (1745): Follies of a Day [from Mariage de Figaro]. C

Tales of the Castle [from Les Veillées du Château by Comtesse de Genlis].

Inchbald (1753): Appearance is against them. D

Johnson (d. 1784): Prayers and Meditations. P
Poetical Works [collected].

Mackenzie (1745): The Lounger [Feb. 1785–Jan. 1787].

Paley (1743): Moral and Political Philosophy. P

Raspe, Rudolf (1737): Baron Munchausen's Travels. P

Reeve, Clara (1729): Progress of Romance. P

Reid (1710): Essay on the Intellectual Powers of Man. P

Smith, Charlotte (1749): Trs. Manon Lescaut.

Warton, Thomas (1728): Ed. Milton's Minor Poems.

Whateley, Thomas (d. 1772): Remarks on Some Characters of Shakespeare. P

Wolcot (1738): Lousiad [compl. 1795]. V
Lyric Odes for 1785.

Thomas De Quincey b.

Thomas Love Peacock b.

John Wilson ('Christopher North') b.

Henry Kirke White b.

Thomas Leland d.

William Whitehead d.

Richard Glover d.

Thomas Warton, jnr., poet-laureate.

The 'Rolliad' satires begin (see 1791).

Francis Grose's 'Dictionary of the vulgar tongue' (reissued as 'Lexicon Balatronicum' 1811).

William Herbert's ed. of Joseph Ames's 'Typographical Antiquities' (see 1749, 1810).

Joseph Strutt, 'Biographical Dictionary of Engravers' (concl. 1786).

John Walter starts 'The Daily Universal Register' (became 'The Times' 1788).

Richard Cumberland starts 'The Observer'.

Moritz, 'Anton Reiser'.

1786

Beckford, William (1759): Vathek [first Eng. trs., perhaps by S. Henley: see 1787]. P

Burgoyne (1722): The Heiress. C
Richard Cœur-de-Lion. D opera.

Burke (1729): Articles of Charge against Warren Hastings. P

Burns (1759): Poems Chiefly in Scottish Dialect [Kilmarnock: see 1787].

Canning, George: The Microcosm [with J. Hookham Frere and J. and R. Smith].

Freneau, Philip (1752): Poems. V

Gilpin (1724): Observations on Cumberland and Westmorland. P

Graves (1715): Lucubrations. P

John Pinkerton, 'Ancient Scottish Poems'.

Samuel Taylor, 'Universal System of Stenography' (adapted by Isaac Pitman in 'Stenographic Shorthand', 1837).

Inchbald (1753): I'll tell you what. D
Macklin (1697?): Man of the World [rev. version of True-born Scotsman]. D
Moore, John (1729): Zeluco. P
Murphy (1727): The Choice, News from Parnassus [in Dramatic Works].
Piozzi, Hester Lynch (Thrale) (1741): Anecdotes of Samuel Johnson. P
Rogers (1763): Ode to Superstition and Other Poems.
Smith, Charlotte (1749): Romance of Real Life.
Tooke, Horne (1736): Diversions of Purley, pt. i (ii 1798, 1805). P
Trimmer (1741): Fabulous Histories [later called History of the Robins]. P
   Œconomy of Charity. P
Williams, Helen Maria (1762): Poems [collected].
Wolcot (1738): Bozzy and Piozzi. V
   Farewell Odes to Academicians. V
   Congratulatory Epistle to James Boswell. V

1787

Adams, John (1735): Defence of the Constitution. P
Bage (1728): Fair Syrian. P
Barlow, Joel (1754): The Vision of Columbus. V
Beattie (1735): Scotticisms. P
Burns (1759): Poems chiefly in Scottish Dialect [Edinburgh and London: see 1786].
   Songs [in James Johnson's Scots Musical Museum, i–vi 1787–1804].
Colman, jnr. (1762): Inkle and Yarico. D musical comedy.
Cowley (1743): Scottish Village. V
Glover (d. 1785): Athenaid. V
Hamilton, Alexander (1757): The Federalist. P
Hawkins, Sir John (1719): Life of Johnson. P
Jephson, Robert (1736): Julia, or the Italian Lover. T
Johnson (d. 1784): Works, ed. Sir John Hawkins [ed. Murphy 1792].
Pye (1745): Poems [collected].
Wolcot (1738): Ode upon Ode. V
   Instructions to a Celebrated Laureat. V
Wollstonecraft (1759): Thoughts on Education of Daughters. P

American Constitution signed.
Mary Mitford b.
Bryan Walter Procter ('Barry Cornwall') b.
Sheridan's Speech against Warren Hastings.
Correspondence begins in 'The World' between Robert Merry ('Della Crusca') and Hannah Cowley ('Anna Matilda').
James Johnson, 'Scots Museum' (concl. 1803).
Henry Headley, 'Select Beauties of Ancient English Poetry'.
Thomas Monro, 'Olla Podrida' (weekly).
Beckford's 'Vathek' in original Fr. in Paris (see 1786).
Bernardin de Saint Pierre, 'Paul et Virginie'.
Goethe, 'Iphigenie auf Tauris'.
Schiller, 'Don Carlos'.
Klopstock, 'Hermanns Tod'.
Herder, 'Gott'.

Bage (1728): James Wallace. P
Brooke (1724): Marian. D opera.
Collins (d. 1759): Ode on Popular Superstitions of the Highlands. V
Crowe, William (1745): Lewesdon Hill. V
Gibbon (1737): Decline and Fall, iv–vi [see 1776, 1781].
Graves (1715): Recollection of the Life of William Shenstone. P
Holcroft (1745): Life of Baron Frederic Trenck [from German]. P
Inchbald (1753): Such things are. C
Child of Nature. D
Johnson (d. 1784): Sermons.
Letters to and from Mrs. Thrale (Piozzi).
Knox (1752): Winter Evenings. P
More (1745): Slavery, a Poem.
Thoughts on the Importance of the Manners of the Great. P
Reeve, Clara (1729): The Exiles. P
Reid (1710): Essay on the Active Powers of Man. P
Smith, Charlotte (1749): Emmeline. P
Whitehead (d. 1785): Collected Poems, ed. William Mason.
Wollstonecraft (1759): Original Stories from Real Life. P

The Young Pretender d.
George Gordon Byron, Lord Byron b.
Richard Harris Barham b.
Sir William Hamilton b.
Thomas Amory d.
Charles Wesley d.
Trial of Warren Hastings, 1788–95.
'Encyclopaedia Britannica', 3rd ed. (concl. 1797).
'The Times' started (see 1785).
Thomas Scott, 'Holy Bible with Notes' (concl. 1792).
Linnean Society founded.
Barthélemy, 'Voyage du jeune Anacharsis en Grèce'.
Goethe, 'Egmont'.
Kant, 'Kritik der praktischen Vernunft'.
Schiller, 'Abfall der Niederlande'.

1789

Bentham (1748): Principles of Morals and Legislation [prtd. 1780]. P
Blake (1757): Songs of Innocence. V
Book of Thel. V
Bowles (1762): Sonnets.
Verses to John Howard.
Cobb, James (1756): Haunted Tower. D opera.
Cumberland (1732): Arundel. P
Darwin, Erasmus (1731): Loves of the Plants [pt. 2 of Botanic Garden: see 1792]. V
Gilpin (1724): Observations on the Highlands of Scotland. P
Macneill, Hector: The Harp. V
Radcliffe (1764): Castles of Athlin and Dunbayne. P
Ramsay, David (1749): History of the American Revolution. P

French Revolution.
Frances Brooke d.
Dr. Richard Price's sermon 'On the love of our country' draws Burke into controversy over the French Revolution.
Bell's 'British Album' with verses by Hannah Cowley, Robert Merry, and others.
'The Mail' (thrice weekly) started.
Vicesimus Knox, 'Elegant Extracts' (poetry: see 1783).

Reynolds, Frederic (1764): The Dramatist. C
Twining, Thomas: Aristotle's Treatise on Poetry. P
Wakefield, Gilbert: Silva Critica [concl. 1795]. P
White (1720): Natural History of Selborne. P

President U.S.A.
Washington.

1790

Alison, Archibald (1757): Essay on Taste. P
Baillie (1762): Fugitive Verses.
Beattie (1735): Elements of Moral Science [vol. ii
    1793]. P
Bewick, Thomas (1753): General History of
    Quadrupeds. P
Blake (1757): Marriage of Heaven and Hell [n.d.].
Bruce, James (1730): Travels to Discover the
    Source of the Nile. P
Burke (1729): Reflections on the French Revolu-
    tion. P
    Speech on Army Estimates. P
Graves (1715): Plexippus. P
Johnson (d. 1784): Letter to Chesterfield. P
    Conversation between George III and Johnson.
    [Parts of Boswell's 'Life': see 1791].
Malone, Edmond: Ed. of Shakespeare [see 1821].
Merry, Robert: Laurel of Liberty. V
More (1745): Estimate of the Religion of the
    Fashionable World. P
Paley (1743): Horæ Paulinæ. P
Pennant (1726): London. P
Radcliffe (1764): A Sicilian Romance. P
Sayers, Frank: Dramatic Sketches of Northern
    Mythology [enlarg. 1792].
Smith, Charlotte (1749): Ethelinde. P
Smollett (d. 1771): Collected Works [later edd.:
    Anderson 1796, Moore 1797, Roscoe 1841,
    Cruikshank 1845, Herbert 1870, Henley
    1899–1901].
Turner, Sharon (1768): History of the Anglo-
    Saxons. P
Williams, Helen Maria (1762): Julia. P
    Letters written in France. P
Wilson, Alexander: Poems.
Wollstonecraft (1759): Morality for Children [trs.
    Salzmann]. P

John Austin b.
Benjamin Franklin d.
Adam Smith d.
Thomas Warton, jnr., d.
Henry James Pye poet-
    laureate.
Wordsworth's first Con-
    tinental tour.
George Ellis, 'Specimens
    of Early English Poets'
    (see 1801).
'The Bee', Dec. 1790–Jan.
    1794.
Goethe, 'Torquato Tasso',
    'Faust, ein Fragment'.
Kant, 'Kritik der Ur-
    theilskraft'.
Lamartine b.

Bentham (1748): Panopticon. P

Boswell (1740): Life of Johnson [ed. 2, 1793, ed. 3, 1799; ed. Croker 1831, Birkbeck Hill 1887, Hill, revised L. F. Powell 1934].

Burke (1729): Letter to a Member of the National Assembly. P

Appeal from the New to the Old Whigs. P

Burns (1759): Tam o' Shanter [in Edinburgh Herald, 18 Mar. and in Grose's Antiquities of Scotland, April]. V

Cowper (1731): Trs. Iliad and Odyssey. V

D'Israeli (1766): Curiosities of Literature, vol. i [ii 1793, iii 1817, iv–v 1823, vi 1834]. P

Ellis, Laurence, Richardson, Tickell, Fitzpatrick: The Rolliad [complete: originally in Morning Herald and in Daily Advertiser from 1784]. V

Franklin, Benjamin (d. 1790): Autobiography, pt. 2 [in French: English version 1817, 1868].

Gilpin (1724): Remarks on Forest Scenery illustrated in the Scenes of New Forest. P

Inchbald (1753): A Simple Story. P

Mackintosh (1765): Vindiciæ Gallicæ. P

Merry, Robert: Lorenzo. P

Paine (1737): Rights of Man, pt. i (ii 1792). P

Radcliffe (1764): Romance of the Forest. P

Reeve, Clara (1729): School for Widows. P

Robertson, William: Disquisition concerning the Knowledge the Ancients had of India. P

Warton, Thomas (d. 1790): Poems on Various Subjects [see 1777].

Henry Hart Milman b.
Michael Faraday b.
John Wesley d.
Richard Price d.
'*The Observer*' (*Sundays only*) *started.*
'*Mother Goose's Melody*' (*anon.*).
Joseph Ritson's '*Ancient Popular Poetry*' (*anthology*).
Francis Grose's '*Antiquities of Scotland*'.
G. Chalmers ('*Francis Oldys*'), '*Life of Thomas Paine*'.
Volney, '*Les Ruines*'.
Schiller, '*Geschichte des dreissigjährigen Krieges*'.

1792

Aikin, John, and Barbauld, Anna: Evenings at Home. P and V

Bage (1728): Man as he is. P

Blake (1757): Song of Liberty [n.d.].

Bligh, Adm. William (1754): Voyage to the South Sea in the Bounty. P

Brackenridge, Hugh Henry (1748): Modern Chivalry [additions in 1804–5, 1815]. P

Burke (1729): Letter to Sir Hercules Langrishe. P
Speeches on Impeachment of Warren Hastings. P

Collected Works [concl. 1827; later edd.: Laurence and King 1803–27; 1839; with correspondence 1852; 1854–5, 1865–7].

Percy Bysshe Shelley b.
John Keble b.
Frederick Marryat b.
Edward John Trelawny b.
Augustus Hare b.
Sir Archibald Alison b.
Sir Joshua Reynolds d.
John Burgoyne d.
Wordsworth in France.
Pitt's attack on slave trade.
Southey expelled from Westminster for article on corporal punishment in '*The Flagellant*'.
Robert Anderson's '*Poets of Great Britain*' (*concl. 1807*).

Darwin (1731): Economy of Vegetation [pt. i of
    Botanic Garden: see 1789]. V
Gilpin (1724): Essays on Picturesque Beauty. P
Gookin, Daniel (d. 1687): Historical Collections of
    the Indians in New England. P
Holcroft (1745): Anna St. Ives. P
    Road to Ruin. C
Hoole, John (1727): Trs. Tasso's Rinaldo. V
Morton (1764?): Columbus. D
Rogers (1763): Pleasures of Memory, with Other
    Poems.
Smith, Charlotte (1749): Desmond. P
Stewart (1753): Philosophy of the Human Mind,
    vol. i [ii 1814, iii 1827]. P
Trimmer (1741): Reflections upon Education of
    Children in Charity Schools. P
Williams, Helen Maria (1762): Letters from
    France containing Anecdotes Relative to the
    Revolution [concl. 1796]. P
Wollstonecraft (1759): Vindication of the Rights
    of Woman. P
Young, Arthur (1741): Travels in France. P

*Joseph Ritson's 'Ancient
Songs' (anthology).*
'The Sun' (daily) started.

1793

Blake (1757): Gates of Paradise.
    Vision of the Daughters of Albion (Prophetic
    Books). P
    America (Prophetic Books). P
Burns (1759): Songs [in George Thomson's Select
    Scottish Airs, i–vi 1793–1841].
    Poems [enlarged ed.: another 1794; see 1787].
Colman, jnr. (1762): The Mountaineers. D
D'Israeli (1766): Dissertation on Anecdotes. P
Godwin (1756): Political Justice. P
Graves (1715): Reveries of Solitude. P and V
Inchbald (1753): Everyone has his fault. D
More (1745): Village Politics. P
Sayers, Frank (1763): Disquisitions, Metaphysical
    and Literary. P
Smith, Charlotte (1749): Old Manor House. P
Stewart (1753): Outlines of Moral Philosophy. P
Whitehead, John (1740?): Life of John Wesley,
    vol. i [ii 1796]. P
Wordsworth (1770): An Evening Walk. V
    Descriptive Sketches. V

John Clare b.
*Felicia Dorothea Hemans
b.*
Gilbert White d.
William Robertson d.
*'The British Critic'
founded by W. Jones
and Robert Nares.*
*Joseph Ritson's 'English
Anthology'.*

*President U.S.A.
Washington (2nd
term).*

Blake (1757): Songs of Experience.
  Songs of Innocence and Experience [n.d.].
  Europe (Prophetic Books). V
  Book of Urizen (Prophetic Books). V
Coleridge (1777): Monody on Chatterton [in
  Cambridge edition of Rowley Poems]. V
Cumberland (1732): The Jew. C
Darwin (1731): Zoonomia. P
Dwight, Timothy (1752): Greenfield Hill. V
Gifford (1756): Baviad. V
Gisborne, Thomas (1758): Walks in a Forest. V
Godwin (1756): Caleb Williams. P
Hayley (1745): Life of Milton [in Boydell's and
  Nicol's ed. of Milton: separately 1796].
Holcroft (1745): Hugh Trevor [concl. 1797]. P
Hurd (1720): Preface to Warburton's Works. P
Knight (1750): The Landscape. V
Mathias, James (1754?): Pursuits of Literature
  [concl. 1797]. V
Mickle, William (d. 1788): Collected Poems, in-
  cluding The Concubine [enlarged 1807].
Paine (1737): Age of Reason, pt. i [ii 1795, iii,
  incl. Essay on Dreams, 1811]. P
Paley (1743): Evidences of Christianity. P
Price, Uvedale (1747): Essay on the Picturesque. P
Radcliffe (1764): Mysteries of Udolpho. P
Southey (1774): Fall of Robespierre [with
  Coleridge]. T
  Trs. Bion and Moschus [with R. Lovell]. V
Taylor, William: Trs. Goethe's Iphigenie.
Wolcot (1738): Works [concl. 1796; later ed.
  1812].

John Gibson Lockhart b.
George Grote b.
William Whewell b.
Anna Jameson b.
Edward Gibbon d.
George Colman, senr., d.
William Cobbett's pamph-
  let 'On the Emigration
  of Dr. Priestley'.
Joseph Ritson's 'Scottish
  Songs' (anthology).
'The Morning Advertiser'
  (daily) started.
Goethe, 'Reineke Fuchs'.

1795

Blake (1757): Book of Los (Prophetic Books). V
  Book of Ahania (Prophetic Books). V
  Song of Los. V
Chatterton (d. 1770): The Revenge: a Burletta.
  Poetical Works [in Anderson's British Poets:
  see 1803].
Coleridge (1772): Conciones ad Populum. P
Cumberland (1732): Henry. P
  Wheel of Fortune. D
D'Israeli (1766): Essay on the Literary Character. P
Edgeworth (1767): Letters for Literary Ladies. P
Gifford (1756): Mæviad. V
Holcroft (1745): Deserted Daughter. C
Landor (1775): Poems.
  Moral Epistle to Earl Stanhope. V
Macneill, Hector: Scotland's Scaith. V
More (1745): Cheap Repository Tracts. P
Paine (1737): First Principles of Government. P

John Keats b.
Thomas Carlyle b.
Thomas Arnold b.
Julius Hare b.
George Darley b.
James Boswell d.
Alexander Wilson's poem
  'Watty and Meg'.
William Ireland's forgery,
  'Miscellaneous Papers
  of Shakespeare', starts
  controversy.
Joseph Ritson's ed. of
  poems of Laurence
  Minot and collection of
  Robin Hood poems.
Lindley Murray's 'Eng-
  lish Grammar'.
Goethe, 'Wilhelm Meisters
  Lehrjahre' (concl.
  1796).

Taylor, William: Trs. Wieland's Dialogues of the Gods.

Wakefield, Priscilla (1751): Juvenile Anecdotes, founded on Facts [concl. 1798].

White (d. 1793): A Naturalist's Calendar. P

Williams, Helen Maria (1762): Paul and Virginia [trs. Bernardin de Saint Pierre]. P

Letters containing a Sketch of the Politics of France. P

Schiller, '*Briefe über ästhetische Erziehung*' (*concl. 1796*).

1796

Bage (1728): Hermsprong. P

Barlow, Joel (1754): Hasty Pudding. V

Burges, James (1752): Birth and Triumph of Love. V

Burke (1729): Letter to a Noble Lord. P

Letters I and II on Regicide Peace [see 1797]. P

Burney, Charles (1726): Life of Metastasio. P

Burney, Frances (1752): Camilla. P

Coleridge (1772): The Watchman [ten nos.].

Poems on Various Subjects [cont. poems by Lamb omitted in 3rd ed.].

Vision of the Maid of Orleans [in Southey's Joan of Arc: re-named Destiny of Nations]. V

Ode on the Departing Year.

Four Sonnets [in Selected Sonnets of Bowles, Lamb, and others].

Colman, jnr. (1762): The Iron Chest. D

D'Israeli (1766): Miscellanies. P

Edgeworth (1767): Parent's Assistant, or Stories for Children, pt. i [complete, with Little Plays, 1800].

Gibbon (d. 1794): Miscellaneous Works, with memoir by himself, ed. Lord Sheffield [concl. 1814].

Holcroft (1745): Man of Ten Thousand. C

Inchbald (1753): Nature and Art. P

Lewis (1775): The Monk. P

Macneill, Hector (1746): Waes o' War. V

Moore, John (1729): Edward. P

Roscoe (1753): Life of Lorenzo de Medici. P

Scott (1771): The Chase, William and Helen [version of Bürger's Leonore]. V

Southey (1774): Joan of Arc. P

Strutt, Joseph (1749): Dresses and Habits of English People [concl. 1799]. P

Taylor, William: Trs. Select Fairy Tales from Wieland.

Trs. Bürger's Leonore. V

White, James (1775): Original Letters of Sir John Falstaff. P

Wollstonecraft (1759): Letters Written from Norway, Sweden, and Denmark. P

Hartley Coleridge b.

Robert Burns d.

James Macpherson d.

Thomas Reid d.

William Beckford starts construction of Fonthill Abbey.

'*The Monthly Magazine*' (*concl. 1843*).

William Ireland's '*Vortigern*' *performed, occasioning controversy.*

George Ellis's ed. of Gregory Lewis Way's trs. of '*Fabliaux*'.

Stephen Jones's '*Biographical Dictionary in Miniature*'.

Goethe, '*Alexis und Dora*'.

Goethe and Schiller, '*Xenien*'.

Jean Paul (Richter), '*Quintus Fixlein*'.

Bewick, Thomas (1753): History of British Birds. P
Burke (1729): Letter to Duke of Portland on Conduct of the Minority in Parliament. P
Thoughts on French Affairs. P
Letter III on a Regicide Peace [Letter IV in Works, 1812: see 1796]. P
Letter on Affairs in Ireland. P
Gifford (editor), **Canning, Frere, Ellis, Pitt, &c.**: The Anti-Jacobin [20 Nov. 1797–9 July 1798; collected edd. of poetry, 1799, 1801, 1852 (ed. Edmonds), 1854 (ed. Gilray), and 1890. Best-known pieces: Needy Knifegrinder, Progress of Man, Loves of the Triangles, The Rovers, and The New Morality].
Godwin (1756): The Enquirer. P
Inchbald (1753): Wives as they were. D
Lee, Harriet (1757): Canterbury Tales, vol. i [with Sophia Lee: concl. 1805]. P
Clara Lennox. P
Lewis (1775): The Minister [from Schiller's Kabale und Liebe]. D
Morton (1764 ?): Cure for the Heart Ache. C
Pinkerton, John (1758): History of Scotland. P
Radcliffe (1764): The Italian. P
Reynolds (d. 1792): Works, ed. Malone [cont. complete series of Discourses, 1769–90].
Southey (1774): Poems.
Letters written in Spain and Portugal. P
Tytler, Alexander Fraser: Essay on Principles of Translation. P
Wilberforce (1759): Practical Christianity. P

Alaric Alexander Watts b.
Samuel Lover b.
Sir Charles Lyell b.
Edmund Burke d.
Horace Walpole d.
Mary Wollstonecraft d.
Charles Macklin d.
William Mason d.
Mary Wollstonecraft Godwin (Shelley) b.
Friendship of Coleridge and Wordsworth (earliest meeting perhaps at Bristol 1795).
John Bell's 'British Theatre'.
Cobbett's 'Porcupine Gazette' (concl. 1799).
Goethe, 'Hermann und Dorothea'. Goethe and Schiller, 'Balladen'.
Tieck, 'Volksmärchen'.
Hölderlin, 'Hyperion' (1797–9).
Schlegel trs. of Shakespeare (1797–1801).
Joseph Warton's ed. of Pope.

President U.S.A.
John Adams.

Baillie (1762): Plays on the Passions, vol. i.
Brown, C. B. (1771): Wieland. P
Coleridge (1772): Fears in Solitude. France, an Ode. Frost at Midnight [see below: Wordsworth]. V
Colman, jnr. (1762): Blue Beard. D
Cowper (1731): Two Poems.
Coxe, William (1747): Memoirs of Sir Robert Walpole. P
Drake, Nathan: Literary Hours. P
Edgeworth (1767): Practical Education. P
Gilpin (1724): Picturesque remarks on Western parts of England and Isle of Wight.
Godwin (1756): Memoirs of Mary Wollstonecraft. P
Ed. Posthumous Works of Mary Wollstonecraft.
Holcroft (1745): He's much to blame. C
Inchbald (1753): Lovers' Vows [from Kotzebue]. D

Wordsworth and Coleridge visit Germany.
Stephen Jones's 'Pronouncing and Explanatory Dictionary' (stereotype ed. 1816).
Schiller, 'Wallensteins Lager'.
Goethe, 'Propyläen des Athenäum' (Periodical, 1798–1800: Manifesto of German Romanticism).

Lamb (1775): Blank Verse [with Charles Lloyd].
    Tale of Rosamond Gray. P
Landor (1775): Gebir. V
Lewis (1775): Castle Spectre. D
Lloyd (1775): Edmund Oliver. P
Malthus (1766): Principle of Population as it
    affects the Future of Society [2nd ed. 1803].
Morton (1764?): Secrets worth Knowing. C
    Speed the Plough. C
Roche, Regina (1764?): Children of the Abbey. P
Rogers (1763): Epistle to a Friend. V
Sheridan (1751): Collected Speeches [later edd.:
    1816, 1842; Speeches on Warren Hastings,
    ed. Bond, 1859–61].
Smith, Charlotte (1749): Minor Morals. P
Sotheby, William: Trs. Wieland's Oberon.
Vancouver, George: Voyage of Discovery. P
Wakefield, Priscilla (1751): Reflections on the
    present condition of the Female Sex. P
Walpole (d. 1797): Works, ed. Berry [cont. first
    instalment of letters to Conway, &c.].
Williams (1762): Tour in Switzerland. P
Wordsworth (1770) **and Coleridge** (1772): Lyrical
    Ballads [Ancient Mariner (see 1817), Tintern
    Abbey, Expostulation and Reply, &c.: see
    1800]. V

1799

Bowles (1762): Battle of the Nile. V
Brown, C. B. (1771): Ormond. P
    Edgar Huntley. P
    Arthur Mervyn [Pt. 2 1800]. P
Campbell (1777): Pleasures of hope. V
Coleridge (1772) **and Southey** (1774): Devil's
    Walk [anon.: acknowledged ed. 1830].
Darwin (1731): Phytologia. P
Glover (d. 1785): Jason. T
Godwin (1756): St. Leon. P
Ireland, William: Vortigern and Rowena. D
    Henry II. D
Jones, Sir William (d. 1794): Works, ed. Lord
    Teignmouth [concl. 1804].
Lewis (1775): Tales of Terror [see 1801]. V
    East Indian [later called Rich and Poor]. C
More (1745): On Modern System of Female
    Education. P
Park, Mungo (1771): Travels in the Interior of
    Africa in 1795–7. P
Scott (1771): Goetz of Berlichingen [trs. Goethe]. T
    Apology for Tales of Terror. V.
Seward (1747): Sonnets.
Sheridan (1751): Pizarro [from Kotzebue]. T
Turner, Sharon (1768): History of England to
    the Norman Conquest [see 1839]. P

Thomas Hood b.
Charles Jeremiah Wells b.
*George Payne Rainsford
    James b.*
George Finlay b.
*Napoleon Buonaparte
    First Consul.*
*'Religious Tract Society'
    founded.*
*Schiller, 'Die Piccolo-
    mini'. 'Wallensteins
    Tod', 'Das Lied von
    der Glocke'.*
Honoré de Balzac b.

Bloomfield, Robert (1766): Farmer's Boy. V
Burns (d. 1796): Works, with Life, New Poems, and Correspondence, ed. Currie [Principal later edd.: Cunningham 1834, Hogg and Motherwell 1834-6, Pickering 1839, Chambers 1856-7 (revised Wallace 1896), Macmillan (ed. A. Smith 1865), Scott Douglas 1877-9, Henley and Henderson 1896].
Coleridge (1772): Poems [in Annual Anthology]. Trs. Schiller's Wallenstein. D
Dibdin, Charles: History of the English Stage. P
Edgeworth (1767): Castle Rackrent. P
Gifford (1756): Epistle to Peter Pindar. V
Malone, Edmond (1741): Ed. Dryden's Prose Works, with Life.
Moore (1779): Trs. Odes of Anacreon.
Scott (1771): Eve of St. John. V
Sotheby, William: Trs. Virgil's Georgics.
Wordsworth (1770) **and Coleridge** (1772): Lyrical Ballads [vol. i poems of 1798; vol. ii new poems and the preface, see also 1815]. V

Thomas Babington Macaulay b.
Edward Bouverie Pusey b.
William Cowper d.
Joseph Warton d.
Mrs. Elizabeth Montagu d.
Mme de Staël, 'De la littérature considerée dans ses rapports avec les institutions sociales'.

1801

Bowles (1762): Sorrows of Switzerland. V
Brown, C. B. (1771): Clara Howard. P
    Jane Talbot. P
Burges, Sir James: Richard the First. V
Burns (d. 1796): Poems ascribed to Robert Burns [incl. Holy Willie, The Jolly Beggars, &c.; ed. Stewart]. V
Cobbett (1762): Porcupine's Works [concl. 1802]. The Porcupine [daily Oct.–Nov.].
Cowper (d. 1800): Poems from the Fr. of Mme de la Motte Guyon, with original poems.
Dibdin, Thomas (1771): The Cabinet. Opera.
Edgeworth (1767): Moral Tales. P
    Belinda. P.   Early Lessons. P
Goldsmith (d. 1774): Works, with Life by Percy [Life by Prior, 1837, by J. Forster 1848, 1854: Works ed. J. W. M. Gibbs, 1884-6].
Graves (1715): Senilities, or Amusements in Prose and Verse.
Hamilton, Elizabeth (1758): Letters on Education. P
Hogg (1770): Scottish Pastorals, Poems, Songs.
Holcroft (1745): Deaf and Dumb. D
Huddesford, George (1749): Collected Poems [Salmagundi, originally pub. 1791, Topsy Turvy 1793, Bubble and Squeak 1799, Crambe Repetita 1799].

John Henry Newman b.
Robert Bage d.
H. J. Todd's Variorum ed. of Milton's Poetical Works (rev. 1808, 1826, 1834).
George Ellis, 'Specimens of Early English Poets' (2nd ed., with Historical Sketch of Progress of English Poetry; 1st ed. in 1790).
Fourth ed. of 'Encyclopaedia Britannica' (Millar editor).
Hardenberg ('Novalis') d.
Schiller, 'Maria Stuart'.
Chateaubriand, 'Atala'.
Lemercier, 'Pinto'.

President U.S.A. Jefferson.

Hunt (1784): Juvenilia. V
Jefferson (1843): Manual of Parliamentary
    Practice. P
Lewis (1775): Tales of Wonder [with contribu-
    tions by Scott, Southey, Leyden, and others:
    includes Tales of Terror 1779]. P and V
  Adelmorn, or the Outlaw. D
  Alphonso, King of Castile. D
Macneill, Hector (1746): Poetical Works [later
    edd.: 1806, 1812, 1856].
Moore (1779): Poems by Thomas Little.
Murphy (1727): Life of David Garrick. P
Opie (1769): Father and Daughter. P and V
Pye (1745): Alfred. V
Sotheby, William (1757): Julian and Agnes. D
Southey (1774): Thalaba. V
Strutt, Joseph (1749): Sports and Pastimes of the
    People of England. P
Wakefield, Priscilla (1751): The Juvenile Travel-
    lers. P
Williams (1762): History of Perourou [dramatized
    as Lady of Lyons by E. B. Lytton]. P
  Sketches of the State of Manners and Opinions
    in the French Republic. P

1802

Baillie (1762): Plays on the Passions, vol. ii.
Bloomfield (1766): Rural Tales. V
Clarke, Adam (1762 ?): Bibliographical Dictionary
    [concl. 1806].
Colman, jnr. (1762): Poor Gentleman. C
Dibdin, Thomas (1776): Introduction to the
    Knowledge of Rare and Valuable Classics. P
Edgeworth (1767): Essay on Irish Bulls (with
    R. L. Edgeworth).
Gifford (1756): Trs. of Juvenal (cont. Auto-
    biography P). V
Holcroft (1745): A Tale of Mystery. D
Lamb (1775): John Woodvil, a tragedy.
Landor (1775): Poetry by author of Gebir.
Opie (1769): Poems.
Paley (1743): Natural Theology. P
Pye (1745): Verses on Several Subjects.
Ritson, Joseph (1752): Bibliographia Poetica. V
Scott (1771): Ed. Border Minstrelsy, vols. i, ii [iii
    1803]. V
Smith (1779): Trevanion. P
Spencer, William Robert (1769): Urania. C

Peace of Amiens.
Winthrop Mackworth
    Praed b.
Letitia Elizabeth Landon b.
Isaac Williams b.
Harriet Martineau b.
Erasmus Darwin d.
Wordsworth's marriage.
William Cobbett starts the
    'Weekly Political Regis-
    ter' (contd. to 1835).
'The Edinburgh Review'
    started by Sydney Smith,
    Jeffrey and Brougham
    (publisher Constable).
Leyden, ed. 'Scottish De-
    scriptive Poems.'
Étienne Dumont's 'Traité
    de la législation civil et
    pénale' based on Ben-
    tham's MSS.
Victor Hugo b.
Chateaubriand, 'Génie du
    christianisme'.
Mme de Staël,'Delphine'.
Schiller, 'Jungfrau von
    Orleans'.
Hardenberg ('Novalis'),
    'Heinrich von Ofter-
    dingen'.

Boswell, Sir Alexander (1775): Songs chiefly in Scottish Dialect.

Bowles (1762): The Picture. V

Burney, James (1750): History of Discoveries in the South Sea [concl. 1817]. P

Chatterton (d. 1770): Collected Works, ed. R. Southey and J. Cottle [ed. Willcox 1842, Skeat 1875, Roberts 1906, Sidney Lee 1906–9: see 1777].

Cowper (d. 1800): Letters [in Life and Posthumous Writings, ed. Hayley. Later and fuller edd. of letters: ed. Hayley 1804, 1809, 1812, ed. J. Johnson 1824, ed. Southey 1834–7, ed. T. Wright 1904].

Darwin (d. 1802): Temple of Nature. V

Dibdin, Charles, senr. (1745): Professional Life of Mr. Dibdin [with 600 songs].

Godwin (1756): Life of Chaucer [including Memoirs of John of Gaunt]. P

Hayley (1745): Life of Cowper. P

Holcroft (1745): Hear both Sides. C

Lancaster, Joseph (1778): Improvements in Education. P

Le Noir, Elizabeth (1755?): Village Annals. P novel.

Leyden, John (1775): Scenes of Infancy. V

Montagu (d. 1762): Works, including Letters [see 1763], Poems [see 1747], and Essays, ed. J. Dallaway [2nd ed. with Letters to Mrs. Hewitt 1817; another ed. with Introductory Anecdotes, ed. Wharncliffe, 1837; another ed., by Moy Thomas, 1861].

Porter, Jane (1776): Thaddeus of Warsaw. P novel.

Reed, Isaac (1742): Ed. of Shakespeare [known as the 1st variorum ed.; revised as the 2nd variorum ed. in 1813].

Repton, Humphrey (1752): Theory and Practice of Landscape Gardening. P

Sayers, Frank (1763): Nugæ Poeticæ [chiefly versifications of Jack the Giant Killer and Guy of Warwick]. V

Southey (1774): Trs. of Amadis of Gaul.

Struthers, John (1776): Anticipation. V

Turner (1768): Vindication of Genuineness of Ancient Poems of Aneurin, Taliesin, &c. P

White (1785): Clifton Grove. V

Woodhouse, James (1735): Norbury Park, and Other Poems.

War with France renewed.
Richard Henry (or Hengist) Horne b.
Thomas Lovell Beddoes b.
George Borrow b.
Robert Surtees b.
Douglas Jerrold b.
Ralph Waldo Emerson b.
Richard Hurrell Froude b.
Edward George Bulwer (Lytton) b.
James Beattie d.
William Cobbett starts 'The Parliamentary Debates' which in 1812 passed on to Hansard.
William Stewart Rose's trs. of 'Amadis de Gaule'.
Klopstock d.
Schiller, 'Braut von Messina'.
Kotzebue, 'Deutscher Kleinstädter'.
Dumas b.
Alfieri d.

Baillie (1762): Miscellaneous Plays [Rayner, Country Inn, Constantine Paleologus].

Blake (1757): Jerusalem. V
　Milton, a Poem. V

Bowles (1762): Spirit of Discovery. V

Brown, Thomas (1778): Poems.
　Observations on the Relation of Cause and Effect [enlarg. ed. 1806; 3rd ed. 1818]. P

Du Bois, Edward: Trs. Decameron with Remarks on Boccaccio. P

Edgeworth (1767): Popular Tales. P
　Modern Griselda. P

Grahame, James (1765): The Sabbath [anon.]. V

Hamilton, Elizabeth (1758): Memoirs of Agrippina. P

Hayley (1745): Triumphs of Music. V

Holcroft (1745): Travels from Hamburg. P

Le Noir, Elizabeth (1755): Village Anecdotes. P

Lewis (1775): Bravo of Venice [from German: dramatized as 'Rugantino' 1805].

Opie (1769): Adeline Mowbray. P

Peacock (1785): Monks of St. Mark. V

Pitt, Earl of Chatham (d. 1778): Letters to his Nephew, Thomas Pitt, ed. Grenville.

Porter, Anna (1780): Lake of Killarney. P

Richardson (d. 1761): Correspondence, ed. with Life by Mrs. Barbauld.

Seward (1747): Memoir of Erasmus Darwin. P

Smith, Charlotte (1749): Conversations introducing Poetry. P

Spencer, William (1769): Year of Sorrow. V

Struthers, John (1776): Poor Man's Sabbath. V

Taylor, Anne and Jane: Original Poems for Infant Minds. V

Nathaniel Hawthorne b.
Sir Richard Owen b.
Benjamin Disraeli b.
William Gilbert b.
Charlotte Lennox d.
Richard Graves d.
John Wilkes d.
Joseph Priestley d.
Scott's ed. of 'The British Drama'.
Napoleon Buonaparte Emperor.
Sainte-Beuve b.
Sénancour, 'Obermann'.
Kant d.
Schiller, 'Wilhelm Tell'.
Goethe, 'Natürliche Tochter'.
Tieck, 'Kaiser Octavianus'.
George Sand b.

Adam, Henry (1735): Discourses on Davilla. P

Anderson, Robert (1770): Ballads in Cumbrian Dialect. V

Brydges, Egerton (1762): Censura Literaria (1805–9). P

Campbell (1777): Collected Poems [later edd.: 1810, 1824, 1828–33, 1837, ed. Hill 1851, Rogers 1871, Rossetti 1871, Robertson 1901].

Cary (1772): Trs. Inferno [see 1814]. V

Colman, jnr. (1762): John Bull [n.d.]. D
Who wants a Guinea? D

Foster, John (1770): Essays. P

Gifford (1756): Ed. of Massinger [another ed. 1813].

Godwin (1756): Fleetwood. P
Fables. P

Graves (d. 1804): The Triflers. P and V

Hayley (1745): Ballads on Anecdotes of Animals [illustr. Blake]. V

Hazlitt (1778): Principles of Human Action. P

Holcroft (1745): Lady of the Rock. D
Memoirs of Bryan Perdue. P

Inchbald (1753): To Marry or not to Marry. C

Johnson (d. 1784): Account of his own Life. P

Knight (1750): Principles of Taste. P

Lamb (1775): King and Queen of Hearts. V

Montgomery (1771): The Ocean. V

Morgan, Sydney, Lady (1783 ?): Novice of St. Dominick. P

Morton (1764 ?): School of Reform. C

Roscoe (1753): Life of Leo X. P

Sayers, Frank (1763): Miscellanies, Antiquarian and Historical. P

Scott (1771): Lay of the Last Minstrel. V

Southey (1774): Madoc. V

Tobin, John (d. 1804): The Honey Moon. C

Trimmer (1741): Comparative View of the Plan of Education promulgated by Mr. Joseph Lancaster. P

Walpole (d. 1797): Reminiscences (written 1788). P

Battles of Trafalgar and Austerlitz.

Frederick Denison Maurice b.

James Martineau b.

William Harrison Ainsworth b.

Arthur Murphy d.

William Paley d.

George Ellis's 'Specimens of Early English Romances in metre'.

William Taylor's trs. of 'Nathan the Wise'.

Correspondence of Lady Hertford and Lady Pomfret, 1738–1741.

Thomas Park's 'British Poets' (1805–9).

Chateaubriand, 'René'.

Schiller d.

Arnim and Brentano, 'Wunderhorn' (1805–8).

President U.S.A.
    Jefferson (2nd term).

Bloomfield (1766): Wild Flowers. V
Bowles (1762): Bowden Hall. V
　Ed. of Pope.
Byron (1788): Fugitive Pieces. V
Combe (1741): Letters of the late Lord Lyttelton.
　P [probably forged].
Edgeworth (1767): Leonora. P
　Letters. P
Franklin (d. 1790): Complete Works in Philo-
　sophy, Politics & Morals. P
Hazlitt (1778): Free Thoughts on Public Affairs. P
Holcroft (1745): The Vindictive Man. C
　Tales in Verse.
Hutchinson, Lucy (1620): Life of Colonel [John]
　Hutchinson [written between 1664 and 1671;
　cont. autobiographical fragment; re-ed., with
　additions, Firth 1904].
Lancaster, Joseph (1778): Plan for educating Ten
　Thousand Poor Children. P
Landor (1775): Simonidea [incl. Gunlung and
　Helga]. V
Lingard (1771): Antiquities of Anglo-Saxon
　Church [see 1845]. P
Montgomery (1771): Wanderer of Switzerland. V
Moore (1779): Epistles, Odes, and Other Poems. V
Morgan, Sydney, Lady (1783 ?): Wild Irish Girl. P
Opie (1769): Simple Tales. P
Peacock (1785): Palmyra. V
Roscoe (1753): Butterfly's Ball and Grasshopper's
　Feast [in the Gentleman's Magazine: Sept.
　1807]. V
Scott (1771): Ballads and Lyrical Pieces. V
　Ed. Diary of Sir Henry Slingsby [abbreviated:
　see 1836].
Struthers, John (1776): The Peasant's Death. V
Webster, Noah (1758): Compendious Dictionary
　of the English Language [his American
　Dictionary of the English Language 1st ed.
　1828].

Elizabeth Barrett (Brown-
　ing) b.
John Stuart Mill b.
Charles James Lever b.
Henry Kirke White d.
Charlotte Smith d.
Charles James Fox d.
William Pitt d.
Mrs. Inchbald's 'British
　Theatre' (contd. 1809).
William Cobbett's 'Par-
　liamentary History of
　England' begins to ap-
　pear.
'The Monthly Repository
　of Theology and General
　Literature' starts (ed.
　Aspland: contd. 1837).

Barlow, Joel (1754): The Columbiad. V

Barrett, Eaton Stannard (1786): All the Talents. V

Byron (1788): Hours of Idleness. V

  Poems on Various Occasions. V

Campbell (1777): Annals of Great Britain. P

Coxe, William (1747): History of the House of Austria. P

Crabbe (1754): Poems [cont. Parish Register and Sir Eustace Percy among new poems].

Cumberland (1732): Memoirs written by Himself. P

Dorset, Catherine (1750?): The Peacock 'At Home'. V

  The Lion's Masquerade. V

Douce, Francis (1757): Illustrations of Shakespeare. P

Godwin (1756): Faulkener. D

Grahame, James (1765): Poems (collected).

Heber (1783): Palestine. V

Hogg (1770): The Mountain Bard. V

Hunt (1784): Critical Essays on the Performers of the London Theatres. P

  Classic Tales, with Critical Essays on the Authors. P

Irving, Washington (1783): Salmagundi [1807–8]. P

Lamb, Mary (1764) **and Charles** (1775): Tales from Shakespeare. P

  Mrs. Leicester's School. P

Lewis (1775): Adelgitha. T

  Feudal Tyrants. P

Malthus (1766): Letter to Whitbred on Poor Laws. P

Maturin (1782): Fatal Revenge. P

Moore (1779): Irish Melodies [1807–34; music by Sir John Stevenson].

Morton (1764?): Town and Country. C

Porter, Anna (1780): Hungarian Brothers. P

Pye (1745): Comments on Commentators of Shakespeare. P

Ramsay, David (1749): Life of Washington. P

Smith, Charlotte (d. 1806): Beachy Head, with Other Poems.

Smith, 'Horace' (1779): Horatio. P

Smith, Sydney (1771): Letters on the Subject of Catholics by Peter Plymley [concl. 1808]. P

Sotheby, William (1757): Saul. V

Southey (1774): Letters from England by Don Espriella. P

  Trs. of Spanish Chronicle of Palmerin of England.

  Specimens of the later English Poets.

Tannahill, Robert (1774): Poems and Songs.

Tobin, John (d. 1804): The Curfew. D

Richard Chenevix Trench b.

Henry Wadsworth Longfellow b.

John Greenleaf Whittier b.

Clara Reeve d.

John Pinkerton's 'Collection of Voyages and Travels' (concl. 1814).

Mme de Staël, 'Corinne'.

Turner, Elizabeth: The Daisy, or Cautionary
    Stories in Verse.
White (d. 1806): Remains, ed. with Life by
    Southey. V
Wordsworth (1770): Poems in Two Volumes [Ode
    to Duty, Intimations of Immortality, Mis-
    cellaneous Sonnets, &c.].

1808

Bryant, William Cullen (1794): The Embargo. V
Burns (d. 1796): Reliques, ed. R. Cromek.
Clarkson, Thomas (1760): History of the Aboli-
    tion of the African Slave Trade. P
Colman, jnr. (1762): Heir at Law (acted 1797). D
    Battle of Hexham. D
    Surrender of Calais. D
Cowper (d. 1800): Trs. of Milton's Italian and
    Latin Poems. V
Dalton, John (1766): New System of Chemical
    Philosophy [concl. 1810]. P
Fox, Charles James (d. 1806): History of the Early
    Part of the Reign of James II. P
Hamilton, Elizabeth (1758): Cottagers of Glen-
    burnie. P
Hemans (1793): Poems.
    England and Spain. V
Hunt (1784): London Theatres [originally in The
    News]. P
Le Noir, Elizabeth (1755?): Clara de Montfier. P
Lewis (1775): Romantic Tales. P
    Venoni, or the Novice of St. Mark. T
Mangin, Edward (1772): Essay on Light Reading.
    P
Maturin (1782): Wild Irish Boy. P
Moore (1779): Corruption, Intolerance. V
Opie (1769): Warrior's Return, and Other Poems.
Scott (1771): Marmion. V
    Ed. of Dryden [re-ed. Saintsbury 1882].
Southey (1774): Trs. of Spanish Romance of the
    Cid. P
Tobin, John (d. 1804): School for Authors. C

Peninsular War begun.
John Home d.
*Leigh Hunt starts 'The
    Examiner' (contd. to
    1821).*
*Rudolf Ackermann's
    'Microcosm of London'
    (concl. 1811; words by
    William Combe and
    W. H. Pyne).*
*Charles Lamb's 'Speci-
    mens of English drama-
    tic Poets'.*
*Mrs. Inchbald's 'British
    Theatre'.*
*Thomas Park's ed. of Har-
    leian Miscellany (concl.
    1813).*
*Catalogue of Harleian
    MSS. by Nares, Ellis,
    and Horne (concl. 1812).*
*Stephen Jones's ed. of
    Thomas Davies's 'Life
    of Garrick', with addi-
    tions (see 1780).*
*C. J. Ingersoll's 'Rights
    and Wrongs of the
    U.S.A.'*
Goethe, 'Faust', pt. i.

Adams, John Quincey (1767): American Principles. P

Blake (1757): Descriptive Catalogue. P

Byron (1788): Imitations and Translations from Classics with Original Poems. V

English Bards and Scotch Reviewers. V

Campbell (1777): Gertrude of Wyoming and Other Poems [2nd ed. 1810]. V

Carter, Elizabeth (d. 1806): Letters to Miss Catherine Talbot and Mrs. Vesey. V

Coleridge (1772): The Friend [cont. to 15 March 1810; reissued with supplementary matter 1812; new and greatly altered ed. 1818]. P

Combe (1741): The Schoolmaster's Tour [in *The Poetical Magazine*: see 1812]. V

Dibdin, Thomas (1776): Bibliomania [enlarg. edd. 1811, 1842]. P

Edgeworth (1767): Tales of Fashionable Life, First series [Eunice, The Dun, Manœuvring, Almeria: see 1812]. P

Freneau, Philip (1752): Poems written during the American Revolutionary War. V

Godwin (1756): Essay on Sepulchres. P

Hobhouse, John (1786): Travels through Albania during 1809–10. P

Hope, Thomas (1770 ?): Costumes of the Ancients. P

Irving, Washington (1783): Diedrich Knickerbocker's History of New York. P

Lamb, Charles (1775) **and Mary** (1764): Poetry for Children. P

Montagu (d. 1800): Letters, vols. i, ii [iii and iv in 1813].

Montgomery (1771): West Indies. V

Moore (1779): The Sceptic. V

More (1745): Cœlebs in Search of a Wife [anon.]. P

Morgan, Sydney, Lady (1783 ?): Woman, or Ida of Athens. P

Porter, Anna (1780): Don Sebastian. P

Wordsworth (1770): Concerning Relations of Great Britain, Spain, and Portugal as affected by the Convention of Cintra. P

William Ewart Gladstone b.
Edgar Allen Poe b.
Oliver Wendell Holmes b.
Alfred Tennyson b.
Alexander William Kinglake b.
Charles Darwin b.
Richard Monckton Milnes (Lord Houghton) b.
Edward Fitzgerald b.
Thomas Gordon Hake b.
Abraham Lincoln b.
Hannah Cowley d.
Anna Seward d.
Thomas Paine d.
Thomas Holcroft d.
'*Quarterly Review*' started with Gifford as editor.
William Cobbett's (later known as Howell's) 'Collection of State Trials' (concl. 1826).
Scott's ed. of Somers Tracts (concl. 1815; see 1748).
Mrs. Inchbald's 'The Modern Theatre' and 'Collection of Farces'.
Rudolf Ackermann's 'Repository of Arts, Literature', etc. (concl. 1828).
Chateaubriand, 'Martyrs'.
Goethe, 'Wahlverwandtschaften'.
August Schlegel, 'Über dramatische Kunst und Literatur' (concl. 1811).

President U.S.A.
Maddison.

Aikin (1781): Epistles on Women. V
Baillie (1762): Family Legend. T
Barrett, Eaton Stannard (1786): Woman, and
    Other Poems. V
Brunton, Mary (1778): Self-Control. P
Brydges, Egerton (1762): British Bibliographer
    [concl. 1814]. P
Clarke, Edward (1769): Travels. P
Conder, Josiah, and others (1789): Associate
    Minstrels. V
Crabbe (1754): The Borough. V
Dibdin, Thomas (1776): Ed. of Joseph Ames's
    Typographical Antiquities [concl. 1819: see
    1749, 1785].
Hawker, Peter (1786): Journal. P
Hogg (1770): Forest Minstrel. V
Lancaster, Joseph (1778): Instructions for form-
    ing a Society for the Education of the
    Labouring Classes. P
Macneill, Hector (1746): Pastoral or Lyric Music
    of Scotland. V
Mitford, Mary (1787): Miscellaneous Poems.
Peacock (1785): Genius of the Thames. V
Pocock, Isaac (1782): Hit or Miss. D
Porter, Jane (1776): The Scottish Chiefs. P
Rogers (1763): Voyage of Columbus [privately
    printed 1808]. V
Scott (1771): Lady of the Lake. V
    Ancient British Drama [anthology].
Seward (d. 1809): Poetical Works, ed. Scott.
Shelley (1792): Original Poetry by Victor and
    Cazire [with Elizabeth Shelley]. V
    Zastrozzi. P
    Posthumous fragments of Margaret Nicholson.
    V
Sotheby, William (1757): Constance de Castille. V
Southey (1774): Curse of Kehama. V
    History of Brazil [concl. 1819]. P
Stewart (1753): Philosophical Essays. P
Taylor, Jane and Ann: Hymns for Infant Minds.
    V
Taylor, William (1765): Tales of Yore [trs. from
    Fr. and Ger.] P
Wordsworth (1770): Topographical Description
    of the Country of the Lakes [in Joseph
    Wilkinson's Select Views in Cumberland: see
    1820, '22]. P

Elizabeth Gaskell b.
Martin Tupper b.
Margaret Fuller b.
*Coleridge lectures on
    Shakespeare.*
*Letters of Marquise du
    Deffand to Horace Wal-
    pole, ed. Berry.*
*Mrs. Barbauld's 'British
    Novelists'.*
*Alexander Chalmers's
    'English Poets'.*
*Robert Cromek's 'Select
    Scottish Songs' and
    'Nithsdale and Gallo-
    way Song'.*
*Leigh Hunt starts 'The
    Reflector' (only four
    numbers).*
*Mme de Staël, 'De l'Alle-
    magne' (1810–13).*
Goethe, 'Pandora'.
*C. J. Ingersoll's 'Inchi-
    quin'.*
*Blake's Canterbury Pil-
    grims (engraving) pub-
    lished.*
Musset b.

Austen (1775): Sense and Sensibility [anon.]. P
Barbauld (1743): Eighteen Hundred and Eleven. V
Female Speaker [P and V anthology].
Bloomfield (1766): Banks of the Wye. V
D'Israeli (1766): Despotism. P
Hunt (1784): Feast of the Poets [in The Reflector: book form 1814]. V
Kerr, Robert: History and Collection of Voyages [concl. 1824]. P
Knowles (1784): Brian Boroihme. D
Lamb (1775): Prince Dorus. V
Mitford, John (1781): Agnes, the Indian Captive and Other Poems. V
Mitford, Mary (1787): Christina. V
Moore (1779): M.P., or The Blue Stocking. D comic opera.
More (1745): Practical Piety. P
Scott, Jonathan (1754): Trs. of the Arabian Nights. P
Scott (1771): Vision of Don Roderick. V
Ed. of Secret History of the Court of James I.
Ed. of Abel Boyer's trs. of Memoirs of Count Grammont [see 1713–14].
Modern British Drama [anthology].
Seward (d. 1809): Correspondence, 1784–1807.
Shelley (1792): Necessity of Atheism. P
St. Irvyne. P
Poetical Essay on Existing State of Things. V
Spencer, William (1769): Poems.
Stewart (1753): Biographical Memoirs. P
Struthers, John (1776): Wintry Day. V
Tighe, Mrs. Mary (1772): Psyche, or the Legend of Love [privately printed 1805]. V
Turner, Elizabeth: The Cowslip, or More Cautionary Stories in Verse.
Warton, Joseph and John: Ed. Poems of Dryden [ed. Christie 1870; Sargeaunt 1910].

Prince of Wales Regent.
William Makepeace Thackeray b.
William Bell Scott b.
Thomas Percy d.
Richard Cumberland d.
Charles Kean d.
Shelley's expulsion from Oxford and marriage with Harriet Westbrook.
National Society for the Education of the Poor founded.
Étienne Dumont's 'Théorie des peines et des récompenses' based on the MSS. of Jeremy Bentham (see 1825).
Edward Mangin's ed. of Richardson.
Chateaubriand, 'Itinéraire'.
Fouqué, 'Undine'.
Gautier b.
Goethe, 'Dichtung und Wahrheit' (concl. 1813).

Baillie (1762): Plays of the Passions, Third series.
Barton (1784): Metrical Effusions. V
Byron (1788): Childe Harold, cantos i and ii (with 20 other poems, including those during his travels and those addressed to Thyrza. Canto iii 1816, iv 1818, complete 1819]. V
　Curse of Minerva. V
Cary (1772): Trs. Purgatorio and Paradiso. V
Combe (1741): Tour of Dr. Syntax in Search of the picturesque [first sep. ed.; originally as 'The Schoolmaster's Tour' in the Poetical Magazine, 1809 ff.: see 1820–1; illustrated by T. Rowlandson]. V
Crabbe (1754): Tales in Verse.
D'Israeli (1766): Calamities of Authors. P
Edgeworth (1767): Tales of Fashionable Life, 2nd series [Vivian, Absentee, Mme de Fleury, Emilie de Coulanges: see 1809]. P
Heber (1783): Poems and Translations. V
Hemans (1793): Domestic Affections, and Other Poems. V
Jones, Stephen (1763): Biographia Dramatica, 3rd ed. [see 1764, 1782]. P
Lancaster, Joseph (1778): Schools for all. P
Landor (1775): Count Julian, a Tragedy.
Maturin (1782): Milesian Chief. P
Mitford, Mary (1787): Blanch of Castile. V
Montgomery (1771): World before the Flood. V
Nichols, John, senr. (1745): Literary Anecdotes of the Eighteenth Century [concl. 1815]. P
Opie (1769): Temper, or Domestic Scenes. P
Peacock (1785): Philosophy of Melancholy. V
Shelley (1792): Address to Irish People. P
　Proposals for Association of Philanthropists for Ireland. P
　Declaration of Rights. P
　Letter to Lord Ellenborough. P
　The Devil's Walk. V
Smith, 'Horace' (1779): Rejected Addresses [with James Smith]. V
Southey (1774) **and Coleridge** (1772): Omniana. P
Tennant, William (1784): Anster Fair [anon.]. V
Wilson (1785): Isle of Palms and Other Poems. V

French retreat from Moscow.
Robert Browning b.
Charles Dickens b.
Edward Lear b.
Samuel Smiles b.
John Forster b.
Horne Tooke d.
Isaac Bickerstaffe d.?
Edmond Malone d.
Shelley's elopement with Mary Godwin.
Roxburghe Club (for reprinting rare English books) founded by Thomas Dibdin and others.
Rudolf Ackermann's 'Westminster Abbey'.
Chalmers's 'General Biographical Dictionary' (enlarg. from ed. of 1761, completed 1817).
Jacob and Wilhelm Grimm, 'Kinder- und Hausmärchen' (concl. 1815).
Hegel, 'Logik' (concl. 1815).
John and L. Hunt's libel in 'Examiner' on Prince Regent.

Aubrey, John (d. 1697): Lives [in Letters Written by Eminent Persons in 17th and 18th Centuries; ed. Clark 1898].

Austen (1775): Pride and Prejudice [anon.]. P

Byron (1788): Bride of Abydos. V
  Waltz [anon.]. V
  Giaour. V

Coleridge (1772): Remorse. D

Cowley (d. 1809): Collected Works.

Coxe, William (1747): Memoirs of Kings of Spain. P

Cunningham, Allan (1784): Songs in Rural Dialect of Scotland. V

Hogg (1770): Queen's Wake. V

Lingard (1771): Collection of Tracts connected with the Civil and Religious Principles of the Catholics. P

Mitford (1787): Poems on the Female Character. V

Moore (1779): Intercepted Letters, or The Two-penny Post Bag. V

More (1745): Christian Morals. P

Northcote, James (1746): Memoirs of Reynolds. P

Opie (1769): Tales of Real Life. P

Owen, Robert (1771): New View of Society [concl. 1816]. P

Pocock, Isaac (1782): Miller and his Men. D

Reresby, Sir John (d. 1689): Travels and Memoirs [see 1734].

Scott (1771): Rokeby. V
  Bridal of Triermain. V

Shelley (1792): Queen Mab. V
  Vindication of Natural Diet. P

Smith, 'Horace' (1779): Horace in London [with James Smith] V

Southey (1774): Life of Nelson. P

Mark Pattison b.
William Aytoun b.
Sir Arthur Helps b.
H. J. Pye d.
Southey becomes poet-laureate.
Leigh Hunt in prison 1813–15.
Wagner b.
Wieland d.
Fouqué, 'Der Zauberring'.

President U.S.A. Maddison (2nd term).

1814

Aikin (1781): Lorimer, a Tale. P

Austen (1775): Mansfield Park [anon.]. P

Barrett, Eaton Stannard (1786): The Heroine. P

Brunton, Mary (1778): Discipline. P

Brydges, Egerton (1762): Restituta: or Titles, Extracts, and Characters of Old Books Revived [concl. 1816]. P

Burney, Frances (1752): The Wanderer. P

Byron (1788): The Corsair. V
  Ode to Napoleon. V
  Lara. V

Cary (1772): Trs. Dante complete [see 1805]. V

Coleridge (1772): Essays on the Fine Arts [in Felix Farley's Journal]. P

Abdication of Napoleon.
Charles Reade b.
Aubrey Thomas De Vere b.
Shelley's departure from England.
Colburn's 'New Monthly Magazine' and 'New British Theatre' (ed. John Galt).
'The British Critic' (new series) begun (became quarterly in 1826; ed. John Newman 1836–41, T. Mozley 1841–3).

D'Israeli (1766): Quarrels of Authors. P

Edgeworth (1767): Patronage. P

Hawker, Peter (1786): Instructions to Young Sportsmen. P

Horne, Thomas (1780): Introduction to Study of Bibliography. P

Hunt (1784): Feast of the Poets [originally in The Reflector 1810]. V

Morgan, Sydney, Lady (1783?): O'Donnel, a National Tale. P

Nicholson, William (1782?): Tales in Verse and Miscellaneous Poems.

Quillinan, Edward (1791): Dunluce Castle. V

Stanzas by Author of Dunluce Castle. P

Reynolds, John Hamilton (1796): Safie, an Eastern Tale. V

Eden of Imagination. V

Richmond, Legh (1772): Annals of the Poor [Dairyman's daughter, Young Cottager, Negro Servant: originally in Christian Guardian between 1809 and 1814]. P

Rogers (1763): Jacqueline [with Byron's Lara]. V

Scott (1771): Waverley [anon.]. P.

Border Antiquities of England and Scotland [concl. 1817]. P

Eyrbiggia Saga [in Weber's Northern Antiquities].

Essays on Chivalry and Romance [in Encyclopaedia Britannica]. P

Ed. of Swift.

Sheil, Richard Lalor (1791): Adelaide, or The Emigrants. D

Shelley (1792): Refutation of Deism. P

Sotheby, William (1757): Song of Triumph on the Peace. V

Five Tragedies [Confession, Orestes (2nd ed., 1st in 1802), Ivan, Death of Darnley, Zamorin and Zama].

Southey (1774): Roderick. V

Odes to the Prince Regent and King of Prussia. V

Stewart (1753): Philosophy of the Human Mind, vol. ii [see 1792, 1827]. P

Struthers, John (1776): Poems, Moral and Religious.

Turner (1768): History of England from Norman Conquest to 1509 [concl. 1823].

Wolcot (1738): The Regent and the King. V

Royalty Fogbound. V

Wordsworth (1770): The Excursion, being a portion of The Recluse [cont. the Essay upon Epitaphs from The Friend of 22 Feb. 1810: The Recluse in 1888].

Capell Lofft's (senr.) 'Laura, or Anthology of Sonnets'.

Thomas Mathias's ed. of Gray.

Rudolf Ackermann's 'University of Oxford'.

Chateaubriand, 'Bonaparte et les Bourbons'.

Fichte d.

Chamisso, 'Peter Schlemihl'.

Boswell, Sir Alexander: Tyrant's Fall. V

Bowles (1762): Missionary of the Andes. V

Burnet (d. 1715): Memorial offered to the Princess Sophia. P

Byron (1788): Hebrew Melodies. V
Collected Works [Murray].

Combe (1741): Life of Napoleon. V
English Dance of Death. V

Cowper (d. 1800): Poems, ed. J. Johnson [later edd.: early poems with anecdotes by Lady Hesketh, ed. J. Croft, 1825, with new letters, ed. Southey, 1834-7, ed. Grimshawe 1835, ed. Bruce 1865 (Aldine), ed. Benham 1889 (Globe), ed. Milford 1905 (Oxford)].

Glen, William (1789): Poems, chiefly Lyrical.

Godwin (1756): Lives of Edward and John Philips. To which are added Collections for the Life of Milton by J. Aubrey, and Life of Milton by Edward Philips. P

Hogg (1770): Pilgrims of the Sun. V

Hubbard (d. 1815): General History of New England. P

Hunt (1784): Descent of Liberty, a Masque. V

Johnstone, Christian (1781): Clan Albin. P

Keightley, Thomas (1789): Outlines of History. P

Knowles (1784): Caius Gracchus. T

Malcolm, Sir John (1769): History of Persia. P

Malthus (1766): Inquiry into Rent. P

Milman (1791): Fazio. D

Moore (1779): National Airs [music by Sir J. Stevenson]. V

More (1745): Essay on Character and Writings of St. Paul. P

Porter, Jane (1776): Pastor's Fireside. P

Scott (1771): Guy Mannering. P
Lord of the Isles. V
Field of Waterloo. V
Paul's Letters to his Kinsfolk. P

Stewart (1753): Dissertation on the Progress of Philosophy, pt. i [pt. ii 1821]. P

Tannahill, Robert (d. 1810): Collected Works [other edd.: 1817, 1822, Ramsay 1838, Semple 1873].

Trench, Melesina (1768): Campaspe, and Other Poems. V

West, Sir Edward (1782): Application of Capital to Land. P

Wordsworth (1770): White Doe of Rylstone [incl. Force of Prayer]. V
Poems including Lyrical Ballads, Miscellaneous Pieces, and (revised) Preface. V

Battle of Waterloo (18 June).

Anthony Trollope b.

Richard William Church b.

George Boole b.

Arthur Penrhyn Stanley b.

Byron married.

Thomas Dibdin's anthology, 'London Theatre' (concl. 1818).

'Encyclopaedia Britannica', 5th ed.

'North American Review' started.

Charles Lloyd's trs. of tragedies of Alfieri.

'The Military Adventures of Johnny Newcome' (illustr. by T. Rowlandson and letterpress probably by David Roberts).

Rudolf Ackermann's 'University of Cambridge.'

Benjamin Constant, 'Adolphe'.

Austen (1775): Emma [anon.]. P
Bentham (1748): Defence of Usury. P
    Chrestomathia. P
Byron (1788): Siege of Corinth. V
    Parisina. V
    Prisoner of Chillon and Other Poems.
    Childe Harold, canto iii. V
    Monody on Death of Sheridan. V
    Poems on his Domestic Circumstances.
Coleridge (1772): Christabel, Kubla Khan, Pains
    of Sleep. V
    The Statesman's Manual, a Lay Sermon. P
Cowper (d. 1800): Memoirs of Early Life, written
    by Himself. P
D'Israeli (1766): Character of James I. P
Heber (1783): Christian Comforter. P
Hogg (1770): Poetic Mirror. V
    Madoc of the Moor. V
Holcroft (d. 1809): Memoirs [completed by
    Hazlitt]. P
Hunt (1784): Story of Rimini. V
Johnson (d. 1784): Diary of a Journey into N.
    Wales in 1774. P
Lamb, Lady Caroline (1785): Glenarvon [anon.:
    called the Fatal Passion, 1865]. P
Maturin (1782): Bertram. D
Moore (1779): Sacred Songs. V
    On the Death of Sheridan. V
Morgan, Sydney, Lady (1783): Florence M'Carthy. P
Opie (1769): Valentine's Eve. P
Peacock (1785): Headlong Hall. P
Quillinan, Edward (1771): Sacrifice of Isabel. V
Ramsay, David (1749): The History of the U.S.A. P
Reynolds, John Hamilton (1796): The Naiad and
    Other Poems.
Scott (1771): Antiquary. P
    Tales of my Landlord [Black Dwarf. Old
    Mortality]. P
Shelley (1792): Alastor and Other Poems [see
    1876]. V
Sheridan (d. 1816): Speeches.
Southey (1774): Carmen Nuptiale. V
    Poet's Pilgrimage to Waterloo. V
    Lay of the Laureate. V
Trench, Melesina (1768): Laura's Dream [anon.]. V
Wilson (1785): City of the Plague and Other
    Poems. V
Wordsworth (1770): Letter to a Friend of Burns
    [James Gray]. P
    Thanksgiving Ode [with other short pieces]. V

Charlotte Brontë b.
Philip James Bailey b.
Sir Theodore Martin b.
Richard Brinsley Sheridan d.
Suicide of Harriet Westbrook and Shelley's marriage with Mary Godwin.
Byron's final departure from England.
Coleridge settles at Highgate.
'Albyn's Anthology' (Scottish Songs), ed. A. Campbell.
Robert Surtees's 'History of Durham' (concl. 1840).
Leigh Hunt's essay on Shelley and Keats entitled 'Young Poets' in 'The Examiner', 1 Dec.
Étienne Dumont's 'Tactique des Assemblées legislatives et Traité de Sophismes politiques' from the MSS. of Bentham.
William Gifford's ed. of Ben Jonson.
John Mitford's ed. of Gray.
Jacob & Wilhelm Grimm, 'Deutsche Sagen' (concl. 1818).
Hegel, 'Philosophie des Rechts'.

Bentham (1748): Table of the Springs of Action [prtd. 1815]. P

Brackenridge, Henry Mane (1786): South America. P

Burges, Sir James (1752): Dramas [collected].

Byron (1788): Manfred. V
Lament of Tasso. V

Carter, Elizabeth (d. 1806): Letters to Mrs. Montagu. P

Chesterfield (d. 1773): Letters to A. C. Stanhope on the education of his Godson [see 1890]. P

Cobbett (1762): English Grammar. P

Coleridge (1772): Sibylline Leaves [first publication of marginal glosses on Ancient Mariner]. V.
Blessed are ye that sow, a Lay Sermon. P
A Hebrew Dirge. V
Biographia Literaria. P
Zapolya. A Christmas Tale. D

Combe (1741): Dance of Life. V

Croly, George (1780): Paris in 1815. V

Dibdin, Thomas (1776): Bibliographical Decameron. P

Drake, Nathan (1766): Shakespeare and his Times. P

Edgeworth (1767): Harington, Ormond. P
Comic Dramas.

Frere (1769): Monks and the Giants, cantos i, ii [iii and iv in 1818; collected ed. 1818; original title Prospectus and Specimen of an intended National Work]. V

Godwin (1756): Mandeville. P

Hazlitt (1778): Characters of Shakespeare's Plays. P
The Round Table [from The Examiner, 1815–17: with Leigh Hunt]. P

Hemans (1793): Modern Greece. V

Hogg (1770): Brownie of Bodsbeck. P
Dramatic Tales. P

Hogg, with Lockhart and Wilson: Translations from Ancient Chaldee MSS. [attack on The Edinburgh Review: in Blackwood's Magazine for October. In the same issue of Blackwood's Lockhart and Wilson attack Coleridge, Shelley, Leigh Hunt, and Keats in article 'The Cockney School of Poets'.]

Henry David Thoreau b.
George Henry Lewes b.
Tom Taylor b.
Branwell Brontë b.
Benjamin Jowett b.
Jane Austen d.
William Hone imprisoned.
William Jerdan starts 'The Literary Gazette'.
'The Scotsman' started.
'Blackwood's Magazine' started in April (ed. William Blackwood: first six numbers called 'Edinburgh Monthly Magazine'; in June number Charles Wolfe's 'Burial of Sir John Moore').
Richard Cumberland's anthology 'The British Drama'.
John Thomas Smith, 'Vagabondiana' (with Introduction by Francis Douce).
Arnim, 'Kronenwächter'.
Mme de Staël d.

President U.S.A. Monroe.

Keats (1795): Poems [Sleep and Poetry, I Stood
    Tiptoe, &c.]. V
Maturin (1782): Manuel. T
    Fredolfo. T
Mill (1773): History of British India [ed. with
    continuation by Horace Hayman Wilson,
    1858). P
Moore (1779): Lalla Rookh. V
Nichols, John (senior) (1745): Illustrations of the
    Literary History of the 18th Century [concl.
    1831: continued by Nichols, jnr., 1848–58]. P
Owen, Robert (1771): Report to the Committee
    on the Poor Law. P
Peacock (1785): Melincourt. P
Porter, Anna (1780): Knight of St. John. P
Priestley (d. 1804): Works, with Memoirs and
    Correspondence, ed. Rutt [concl. 1832].
Ricardo (1772): Principles of Political Economy
    and Taxation. P
Scott (1771): Harold the Dauntless. V
    Ballad of the Noble Moringer [in Edinburgh
    Annual Register]. V
Sheil, Richard Lalor (1791): The Apostate. T
Shelley (1792): Proposal for putting Reform to the
    Vote [anon.]. P
  Address to the People on the Death of Princess
    Charlotte. P
  History of a Six Weeks' Tour [with Mrs.
    Shelley]. P
  Laon and Cythna [see 1818]. V
Southey (1774): Wat Tyler [written 1794: a
    pirated and a genuine ed. in 1817]. D
  Letter to W. Smith. P
  Ed. of Malory.
Wolcot (1738): Epistle to Emperor of China. V

Aikin (1781): Memoirs of the Court of Queen Elizabeth. P

Austen (d. 1817): Northanger Abbey, Persuasion [with biography by Henry Austen]. P

Barton (1784): The Convict's Appeal. V
Poems by an Amateur. V

Bowdler, Thomas (1754): The Family Shakespeare.

Burges, Sir James: The Dragon Knight. V

Byron (1788): Childe Harold, canto iv. V
Beppo. V
Suppressed Poems [English Bards and Scotch Reviewers, Land of the Gaul, Windsor Poetics: published by Galignani].

Coleridge (1772): Essay on Method [in Encyclopaedia Metropolitana: reprtd. 1845]. P

Coxe, William (1747): Memoirs of the Duke of Marlborough. P

Dwight, Timothy (d. 1817): Theology Explained. P

Egan (1772): Boxiana, vols. i, ii [iii 1821, iv 1824]. P

Evelyn (d. 1706): Diary 1641–1706, ed. Bray [later edd.: Upcott 1827, Wheatley 1879, 1906, Dobson 1906].

Ferrier, Susan (1782): Marriage. P

Hallam (1777): Europe during the Middle Ages. P

Hazlitt (1778): Lectures on the English Poets. P
Review of the English Stage. P

Hemans (1793): Translations from Camoens and Other Poets. V

Horne, Thomas (1780): Introduction to the Study of the Scriptures. P

James Anthony Froude b.
Emily Brontë b.
John Mason Neale b.
Matthew Gregory Lewis d.
Isaac D'Israeli d.
Shelley's final departure from England. Attack on Keats (probably by Lockhart) in 'Blackwood's Magazine' for August.
Attack on Keats (probably by Gifford) in 'Quarterly Review' in September (in a number dated April: see 1819).

Hunt (1784): Foliage. V
    Literary Pocket Book [miscellany: concl. 1822].
Keats (1795): Endymion. V
Lamb (1775): Collected Works [later fuller col-
    lections: Talfourd 1838–40, Shepherd 1874,
    Fitzgerald 1875, Ainger 1899–1900, Lucas
    1903–5, Macdonald 1903, Hutchinson 1908].
Maturin (1782): Women, or Pour et Contre. P
Milman (1791): Samor. V
Mitford, John ('**Alfred Burton**') (1782): Adven-
    tures of Johnny Newcombe in the Navy
    [illustrated by T. Rowlandson]. V
    Poems of a British Sailor. V
Moore (1779): Fudge Family in Paris. V
Newman (1801): St. Bartholomew's Eve [with
    J. W. Bowden]. V
Opie (1769): New Tales. P
Peacock (1785): Nightmare Abbey. P
    Rhododaphne, or the Thessalian Spell. V
Pocock, Isaac (1782): Rob Roy Macgregor. D
Scott (1771): Tales of my Landlord, 2nd series
    [Rob Roy, Heart of Midlothian]. P
Sheil, Richard Lalor (1791): Bellamira. T
Shelley, Mary (1797): Frankenstein. P
Shelley (1792): Revolt of Islam [originally printed
    as Laon and Cythna, 1817]. V
Sherwood, Mary (1775): Fairchild Family, pt. i
    (ii 1842, iii 1847). P
Sotheby, William (1757): Farewell to Italy, and
    Occasional Poems.
Struthers, John (1776): The Plough. V
Walpole (d. 1797): Letters to George Montagu. P
    Letters to William Cole. P

Balfour, Alexander (1767): Campbell. P

Bentham (1748): Radical Reform Bill. P

Brackenridge, Henry Marie (1786): Voyage to South America. P

Brunton, Mary (d. 1818): Literary Remains [incl. Emmeline] with Correspondence and Life, ed. A. Brunton.

Byron (1788): Mazeppa [with fragment of Vampire]. V

Don Juan, cantos i and ii. V

Crabbe (1754): Tales of the Hall. V

Field, Barron (1786): First Fruits of Australian Poetry. V

Hazlitt (1778): Lectures on English Comic Writers. P

Political Essays, with Sketches of Public Characters. P

Letter to William Gifford [in reply to G.'s attack on Keats: see 1818]. P

Hemans (1793): Tales and Historic Scenes. V

Meeting of Bruce and Wallace. V

Hone, William (1780): Political House that Jack built. P

Hope, Thomas (1770?): Anastasius. P

Hunt (1784): Hero and Leander, Bacchus and Ariadne. V

The Indicator [journal: concl. 1821].

Irving, Washington (1783): Sketch Book. P

Keats (1795): Ode to a Nightingale [in Annals of the Fine Arts, July]. V

Leyden, John (d. 1811): Poetical Remains, ed. with Memoir by James Morton.

Lingard (1771): History of England [concl. 1830]. P

Lloyd, Charles (1775): Nugae Canorae. V

Peterloo massacre.
Queen Victoria b.
Charles Kingsley b.
John Ruskin b.
James Russell Lowell b.
Arthur Hugh Clough b.
Mary Ann Evans ('George Eliot') b.
Herman Melville b.
Walt Whitman b.
John Wolcot ('Peter Pindar') d.
'Harp of Caledonia', ed. John Struthers.
William Whewell's 'Treatise on Mechanics'.
William Tennant's ed. of Allan Ramsay.
Thomas Campbell's 'Specimens of British Poets'.
James Hogg's 'Jacobite Relics of Scotland' (verse anthology, 2nd vol. 1821).
Kotzebue d.
Goethe, 'West-Oestliche divan'.
Schopenhauer, 'Wille und Vorstellung'.

Lockhart (1794): Peter's Letters to his Kinsfolk.
   P
Macaulay (1800): Pompeii. V
Mitford (1787): Our Village [in The Lady's
   Magazine: in book form 1824-6-8-30-2].
Moncrieff, William (1794): Dandy Family. D
Montgomery (1771): Greenland. V
Moore (1779): Tom Crib's Memorial to Congress.
   V
More (1745): Moral Sketches of Prevailing
   Opinions of Manners. P
Procter (1787): Dramatic Scenes, and Other
   Poems. V
Reynolds, John Hamilton (1796): One, Two
   Three, Four, Five. D
   Peter Bell [travesty of Wordsworth's poem]. V
Rogers (1763): Human Life. V
Ross, Sir John (1777): Voyage of Discovery for
   exploring Baffin's Bay and NW. Passage. P
Russell, Lord John (1792): Life of Lord William
   Russell. P
Scott (1771): Tales of my Landlord, 3rd series
   [Bride of Lammermoor. Legend of Mon-
   trose]. P
   Ivanhoe [bears date 1820]. P
   Description of Regalia of Scotland. P
Sheil, Richard Lalor (1791): Evadne. D
Shelley (1792): Rosalind and Helen, and Other
   Poems. V
   Cenci. T
Whately, Richard (1787): Historic Doubts rela-
   tive to Napoleon Buonaparte. P
Wordsworth (1770): Peter Bell [with four son-
   nets]. V
   The Waggoner [with sonnets]. V

Anderson, Robert (1770): Poetical Works.

Barrett, E. B. (Browning) (1806): Battle of Marathon. V

Barton (1784): Poems [2nd ed., with additions, 1821; 4th ed., with additions, 1825].

Belzoni, Giovanni (1778): Observations and Discoveries within Pyramids, Tombs, &c., in Egypt and Nubia. P

Brown, Thomas (d. 1820): Physiology of the Human Mind. P

Collected Poems [cont. Paradise of Coquettes, pub. 1814, Wanderer in Norway, 1815, Warfiend, 1816, Bower of Spring, 1817, Agnes, 1818, Emily, 1819, and Other Poems].

Byron (1788): Marino Faliero. T

Clare (1793): Poems, Descriptive of Rural Life. V

Combe (1741): Second Tour of Dr. Syntax in Search of Consolation [see 1812, 1821]. V

Crabbe (1754): Collected Works [later collections: ed. his son, with letters, journals, and life, 1834, ed. Ward 1905, ed. Carlyle 1908].

Croly, George (1786): Angel of the World. V
May Fair. V

Edgeworth, Richard Lovell (d. 1817): Memoirs [completed by Maria Edgeworth]. P

Foster, John (1770): On the Evils of Popular Ignorance. P

Galt (1779): Ayrshire Legatees. P

Godwin (1756): Of Population, in answer to Mr. Malthus. P

Hemans (1793): The Sceptic. V

Heraud, John (1799): Legend of St. Loy and Other Poems. V
Tottenham, a Poem.

Hogg (1770): Winter Evening Tales. P

Hunt (1784): Trs. Tasso's Amyntas. V

Irving, Washington (1783): The Sketch Book of Geoffrey Crayon. P

Keats (1795): La Belle Dame sans Merci [in The Indicator]. V
Lamia, Isabella, Eve of St. Agnes, Hyperion, and Other Poems. V

Knowles (1784): Virginius. D

Lamb (1775): Essays of Elia [in London Magazine, between Aug. 1820 and Dec. 1822; separately 1823: see 1832]. P

Accession of George IV.
Trial of Queen Caroline.
Anne Brontë b.
Herbert Spencer b.
Ebenezer Jones b.
John Tyndall b.
Dion Boucicault b.?
Jean Ingelow b.
William Hayley d.
'*London Magazine*' (*1820–9*) *started, ed. John Scott, who attacks Lockhart and other critics of* '*Blackwood's*' (*see 1821*).
'*Retrospective Review*' (*1820–8*) *started.*
'*John Bull*' *started, ed. Theodore Hook.*
Charles Knight's weekly, '*The Plain Englishman*' (*1820–2*) *started.*
Blake, '*Inventions to the Book of Job*'.
Lamartine, '*Méditations*'.

Landor (1775): Idyllia Heroica Decem [pub. at Pisa].

Luttrell, Henry (1765?): Advice to Julia [3rd ed. entitled Letters to Julia, 1822]. V

Lytton (1803): Ismael and Other Poems. V

Malthus (1766): Principles of Political Economy [2nd ed., revised, with memoir by Otter, 1836]. P

Maturin (1782): Melmoth the Wanderer. P

Milman (1791): Fall of Jerusalem. D

Moncrieff, William (1794): Lear of the Private Family. D

Moultrie, John (1799): My Brother's Grave. V
Godiva. V

Opie (1769): Tales of the Heart. P

Peacock (1785): Four Ages of Poetry [in Ollier's Literary Pocket Book: provoked Shelley's Defence of Poetry, written 1821, first pub. in Works 1840]. P

Procter (1787): Marcian Colonna, with Three Dramatic Scenes, and Other Poems.
A Sicilian Story and Other Poems.

Reynolds, John Hamilton (1796): The Fancy, or Poetical Remains of Peter Corcoran [cont. Fields of Tothill]. V

Scott (1771): The Monastery. P
The Abbot. P
Miscellaneous Poems, collected [other edd.: 1821–7–30, Lockhart 1833, Palgrave 1866, Rossetti 1870, Robertson 1904, Lang 1905].

Shelley (1792): Œdipus Tyrannus. V
Prometheus Unbound and Other Poems.

Southey (1774): Life of John Wesley. P

Spence (d. 1768): Anecdotes [both Singer's and Malone's edd.]. P

Walpole (d. 1797): First collected ed. of Correspondence [later and fuller collections: Wright 1840, Cunningham 1857–9, Toynbee 1903].

Wordsworth (1770): The River Duddon, a Series of Sonnets. Vaudracour and Julia, and other Poems. Topographical Description of the Country of the Lakes [see 1810, '22].

Baillie (1762): Metrical Legends. V

Beddoes (1803): The Improvisatore, with Other Poems.

Bryant, William Cullen (1794): Poems.

Byron (1788): Prophecy of Dante. V

    Sardanapalus, a Tragedy; The Two Foscari, a Tragedy; Cain, a Mystery.

    Don Juan, iii–v. V

    Letter on W. L. Bowles's Strictures on Pope.

Clare (1793): Village Minstrel, and Other Poems.

Cobbett (1762): Monthly Religious Tracts [afterwards called Twelve Sermons. Concl. 1822]. P

    American Gardener [altered as English Gardener, 1827]. P

    Cottage Economy. P

Combe (1741): Third Tour of Doctor Syntax in Search of a Wife [see 1812, 1820]. V

Cooper, James Fenimore (1789): The Spy. P

De Quincey (1785): Confessions of an Opium Eater [in London Magazine, Oct. and Nov.; separately 1822, enlarg. 1856].

Dibdin, Thomas (1776): Bibliographical Tour in France and Germany. P

Dwight, Timothy (1752): Travels in New England and New York. P

Egan (1772): Life in London [illustr. George and Robert Cruikshank: see 1828]. P

Galt (1779): Annals of the Parish. P

Gifford (1756): Trs. Satires of Persius. V

Hall, John Vine (1774): Sinner's Friend. P

Hazlitt (1778): Lectures on Elizabethan Drama. P

    Table Talk [concl. 1822].

Hunt (1784): The Months. P

Greek War of Liberation begins.

Henry Thomas Buckle b.

George John Whyte-Melville b.

John Keats d.

Hester Lynch (Thrale) Piozzi d.

John Scott, editor of 'London Magazine', killed in duel following controversy with Lockhart and others of 'Blackwood's'.

'Manchester Guardian' started.

Rudolf Ackermann's 'The World in Miniature' (illustr. T. Rowlandson and W. H. Pyne).

John Struthers's 'British Minstrel' (anthology).

William Moncrieff's 'Tom and Jerry', dramatic adaptation of Pierce Egan's 'Life in London' produced.

Goethe, 'Wilhelm Meisters Wanderjahre'.

Baudelaire b.

President U.S.A. Monroe (2nd Term).

Landon (1802): Fate of Adelaide. V
Lloyd, Charles (1775): Desultory Thoughts in London, Titus Gisippus, and Other Poems. V
    Poetical Essays on the Character of Pope. V
Lockhart (1794): Valerius, a Roman Story. P
Macaulay (1800): Evening. V
Malone (d. 1812): Ed. Shakespeare, completed by James Boswell, jnr. [see 1790].
Mill (1773): Elements of Political Economy. P
Parry, William Edward (1790): Journal of a Voyage for Discovery of NW. Passage in 1795–7 [concl. 1824: see 1824, 1826]. P
Procter (1787): Mirandola, a Tragedy. V
Reynolds, John Hamilton (1796): Garden of Florence and Other Poems [incl. Romance of Youth and Sonnets]. V
Russell, Lord John (1798): Essay on English Constitution. P
Scott (1771): Kenilworth. P
    Biographies [in Ballantyne's Novelists]. V
    Account of George IV's Coronation. V
    Edition of Fielding's Novels. V
Shelley (1792): Epipsychidion. V
    Adonais. V
Smith, 'Horace' (1779): Amarynthus the Nympholept. D
Southey (1774): Carmen Triumphale. V
    Vision of Judgment [provoked Byron's Vision of Judgment 1823]. V
    Expedition of Orsua, and the Crimes of Aguirre. P
    Life of Cromwell [in Quarterly Review]. P
Waldegrave, James, Earl (d. 1763): Memoirs [1754–8]. P

Aikin (1781): Memoirs of the Court of James I. P

Barton (1784): Napoleon and Other Poems. V

Beddoes (1803): Bride's Tragedy. D

Bentham (1748): Influence of Natural Religion upon Temporal Happiness. P

Bloomfield (1766): May Day with the Muses. V

Bowles (1762): Grave of the Last Saxon. V

Byron (1788): Werner, a Tragedy.
The Vision of Judgment [in The Liberal: see 1821, Southey]. V

Croly, George (1780): Catiline. T

Cunningham, Allan (1784): Sir Marmaduke Maxwell. D
Traditional Tales of English and Scottish Peasantry.

Darley, George (1795): Errors of Ecstacie. V

De Vere, Sir Aubrey (1788): Julian the Apostate. V

Digby, Kenelm (1800): Broad Stone of Honour [enlarged 1826–7]. P

Galt (1779): Steamboat. P
The Provost. P.　　Sir Andrew Wylie. P

Grattan, Henry (d. 1820): Speeches, ed. his son [ed. Madden 1845]. Miscellaneous Works.

Hemans (1793): Welsh Melodies. V

Hogg (1770): Three Perils of Man. P

Irving, Washington (1783): Bracebridge Hall. P

Lamb, Lady Caroline (1785): Graham Hamilton. P

Lloyd, Charles (1775): Duke d'Ormond. T
Beritola. V

Lockhart (1794): Adam Blair. P

Milman (1791): Martyr of Antioch. V
Belshazzar. V

Opie (1769): Madeline. P

Peacock (1785): Maid Marian. P

Rhodes, William Barnes (1772): Bombasto Furioso. D burlesque.

Rogers (1763): Italy, pt. i (ii 1828; complete 1830). V

Scott (1771): The Pirate. P
Fortunes of Nigel. P
Peveril of the Peak. P.　　Halidon Hill. V

Shelley (1792): Hellas. V lyrical drama.

Walpole (d. 1797): Memoirs of the Last Ten Years of the Reign of George II. P

Wells (1799?): Stories after Nature. V

Wilson (1785): Lights and Shadows of Scottish Life. P

Wilson, Lockhart, Hogg, and Maginn: Noctes Ambrosianae [in Blackwood, 1822–35]. P

Wordsworth (1770): Ecclesiastical Sketches. V
Memorials of a Tour on the Continent. V
Description of the Scenery of the Lakes [see 1810, 1820, 1835]. P

Matthew Arnold b.
Sir Henry Maine b.
Thomas Hughes b.
David Masson b.
Sir Francis Galton b.
Percy Bysshe Shelley d.
Leigh Hunt starts 'The Liberal' (4 nos. 1822–3).
'Sunday Times' started.
Robert Nares's 'Glossary'.
Reginald Heber's ed. of Jeremy Taylor (rev. C. P. Eden 1847–52).
Francis Place's 'Illustrations and Proofs of the Principle of Population'.

Baillie (1762): Poetic Miscellanies [cont. poems by Scott, Mrs. Hemans, Miss Fanshawe, &c.].

Berkeley (d. 1753): Three Dialogues between Hylas and Philonous. P

Bowles (1762): Ellen Gray. V

Bowles, Caroline (1786): Tales of the Factories. V

Byron (1788): Age of Bronze. V
  Island. V
  Don Juan, vi–xiv. V
  Contributions to The Liberal [Vision of Judgment, Letter to the editor of my Grandmother's Review, Epigrams on Castlereagh, Heaven and Earth, The Blues, Morgante Maggiore]. V

Carlyle (1795): Life of Schiller [in London Magazine, 1823–4; separately 1825]. P

Cooper, James Fenimore (1789): The Pioneers. P
  The Pilot. P

De Quincey (1785): Letters to a Young Man whose Education has been neglected [in London Magazine, Jan., Feb., Mar., and May]. P

De Vere, Sir Aubrey (1788): Duke of Mercia. D
  Lamentation of Ireland and Other Poems. V

Franklin, Sir John (1786): Narrative of a Journey to Polar Sea in 1819–22 [see 1828]. P

Galt (1779): The Entail. P
  Gathering of the West. P

Hazlitt (1778): Liber Amoris. P
  Characteristics. P

Hogg (1770): Three Perils of Women. P

Hunt (1784): Literary Examiner [27 nos.].
  Ultra-Crepidarius, a Satire on W. Gifford. V

Lamb, Lady Caroline (1785): Ada Reis, a Tale. P

Lamb (1775): Essays of Elia [collected: see 1820, 1833]. P

Lloyd, Charles (1775): Poems.

Lockhart (1794): Reginald Dalton. P
  Ancient Spanish Ballads [trs.]. V

Lytton (1803): Delmour and Other Poems.

Mitford (1787): Julian. D

Moore (1779): Fables for the Holy Alliance. V
  Loves of the Angels. V

Procter (1787): Flood of Thessaly, Girl of Provence and Other Poems.

Scott (1771): Quentin Durward. P

Shelley (d. 1822): Poetical Pieces. V

Shelley, Mary (1797): Valperga. P

Southey (1774): History of Peninsular War [concl. 1832].

Tennant, William (1784): Cardinal Bethune. T

Watts (1797): Poetical Sketches. V

Wilson (1785): Trials of Margaret Lyndsay. P

Edward Augustus Freeman b.
Charlotte Mary Yonge b.
Coventry Patmore b.
Friedrich Max Müller b.
Ann Radcliffe d.
Bannatyne Club founded, with Scott as president.
'Encyclopaedia Britannica', 6th ed.
Jeremy Bentham's 'Rationale of Judicial Evidence' in Dumont's 'Traité des preuves judiciaires' (see 1827).
Dumont's 'De l'organisation judiciaire et codification' (based on Bentham's MSS.).
John Cumberland's 'BritishTheatre'(anthology).
William Whewell's 'Treatise on Dynamics'.
Joseph Bosworth's 'Anglo-Saxon Grammar'.
William Stewart Rose's trs. of 'Orlando Inamorato' (concl. 1831).
'The Lancet' (weekly).
Lamartine, 'Nouvelles Méditations'.
Renan b.

Barton (1784): Poetic Vigils. V

Bentham (1748): Book of Fallacies. P

Byron (d. 1824): Don Juan, xv–xvi. V
Deformed transformed. V

Campbell (1777): Theodoric and Other Poems.

Carlyle (1795): Trs. Goethe's Wilhelm Meister's Apprenticeship [see 1827]. P

Cobbett (1762): History of the Protestant Reformation [concl. 1827]. P

De Quincey (1785): Dialogue of the Three Templars [in London Magazine, Apr. and May]. P

Ferrier (1782): Inheritance. P

Godwin (1756): History of the Commonwealth of England [concl. 1828]. P

Gore, Catherine (1799): Theresa Marchmont. P

Hazlitt (1778): Sketches of the Principal Picture-galleries of England [enlarg. as Criticisms on Art, 1843–4].

Hogg (1770): Confessions of a Justified Sinner [later called ' Of a Fanatic ']. P

Irving, Washington (1783): Tales of a Traveller. P

Johnson, John (1777): Typographia, or the Printer's Instructor. P

Landon (1802): Improvisatrice. V

Landor (1775): Imaginary Conversations, i, ii [iii–iv 1828, v 1829]. P

Lockhart (1794): History of Matthew Wald. P

Maturin (1782): Albigenses. P

Medwin, Thomas (1788): Journal of Conversations with Lord Byron.

Mitford (1787): Our Village [concl. 1832]. P

Moncrieff, William (1794): Cataract of the Ganges. D

Moore (1779): Memoirs of Captain Rock. P

Morier, James (1780 ?): The Adventures of Hajji Baba of Ispahan. P

Parry, William Edward (1790): Journal of a Second Voyage for Discovery of NW. Passage in 1821–3 [see 1821, 1826].

Scott (1771): Redgauntlet. P
St. Ronan's Well. P
Ed. Richardson's Novels.

Shelley (d. 1822): Posthumous Poems, ed. Mary Shelley [incl. Julian and Maddalo, Witch of Atlas, Triumph of Life, Epistle to Maria Gisborne].

Southey (1774): Book of the Church. P

Thompson, William (1785 ?): Enquiry into the Principles of the Distribution of Wealth. P

Wells (1799): Joseph and his Brethren [by ' H. L. Howard ': revised by Swinburne 1876]. V

George MacDonald b.

Sydney Thompson Dobell b.

Francis Turner Palgrave b.

William Wilkie Collins b.

William Allingham b.

Lord Byron d.

'Westminster Review' started (later amalgamated with 'London Review').

'The Literary Souvenir' started (ed. Alaric Watts; concl. 1838).

'Grimm's Tales' (concl. 1826; illustr. G. Cruikshank).

William Roscoe's ed. of Pope.

Bentham (1748): Rationale of Reward [from the Fr. of Étienne Dumont: see 1811]. P
Brougham, Henry (1778): Practical Observations on Education. P
Byron (d. 1824): Correspondence, ed. R. C. Dallas.
Coleridge (1772): Aids to Reflection. P
Coleridge, Sara (1802): Trs. Bayard's Memoirs.
Conder, Josiah (1789): Modern Traveller. P
Croker, Thomas Crofton (1798): Fairy Legends and Traditions of South Ireland. P
Cunningham, Allan (1784): Songs of Scotland. V
De Quincey (1785): Walladmor. P
Egan (1772): Life of an Actor. P
Galt (1779): The Omen. P
Gamba, Count Peter: Lord Byron's Last Journey. P
Hazlitt (1778): Spirit of the Age. P
Select Poets of Great Britain. V
Hemans (1793): Forest Sanctuary [2nd ed. 1829 cont. Casabianca]. V
Lays of Many Lands. V
Hood (1799) and Reynolds (1796): Odes and Addresses to Great People. V
Knowles (1784): William Tell. D
Landon (1802): The Troubadour and Other Poems.
Lauder, Sir Thomas (1784): Lochindhu. P
Lytton (1803): Sculpture. V
Macaulay (1800): Essay on Milton (in Edin. Rev.). P
McCulloch, John Ramsay (1789): Principles of Political Economy. P
Mill, James (1773): Essays on Government [concl. 1828].
Moore (1775): Life of Sheridan. P
Evenings in Greece. V
Nicholson, John (1790): Airedale in Ancient Times. V
Opie (1769): Tales of the Pemberton Family.
Pepys (d. 1703): Diary, ed. Smith and Braybrook [later edd.: 1828–48–54; Bright (with new material) 1875–9; Wheatley 1893–9].
Scott (1771): The Betrothed, The Talisman. P
Smith, 'Horace' (1779): Gaieties and Gravities. P
Sotheby, William (1757): Poems.
Southey (1774): Tale of Paraguay. V
Wade, Thomas (1805): Tasso, and Other Poems.
Walpole (d. 1797): Letters to Earl of Hertford and Rev. Henry Zouch [in Works, vol. ix].
Ward, Robert Plumer (1765): Tremaine. P
Waterton, Charles (1782): Wanderings in South America. P
Wilson (1785): The Foresters. P
Wolfe, Charles (d. 1823): Remains.

Thomas Henry Huxley b
William Stubbs b.
Richard Doddridge Blackmore b.
Anna Barbauld d.
Samuel Parr d.
Charles Molloy Westmacott's 'The English Spy' (illustr. R. Cruikshank, T. Rowlandson and others).
John Poole's 'Paul Pry' acted.
Alexander Dyce's 'Specimens of British Poetesses' (anthology).
Richter d.

President U.S.A.
John   Quincey
Adams.

Baillie (1762): The Martyr. T
Barrett, E. B. (Browning) (1806): Essay on Mind, with Other Poems.
Barton (1784): Devotional Verse.
Bowdler, Thomas: Gibbon's Decline and Fall, with omissions of passages of irreligious or immoral tendency. P
Cooper, James Fenimore (1789): The Last of the Mohicans. P
Darley, George (1795): Labours of Idleness. P
De Quincey (1785): Trs. Lessing's Laocoon [in Blackwood's, Nov.]. P
Disraeli (1804): Vivian Grey, pt. i [ii. 1827]. P
    Modern Dunciad [in Star Chamber]. V
Galt (1779): Last of the Lairds. P
Gleig (1796): The Subaltern. P
Grant Duff, James (1798): History of the Mahrattas. P
Hazlitt (1778): The Plain Speaker. P
    Journey through France and Italy. P
    Conversations of James Northcote [in Colburn's New Monthly Magazine; separately 1830; ed. Gosse 1894]. P
Hogg (1770): Queen Hynde. V
Hood (1799): Whims and Fancies, 1st series [see 1827]. P and V
Hook, Theodore (1788): Sayings and Doings [collective title for Passion and Principle, Cousin William, Gervase Skinner, Martha the Gipsy, and five other novels pub. between 1826 and 1829]. P
Jameson, Anna (1794): Diary of an Ennuyée. P
Lister, Thomas Henry (1800): Granby. P
Macnish, Robert (1802): Metempsychosis [in Blackwood's]. P
Milman (1791): Anne Boleyn. V
Mitford (1787): Foscari. T
Montgomery (1771): Pelican Island. V
Parry, William Edward (1790): Journal of a Third Voyage for Discovery of NW. Passage in 1824–5 [see 1821, 1824].
Patmore, Peter (1786): Rejected Articles. P
Porter, Jane and Anna: Tales round a Winter Hearth. P
Scott (1771): Woodstock. P
Shelley, Mary (1797): The Last Man. P
Smith, 'Horace' (1779): Brambletye House. P
    Tor Hill. P
Southey (1774): Vindiciae Ecclesiae Anglicanae. P
Turner (1768): History of the Reign of Henry VIII. P
Whately, Richard (1787): Logic. P

Walter Bagehot b.
William Gifford d.
Reginald Heber d.
'Encyclopaedia Metropolitana'.
William Hone's 'Everyday Book' (concl. 1827).
Samuel Singer's ed. of Shakespeare.
Archibald Constable's 'Miscellany of original and selected publications' (concl. 1835).
Burke's 'Peerage and Baronetage', 1st ed.

Barton (1784): Widow's Tale and Other Poems.
Bentham (1748): Rationale of Evidence, ed. J. S. Mill [see 1823]. P
Burke (d. 1797): Correspondence with Dr. French Laurence.
Carlyle (1795): German Romance [vol. i Musaeus and Fouqué; ii Tieck and Hoffman; iii Richter; iv Wilhelm Meister]. P
  Wotton Reinfried, Fragment of a Novel. P
Clare (1793): Shepherd's Calendar. V
Cooper, James Fenimore (1789): The Prairie. P
Crowe, William (1745): English Versification. P
Dana, Richard Henry (1787): The Buccaneer and Other Poems.
Darley, George (1795): Sylvia, or the May Queen. V
De Quincey (1785): Murder as one of the Fine Arts, pt. i [in Blackwood's]. P
Digby, Sir Kenelm (d. 1665): Private Memoirs. P
Egan (1772): Anecdotes of the Turf. P
Hallam (1777): Constitutional History. P
Hare, Julius and Augustus: Guesses at Truth. P
Heber (d. 1826): Hymns. V
Hood (1799): Plea of Midsummer Fairies. V
  Whims and Oddities, 2nd series. P and V
  National Tales.
Keble (1792): Christian Year. V
Landon (1802): Golden Violet. V
Luttrell, Henry (1765 ?): Crockford House. V
Lytton (1803): Falkland. P
  O'Neil, or the Rebel. V
Macnish, Robert (1802): Anatomy of Drunkenness. P
Mitford (1787): Dramatic Scenes, Sonnets, &c. V
Moore (1779): The Epicurean. P
Poe (1809): Tamerlane and Other Poems. V
Pollok, Robert (1798): The Course of Time. V
Scott (1771): Chronicles of the Canongate [Highland Widow, Two Drovers, Surgeon's Daughter]. P
  Life of Napoleon Buonaparte. P
  Miscellaneous Prose Works [later edd.: 1834–71, 1836].
  Ed. George Bannatyne Miscellany.
Smith, 'Horace' (1779): Reuben Apsley. P
Stewart (1753): Philosophy of the Human Mind, vol. iii [see 1792, 1814]. P
Taylor, Sir Henry (1800): Isaac Comnenus. D
Tennyson (1809): Poems by Two Brothers [with Charles Tennyson].
Ward, Robert Plumer (1765): De Vere, or the Man of Independence. P

University of London founded.
Edward Bradley ('Cuthbert Bede') b.
William Blake d.
Helen Maria Williams d.
Thomas Arnold becomes Head Master of Rugby.
'The Evening Standard' started.
William John Thoms's ed. of Early English Prose Romances (concl. 1828).
William Gifford's ed. of John Ford.
William Hone's 'Table Book' (concl. 1828).

Barton (1784): A New Year's Eve. V

Blanchard, S. L. (1804): Lyric Offerings. V

Bowles (1762): Days Departed. V

Bury, Lady Charlotte (1775): Flirtation. P

Carlyle (1795): Essay on Burns [in Edinburgh Review, Dec.].

Combe, George (1788): Constitution of Man. P

Cooper, James Fenimore (1789): The Red Rover. P

Disraeli (1804): Voyage of Captain Popanilla. P

D'Israeli (1766): Life and Reign of Charles I. P

Drake, Nathan (1766): Memorials of Shakespeare. P

Egan (1772): Finish to the Adventures of Tom, Jerry, and Logic [concl. of Life in London, 1821; illustr. R. Cruikshank]. P

Franklin, John (1786): a Second Expedition to the Polar Sea in 1825-7 [see 1823]. P

Hazlitt (1778): Life of Napoleon Buonaparte, vols. i–ii [iii–iv 1830; i–iv complete 1852]. P

Heber (d. 1826): Journey through India. P

Hemans (1793): Records of Women and Other Poems.

Hunt (1784): Lord Byron and his Contemporaries. P

The Companion [28 nos.].

Landor, Robert Eyres (1781): Impious Feast. V

Landor (1775): Imaginary Conversations, iii–iv [see 1824]. P

Lockhart (1794): Life of Robert Burns. P

Lytton (1803): Pelham. P

Malcolm, Sir John: Sketches of Persia. P

Moir, David Macbeth (1798): Mansie Wauch. P

Montgomery, Robert (1807): Omnipresence of the Deity. V

Moore (1779): Odes upon Cash, Corn, Catholics. V

Morier (1780?): Hajji Baba in England. P

Napier (1785): History of Peninsular War. P

Parr, Samuel (d. 1825): Collected Works.

Parry, William Edward (1790): Narrative of an Attempt to reach the N. Pole. P

Scott (1771): Tales of a Grandfather, 1st series [see 1829, 1830]. P

Chronicles of Canongate, 2nd series [cont. Fair Maid of Perth]. P

My Aunt Margaret's Mirror, The Tapestried Chamber, The Laird's Jock [in The Keepsake]. P

Religious Discourses by a Layman. P

Smith, John Thomas (1766): Nollekens and his Times [ed. Edmund Gosse 1894]. P

Stewart (d. 1828): Philosophy of the Active and Moral Powers of Man. P

Tytler (1791): History of Scotland. P

Whately, Richard (1787): Rhetoric. P

Dante Gabriel Rossetti b.

George Meredith b.

Mrs. Margaret Oliphant b.

Dugald Stewart d.

'The Spectator' (weekly) started.

'The Athenaeum' (weekly) started.

Thomas Richardson's 'New Minor Drama' (anthology: concl. 1831).

Alaric Watts's 'Poetical Album and Register of Modern Fugitive Poetry', 1st series (2nd series 1829).

Julius Hare, Connop Thirlwell, and others, trs. Niebuhr's 'History of Rome' (concl. 1832).

Washington Irving, 'History of the Life and Voyages of Christopher Columbus'.

William Taylor, 'Historic Survey of German Poetry, with Translations' (concl. 1830).

Taine b.

Adams, John Quincey (1767): Correspondence. P
Arnold (1795): Sermons [later collections: Christian Life, 1841–2; Interpretation of Scriptures, 1845. Collected ed. 1878]. P
Carlyle (1795): Signs of the Times [in Edinburgh Review, June]. P
Croly, George (1780): Salathiel. P
Cunningham, Allan (1784): Lives of British Painters [concl. 1833]. P
Dibdin, Thomas: The Library Companion. P
Elliott (1781): Village Patriarch. V
Fanshawe, Lady Anne (d. 1680): Memoirs written by herself, with extracts from Correspondence of Sir Richard Fanshawe. P
Heber (d. 1826): Sermons preached in England.
Hogg (1770): The Shepherd's Calendar. V
Hood (1799): Eugene Aram's Dream [in The Gem]. V
  Epping Hunt. V
Irving, Washington (1783): Chronicle of the Conquest of Granada. P
Jefferson (d. 1826): Autobiography.
Jerrold (1803): Black-eyed Susan [acted]. D
Landon (1802): Venetian Bracelet. V
Landor (1775): Imaginary Conversations, v [see 1824]. P
Lytton (1803): The Disowned. P
  Devereux. P
Marryat (1792): Frank Mildmay. P
Mill, James (1773): Analysis of the Human Mind. P
Milman (1791): History of the Jews. P
Peacock (1785): Misfortunes of Elphin. P
Poole, John (1786 ?): Lodgings for Single Gentlemen [acted]. D
Scott, Michael (1789): Tom Cringle's Log [in Blackwood's, Sept. 1829–Aug. 1833; separately, 1836]. P
Scott (1771): Anne of Geierstein. P
  History of Scotland [concl. 1830]. P
  Tales of a Grandfather, 2nd series. P
Southey, Caroline (1786): Chapters on Church Yards. V
Southey (1774): Sir Thomas More. P
  All for Love, Pilgrim to Compostella. V
Taylor, Isaac (1787): Natural History of Enthusiasm. P
Tennyson (1809): Timbuctoo. V
Turner (1768): History of the Reigns of Edward VI, Mary, and Elizabeth. P
Wade, Thomas (1805): Woman's Love. D

Samuel Rawson Gardiner b.
Thomas William Robertson b.
Charles Knight's 'Library of Entertaining Knowledge'.
Murray's 'Family Library'.
Sir William Hamilton's article, 'The Philosophy of the Unconditioned', in 'Edinburgh Review', October.

President U.S.A. Jackson.

Alcott, Amos Bronson (1799): Infant Instruction. P
Bentham (1748): Rationale of Punishment. P
    Constitutional Code for All Nations. P
Byron (d. 1824): Letters and Journals, with Life
    by Thomas Moore [see 1832].
Carleton, William (1794): Traits and Stories of
    the Irish Peasantry, 1st series [2nd 1833; new
    ed. with notes and illustrations 1843-4]. P
Channing, William Ellery (1780): Remarks on
    American Literature. P
Cobbett (1762): Rural Rides. P
    Advice to Young Men. P
Coleridge (1772): On Constitution of Church and
    State. P
Forster, Thomas (ed.): Original Letters of Locke,
    Sidney, and Shaftesbury.
Frere (1769): Fables for Five Years Old. P
Galt (1779): Lawrie Todd. P
    Life of Byron. P
Godwin (1756): Cloudesley, a Tale. P
Gore, Catherine (1799): Manners of the Day. P
Hemans (1793): Songs of the Affection. V
Heraud, John Abraham: Descent into Hell. V
Herschel, Sir John (1792): Preliminary Discourse
    on the Study of Natural Philosophy. P
Hood (1799): Comic Annual [1830-9; 1842].
Hook, Theodore (1788): Maxwell. P
Hunt (1784): The Tatler [Sept. 1830-Feb. 1832].
    Chat of the Week [13 nos.].
James, G. P. R. (1799): De l'orme. P
Jerrold (1803): Sally in our Alley [acted]. C
Keightley, Thomas (1789): History of the War of
    Greek Independence. P
Lamb (1775): Album Verses.
Lyell, Sir Charles (1797): Principles of Geology
    [concl. 1833]. P
Lytton (1803): Paul Clifford. P
Macaulay (1800): Essay on Robert Montgomery
    (in Edin. Rev.). P
Mackintosh (1765): History of England. P
    Life of Sir Thomas More. P
    Progress of Ethical Philosophy [in Encyclo-
        paedia Britannica; separately, ed. Whewell,
        1836]. P
Maginn, William (1793): Gallery of Illustrious
    Literary Characters [in Fraser's Magazine,
    1830-8; separately 1873]. P
Marryat (1792): King's Own. P
Martineau (1802): Traditions of Palestine. P
Mitford (1787): Stories of American Life. P
Montgomery, Robert (1807): Satan. V
    Puffiad. V

Accession of William IV.
Reform Bill, 1830-2.
Christina Rossetti b.
Alexander Smith b.
Henry Kingsley b.
Thomas Edward Brown b.
William Hazlitt d.
'Fraser's Magazine'
    (1830-82; followed
    by Longman's Maga-
    zine).
Lardner's 'Cabinet Cyclo-
    paedia' (concl. 1849)
    and 'Cabinet Library'
    (concl. 1832).
'Encyclopaedia Britan-
    nica', 7th ed. (concl.
    1842).
French 'Revolution of
    July'.
Comte, 'Cours de philo-
    sophie positive'.
Hugo, 'Hernani'.

Moore (1779): Legendary Ballads. V
  Life of Byron [see Byron, above]. P
Scott (1771): Letters on Demonology and Witch-
    craft [in Murray's Family Library]. P
  House of Aspen [in The Keepsake].
  Doom of Devorgoil, Auchindrane. D
  Essays on Ballad Poetry. P
  Tales of a Grandfather, series III and IV
    [England and France].
Shelley, Mary (1797): Perkin Warbeck. P
Tennyson (1809): Poems, chiefly Lyrical.
Wade, Thomas (1805): Jew of Arragon. D
Webster, Daniel (1782): Speeches of Forensic
    Arguments. P

1831

Bell, Henry Glassford (1803): Summer and Winter
    Hours. V
Brewster, Sir David (1781): Treatise on Optics. P
Collier, John Payne (1789): History of English
    Dramatic Poetry and Annals of the Stage. P
Disraeli (1804): The Young Duke. P
Elliott (1781): Corn-Law Rhymes. V
  Love, a Poem.
Erskine, Thomas (1788): The Brazen Serpent. P
Ferrier (1782): Destiny. P
Galt (1779): Lives of the Players. P
Garrick (d. 1779): Private Correspondence, ed.
    with Memoir by Boaden [concl. 1832.
    Further unpub. correspondence, ed. G. P.
    Baker, 1907].
Godwin (1756): Thoughts on Man. P
Gore, Catherine (1799): School for Coquettes. C
  Mothers and Daughters. P
Grote (1794): Parliamentary Reform. P
Hogg (1770): Songs. V
Landon (1802): Romance and Reality. P
Lover, Samuel (1797): Legends and Stories of
    Ireland. P
Macaulay (1800): Essay on Boswell [in Edin.
    Rev.]. P
Moore (1779): Summer Fête. V
  Life of Lord Edward Fitzgerald. P
Peacock (1785): Crotchet Castle. P
Poe (1809): Al Araaf, Tamerlane, and Other
    Poems. V.   Poems. V
Porter, Jane (1776): Sir Edward Seaward's Narra-
    tive of his Shipwreck. P
Trelawny, Edward John (1792): Adventures of a
    Younger Son. P
Whitehead, Charles (1804): The Solitary. V
Whittier (1807): Legends of New England. V

*William Hale White
  ('Mark Rutherford') b.*
*Edward Robert Bulwer,
  Earl Lytton ('Owen
  Meredith') b.*
*Charles Stuart Calverley
  b.*
Henry Mackenzie d.
William Roscoe d.
*First meeting of the British
  Association.*
*John Cumberland's
  'Minor Theatre' (anth.).*
*Charles Knight's 'Results
  of Machinery' and
  'Capital and Labour'
  (reprtd. together as
  'Knowledge is Power',
  1855).*
*John Wilson Croker ed.
  Boswell's 'Life of John-
  son'.*
*Sotheby, trs. of Homer
  [concl. 1834].*
Hegel d.

Austin, John (1790): Province of Jurisprudence. P

Bell, Henry Glassford (1803): My Old Portfolio. V

Brackenridge, Henry Marie (1786): Letters to the Public. P

Bryant, William Cullen (1794): Poems.

Burney, Frances (1752): Memoirs of Dr. Burney. P

Byron (d. 1824): Works, with Letters, Journals, and Life by Thomas Moore [concl. 1835. New and rev. ed., E. H. Coleridge and Prothero, 1898–1904].

Darwin (1809): Narrative of the Surveying Voyages of H.M.S. Adventure and Beagle [concl. 1836; 2nd ed. 1845; 3rd ed. 1860].

De Quincey (1785): Klosterheim. P

Disraeli (1804): Contarini Fleming. P

Genest, John: Account of the English Stage. P

Hawker (1803): Records of the Western Shore. V

Hunt (1784): Poetical Works [2nd ed. 1844; ed. L. S. Adams 1857; Thornton Hunt 1860; Milford 1922].

    Sir Ralph Esher. P

    Christianism [privately prtd. Reissued as Religion of the Heart 1853]. P

Irving, Washington (1783): The Alhambra. P

James, G. P. R.: Henry Masterton. P

Jameson, Anna (1794): Characteristics of Women. P

Jerrold (1803): Rent Day. D

Knowles (1784): The Hunchback. D

Lytton (1803): Eugene Aram. P

Martineau (1802): Illustrations of Political Economy [concl. 1834]. P

Montgomery, Robert (1807): The Messiah. V

Procter (1787): English Songs. V

Scott (1771): Tales of My Landlord, 4th series [Count Robert of Paris. Castle Dangerous]. P

Shelley (d. 1822): Masque of Anarchy [with Preface by Leigh Hunt]. V

Stanhope, Fifth Earl (1805): History of the War of Succession in Spain. P

Tennyson (1809): Poems [Lady of Shalott, Miller's Daughter, Œnone, Palace of Art, Lotos-Eaters, Dream of Fair Women, &c.: bears date 1833].

Trollope, Frances (1780): Domestic Manners of the Americans. P

Warren, Samuel (1807): Passages from the Diary of a Late Physician [concl. 1838; originally in Blackwood's from 1830]. P

Charles Lutwidge Dodgson ('Lewis Carroll') b.

Sir Leslie Stephen b.

Theodore Watts-Dunton b.

Sir Edwin Arnold b.

Sir Walter Scott d.

Jeremy Bentham d.

George Crabbe d.

Sir James Mackintosh d.

'Chambers's Journal.'

'Tait's Edinburgh Magazine.'

Hugh James Rose founds 'The British Magazine' (concl. 1849).

Robert Chambers's 'Biographical Dictionary of Eminent Scotsmen' (concl. 1834).

Benjamin Thorpe's ed. of Cædmon with Eng. translation and notes.

Goethe d.

President U.S.A. Jackson (2nd Term).

Aikin, Lucy (1781): Memoirs of the Court of Charles I. P

Alison, Sir Archibald (1792): History of Europe, 1789–1815 [concl. 1842: see 1852]. P

Barrett, E. B. (Browning) (1806): Prometheus Bound, trs. from Æschylus [cont. miscellaneous poems: see 1850]. V

Browning, R. (1812): Pauline. V

Carlyle (1795): Sartor Resartus [in Fraser's Magazine, Nov. 1833–Aug. 1834; separately 1838]. P

Coleridge, Hartley (1796): Poems [Leonard and Susan, Sonnets].

   Biographia Borealis [called Worthies of Yorkshire and Lancashire 1836]. P

Dana, Richard Henry (1787): Poems and Prose Writings.

Disraeli (1804): Wondrous Tale of Alroy, Rise of Iskander. P

   Ixion in Heaven [in Colburn's New Monthly]. P

Hayward, Abraham (1801): Trs. Goethe's Faust. P

Hemans (1793): Hymns on the Works of Nature. V

Knowles (1784): The Wife. D

Lamb (1775): Last Essays of Elia. P

Lytton (1803): Godolphin. P

   England and the English. P

Macaulay (1800): Essay on Walpole [in Edin. Rev.]. P

Montgomery, Robert (1807): Woman, and Other Poems.

Moore (1779): Travels of an Irish Gentleman in Search of a Religion. P

Newman (1801): Arians of the Fourth Century. P

Newman, Pusey, John and Thomas Keble, R. H. Froude, Marriott, Palmer, Perceval: Tracts for the Times [90 nos. from 1833 to 1841]. P

Nyren, John: The Young Cricketer's Tutor. P

Shelley (d. 1822): Shelley Papers, with Memoir by Thomas Medwin.

Southey (1774): Lives of British Admirals [contd. by W. Bell 1840]. P

   Ed. Works of Cowper.

Walpole (d. 1797): Letters to Sir Horace Mann, 1741–60, ed. Dover [see 1843].

Hannah More d.
William Wilberforce d.
Arthur Henry Hallam d.
Richard Watson Dixon b.
The Oxford Movement commences with Keble's sermon, 'National Apostasy', on 14 July.
Charles Knight's 'Penny Cyclopaedia' (concl. 1844).

Ainsworth (1805): Rookwood. P

Bancroft, George (1800): History of the United States, vol. i [completed in 10 vols. in 1874].

Beckford (1759): Letters from Various Parts of Europe [incl. those of 1783 repub. with omissions, and adding new letters from Spain and Portugal]. P

Bentham (d. 1832): Deontology, ed. John Bowring. P

Blessington, Lady (1789): Conversations with Lord Byron. P

Brackenridge, Henry Marie (1786): Recollections. P

Brydges, Egerton (1762): Autobiography. P

Campbell (1777): Life of Mrs. Siddons. P

Crabbe (d. 1832): Poetical Works [cont. Letters, Journals, and Unpub. Poems, ed., with Life, by his son, see 1820; with more unpub. poems, ed. Ward, 1905].

Cunningham, Allan (1784): Ed. of Burns.

Disraeli (1804): Infernal Marriage [in Colburn's New Monthly]. P

Revolutionary Epic. V

Edgeworth (1767): Helen. P.   Orlandino. P

Elliott, Charlotte (1789): The Invalid's Hymn Book. V

Godwin (1756): Lives of Necromancers. P

Hallam, Arthur Henry (d. 1833): Essays and Remains.

Heraud, John (1799): Judgment of the Flood. V

Hogg (1770): Familiar Anecdotes of Sir Walter Scott. P

Hood (1799): Tylney Hall. P

Hunt (1784): Leigh Hunt's London Journal [concl. 1835].

The Indicator and The Companion [selections].

Landor (1775): Citation and Examination of William Shakespeare touching deer-stealing. Conference of Edmund Spenser with the Earl of Essex. P

Lytton (1803): Last Days of Pompeii. P

Marryat (1792): Peter Simple. P

Jacob Faithful. P

Martineau (1802): Illustrations of Taxation. P

More (d. 1833): Memoirs of Life and Correspondence, ed. Roberts.

Myers, Frederic (1811): Catholic Thoughts [privately printed. First pub. 1873]. P

Place, Francis (1771): Improvement of the Working People. P

Planché (1796): History of British Costumes. P

Pringle, Thomas (1789): African Sketches. P and V

William Morris b.
Lord Acton b.
Sir John Seeley b.
George Du Maurier b.
James Thomson b.
Henry James Byron b.
Charles Farrar Browne b.
Samuel Taylor Coleridge d.
Charles Lamb d.
Thomas Malthus d.
Augustus Hare d.
Surtees Society founded.
William Thomas Lowndes, 'Bibliographer's Manual'.

Scott, Michael (1789): Cruise of the Midget [in Blackwood's, Mar. 1834–June 1835; separately 1836].

Sigourney, Lydia Huntley (1791): Letters to Young Ladies.
Poems.

Somerville, Mary (1780): Connection of the Physical Sciences. P

Southey (1774): The Doctor [concl. 1847; vols. vi and vii, ed. J. W. Warter]. P

Taylor, Sir Henry (1800): Philip von Artevelde. D

Whitehead, Charles (1804): Autobiography of Jack Ketch. P
Lives and Exploits of English Highwaymen. P

Wilson, John Mackay (1804): Tales of the Borders [concl. 1840]. P

1835

Browning, R. (1812): Paracelsus. V

Callcott, Maria, Lady (1785): Little Arthur's History of England. P

Channing, William Ellery (1780): Slavery. P

Clare (1793): The Rural Muse. V

Cobbett (d. 1835): Legacy to Parsons. P
Legacy to Labourers. P

Coleridge (d. 1834): Specimens of Table Talk, ed. H. N. Coleridge [enlarg. ed. T. Ashe 1884].

Coleridge, Hartley (1796): Lives of Illustrious Worthies. P

Darley (1795): Nepenthe. V

Dickens (1812): Sketches by Boz, 1st series. P

Hunt (1784): Captain Sword and Captain Pen. V

Longfellow (1807): Outre Mer. P

Lytton (1803): Rienzi. P

Mitford (1787): Belford Regis. P

Moore (1779): The Fudges in England. V
History of Ireland [concl. 1846]. P

Procter (1787): Life of Edmund Kean. P

Shelley, Mary (1797): Lodore. P

Simms, William Gilmore (1806): The Yemassee. P
The Partisan. P

Thirlwall, Connop (1797): History of Greece [concl. 1844].

Wade, Thomas (1805): Mundi et Cordis Carmina. V

Wordsworth (1770): Yarrow Revisited, and Other Poems.
Lines after the Death of Charles Lamb [n.d.]. V
Guide through the Lakes [enlarg. from Description of Scenery of the Lakes, 1822]. P

Alfred Austin b.
Samuel Clemens ('Mark Twain') b.
Samuel Butler b.
Walter Skeat b.
James Hogg (Ettrick Shepherd) d.
William Cobbett d.
Felicia Dorothea Hemans d.
Chambers's 'Information for the People'.
Vigny, 'Chatterton'.

Bayly, Thomas Haynes (1797): Perfection, a Farce.
Bowles, Caroline (1786): The Birthday. V
Browning, R. (1812): Porphyria's Lover, Johannes Agricola [in Monthly Repository]. V
Channing, William Ellery (1780): Abolitionist. P
Coleridge (d. 1834): Literary Remains, ed. H. N. Coleridge [concl. 1838]. P and V
Letters, Conversations, and Recollections, by T. Allsop. P
Croker (1780): Johnsoniana.
Dickens (1812): Sketches by Boz, 2nd series. P
Pickwick Papers [monthly from April 1836 to Nov. 1837; collected 1837]. P
Emerson (1803): Nature. P
Forster, John (1812): Lives of the Statesmen of the Commonwealth, vol. i [complete 1840]. P
Gore, Catherine (1799): Mrs. Armytage. P
Diary of a Désennuyée. P
Hazlitt (d. 1830): Literary Remains, with Memoir by his son [see 1839].
Holmes, Oliver Wendell (1809): Poems. V
Hook, Theodore (1788): Jack Brag. P
Landon (1802): Traits and Trials of Early Life. P
Landor (1775): Pericles and Aspasia. P and V
Satire on Satirists and Admonition to Detractors [on Wordsworth]. P
Lane, Edward William (1801): Manners and Customs of Modern Egyptians. P
Lockhart (1794): Life of Scott [concl. 1838]. P
Lytton (1803): Duchesse de la Vallière. D
Mahony, Francis Sylvester (1804): Reliques of Father Prout [enlarg. 1860: see 1876].
Marryat (1792): Mr. Midshipman Easy. P
Japhet in Search of a Father. P
Newman, Keble, Williams, R. H. Froude, Bowden, and Wilberforce: Lyra Apostolica [179 poems; 109 by Newman].
Slingsby, Sir Henry (d. 1658): Diary, ed. Daniel Parsons [first complete ed.: see Scott 1806].
Stanhope, Fifth Earl (1805): History of England from the Peace of Utrecht to the Peace of Versailles, 1713–83 [concl. 1853]. P
Talfourd, Sir Thomas Noon (1795): Ion, a Tragedy. D
Taylor, Sir Henry (1800): The Statesman. P
Temple (d. 1699): Memoirs of Life, Works, and Correspondence, ed. T. P. Courtenay [cont. extracts from Dorothy Osborne's letters now first pub.: see 1888].
Whitehead, Charles (1804): The Cavalier. D

Sir William Gilbert b.
Francis Bret Harte b.
Isabella Mary Mayson (Mrs. Beeton) b.
William Godwin d.
James Mill d.
George Colman jnr. d.
Richard Hurrell Froude d.
'The Dublin Review.'
Keble, ed. of Richard Hooker (rev. Church and Paget 1888).

Ainsworth (1805): Crichton. P

Apperley, Charles ('Nimrod') (1773): Memoirs of the Life of John Mytton. P

Browning, R. (1812): Strafford. T

Carlyle (1795): French Revolution. P
Lectures on German Literature. P

Coleridge, Sara (1802): Phantasmion. P and V

Cooper, James Fenimore (1789): Gleanings in Europe. P

Dickens (1812): Mudfog Papers [in Bentley's Miscellany, 1837–9; collected 1880]. P
Oliver Twist [in Bentley's Miscellany, 1837–8; collected 1838]. P
The Strange Gentleman, a Comic Burletta.
The Village Coquettes, a Comic Opera.

Disraeli (1804): Henrietta Temple. P
Venetia. P

Hallam (1777): Literature of Europe during the 15th, 16th, and 17th Centuries [concl. 1839]. P

Hare (d. 1834): Alton Sermons.

Hawthorne (1804): Twice-Told Tales [2nd series 1842]. P

Horne (1803): Cosmo de Medici. T
Death of Marlowe. T

Hunt (1784): Monthly Repository [9 nos.].

Knowles (1784): The Love-Chase. C

Lamb (d. 1833): Letters, ed. with Life by T. N. Talfourd [more letters in Final Memorials of Lamb, ed. Talfourd 1848, ed. by W. C. Hazlitt 1886, Purnell 1870, Harper 1907, Lucas 1935].

Landon (1802): Ethel Churchill. P

Landor (1775): Pentameron and Pentalogia. P and V
High and Low Life in Italy [in Monthly Repository, Aug. 1837–Apr. 1838]. P and V
Literary Hours, by Various Friends, ed. J. Ablett [cont. Six Imaginary Conversations and other contributions by L.].

Lover, Samuel (1797): Rory O'More. P

Lytton (1803): Ernest Maltravers [see 1838]. P

Macaulay (1800): Essay on Bacon [Edin. Rev.]. P

Mill, James (d. 1836): Principles of Toleration. P

Newman (1801): Parochial Sermons [concl. 1842].

Peacock (1785): Paper Money Lyrics. V

Ruskin (1819): Poetry of Architecture [in Loudon's Architectural Magazine]. P

Thackeray (1811): The Professor [in Bentley's Miscellany]. P
Yellowplush Papers [Fraser's Mag. 1837–8]. P

Trollope, Frances (1780): Vicar of Wrexhill. P

Whewell (1794): The Inductive Sciences. P

Whittier (1807): Poems [2nd series 1865]. V

Accession of Queen Victoria.
Camden Society founded.
Algernon Charles Swinburne b.
John Richard Green b.
William Dean Howells b.
Benjamin Webster, 'Acting National Drama' (anthology: concl. 1853).
Charles Knight's 'Pictorial History of England' (concl. 1844).
Bentley's 'Miscellany' (concl. 1868).
Joseph Cottle, Early Recollections of S. T. Coleridge.

President U.S.A.
Van Buren.

Arnold (1795): Early History of Rome [concl. 1843: see 1845].

Barrett, E. B. (Browning) (1806): The Seraphim. V

Bentham (d. 1832): Collected Works, ed. J. Bowring [concl. 1843].

Bethune, Alexander (1804): Tales and Sketches of the Scottish Peasantry.

Bury, Lady Charlotte (1775): Diary Illustrative of the Times of George IV.

Carlyle (1795): Lectures on History of Literature. P Essay on Scott [in Westminster Review]. P

Cooper, James Fenimore (1789): Home as Found. P

Dibdin, Thomas (1776): Bibliographical Tour in the Northern Counties of England. P

Dickens (1812): Memoirs of Joseph Grimaldi. P Sketches of Young Gentlemen. P Nicholas Nickleby [monthly from Apr. 1838 to Oct. 1839; collected 1839]. P

Froude, R. H. [d. 1836]: Remains, ed. Keble and Newman [pt. ii ed. Keble and Mozley 1839].

Guest, Lady Charlotte (1812): Mabinogion. P

Guest, Edwin (1800): History of English Rhythms [ed. Skeat 1882]. P

Hood (1799): Hood's Own, or Laughter from Year to Year [miscellany].

Jerrold (1803): Men of Character. P

Lane, Edward (1801): Trs. of Arabian Nights [from the Fr. of Galland; concl. 1840; ed. E. S. Poole 1859, S. Lane-Poole 1891]. P

Lyell, Sir Charles (1797): Elements of Geology. P

Lytton (1803): Alice, or the Mysteries [afterwards with Maltravers (see 1837) as Eleusinia]. P Lady of Lyons. D. Richelieu. D

Macaulay (1800): Essay on Temple [in Edin. Rev.]. P

Milnes, Richard Monckton (1809): Poems of Many Years.

Newman (1801): Doctrine of Justification. P

Prescott (1796): Ferdinand and Isabella. P

Scott, William Bell (1811): Hades, or the Transit. V

Surtees (1803): Jorrocks's Jaunts and Jollities [orig. in New Sporting Mag. 1831–4]. P

Thackeray (1811): Some Passages in the Life of Major Gahagan [in New Monthly Magazine]. P

Trollope, Frances (1780): Widow Barnaby. P

Tupper (1810): Proverbial Philosophy, 1 series [II 1842, III 1867, I–IV complete 1876]. V

Williams (1802): The Cathedral. V Thoughts in Past Years [enlarg. 1852]. V

Wordsworth (1770): Sonnets, with a few additional ones now first printed.

William Edward Lecky b.

Henry Sidgwick b.

James Bryce (Viscount Bryce) b.

John Morley (Viscount Morley) b.

Thomas Morton d.

Letitia Elizabeth Landon d.

English Historical Society founded.

Camden Society publications begin (First Series, 1838–72; New Series, 1871–97).

Joseph Bosworth, 'Anglo-Saxon Dictionary'.

Charles Knight, 'Pictorial Shakespeare' (concl. 1841).

Thomas Campbell, ed. of Shakespeare.

Milman, ed. Gibbon's 'Decline and Fall'.

Newman, Pusey, and Keble (editors); Church, Copeland, and others: Library of the Fathers of the Catholic Church (concl. 1885).

Ainsworth (1805): Jack Sheppard. P
Bailey (1816): Festus [11th or jubilee ed. considerably enlarged 1889]. V
Carlyle (1795): European Revolutions. P
  Chartism. P
  Critical and Miscellaneous Essays [collected].
Disraeli (1804): Tragedy of Count Alarcos. V
Domett, Alfred (1811): Venice. V
Faraday (1791): Experimental Researches in Electricity [concl. 1855]. P
Frere (1769): The Frogs [trs. Aristophanes: see 1840]. V
Grant, Sir Robert (d. 1838): Sacred Poems.
Hazlitt (d. 1830): Sketches and Essays, collected by his son [new ed. entitled Men and Manners; Sketches and Essays 1852]. P
  Winterslow; Essays and Characters written there, collected by his son. P
Hemans (d. 1835): Collected Works.
Hood (1799): Up the Rhine. P
Hook, Theodore (1788): Births, Marriages, and Deaths. P
Landor (1775): Andrea of Hungary. Giovanna of Naples. D
Lever (1806): Harry Lorrequer. P
Longfellow (1807): Hyperion. P
  Voices of the Night. V
Marryat (1792): Phantom Ship. P
Martineau (1802): Deerbrook. P
Milman (1791): Life of Gibbon. P
  Poetical Works.
Moore (1779): Alciphron. V
Shelley (d. 1822): Poetical Works, ed. Mrs. Shelley [ed. Rossetti 1870–78–88; Forman 1876–82–92; Dowden 1890–96–1900; Hutchinson 1904–5–7].
Smith, Sydney (1771): Works [concl. 1840; incl. Letters of Peter Plymley 1807–8, Three Letters to Archdeacon Singleton 1837–8–9, The Ballot 1839, Edinburgh Review articles].
Sterling, John (1806): Poems.
Taylor, Meadows (1808): Confessions of a Thug. P
Thackeray (1811): Catherine [in Fraser's Magazine 1839–40]. P
  Stubbs's Calendar, or the Fatal Boots [in Cruikshank's Comic Annual]. P
Williams (1802): Hymns translated from the Parisian Breviary. V

Walter Pater b.
Louise De La Ramée ('Ouida') b.
William de Morgan b.
John Galt d.
Winthrop Mackworth Praed d.
'*The New General Biographical Dictionary*' (*projected by Hugh James Rose*) *appears.*
John Thomas Smith's '*Cries of London*' (*illustr. by himself and J. Bowyer Nichols*).
First authentic ed. of Saint-Simon's Memoirs (*many pirated edd. in 18th century*).
Lowndes, '*The British Librarian*' [*concl. 1842*].

Ainsworth (1805): Tower of London. P

Barham, Richard (1788): Ingoldsby Legends, Series I [Series II and III 1847]. V

Browning, R. (1812): Sordello. V

Clive, Caroline (1801): IX Poems by V.

Coleridge (d. 1834): Confessions of an Enquiring Spirit, ed. H. N. Coleridge. P

Cooper, James Fenimore (1789): The Pathfinder. P

Dana, Richard Henry (1815): Two Years before the Mast. P

Darwin (1809): Voyage of H.M.S. Beagle. P

Dickens (1812): Sketches of Young Couples. P
Master Humphrey's Clock, Old Curiosity Shop, Barnaby Rudge [weekly from Apr. 1840 to Nov. 1841; collected 1840–1]. P

D'Israeli (1766): Amenities of Literature. P

Elliott, Charlotte (1789): Hours of Sorrow. V

Frere (1769): Trs. Acharnians, Knights, and Birds of Aristophanes [see 1839]. V

Hawker (1803): Ecclesia. V

Hunt (1784): The Seer [concl. 1841].
Legend of Florence. D
Prefaces to Moxon's edd. of Wycherley, Congreve, Vanbrugh, Farquhar, and Sheridan. P

Landor (1775): Fra Rupert. D

Lytton (1803): Money. D

Macaulay (1800): Essay on Clive [in Edin. Rev.]. P

Milman (1791): Christianity under the Empire. P

Pepys (d. 1703): Life, Journals, Correspondence, ed. John Smith.

Poe (1809): Tales of the Arabesque and Grotesque. P

Shelley (d. 1822): Letters and Miscellaneous Prose, ed. Mrs. Shelley [new ed. 1852; Collected Prose, ed. Forman, 1880. Collected Letters, ed. Dobell 1908, Ingpen 1912].

Strickland, Agnes and Elizabeth: Lives of the Queens of England [concl. 1848]. P

Thackeray (1811): Bedford Row Conspiracy [in New Monthly Magazine]. P
A Shabby Genteel Story [in Fraser's Magazine]. Paris Sketch Book. P
Essay on Genius of George Cruikshank. P
Barber Cox and the Cutting of his Comb. P
Character Sketches. P

Walpole (d. 1797): Collected Letters, ed. Wright [Letters to the Misses Berry now first pub.].

Whewell (1794): Philosophy of the Inductive Sciences. P

Wilberforce, Samuel (1808): Agathos. P

Williams and Copeland (editors); **Newman,** and others: Plain Sermons by authors of the Tracts for the Times [concl. 1848].

Marriage of Queen Victoria and Prince Albert.

John Addington Symonds b.

Austin Dobson b.

Thomas Hardy b.

Wilfrid Scawen Blunt b.

Frances Burney d.

Percy Society founded.

Parker Society founded.

First Eng. trs. of Ranke's 'History of the Popes during the 16th and 17th centuries'.

'The Dial' started (ended 1844).

Hartley Coleridge, edd. of Massinger and Ford.

Zola b.

Ainsworth (1805): Guy Fawkes. P
  Old Saint Paul's. P
Borrow (1803): ·The Zincali, or Account of the
  Gypsies of Spain. P
Boucicault (1820 ?): London Assurance. D
Browning, R. (1812): Pippa Passes [no. 1 of Bells
  and Pomegranates]. V
Carlyle (1795): Heroes, Hero-Worship, and the
  Heroic in History. P
Channing, William Ellery (1780): Works. P
Cooper, James Fenimore (1789): The Deerslayer. P
Crowe, Catherine (1800 ?): Adventures of Susan
  Hopley. P
Dickens (1812): Pic-Nic Papers, by various hands
  [cont. The Lamp-Lighter by Dickens].
Elphinstone, Mountstuart (1779): History of India
  [enlarg. ed., F. B. Cowell, 1866].
Emerson (1803): Essays: 1st series [2nd series
  1844].
Gore, Catherine (1799): Cecil. P
Heber (d. 1826): Poetical Works [collected].
Helps, Sir Arthur (1813): Essays written in the
  Intervals of Business. P
Hunt (1784) and others: Chaucer Modernized. V
Key, Francis Scott (1780): The Star-Spangled
  Banner. V
Lever, Charles James (1806): Charles O'Malley. P
Lowell (1819): A Year's Life. V
Macaulay (1800): Essay on Warren Hastings [in
  Edin. Rev.]. P
Marryat (1792): Masterman Ready. P
Marston, John Westland (1819): Patrician's
  Daughter. D
Martineau (1802): The Playfellow, a Series of
  Tales. P
  The Hour and the Man. P
Miller, Hugh (1802): Old Red Sandstone. P
Thackeray (1811): History of Samuel Titmarsh
  and the Great Hoggarty Diamond [in
  Fraser's Magazine; separately 1849]. P
  Second Funeral of Napoleon, Chronicle of the
  Drum. P
  Comic Tales and Sketches [reprt. of earlier
  writings]. P
Trench (1807): Notes on the Parables. P
  Poems.
Ward, Robert Plumer (1765): De Clifford, or the
  Constant Man. P
Warren, Samuel (1807): Ten Thousand a Year
  [originally in Blackwood's from 1839]. P

William Black b.
William Henry Hudson b.
Sir Henry Morton Stanley
  (John Rowlands) b.
'*The Christian Remem-*
  brancer' (concl. 1868).
'*Punch' started.*
Shakespeare   Society,
  1841–53.
Last 'Tract of the Times'
  (No. 90) by Newman.

President U.S.A.
Tyler.

Apperley, Charles ('Nimrod') (1773): Life of a Sportsman. P

Arnold (d. 1842): Study of Modern History. P

Browning (1812): King Victor and King Charles [no. 2 of Bells and Pomegranates]. V
Dramatic Lyrics [no. 3 of above]. V

Bryant, William Cullen (1794): The Fountain. V

Burney (d. 1840): Diary and Letters, 1778–1840, ed. Charlotte Barrett [concl. 1846: see 1889].

Campbell (1777): Pilgrim of Glencoe. V
Frederick the Great and his Times. P

Channing, William Ellery (d. 1842): The Duty of the Free States. P

Dickens (1812): American Notes for General Circulation. P

Drummond (d. 1649): Conversations with Ben Jonson in 1619, ed. from original MS. by David Laing [see 1711]. P

Hunt (1784): The Palfrey. V

Longfellow (1807): Ballads and Other Poems. V
Poems on Slavery. V

Lover (1797): Handy Andy. P

Lytton (1803): Zanoni. P
Eva, and Other Tales and Poems. V

Macaulay (1800): Lays of Ancient Rome [Ivry, first pub. in Quarterly Magazine in 1833, and Armada, first pub. in Friendship's Offering in 1833, added in 1848]. V

Manning, Henry Edward (1808): Sermons [collected; concl. 1850].

Marryat (1792): Percival Keene. P

Montgomery, Robert (1807): Luther, a Poem.

Taylor, Sir Henry (1800): Edwin the Fair. D

Tennyson (1809): Poems [among new pieces: Locksley Hall, Morte d'Arthur, Ulysses, Two Voices, Godiva, Sir Galahad, Vision of Sin, 'Break, break, break', &c.].

Thackeray (1811): Sultan Stork [in Ainsworth's Magazine]. P
Fitz-Boodle Papers [in Fraser's Magazine 1842–3]. P

Trench (1807): Poems from Eastern Sources, V
Genoveva, a Poem.

Tupper (1810): Proverbial Philosophy, 2nd series [see 1838]. V

Whitehead, Charles (1804): Richard Savage. P

Williams (1802): The Baptistry. V

Wilson (1785): Recreations of Christopher North. P

Wordsworth (1770): Poems chiefly of Early and Late Years, including The Borderers.

William James b.

Thomas Arnold d.

Allan Cunningham d.

'Biographical Dictionary', ed. George Long (concl. 1844).

'Dictionary of Greek and Roman Antiquities', ed. Sir William Smith.

William Thoms's ed. of Stow's 'Survey of London'.

'Illustrated London News' started.

John Payne Collier, ed. of Shakespeare (concl. 1844).

Copyright Act extends term of copyright to 42 years from publication or 7 years after the Author's death, whichever is the longer. See 1709, 1774, 1911.

Ainsworth (1805): Windsor Castle. P
Bethune, Alexander (1804): The Scottish Peas-
    ant's Fireside.
Borrow (1803): Bible in Spain. P
Browning, R. (1812): Return of the Druses [no. 4
    of Bells and Pomegranates]. D
    Blot on the Scutcheon [no. 5 of above]. D
Carlyle (1795): Past and Present. P
Church (1815): Life of St. Anselm [enlarg. 1870]. P
Dickens (1812): A Christmas Carol in Prose. P
    Martin Chuzzlewit [monthly from Jan. 1843 to
    July 1844; collected 1844]. P
Gore, Catherine (1799): The Banker's Wife. P
Hawker (1803): Reeds Shaken by the Wind. V
Hood (1799): Song of the Shirt [in Punch]. V
Horne (1803): Orion, an Epic Poem.
Hunt (1784): One Hundred Romances of Real
    Life. P
Jerrold (1803): Punch's Letters to his Son. P
Jones, Ebenezer (1820): Studies of Sensation and
    Event. V
Knowles (1784): The Secretary. D
Longfellow (1807): The Spanish Student. D
Lytton (1803): Last of the Barons. P
Macaulay (1800): Critical and Historical Essays. P
Martineau (1805): Endeavours after the Christian
    Life, 1st series [2nd 1847]. P
Mill, John Stuart (1806): System of Logic. P
Neale, John Mason (1818): Hymns for Children.
Prescott (1796): The Conquest of Mexico. P
Prichard, James Cowles (1786): Natural History
    of Man. P
Ruskin (1819): Modern Painters, vol. i [ii 1846,
    iii–iv 1856, v 1860]. P
Sidney, Henry, Earl of Romney (1641–1704): Diary
    of the Time of Charles II, ed. A. W. Blencowe.
Spencer (1820): Proper Sphere of Government. P
Surtees (1803): Handley Cross, or the Spa Hunt
    [expanded into Handley Cross, or Mr. Jor-
    rocks's Jaunts 1854]. P
Thackeray (1811): Irish Sketchbook. P
    Men's Wives [in Fraser's Magazine]. P
    Bluebeard's Ghost [in Fraser's Magazine].
Walpole (d. 1797): Letters to Sir Horace Mann,
    1760–85 [see 1833].

Henry James b.
Edward Dowden b.
*Frederic William Henry
    Myers b.*
*Charles Montagu Doughty
    b.*
*Sir William Reynell
    Anson b.*
Robert Southey d.
Wordsworth poet-laureate.
*Condemnation and sus-
    pension of Pusey by
    Oxford University after
    his sermon, 'Holy Eu-
    charist', preached on 14
    May.*
*'The Economist' started
    by James Wilson.*
*Liddell and Scott's 'Greek-
    English Lexicon' (7th
    ed. 1883, 8th ed. 1897).*
*Charles Knight's 'Shake-
    speare's Biography'.*
*Anna Swanwick, trs.
    Selections from Dramas
    of Goethe and Schiller
    [see 1850].*
*Owen, 'Comparative Ana-
    tomy and Physiology of
    Invertebrate Animals'
    (concl. 1846); enlarg.
    1855.*

Barnes, William (1801): Poems of Rural Life in Dorset Dialect [a second collection 1859; third 1863; collected 1879].

Barrett, E. B. (Browning) (1806): Poems.

Browning, R. (1812): Colombe's Birthday [no. 6 of Bells and Pomegranates]. D

Bryant, William Cullen (1794): The White-Footed Deer. V

Burke (d. 1797): Correspondence 1744–97, ed. Fitzwilliam and Bourke.

De Quincey (1785): Logic of Political Economy. P

Dickens (1812): The Chimes, a Goblin Story. P

Disraeli (1804): Coningsby. P

Finlay, George (1799): Greece under the Romans [first pt. of History of Greece: see 1877]. P

Fuller, Margaret (1810): Summer on the Lakes. P

Haydon, Benjamin (1786): Lectures on Painting and Design [concl. 1846]. V

Hood (1799): Whimsicalities. P and V
Hood's Magazine and Comic Miscellany [concl. 1848].

Horne (1803): New Spirit of the Age. P

Hunt (1784): Collected Poems, 2nd ed., with Additions [see 1832].

James, G. P. R. (1799): Col. Novels [concl. 1849].

Jeffrey, Francis, Lord Jeffrey (1773): Contributions to Edinburgh Review [concl. 1853].

Jerrold (1803): Story of a Feather. P

Kinglake (1809): Eothen. P

Lever (1806): Tom Burke of Ours. P
Arthur O'Leary. P

Lowell (1819): Poems. V

Mill (1806): Essays on Some Unsettled Questions of Political Economy. P

Milnes (Lord Houghton) (1809): Palm Leaves. V

Newman (editor), Church, Dalgairns, Meyrick, Pattison, Faber, Froude, Coffin, Ornsby, Walker, Oakeley, Barrow: Lives of the English Saints.

Patmore (1823): Poems.

Sewell, Elizabeth (1815): Amy Herbert. P

Sleeman, Sir William (1788): Rambles and Recollections of an Indian Official. P

Stanley (1815): Life of Arnold. P

Thackeray (1811): Luck of Barry Lyndon [in Fraser's Magazine. Reprtd. in Miscellanies 1855, and as Memoirs of B. L. 1856]. P
History of the next French Revolution. P

Warburton, Bartholomew Elliot (1810): The Crescent and the Cross. P

Ward, William George (1812): Ideal of a Christian Church. P

Edward Carpenter b.
Andrew Lang b.
Robert Bridges b.
William Beckford d.
Thomas Campbell d.
Henry Francis Cary d.
Keble's 'Prælectiones Academicæ'.
Caxton Society founded.
W. J. Thoms's ed. of 'Reynard the Fox' from Caxton.
'North British Review' (concl. 1871).
Robert Chambers's 'Cyclopaedia of English Literature'.
Sir William Smith's 'Dictionary of Greek and Roman Biography and Mythology' (concl. 1849).
Charles Knight's 'Weekly Volumes' and 'Old England'.
Robert Chambers,'Vestiges of the Natural History of Creation'.

Arnold (d. 1842): History of the Later Roman Commonwealth [see 1838]. P

Miscellaneous Works, ed. Arthur Stanley.

Aytoun (1813) **and Martin** (1816): Bon Gaultier Ballads [in Tait's and Fraser's Magazines 1842–4; later collections 1849, 1855]. V

Browning, R. (1812): Dramatic Romances and Lyrics [no. 7 of Bells and Pomegranates]. V

Carlyle (1795): Ed. Letters and Speeches of Cromwell [ed. Lomas 1904]. P

Cooper, Thomas (1805): Purgatory of Suicides. V

Dickens (1812): Cricket on the Hearth. P

Disraeli (1804): Sybil. P

Ford, Richard (1796): Handbook for Travellers in Spain. P

Fuller, Margaret (1810): Woman in the 19th Century. P

Henslowe, Philip (d. 1616): Diary, 1592–1603, ed. J. P. Collier [Extracts in Malone's ed. of Shakespeare, 1790–1821. Ed. Greg, 1904–8].

Jerrold (1803): Time Works Wonders [acted]. D
Punch's Complete Letter-Writer. P

Lewes (1817): Biographical History of Philosophy [concl. 1846]. P

Lowell (1819): Conversations on some of the Old Poets. P

Lytton (1803): New Timon [completed 1847]. V

Martineau (1802): Dawn Island. P
Forest and Game Law Tales. P

Newman (1801): Essay on Development of Christian Doctrine. P

Poe (1809): Tales of Mystery and Imagination. P
The Raven. V

Smith, John Thomas (d. 1833): Book for a Rainy Day [ed. W. Whitten 1905]. P

Southey (d. 1843): Oliver Newman and other Poetical Remains, ed. Hill.

Thackeray (1811): Legend of the Rhine [in Cruikshank's Table-Book, June to Dec.]. P
Diary of Jeames de la Pluche [Punch 1845–6]. P

Walpole (d. 1797): Memoirs of the Reign of George III, ed. Denis le Marchant [New ed. by G. F. R. Barker 1894]. P

Whewell (1794): Elements of Morality. P

Williams (1802): Sacred Verses.

George Saintsbury b.
Sidney Colvin b.
Thomas Hood d.
Sydney Smith d.
Richard Harris Barham d.
The Oxford Movement reaches a crisis with the condemnation by the University of William Ward's 'Ideal of a Christian Church' (pub. 1844) and the degradation of the author: Newman joins the Church of Rome on 9 October.
Meeting of Robert Browning and Elizabeth Barrett.
Mrs. Cowden Clarke, 'Concordance to Shakespeare's Plays'.
'Encyclopaedia Metropolitana.'
Joseph Hunter, 'New Illustrations of Shakespeare'.
Walter Farquhar Hook, 'Dictionary of Ecclesiastical Biography' (concl. 1852).
Lingard, 'History and Antiquities of Anglo-Saxon Church' (enlarg. from 'Antiquities of Anglo-Saxon Church', 1806).

President U.S.A.
Polk.

Blanchard, Laman (d. 1845): Sketches from Life. P
Brontë, Charlotte (1816), **Emily** (1818), **and Anne**
(1820): Poems by Currer, Ellis, and Acton
Bell.
Browning, R. (1812): Luria, A Soul's Tragedy
[no. 8 of Bells and Pomegranates]. D
Bells and Pomegranates, 1841–6, reprtd.
Dickens (1812): Pictures from Italy [originally in
Daily News, Jan. to Mar. 1846]. P
Battle of Life. P
Dombey and Son [monthly from Oct. 1846 to
Apr. 1848; collected 1848]. P
Fuller, Margaret (1810): Literature and Art. P
'George Eliot' (1819): Trs. Strauss's Life of Jesus. P
Grote (1794): History of Greece, vols. i–ii [con-
cluded 1856]. P
Hawker (1803): Echoes from Old Cornwall. V
Hawthorne (1804): Mosses from an Old Manse. P
Hume (d. 1776): Life and Correspondence, ed.
Burton [Letters, ed. Greig 1932].
Hunt (1784): Wit and Humour selected from
English Poets.
Stories from Italian Poets, with Lives of
Writers. P
Jerrold (1803): Mrs. Caudle's Curtain Lectures
[repub. from Punch]. P
Chronicles of Clovernook. P
Keble (1792): Lyra Innocentium. V
Landor, Robert Eyres (1781): Fawn of Sertorius. P
Lear (1812): Book of Nonsense. V
Longfellow (1807): The Belfry of Bruges. V
Lytton (1803): Lucretia, or Children of the Night.
P
Marryat (1792): Privateer's Man. P
Martineau (1802): The Billow and the Rock. P
Melville (1819): Typee. P
Owen (1804): British Fossil Mammals and Birds. P
Ruskin (1819): Modern Painters, vol. ii [see 1843]. P
Smith, H. (1779): Poetical Works [collected].
Thackeray (1811): Cornhill to Cairo. P
Snobs of England [in Punch 1846–7; separately,
as Book of Snobs, 1848]. P
Mrs. Perkins's Ball [1847].
Trench (1807): Notes on the Miracles of Our Lord. P
Walpole (d. 1797): Memoirs of the Reign of King
George II, ed. Lord Holland [see 1822].
Webster, Daniel (1782): Bunker Hill Speeches.
Whewell (1794): Lectures on Systematic Moral-
ity. P

Francis Herbert Bradley
b.
John Hookham Frere d.
Marriage of Browning and
Elizabeth Barrett.
Hakluyt Society founded.
Bohn's 'Standard
Library'.
'The Guardian' started.
'The Daily News' started
by Dickens.
John Thomas Smith,
'Antiquarian Rambles
in the Streets of Lon-
don'.
Lord Campbell, 'Lives of
Lord Chancellors and
Keepers of the Great
Seal of England' (concl.
1847).

Barham (d. 1845): Ingoldsby Legends, 2nd and 3rd series [see 1840]. P and V

Boole, George (1815): Mathematical Analysis of Logic. P

Brontë, Anne (1820): Agnes Grey [by 'Acton Bell']. P

Brontë, Charlotte (1816): Jane Eyre [by 'Currer Bell']. P

Brontë, Emily (1818): Wuthering Heights [by 'Ellis Bell': pub. with Agnes Grey above]. P

Crowe, Catherine (1800 ?): Story of Lilly Dawson. P

Disraeli (1804): Tancred. P

Emerson (1803): Poems. V

Evelyn (d. 1706): Life of Mrs. Godolphin, ed. Bishop Wilberforce. P

Froude (1818): Shadows of the Clouds. P

Gaskell (1810): The Sexton's Hero, Christmas Storms & Sunshine [Howitt's Journal, 1847]. P

Helps, Sir Arthur (1813): Friends in Council, 1st series [concl. 1859]. P

Hunt (1784): Men, Women, & Books [selections]. P

Keble (1792): Sermons. P

Landor (1775): Hellenics, enlarged and completed [repub. with alterations 1859]. V

Lever (1806): The Knight of Gwynne. P

Lewes (1817): Ranthorpe. P

Longfellow (1807): Evangeline. V

Medwin, Thomas (1788): Life of Shelley. P

Melville (1819): Omoo. P

Morton, John Maddison (1811): Box and Cox [acted]. C

Prescott (1796): The Conquest of Peru. P

Surtees (1803): Hawbuck Grange. P

Taylor, Sir Henry (1800): Notes from Life. P
Eve of the Conquest and Other Poems.

Tennyson (1809): The Princess [3rd ed. with Songs added 1850]. V

Thackeray (1811): Vanity Fair [serially Jan. 1847 to July 1848; collected 1848]. P
Punch's Prize Novelists [3 Apr. to 9 Oct. 1847; later Novels by Eminent Hands]. P

Trollope (1815): Macdermots of Ballycloran. P

Whewell (editor), **Herschel, Hare, Lockhart, Hawtrey**: English Hexameter Translations.

Williams (1802): The Altar. V

Alice Thompson (Mrs. Meynell) b.

Sharon Turner d.

Layamon's 'Brut' ed. by Sir Frederick Madden.

Bohn's 'Antiquarian Library' and 'Scientific Library'.

Marx's Communist Manifesto.

Foundation of Communist League.

Adams, John Quincey (d. 1848): Poems of Religion and Society.

Ainsworth (1805): Lancashire Witches. P

Aytoun (1813): Lays of Scottish Cavaliers. V

Brontë, A. (1820): Tenant of Wildfell Hall. P

Clough (1819): Bothie of Toper-na-Fuosich [later Tober-na-Vuolich]. V

Coleridge (d. 1834): Hints towards a Comprehensive View of Life, ed. S. B. Watson. P

Crowe, Catherine (1800 ?): Night Side of Nature. P

Dickens (1812): The Haunted Man. P

Fairfax, Thomas, Lord Fairfax (d. 1671): Correspondence, ed. Johnson and Bell [concl. 1849].

Forster, John (1812): Life and Adventures of Oliver Goldsmith [enlarg. as Life and Times, &c., 1854]. P

Gaskell (1810): Mary Barton. P

Grant, James (1822): Adventures of an Aide-de-Camp. P

Hervey, John, Lord Hervey (d. 1743): Memoirs of the Reign of George II, ed. J. W. Croker.

Hunt (1784): Jar of Honey from Mount Hybla. V
The Town. P

Jameson, Anna (1794): Sacred and Legendary Art. P

Keats (d. 1821): Life, Letters, and Literary Remains, ed. Lord Houghton [rev. 1867].

Kingsley (1819): Saint's Tragedy. D

Landor (1775): Imaginary Conversation of King Carlo-Alberto and the Duchess of Belgioioso. P
Italics. V

Lowell (1819): The Biglow Papers [2nd series 1860]. V
A Fable for Critics. V.   Vision of Sir Launfal. V

Lytton (1803): Harold. P
King Arthur. V

Mill (1806): Principles of Political Economy. P

Newman (1801): Loss and Gain. P

Pusey (1800): Parochial Sermons, vol. i [ii 1853, iii 1869].

Rich, Mary, Countess of Warwick (d. 1678): Autobiography, ed. T. C. Croker.

Sterling, John (d. 1844): Essays and Tales. P

Thackeray (1811): A Little Dinner at Timmins's. P
History of Pendennis [serially Nov. 1848 to Dec. 1850; collected 1849–50]. P
Our Street. P

Trollope (1815): The Kellys and the O'Kellys. P

Walpole (d. 1797): Letters to Countess of Ossory. 1769–97, ed. R. Vernon Smith.

Bernard Bosanquet b.
Arthur James Balfour, Earl of Balfour b.
Richard Jefferies b.
George John Romanes b.
Branwell Brontë d.
Emily Brontë d.
Frederick Marryat d.
Isaac D'Israeli d.
Formation of the Pre-Raphaelite Brotherhood by Rossetti, Madox Brown, Woolner, Holman Hunt, and Millais, 1848–9.
Thomas Lacy, 'Acting Edition of Plays' (concl. 1873).
Bohn's 'Classical Library'.
Chambers's 'Instructive and Entertaining Library'.
Revolution in France.
Chateaubriand d.

Arnold (1822): Strayed Reveller and Other Poems.

Barton (d. 1849): Selections from Poems and Letters, ed. Lucy Barton.

Brontë, C. (1816): Shirley. P

Campbell, Lord (1779): Lives of the Chief Justices of England [concl. 1857]. P

Clough (1819): Ambarvalia [with Thomas Burbidge]. V

Coleridge (d. 1834): Notes and Lectures on Shakespeare and some of the Old Dramatists, ed. Sara Coleridge [ed. from notes by J. P. Collier 1856; ed. T. Ashe 1885]. P

Curzon, Robert (1810): Visit to the Monasteries in the Levant. P

Dickens (1812): David Copperfield [monthly from May 1849 to Nov. 1850; collected 1850]. P

Emerson (1803): Miscellanies. P

Freeman (1823): Study of History. P

Froude (1818): Nemesis of Faith. P

Herschel, Sir John (1792): Outlines of Astronomy. P

Hunt (1784): Readings for Railways. P

Jerrold (1803): A Man made of Money. P

Macaulay (1806): History of England, vols. i–ii [iii–iv 1855; ed. Lady Trevelyan 1861]. P

Manning, Anne (1807): Mary Powell [with a sequel, Deborah's Diary, 1859]. P

Marston, John Westland (1819): Strathmore. D

Martineau (1802): History of England during the Thirty Years' Peace, 1815–1845. P

Household Education. P

Melville (1819): Mardi. P. Redburn. P

Owen (1804): History of British Fossil Reptiles [concl. 1884]. P

Parkman, Francis (1823): California and Oregon Trail. P

Ruskin (1819): Seven Lamps of Architecture. P

Southey (d. 1843): Commonplace Book, ed. J. W. Warter [concl. 1851]. P

Life and Correspondence, ed. C. C. Southey. P

Stephen, Sir James (1789): Essays in Ecclesiastical Biography. P

Thackeray (1811): Dr. Birch and his Young Friends. P

Thoreau (1817): A Week on the Concord. P

Wakefield, Edward Gibbon (1796): A View of the Art of Colonization. P

Wesley, Charles (d. 1788): Journal, 1736–56, with Selections from Correspondence, ed. Jackson.

Whitehead, Charles (1804): The Solitary and Other Poems [collected].

William Ernest Henley b.
Edmund Gosse b.
Horace Smith d.
Maria Edgeworth d.
Hartley Coleridge d.
Thomas Lovell Beddoes d.
Ebenezer Elliott d.
Anne Brontë d.
Bernard Barton d.
Edgar Allan Poe d.
'*Notes and Queries*' *founded by William John Thoms.*
'*Household Words*' (*weekly*) *started by Dickens.*
Charles Knight, 'Studies of Shakespeare'.
Sir Austen Layard, 'Nineveh and its Remains'.
William Smith, trs. Works of Fichte (*collected; separately 1845–9*).

President U.S.A.
Taylor.

Alison, Sir Archibald (1792): Essays, Political, Historical and Miscellaneous.

Allingham, William (1824): Poems.

Beddoes (d. 1849): Death's Jest Book. V

Browning, E. B. (1806): Poems [cont. Sonnets from the Portuguese and entirely new version of Prometheus Bound: see 1833].

Browning, R. (1812): Christmas Eve and Easter Day. V

Bryant, William Cullen (1794): Letters of a Traveller. P

Carlyle (1795): Latter-Day Pamphlets. P

Church, Richard William (1815): Dante [in Christian Remembrancer: repub. 1878]. P

Coleridge (d. 1834): Essays on His Own Times, ed. Sara Coleridge.

Collins (1824): Antonia, or the Fall of Rome. P

Dobell (1824): The Roman, a Dramatic Poem.

Emerson (1803): Representative Men. P

Gaskell (1810): Moorland Cottage. P

Grant, James (1822): The Scottish Cavalier. P

Hawthorne (1804): The Scarlet Letter. P

Hunt (1784): Autobiography [enlarg. ed. Thornton Hunt 1860; ed. Ingpen 1903].
Leigh Hunt's Journal [1850-1].

Kingsley (1819): Alton Locke, Tailor and Poet. P

Landon (d. 1838): Collected Poems.

Longfellow (1807): Seaside and Fireside. V

Lytton (1803): The Caxtons. P

Marston, John Westland (1819): Philip of France. D
Marie de Méraine. D

Melville (1819): White Jacket. P

Merivale, Charles (1808): History of the Romans under the Empire [concl. 1864]. P

Neale, John Mason (1818): History of the Holy Eastern Church. P

Newman, F. W. (1807): Phases of Faith. P

Poe (d. 1849): Works. P and V

Rossetti (1828) and others: The Germ [four nos., Jan.–Apr. R.'s contributions: Hand and Soul, My Sister's Sleep, Blessed Damozel (original version), Carillon, Sonnets for Pictures, &c.].

Senior, William Nassau (1790): Political Economy. P

Smedley, Francis Edward: Frank Fairleigh. P

Spencer (1820): Social Statics. P

Tennyson (1809): In Memoriam. V

Thackeray (1811): The Kickleburys on the Rhine [2nd ed. with Preface, 1851]. P
Rebecca and Rowena. P

Watts (1797): Lyrics of the Heart. V

Wordsworth (d. 1850): The Prelude [1805 version, ed. E. de Sélincourt pub. 1926]. V

Robert Louis Stevenson b.
Frederic William Maitland b.
Lafcadio Hearn b.
Augustine Birrell b.
William Wordsworth d.
Francis, Lord Jeffrey d.
William Lisle Bowles d.
Tennyson poet-laureate.
Sir William Smith, 'New Classical Dictionary'.
Joseph Hunter, 'Milton: A Sheaf of Gleanings after his Biographers and Annotators'.
Sir Frederick Madden ed. Wiclif's 'Bible'.
'Harper's Magazine' started.
Honoré de Balzac d.
John Stuart Blackie, trs. of Æschylus.
Anna Swanwick, trs. Goethe's 'Egmont and Faust', pt. i (pt. ii in 1878: see 1843).

President U.S.A.
Fillmore.

Beddoes (d. 1849): Collected Poems, ed. Kelsall [ed. Gosse 1890, Colles 1907].

Borrow (1803): Lavengro. P

Browning, E. B. (1806): Casa Guidi Windows. V

Carlyle (1795): Life of John Sterling. P
Excursion (futile enough) to Paris. P

Coleridge, H. (d. 1849): Poems, ed. Derwent Coleridge [ed. Bailey-Kempling 1903].
Prose Remains, ed. Derwent Coleridge.

Dickens (1812): Child's History of England [in Household Words, Jan. 1851–Dec. 1853; collected 1852–4]. P

Fitzgerald, Edward (1809): Euphranor, a Dialogue on Youth. P

Hawthorne (1804): House with Seven Gables. P
The Snow Image. P

Helps, Sir Arthur (1813): Companions of my Solitude. P

Hunt (1784): Table-Talk [with Imaginary Conversations of Pope and Swift].

Jerrold (1803): Collected Works [concl. 1854].

Kingsley (1819): Yeast [in abridged form in Fraser's Magazine 1848]. P

Layard, Sir Austen (1817): Popular Account of Discoveries at Nineveh. P

Longfellow (1807): The Golden Legend. D

Lytton (1803): Not so bad as we seem. D

Manning, Anne (1807): Household of Sir Thomas More. P

Mansel, Henry Longueville (1820): Prolegomena Logica. P

Melville (1819): Moby Dick. P

Meredith (1828): Poems [incl. first version of Love in the Valley].

Napier, Sir William Francis (1785): History of Sir Charles Napier's Administration of Scinde. P

Parkman, Francis (1823): Conspiracy of Pontiac. P

Ruskin (1819): King of the Golden River. P
Pre-Raphaelitism. P
Stones of Venice, vol. i [ii–iii 1853]. P
Examples of the Architecture of Venice. P
Notes on the Construction of Sheepfolds. P

Trench (1807): Study of Words. P

Walpole (d. 1797): Letters to Mason, ed. Mitford.

Wordsworth (d. 1850): Memoirs, dictated by himself, ed. Christopher Wordsworth.

The Great Exhibition.
Coup d'état: Louis Napoleon Emperor.
Mary Augusta Arnold (Mrs. Humphry Ward) b.
Henry Arthur Jones b.
Sir Oliver Lodge b.
Andrew Cecil Bradley b.
Joanna Baillie d.
John Lingard d.
J. M. W. Turner d.
H. N. Hudson's ed. of Shakespeare (concl. 1856; repub. as Harvard ed. 1881).
J. Mitford's ed. of Milton's Works (prose and verse).
Robert Chambers's ed. of Burns.
'Atlantic Monthly' started.

Alison, Sir Archibald (1792): History of Europe, 1815–52 [concl. 1859: see 1833]. P
Life of Marlborough. P
Arnold (1822): Empedocles on Etna, and other Poems [Tristram and Iseult, A Summer Night, Youth of Nature, Youth of Man, Isolation, &c.].
Browning, R. (1812): Essay on Shelley. P
Creasy, Sir Edward Shepherd (1812): Fifteen Decisive Battles of the World. P
Dickens (1812): Bleak House [monthly from Mar. 1852 to Sept. 1853; collected 1853]. P
Disraeli (1804): Life of Lord George Bentinck. P
Hamilton (1788): Philosophy and Literature. P
Hawthorne (1804): A Wonder Book for Boys and Girls. P
The Blithedale Romance. P
Hayward, Abraham (1801): Art of Dining. P
Holland, Lord (d. 1840): Memoirs of the Whig Party. P
Kingsley (1819): Phaethon. P
Martineau (1802): Merdhen, the Manor and the Eyrie, and Old Landmarks and Old Laws. P
Melville (1819): Pierre. P
Miller, Hugh (1802): My Schools and Schoolmasters. P
Mitford (1787): Recollections of a Literary Life. P
Newman (1801): Scope and Nature of University Education [later ed. Idea of a University]. P
Reade, Charles (1814) and **Taylor, Tom**: Masks and Faces [acted]. D
Stowe, Harriet Beecher (1811): Uncle Tom's Cabin. P
Stirling-Maxwell, Sir William (1818): Cloister Life of the Emperor Charles V [enlarg. 1891]. P
Tennyson (1809): Ode on Death of Wellington. V
Thackeray (1811): History of Henry Esmond. P

George Moore b.
Thomas Moore d.
John Cassell's 'The Popular Educator' (concl. 1855).
John Payne Collier's 'Notes and Emendations to the Plays of Shakespeare' starts the controversy leading to his exposure.

1853

Arnold (1822): Poems [among new pieces: Sohrab and Rustum, Scholar Gipsy, Requiescat].
Blackmore (1825): Poems by Melanter. V
Brontë, C. (1816): Villette. P
Burton, John Hill (1809): History of Scotland [concl. 1870]. P
Coleridge (d. 1834): Notes on English Divines, ed. Derwent Coleridge.
Notes, Theological, Political, and Miscellaneous, ed. Derwent Coleridge.

Crimean War 1853–6.
Sir Hall Caine b.
Amelia Opie d.
Charles Knight, 'English Cyclopaedia' (concl. 1861).
'Bohn's British Classics.'
'Cassell's Classical Library.'
'Encyclopaedia Britannica', 8th ed. (concl. 1860).

'Cuthbert Bede' (1827): Adventures of Mr. Verdant Green, pt. i [ii 1854, iii 1857]. P

De Quincey (1785): Collected Works [concl. 1860; enlarg. 1862–78; enlarg. ed. D. Masson 1889–90].

Fitzgerald (1809): Trs. Six Dramas of Calderon [see 1865]. V

Fox (d. 1806): Memorials and Correspondence, ed. Earl Russell [concl. 1857].

Gaskell (1810): Ruth. P
Cranford [originally in Household Words, 13 Dec. 1851–21 May 1853]. P

Hawthorne (1804): Tanglewood Tales. P

Haydon, Benjamin Robert (d. 1846): Autobiography and Journals, ed. Tom Taylor.

Kingsley (1819): Hypatia. P

Landor (1775): Last Fruit off an Old Tree. P and V

Lewes (1817): Comte's Philosophy of Sciences. P

Lytton (1803): My Novel. P

Manning, Anne (1807): Cherry and Violet. P

Martineau (1802): Philosophy of Comte, translated and condensed. P

Maurice (1805): Theological Essays. P

Moore (d. 1852): Memoirs, Journals, and Correspondence, ed. Earl Russell [concl. 1856].

Patmore (1823): Tamerton Church Tower. V

Reade (1814): Peg Woffington. P
Christie Johnstone. P

Ruskin (1819): Architecture and Painting. P
Stones of Venice, ii–iii [i 1851]. P

Smith, Alexander (1830): Life Drama. V

Surtees (1803): Mr. Sponge's Sporting Tour [3rd ed. Soapey Sponge's Sporting Tour 1893]. P

Thackeray (1811): English Humorists of the 18th Century. P
The Newcomes [serially from Oct. 1853 to Aug. 1855; collected 1854–5]. P

Trench (1807): Lessons in Proverbs. P

Verney: Letters and Papers of the Verney Family to the end of the year 1639, ed. J. Bruce.

Wallace, Alfred Russel (1823): Travels on the Amazon and Rio Negro. P

Whewell, William (1794): Of the Plurality of Worlds [2nd ed. with Supplement, A Dialogue on the Plurality of Worlds 1854]. P

Whyte-Melville (1821): Captain Digby Grand. P

Yonge (1823): Heir of Redclyffe. P

J. O. Halliwell-Phillipps,
  ed. Shakespeare.
Johann Tieck d.
Francis William Newman,
  trs. Odes of Horace.

President U.S.A.
  Pierce.

Ainsworth (1805): Star Chamber. P
Flitch of Bacon. P
Allingham (1824): Day and Night Songs. V
Aytoun (1813): Firmilian. V
Church (1815): Essays and Reviews. P
Cooke, John E. (1830): Youth of Jefferson. P
Dickens (1812): Hard Times [in Household Words and separately]. P
Dobell (1824): Balder. V
Ferrier, James Frederick (1808): Institutes of Metaphysic. P
Forster, John (1812): Life and Times of Oliver Goldsmith [see 1848]. P
Keats (d. 1821): Poetical Works, with Memoir, ed. Lord Houghton [new ed. 1861: see 1883].
Macaulay (1800): Speeches, corrected by himself.
Massey, Gerald (1828): Ballad of Babe Christabel. V
May, Sir Thomas (1815): Rules, Orders, and Forms of Procedure of the House of Commons.
Milman (1791): Latin Christianity [concl. '55]. P
Mitford (1787): Atherton, and Other Tales. P
Owen (1804): Geology and Inhabitants of the Ancient World. P
Patmore (1823): The Betrothal [pt. i of Angel in the House: see 1856–60–62]. V
Patmore, Peter George (1786): My Friends and Acquaintances. P
Rossetti, William Michael (ed.): Ruskin, Rossetti, and Pre-Raphaelitism [Papers: concl. 1861].
Scott, W. B. (1811): Poems. V
Shillaber, Benjamin (1814): Life and Sayings of Mrs. Partington. P
Smedley, Francis Edward (1818): Harry Coverdale's Courtship. P
Stanley, Arthur Penrhyn (1815): Memorials of Canterbury. P
Stewart (d. 1828): Works, ed. Sir William Hamilton and John Veitch [concl. 1858].
Surtees (1803): Handley Cross, or Mr. Jorrocks's Hunt [illustr. Leech; originally monthly Mar. 1853 to Oct. 1854: see 1843]. P
Tennyson (1809): Charge of the Light Brigade [in The Examiner, 9 Dec.; separately 1855]. V
Thoreau (1817): Walden, or Life in the Woods. P
Whyte-Melville (1821): General Bounce. P
Williams, Isaac (1802): The Christian Seasons. V
Wiseman, Nicholas (1802): Fabiola. P
Yonge (1823): The Little Duke. P

Caroline Cody (Marie Corelli) b.
John Gibson Lockhart d.
John Wilson ('Christopher North') d.
Susan Ferrier d.
James Montgomery d.
Working Men's College.
George Eliot lives with G. H. Lewes.
Sir William Smith's 'Dictionary of Greek and Roman Geography' (concl. 1857).
Constable's 'Miscellany of Foreign Literature' (concl. 1855).
George Boole, 'Analysis of the Laws of Thought on which are founded the Mathematical Theories of Logic and Probabilities'.
George Eliot, trs. Feuerbach's 'Essence of Christianity'.

Arnold (1822): Poems, second series.
Bailey, Samuel (1791): Philosophy of the Human Mind. P
Bain, Alexander (1818): Senses and Intellect. P
Bancroft, George (1800): Literary and Historical Miscellanies. P
Blanchard, Laman (d. 1845): Corporation Characters. P
Browning, R. (1812): Men and Women. V
Burton, Sir Richard (1821): Pilgrimage to El-Medinah and Mecca [concl. 1856]. P
Clive, Caroline (1801): Paul Ferroll. P
Dickens (1812): Little Dorrit [monthly from Dec. 1855 to June 1857; collected 1857]. P
Gaskell (1810): Lizzie Leigh, and Other Tales. P
North and South [originally in Household Words, Sept. 1854–Jan. 1855]. P
Hunt (1784): The Old Court Suburb. P
Stories in Verse.
Irving (1783): Life of George Washington [completed 1859]. P
Jowett (1817): Commentary to St. Paul's Epistles to the Thessalonians, Galatians, & Romans. P
Kingsley (1819): Westward Ho! P
Glaucus, or the Wonders of the Shore. P
Lewes (1817): Life of Goethe. P
Lewis, Sir George Cornewall (1806): Credibility of Early Roman History. P
Longfellow (1807): Hiawatha. V
Macaulay (1800): History of England, vols. iii–iv [see 1849, 1861]. P
Macdonald, George (1824): Within and Without. V
Maurice, Frederick Denison (1805): Plan of a Female College. P
Melville (1819): Israel Potter. P
Meredith (1828): Shaving of Shagpat. P
Motley, John Lothrop (1814): The Rise of the Dutch Republic. P
'Owen Meredith' (1831): Clytemnestra. V
Peacock (1785): Memoirs of Shelley [in Fraser's Magazine 1855–60; collected in Works, 1875, vol. iii].
Prescott (1796): Philip II [completed 1858]. P
Taylor, Tom (1817): Still Waters run Deep. D
Tennyson (1809): Maud and Other Poems.
Thackeray (1811): The Rose and the Ring. V
Miscellanies in Prose and Verse [collected].
Trench (1807): English Past and Present. P
Alma and Other Poems.
Trollope (1815): The Warden. P
Whitman, Walt (1819): Leaves of Grass. V
Wilson (d. 1854): Collected Works, ed. Ferrier.
Yonge (1823): The Lances of Lynwood. P

William Paton Ker b.
William Sharp ('Fiona Macleod') b.
Oliver Madox Brown b.
Arthur Pinero b.
Samuel Rogers d.
Charlotte Brontë d.
Julius Hare d.
Mary Mitford d.
Sir William Smith, 'Latin and English Dictionary'.
'Saturday Review' started.
'Daily Chronicle' started.
'Daily Telegraph' started.
Charles Knight, 'Knowledge is Power' (see 1831).
Thomas Keightley, 'Life, Opinions, and Writings of John Milton'.
William Chappell, ed. 'Popular Music of Olden Time' (concl. 1859; rev. Wooldridge, 1893).
Benjamin Thorpe, ed. of 'Beowulf', with Translation and Commentary.

Bradford, William (d. 1657): History of Plimouth Plantations. P

Carlyle (1795): Collected Works [later edd. 1869–71; 1871–4; 1885–7; Traill 1897–1901].

Curtis, George William (1824): Prue and I. P

Dobell (1824): England in Time of War. V

Emerson (1803): English Traits. P

Froude (1818): History of England, vols. i–ii [iii–iv 1858, v–vi 1860, vii–viii 1863, ix–x 1866, xi–xii 1870]. P

Kingsley (1819): The Heroes. P

Landor (1775): Antony and Octavius. P

Melville (1819): Piazza Tales. P

Mulock, Dinah Maria (1826): John Halifax, Gentleman. P

Newman (1801): Callista. P

Patmore (1823): The Espousals [pt. ii o Angel in the House: see 1854–60–62]. V

Reade (1814): It is Never too Late to Mend. P

Rogers (d. 1855): Recollections, ed. Sharpe.

Rossetti (1828), Morris (1834), and others: Oxford and Cambridge Magazine [R. cont: Burden of Nineveh, Blessed Damozel, Staff and Scrip. M. cont: Winter Weather, Riding Together, Chapel in Lyoness, Pray but one prayer for me, prose tales and articles]. P and V

Ruskin (1819): Modern Painters, iii–iv [see 1843]. P

Schoolcraft, Henry Rowe (1793): The Myth of Hiawatha. P

Stanley (1815): Sinai and Palestine. P

Yonge (1823): Daisy Chain. P

Oscar Wilde b.
George Bernard Shaw b.
William Archer b.
Sir William Hamilton d.
Hugh Miller d.
Charles Knight's 'Popular History of England' (concl. 1862).
John Stuart Blackie, 'Lays and Legends of Ancient Greece'.
Joseph Bosworth's ed. of King Alfred's Orosius.
G. W. Thornbury, 'Shakespeare's England'.
Heine d.

1857

Bacon (d. 1626): Works, ed. Ellis, Spedding, and Heath [concl. 1874].

Borrow (1803): Romany Rye. P

Boswell (d. 1795): Letters to Temple [Letters, ed. Tinker 1924].

Brontë, C. (d. 1855): The Professor. P

Browning, E. B. (1806): Aurora Leigh. V

Buckle (1821): History of Civilization in England, vol. i [ii 1861; together, 1866]. P

Gaskell (1810): Life of Charlotte Brontë. P

Hughes (1822): Tom Brown's Schooldays. P

Kingsley (1819): Two Years Ago. P

Lawrence, George Alfred: Guy Livingstone. P

Livingstone, David (1813): Missionary Travels in South Africa. P

Locker-Lampson (1821): London Lyrics. V

Luttrell, Narcissus (d. 1752): Brief Relation of State Affairs from 1678 to 1714. P

Macdonald (1824): Poems.

Indian Mutiny.
Joseph Conrad b.
George Gissing b.
John Davidson b.
Douglas Jerrold d.
Matthew Arnold Professor of Poetry at Oxford.
Rossetti visits Oxford and meets Burne - Jones, Morris, and Swinburne.
'Calendar of State Papers,' ed. Mary Everett Green and others, begun.
'The Standard' started.
'The Christian World' started.
Alexander Dyce, ed. of Shakespeare.
Musset d.

Marston, John Westland (1819): A Life's Ransom. D
Melville (1819): The Confidence Man. P
Meredith (1828): Farina. P
Miller (d. 1856): Testimony of the Rocks. P
Newman (1801): Sermons on Various Occasions.
'Owen Meredith' (1831): The Wanderer. V
Ruskin (1819): Political Economy of Art. P
Smith, Alexander (1830): City Poems.
Smith, William Henry (1808): Thorndale. P
Spencer (1820): Essays, series I [II 1863, III 1874].
Story, Robert (1795): Poetical Works [collected].
Thackeray (1811): The Virginians [monthly from
   Nov. 1857 to Oct. 1859; collected 1858–9]. P
   Christmas Books [collected]. P
Trollope (1815): Barchester Towers. P
Walpole (d. 1797): Letters, ed. Cunningham
   [concl. 1859; ed. Toynbee, 1903–5].

President U.S.A.
Buchanan.

1858

Arnold (1822): Merope. D
Brown, John (1810): Horæ Subsecivæ, vol. i
   [ii 1861, iii 1882]. P
Carlyle (1795): Friedrich II (Frederick the Great),
   vols. i–ii [iii 1862, iv 1864, v–vi 1865]. P
Clough (1819): Amours de Voyage. V
Cory, William Johnson (1823): Ionica [2nd vol.
   1877; enlarg. edition 1891]. V
Farrar (1831): Eric, or Little by Little. P
Forster, John (1812): Essays [collected]. P
'George Eliot' (1819): Scenes of Clerical Life
   [in Blackwood's, 1857]. P
Gladstone (1809): Studies on Homer. P
Hare (d. 1855): Sermons.
Hogg, Thomas (1792): Life of Shelley. P
Holmes (1809): The Autocrat of the Breakfast-
   Table. P and V
Kingsley (1819): Andromeda, and Other Poems.
Landor (1775): Dry Sticks Fagoted. V
Leyden, John (d. 1811): Poems and Ballads.
Longfellow (1807): Courtship of Miles Standish. V
Lytton (1803): What will he do with it. P
Macdonald (1824): Phantastes. P
Marston, John Westland (1819): A Hard Struggle. D
Morris (1834): Defence of Guenevere. V
Procter, Adelaide (1825): Legends and Lyrics.
Sleeman, Sir William (d. 1856): A Journey
   through the Kingdom of Oudh. P
Trelawny, Edward John (1792): Recollections of
   Last Days of Shelley and Byron. P
Trollope (1815): Doctor Thorne. P
   The Three Clerks. P.
Wiseman, Nicholas (1802): Recollections of the
   Last Four Popes. P

Sir William Watson b.
Robert Owen d.
William Aytoun, 'Ballads
*   of Scotland' (anthology).*
Dickens begins his public
*   readings.*
First volume of the 'Rolls
*   Series' published.*
Aytoun and Martin, trs.
*   Poems and Ballads of*
*   Goethe.*

Arnold (1822): England and the Italian question. P
Bain, Alexander (1818): Emotions and Will. P
Boole (1815): Differential Equations [concl. 1865].
Boyd, A. K. H. (1825): Recreations of a Country Parson. P
Brown, John (1810): Rab and his Friends. P
Darwin (1809): Origin of Species. P
Dickens (1812): Tale of Two Cities [in All the Year Round, Apr.–Nov.; also separately]. P
Fitzgerald (1809): Rubáiyát of Omar Khayyám [2nd ed. much altered 1868; 3rd ed. 1872; 4th ed. 1879]. V
Gaskell (1810): Round the Sofa. P
'George Eliot' (1819): Adam Bede. P
The Lifted Veil [in Blackwood's]. P
Holmes (1809): The Professor at the Breakfast-Table. P and V
Hughes (1822): Scouring of the White Horse. P
Kingsley, Henry (1830): Recollections of Geoffrey Hamlyn. P
Lewes (1817): Physiology of Common Life. P
Mackay, Charles (1814): Collected Songs.
Masson (1822): Life of Milton [concl. 1880]. P
Meredith (1828): Ordeal of Richard Feverel. P
Mill (1806): On Liberty. P
Thoughts on Parliamentary Reform. P
Dissertations and Discussions, vols. i–ii [iii 1867, iv 1876]. P
Norton, Charles Eliot (1827): Notes of Travel. P
Ruskin (1819): The Two Paths. P
Elements of Perspective. P
Sewell, Mary (1797): Children of Summerbrook. V
Shaftesbury (d. 1683): Memoirs, Letters, and Speeches, ed. W. D. Christie.
Shelley (d. 1822): Memorials, ed. Lady Shelley.
Smiles, Samuel (1812): Self-Help. P
Tennyson (1809): Idylls of the King [Enid, Vivien, Elaine, Guinevere: see 1869, 1872]. V
Trench (1807): Select Glossary of English Words.
Trollope (1815): The Bertrams. P
Walpole (d. 1797): Journal of the Reign of George III, 1771–83, ed. John Doran [new ed. by A. F. Steuart 1910].

War of Italian Liberation.
Garibaldi in Sicily.
Kenneth Grahame b.
Lady Gregory b.
Francis Thompson b.
Arthur Conan Doyle b.
Alfred Edward Housman b.
Sir Sidney Lee b.
Havelock Ellis b.
Thomas de Quincey d.
Leigh Hunt d.
Lord Macaulay d.
Henry Hallam d.
John Austin d.
'Chambers's Encyclopaedia' (concl. 1868).
Chambers's 'Domestic Annals of Scotland' (concl. 1861).
Dickens starts 'All the Year Round' (weekly).
'Macmillan's Magazine' started.
'Sporting Life' started.
Thomas Keightley, ed. of Milton.

Boole (1815): Calculus of Finite Differences. P
Boucicault, Dion (1820?): Colleen Bawn. D
Bright, William (1824): History of the Church,
　A.D. 313–457. P
Browning, E. B. (1806): Poems before Congress.
Campbell, John Francis: Popular Tales of the
　West Highlands [concl. 1862]. P
Collins (1824): Woman in White. P
Dickens (1812): Great Expectations [in All the
　Year Round, 1860–1; collected 1861]. P
　Uncommercial Traveller [enlarg. 1866]. P
　Hunted Down [in All the Year Round]. P
Doran, John: Their Majesties' Servants. P
Dundonald, Thomas Cochrane, 10th Earl of (d.
　1860): Autobiography of a Seaman. P
Emerson (1803): The Conduct of Life. P
Gaskell (1810): Right at Last, and Other Tales. P
'George Eliot' (1819): Mill on the Floss. P
Hawthorne (1804): The Marble Faun. P
Hook, Walter Farquhar (1798): Lives of the
　Archbishops of Canterbury [concl. 1876]. P
Howells, W. Dean (1837): Columbus. P
Hunt (d. 1859): Poetical Works, rev. by himself
　and ed. Thornton Hunt [ed. Milford 1922].
Macaulay (d. 1859): Miscellaneous Writings, ed.
　T. F. Ellis.
Motley (1814): The History of the United
　Netherlands, vol. i [vols. ii and iii in 1867].
'Owen Meredith' (1831): Lucile. V
Patmore (1823): Faithful for Ever [pt. iii. of
　Angel in the House: see 1854–6–62]. V
Peacock (1785): Gryll Grange [in Fraser's Maga-
　zine; separately 1861]. P
Pusey (1800): The Minor Prophets. P
Rogers (d. 1855): Table Talk, ed. Dyce. P
Roscoe, William Caldwell (d. 1859): Poems and
　Essays, ed. R. H. Hutton.
Ruskin (1819): Modern Painters, vol. v [see 1843].
Swinburne (1837): The Queen Mother, Rosa-
　mond. D
Thackeray (1811): Lovel the Widower [in Corn-
　hill; separately 1861]. P
　The Four Georges [in Cornhill; sep. 1861].
Timrod, Henry (1829): Poems.
Trollope (1815): Castle Richmond. P
Tyndall, John (1820): Glaciers of the Alps. P
Whyte-Melville (1821): Holmby House. P
Wilson (editor), Temple, Williams, Powell, Patti-
　son, Jowett, Goodwin: Essays and Reviews. P
Yonge (1823): Pigeon Pie. P

Sir James Barrie b.
William Ralph Inge b.
Anna Jameson d.
George Payne Rainsford
　James d.
Sir William Napier d.
Ebenezer Jones d.
'Cornhill　　Magazine'
　(Thackeray editor up
　to 1862) started.
Thomas Corser, 'Collec-
　tanea　Anglo-Poetica'
　(concl. 1880).
Charles Bradlaugh starts
　the 'National Reformer'
　(concl. 1891).
Theodore Martin, trs. of
　Horace's Odes.
'London Review' (weekly;
　concl. 1869).
Wilberforce–Huxley　de-
　bate at British Associa-
　tion meeting at Oxford.
Schopenhauer d.

Arnold (1822): On Translating Homer: [see 1862]. P

Popular Education of France. P

Beeton, Mrs. (1836): Book of Household Management [originally pub. in parts 1859-60]. P

Buckle (1821): History of Civilization, vol. ii [see 1857]. P

Channing, William Henry (1810): The Civil War in America. P

Dixon (1833): Christ's Company. V

Du Chaillu, Paul (1835): Explorations in Equatorial Africa. P

'George Eliot' (1819): Silas Marner. P

Holmes (1809): Elsie Venner. P

Hughes (1822): Tom Brown at Oxford. P

Hunt (d. 1859): A Saunter through the West End. P

Kingsley, Henry (1830): Ravenshoe. P

Macaulay (d. 1859): History of England, vol. v, ed. Lady Trevelyan [see 1849-55]. P

Maine (1822): Ancient Law. P

Max Müller (1823): Science of Language [concl. 1863]. P

May, Sir Thomas (1815): Constitutional History of England [concl. 1863]. P

Meredith (1828): Evan Harrington [originally in Once a Week 1860]. P

Mill (1806): Representative Government. P

Utilitarianism [in Fraser's Magazine; separately 1863]. P

Palgrave (1824): Golden Treasury [rev. and enlarg. 1896]. V

Piozzi (d. 1821): Autobiography, Letters, &c., ed. Hayward. P

Reade (1814): The Cloister and the Hearth [as A Good Fight in Once a Week 1859]. P

Rossetti (1828): Early Italian Poets [translations; revised as Dante and his Circle, 1874]. V

Sewell, Mary (1797): Stories in Verse.

Smith (1830): Edwin of Deira. V

Smith, William Henry (1808): Gravenhurst. P

Spencer (1820): Education. P

Stanhope, Fifth Earl of (1805): Life of William Pitt [concl. 1862].

Stanley (1815): History of the Eastern Church. P

Tennent, Sir James (1804): Natural History of Ceylon. P

Thackeray (1811): Adventures of Philip [in Cornhill 1861-2; separately 1862]. P

Trollope (1815): Framley Parsonage. P

Wood, Mrs. Henry (1814): East Lynne. P

Goldsworthy Lowes Dickinson b.
Mary Coleridge b.
Rabindranath Tagore b.
Maurice Hewlett b.
Walter Raleigh b.
Prince Albert d.
Elizabeth Barrett Browning d.
Arthur Hugh Clough d.
William Blades's 'Life and Typography of Caxton' (concl. 1863).
Benjamin Thorpe's ed. of 'Anglo-Saxon Chronicle'.
James Spedding's 'Life and Letters of Francis Bacon', 1861-74.
Outbreak of American Civil War (ended 1865).

President U.S.A. Lincoln.

Arnold (1822): On Translating Homer, Last Words [see 1861]. P

Austin, Alfred (1835): Human Tragedy. V

Borrow (1803): Wild Wales. P

Braddon, Mary (1837): Lady Audley's Secret. P

Browning, E. B. (d. 1861): Last Poems, ed. R. Browning.

Burton, John Hill (1809): The Book Hunter. P

Calverley (1831): Verses and Translations.

Carlyle (1795): Friedrich II, vol. iii [see 1858]. P

Clough (d. 1861): Collected Poems, with Memoir by F. T. Palgrave [ed. Milford, 1910].

Colenso, John William (1814): The Pentateuch Examined [concl. 1879]. P

Collins (1824): No Name. P

Cook, Edward Dutton (1829): Trials of the Tredgolds. P

Darwin (1809): On the Contrivances by which Orchids are fertilized. P

Faber, Frederick (1814): Hymns [complete ed.].

Farrar, Frederick William (1831): St. Winifred's, or the World of School. P

'George Eliot' (1819): Romola [in Cornhill, July 1862–Aug. 1863; separately 1863]. P

Howe, Julia Ward (1819): Battle Hymn of the Republic. V

Hunt (d. 1859): Correspondence, ed. T. Hunt.

Lytton (1803): A Strange Story. P

Meredith (1828): Modern Love. Poems of the English Roadside. V

Patmore (1823): Victories of Love [pt. 4 of Angel in the House: see 1854–6–60]. V

Rossetti, Christina (1830): Goblin Market and Other Poems.

Ruskin (1819): Unto this Last [in the *Cornhill*]. P

Sewell, Mary (1797): Patience Hart's Experiences in Service. P

Shelley (d. 1822): Relics of Shelley, ed. Richard Garnett.

Spencer (1820): A System of Synthetic Philosophy: First Principles. P

Stephen, Sir James Fitzjames (1829): Essays by a Barrister. P

Swinburne (1837): Dead Love [in Once a Week]. P

Taylor, Sir Henry (1800): St. Clement's Eve. D

Trollope (1815): Orley Farm. P

Wood, Mrs. Henry (1814): The Channings. P

Sir Henry Newbolt b.
Eden Phillpotts b.
Montagu Rhodes James b.
Henry Thomas Buckle d.
James Sheridan Knowles d.
Robert Chambers's 'Book of Days' (miscellany).
George Long's trs. of Marcus Aurelius.
John Payne Collier, ed. of Spenser.

Aldrich, Thomas Bailey (1836): Poems. V

Ashworth, John (1813): Strange Tales. P

Austin (d. 1859): Lectures on Jurisprudence. P

Bates (1825): The Naturalist on the Amazon. P

Blake (d. 1827): Life by Gilchrist and Selections from Works, ed. D. G. Rossetti.

Brown, John (1810): Marjorie Fleming. P

Browning, E. B. (d. 1861): The Greek Christian Poets and the English Christian Poets. P

Butler (1835): A First Year in Canterbury Settlement. P

Conington, John (1825): Trs. Odes of Horace. V

Cooke (1830): Life of Stonewall Jackson. P

Freeman (1823): History of Federal Government. P

Gardiner (1829): History of England from the Accession of James I [see 1883]. P

Gaskell (1810): A Dark Night's Work. P
 Sylvia's Lovers. P
 Crowley Castle [in All the Year Round]. P

Hawthorne (1804): Our Old Home. P

Huxley (1825): Man's Place in Nature. P

Ingelow, Jean (1820): Poems [a second series of Poems 1876, third series 1885].

Kinglake (1809): Invasion of the Crimea, vols. i–ii [iii–iv 1868, v 1875, vi 1880, vii–viii 1887]. P

Kingsley (1813): Water Babies. P

Landor (1775): Heroic Idylls. V

Le Fanu (1814): The House by the Churchyard. P

Lincoln (1809): Gettysburg Address. P

Longfellow (1807): Tales of a Wayside Inn. V

Lyell (1797): Antiquity of Man. P

Manning, Henry Edward (1803): Sermons on Several Subjects [concl. 1873].

Marston, John Westland (1819): Donna Diana. D

Maurice (1805): Claims of the Bible and of Science. P

Mill (1806): Utilitarianism [reprtd. from Fraser's Magazine 1861]. P

Oliphant, Mrs. (1828): Salem Chapel [series 1 of Chronicles of Carlingford]. P
 The Rector and the Doctor's Family [series 11 of above]. P

Reade (1814): Hard Cash. P

Reid (d. 1796): Works, ed. Hamilton and Mansel.

Smith, Alexander (1830): Dreamthorp. P

Speke, John Hanning (1827): Journal of Discovery of the Source of the Nile. P

Stanley (1815): History of Jewish Church. P

Thackeray (1811): Roundabout Papers [collected from Cornhill 1860–3].

Thoreau (d. 1862): Excursions. P

Whyte-Melville (1821): The Gladiators. P

Woolner, Thomas (1825): My Beautiful Lady. V

William Wymark Jacobs b.

Sir Arthur T. Quiller-Couch b.

William Makepeace Thackeray d.

Richard Whately d.

'*The Church Times*' (*weekly*).

Cambridge Shakespeare, ed. Clarke, Glover, and Wright (concl. 1866; new edd.: 1887, 1893).

Tyndall, 'Heat considered as a Mode of Motion' (later edd., each altered and enlarg., 1865–8–70–5–80).

Sir William Smith, 'Dictionary of the Bible'.

Edward Lane, 'Arabic-English Lexicon' (concl. 1892).

Taine, 'Histoire de la Littérature Anglaise' (concl. 1864; see 1872).

Renan, 'La Vie de Jésus'.

Allingham (1824): Laurence Bloomfield in Ireland. V
The Ballad Book [Golden Treasury Series].
Arnold (1822): A French Eton. P
Babbage, Charles (1792): Passages from the Life of a Philosopher. P
Browning (1812): Dramatis Personae. V
Bryce (1838): Holy Roman Empire. P
Burton, John Hill (1809): Scot Abroad. P.
Cobbe, Francis Power (1822): Broken Lights. P
Carlyle (1795): Friedrich II, vol. iv [see 1858]. P
Cowper, Mary, Countess (d. 1724): Diary, 1714–20.
Dickens (1812): Our Mutual Friend [monthly May 1864 to Nov. 1865; collected 1865]. P
Dixon, Richard Watson (1833): Historical Odes. V
Forster (1812): Life of Sir John Eliot. P
Gaskell (1810): Cousin Phillis and Other Tales. P
'**George Eliot**' (1819): Brother Jacob [in Cornhill]. P
Hawker, R. S. (1803): Quest of the Sangraal. V
Huxley (1825): On the Classification of Animals. On the Vertebrate Skull. P
Le Fanu, Joseph Sheridan (1814): Uncle Silas. P
Long, George (1800): Decline of the Roman Republic [concl. 1874]. P
Lowell (1819): Fireside Travels. P
Meredith (1828): Emilia in England [called Sandra Belloni 1889]. P
Newman (1801): Apologia pro vita sua [repub. with passages dealing with Kingsley as History of my Religious Opinions 1865; original title readopted in later edd.].
Payn, James (1830): Lost Sir Massingberd. P
Praed (d. 1839): Poetical Works, ed. Derwent Coleridge [American edd. 1844, '57].
Robertson (1829): David Garrick [acted]. D
Spencer (1820): Principles of Biology, vol. i [ii 1867; enlarg. 1898–9]. P
Stanley, Edward, Earl of Derby (1799): Trs. of Iliad. V
Tennyson (1809): Idylls of the Hearth [later called Enoch Arden].
Thackeray (d. 1863): Denis Duval [in Cornhill; separately 1867]. P
Thoreau (d. 1862): Maine Woods. P
Cape Cod. P
Trollope (1815): The Small House at Allington. P
Can you forgive her? P
Westcott (1825): The Bible and the Church. P
Whateley (d. 1863): Miscellaneous Remains. P

Stephen Phillips b.
Leonard Trelawny Hobhouse b.
Israel Zangwill b.
Walter Savage Landor d.
Alaric Alexander Watts d.
John Clare d.
Robert Smith Surtees d.
George Boole d.
Adelaide Procter d.
Nathaniel Hawthorne d.
Controversy between Charles Kingsley and Newman starts with K.'s review of Froude's 'History of England' in 'Macmillan's Magazine' for January: K.'s pamphlet 'What then does Dr. Newman mean?' draws forth N.'s 'Apologia'.
'The Month' started.
Early English Text Society founded by F. J. Furnivall.
Henry Morley's 'English Writers' (vol. i before Chaucer, vol. ii up to Dunbar) 1864–7 (see 1887).

Alcott, Amos Bronson (1799): Ralph Waldo Emerson [2nd edition 1888]. P

Arnold (1822): Essays in Criticism, 1st series [see 1888]. P

Berry, Mary (d. 1852): Extracts from Journals and Correspondence.

Browne, Charles Farrar (1834): Artemus Ward: his Travels. P

Carlyle (1795): Friedrich II, vols. v–vi [see 1858]. P

Clough (d. 1861): Letters and Remains.

Fitzgerald (1809): The Mighty Magician, Such Stuff as Dreams are made of [trs. from Calderon: see 1853]. V

Gaskell (d. 1865): The Grey Woman. P

Grote (1794): Plato and other Companions of Sokrates. P

Grote, John (1813): Exploratio Philosophica. P

Kingsley, Henry (1830): The Hillyars and Burtons. P

Lecky (1838): Rise and Influence of the Spirit of Rationalism in Europe. P

'Lewis Carroll' (1832): Alice in Wonderland. P

Lincoln (1809): Second Inaugural Address. P

Longfellow (1807): Trs. Divine Comedy. V

Lowell (1819): Commemoration Ode. V

Martin (1816): Trs. Faust, pt. i [ii. 1886]. V

Meredith (1828): Rhoda Fleming. P

Neale, John Mason (1818): Hymns. V

Newman (1801): Dream of Gerontius [in The Month; separately 1866]. V

Oliphant, Laurence (1829): Piccadilly [in Blackwood's; separately, 1870]. P

'Ouida' (1839): Strathmore. P

Owen (1804): Memoir on the Gorilla. P

Palgrave, William Gifford (1826): A Year's Journey through Central and Eastern Arabia. P

Parkman, Francis (1823): Pioneers of France. P

Pusey (1800): Eirenicon, pt. i [ii. 1869, iii 1870]. V

Ruskin (1819): Sesame and Lilies. P

Seeley (1834): Ecce Homo. P

Shaw, H. W. (1818): Josh Billings, his sayings. P

Smith, Goldwin (1823): England and America. P

Stirling, James Hutchinson (1820): Secret of Hegel. P

Swinburne (1837): Atalanta in Calydon. D
Chastelard. D

Trench, Richard (1807): Poems [collected].
Gustavus Adolphus. P

Whitman (1819): Drum-Taps. V
Sequel to Drum-Taps. V

Whittier (1807): Poems. V

Rudyard Kipling b.
William Butler Yeats b.
A. E. W. Mason b.
Laurence Housman b.
Isaac Williams d.
Elizabeth Gaskell d.
Mrs. Beeton d.
William Aytoun d.
Charles Cavendish Fulke Greville d.
'The Argosy' started.
'Fortnightly Review' ,,
'Pall Mall Gazette' ,,
'Sporting Times' ,,
'Nation' (American) ,,
Cassell's 'Illustrated History of England'.
John Payne Collier, 'Bibliographical and Critical Account of the Rarest Books in the English Language'.
Joseph Barber Lightfoot, 'Commentary on St. Paul's Epistle to the Galatians'.
Viscount Milton and W. B. Cheadle, 'The North-West Passage by Land'.
Assassination of Abraham Lincoln.

President U.S.A. Johnson.

Baker, Sir Samuel (1821): The Albert Nyanza and Exploration of Nile Sources. P
Bell, Henry Glassford (1803): Romances. V
Blackmore (1825): Cradock Nowell. P
Carlyle (1795): On the Choice of Books. P
Collins (1824): Armadale. P
Conington, John (1825): Trs. Æneid. V
Dallas, Eneas Sweetland (1828): The Gay Science. P
Doyle, Sir Francis (1810): Return of the Guards. P
Gaskell (d. 1865): Wives and Daughters [completed by F. Greenwood: originally in Cornhill 1864–6]. P
'George Eliot' (1819): Felix Holt. P
Hinton, James (1822): Mystery of Pain. P
Howells, W. Dean (1837): Venetian Life. P
Kingsley (1813): Hereward the Wake. P
Lytton (1803): Lost Tales of Miletus. V
Macaulay (d. 1859): Collected Works, ed. Lady Trevelyan.
Mansel (1820): Philosophy of the Conditioned. P
Marston, John Westland (1819): Favourite of Fortune. D
Melville (1819): Battle Pieces. V
Neale (d. 1866): Sequences, Hymns, and other Ecclesiastical Verses.
'Ouida' (1839): Chandos. P
Owen (1804): Memoir on the Dodo. P
   On the Anatomy of Vertebrates. P
Procter (1787): Charles Lamb [concl. 1868]. P
Reade (1814): Griffith Gaunt [originally in Argosy 1865]. P
Rogers, J. E. Thorold (1823): History of Agriculture and Prices in England, vols. i–ii [iii–iv 1882, v–vi 1887, vii 1902]. P
Rossetti, Christina (1830): Prince's Progress and Other Poems.
Ruskin (1819): Ethics of the Dust. P
   Crown of Wild Olive. P
Swinburne (1837): Poems and Ballads, 1st series [see 1878, 1889].
   Notes on Poems and Reviews. P
Thoreau (d. 1862): A Yankee in Canada. P
Trollope (1815): The Belton Estate. P
Webster, Augusta (1837): Dramatic Studies. V
Westcott (1825): Gospel of Resurrection. P
Whittier (1807): Snow-Bound. V
Yonge (1823): The Dove in the Eagle's Nest. P

Herbert George Wells b.
Gilbert Murray b.
Thomas Love Peacock d.
John Keble d.
William Whewell d.
John Mason Neale d.
Jane Welsh Carlyle d.
Richard Morris, ed. of Chaucer and 'Specimens of Early English' (concl. 1872).
'Contemporary Review' started.
'Aunt Judy's Magazine' started.
Sir William Rowan Hamilton, 'Elements of Quaternions'.

Arnold (1822): New Poems [Thyrsis, A Southern Night, Saint Brandan, &c.].
On the Study of Celtic Literature. P
Bagehot (1826): English Constitution. P
Bailey (1816): The Universal Hymn. V
Browne, Charles Farrar (1834): Artemus Ward in London. P
Carlyle (1795): Shooting Niagara [in Macmillan's Magazine]. P
Dixon, William Hepworth (1821): New America. P
Emerson (1803): May Day and other pieces. V
Freeman (1823): History of Norman Conquest of England [concl. 1879]. P
Froude (1818): Short Studies on Great Subjects, series I [II 1871, III 1877, IV 1883]. P
Harte (1836): The Lost Galleon. V
Condensed Novels. V
Hazlitt (d. 1830): Memoirs, by W. C. Hazlitt.
Holmes (1809): The Guardian Angel. P
Howells (1837): Italian Journeys. P
Ingelow (1820): Story of Doom. V
Keble (d. 1866): Sermons. P
Lanier, Sidney (1842): Tiger Lilies. P
Liddon, Henry Parry (1829): Divinity of Our Lord and Saviour [Bampton Lecture, 1866].
Longfellow (1807): Flower-de-Luce. V
'Mark Twain' (1835): The Celebrated Jumping Frog. P
Marston, John Westland (1819): Hero of Romance. D
Max Müller (1823): Chips from a German Workshop [concl. 1875]. P
Meredith (1828): Vittoria. P
Morris (1834): Life and Death of Jason. V
Myers (1843): St. Paul. V
'Ouida' (1839): Under Two Flags. P
'Owen Meredith' (1831): Poetical Works.
Parkman, Francis (1827): The Jesuits in North America. P
Pater (1839): Essay on Winckelmann [in Westminster Review].
Robertson (1829): Caste [acted]. D
Ruskin (1819): Time and Tide. P
Seebohm, Frederic (1833): Oxford Reformers. P
Smith, Goldwin (1823): Three English Statesmen. P
Swinburne (1837): Song of Italy. V
Appeal to England. V
Thackeray, Anne Isabella (1837): The Village on the Cliff. P
Thackeray (d. 1863): Collected Works [concl. 1869].

Arnold Bennett b.
Pearl Mary Craigie ('John Oliver Hobbes') b.
George William Russell ('Æ') b.
Lionel Johnson b.
John Galsworthy b.
Charles Edward Montague b.
Alexander Smith d.
Sir Archibald Alison d.
Michael Faraday d.
Alaric Watts's 'The Laurel and the Lyre' (anthology of fugitive verse).
Walter Skeat's ed. of 'Piers Plowman' (concl. 1884).
William Carew Hazlitt, 'Handbook to the Popular Poetical and Dramatic Literature of Great Britain'.
William Thomson, Lord Kelvin, and Peter Guthrie Tait, 'Natural Philosophy'.
Marx, 'Das Kapital', 1st vol. published.
Baudelaire d.

Trollope (1815): Last Chronicle of Barset [in parts 1866]. P
  The Claverings. P.   Nina Balatka. P
Tupper (1810): Proverbial Philosophy, series III [see 1838]. V
Tyndall (1820): Lectures on Sound. P
Whittier (1807): Maud Muller. V

1868

Ainsworth (1805): South Sea Bubble. P
Alcott, Amos Bronson (1799): Tablets. P
Alcott, Louisa (1832): Little Women. P
Arnold (1822): Schools and Universities on the Continent. P
Browne, Charles Farrar (1834): Artemus Ward: his book. P
Browning (1812): The Ring and the Book. V
Byron (1834): Uncle Dick's Darling [acted]. D
Church (1815): Oxford Sermons. P
Collins (1824): The Moonstone. P
Darwin (1809): Variation of Animals and Plants under Domestication. P
Digby, Sir Kenelm (d. 1665): Journal of the Scanderoon Voyage in 1628. P
Dilke, Charles Wentworth (1843): Greater Britain. P
'George Eliot' (1819): Spanish Gypsy. V
Helps (1813): Realmah. P
Lightfoot, Joseph Barber (1828): Commentary on St. Paul's Epistle to the Philippians. P
Longfellow (1807): New England Tragedies. V
Lowell (1819): Under the Willows. V
Mackay, Charles (1814): Poetical Works.
Martineau, J. (1805): Essays, Philosophical and Theological.
Maurice (1805): The Conscience. P
Milman (d. 1868): Ed. Annals of St. Paul's. P
Morris (1834): Earthly Paradise, vol. i [ii. 1869, iii 1870]. V
Newman (1801): Verses on various Occasions. Collected Works [concl. 1881].
Stanley (1815): Memorials of Westminster Abbey. P
Swinburne (1837): Siena. V
  William Blake. P
  Notes on the Royal Academy. P
Victoria, Queen (1819): Leaves from a Journal of our Life in the Highlands [ed. Sir A. Helps]. P

Gertrude Lowthian Bell b.
Henry Hart Milman d.
Lord Brougham d.
The Ballad and Chaucer Societies founded by F. J. Furnivall.
The Royal Historical Society founded.
Edward Arber's series of 'English Reprints' (concl. 1870) starts with Milton's 'Areopagitica'.
F. J. Furnivall and J. W. Hales's ed. of the Percy Ballads MS.
F. J. Furnivall, ed. of 'Canterbury Tales' (six-text ed.).
A. B. Grosart, 'Fuller Worthies Library' (39 vols., concluded 1876; edd. of Sir John Davies, Fulke Greville, Henry Vaughan, Andrew Marvell, George Herbert, Richard Crashaw, John Donne, Robert Southwell, Sir Philip Sidney, and others).
Alexander Bain, 'Mental and Moral Science'.
Philip Stanhope Worsley and John Conington, trs. Iliad (W.'s share, bks. i–xii, previously in 1865).

Alcott, Louisa (1832): Good Wives. P
Arnold (1822): Collected Poems [incl. Rugby Chapel, now first pub.].
    Culture and Anarchy. P
Beecher, Henry Ward (1813): Sermons.
Blackmore (1825): Lorna Doone. P
Browne (1834): Artemus Ward's Panorama. P
Clough (d. 1861): Poems and Prose Remains, with Selection from Letters, ed. by his Wife.
Ewing, Juliana Horatia (1841): Mrs. Overtheway's Remembrances. P
Forster (1812): Life of Landor. P
Galton, Sir Francis (1822): Hereditary Genius. P
'George Eliot' (1819): Agatha, a Poem.
Gilbert (1836): Bab Ballads. V
Guiccioli, Teresa: Recollections of Lord Byron [Eng. trs.; original French 1868]. P
Hawker, R. S. (1803): Cornish Ballads. V
Keble (d. 1866): Sermons on Baptismal Service. Miscellany Poems, ed. Moberley.
Lecky (1838): History of European Morals. P
'Lewis Carroll' (1832): Phantasmagoria. P
Lightfoot (1828): Apostolic Fathers, pt. i.
'Mark Twain' (1835): Innocents Abroad. P
Maurice (1805): Lectures on Social Morality. P
Mill (1806): On the Subjection of Women. P
Morris (1834): Earthly Paradise, vol. ii [see 1868]. V
    Trs. Grettir's Saga. P
'Owen Meredith' (1831): Orval, or the Fool of Time. V
Reade (1814): Foul Play [with Dion Boucicault: dramatic version produced in 1868, and in 1877 as Scuttled Ship]. P
Robinson, Henry Crabb (d. 1867): Diary (selections), ed. T. Sadler.
Ruskin (1819): Queen of the Air. P
Stubbs, William, and Haddan, A. W.: Ed. Councils and Ecclesiastical Documents of Great Britain and Ireland. P
Tennyson (1809): Holy Grail and Other Poems [New Arthurian poems: Holy Grail, Coming of Arthur, Pelleas and Ettarre, Passing of Arthur; non-Arthurian: Lucretius, Higher Pantheism, Northern Farmer (new style), &c.: see 1859, 1872].
Thornton, William Thomas (1813): On Labour. P
Trollope (1815): Phineas Finn. P
Wallace (1823): The Malay Archipelago. P

Laurence Binyon b.
Harleian Society founded.
'Nature' started.
'The Academy' started.
'The Graphic' started.
Thomas Arnold (jnr.), ed. of the English Works of Wycliffe (concl. 1871).
William Chappell, ed. of Roxburghe Ballads, vols. i–iii (1869–79); see 1883).
E. A. Abbott, 'Shakesperian Grammar' (new ed. 1897).
Sainte-Beuve d.
Lamartine d.

President U.S.A. Grant.

Aldrich, Thomas Bailey (1836): The Story of a Bad Boy. P

Arnold (1822): St. Paul and Protestantism. P

Church (1815): Life of St. Anselm [enlarg. from ed. of 1843]. P

Collins (1824): Man and Wife. P

Cox, George William (1827): Mythology of Aryan Nations. P

Dickens (d. 1870): Mystery of Edwin Drood [unfinished; monthly Apr.–Sept.]. P

Disraeli (1804): Lothair. P

Emerson (1803): Society and Solitude. P

Ewing, Juliana Horatia (1841): The Brownies. P

Grote, John (d. 1866): Utilitarian Philosophy. P

Harte (1836): The Luck of Roaring Camp, and Other Sketches. P

Hunt (d. 1858): A Day by the Fire, and other papers hitherto uncollected. P

Huxley (1825): Lay Sermons, Addresses, and Reviews. P

Keble (d. 1866): Letters of Spiritual Counsel. P

Lowell (1819): The Cathedral. V
 Among my Books. P

Miller, Joaquin (1839): Pacific Poems. V

Milman (d. 1868): Savonarola, Erasmus, and other Essays, ed. A. Milman. P

Morris (1834): Earthly Paradise, vol. iii [see 1868]. V
 Trs. Volsunga Saga [with E. Magnússon]. P

Newman (1801): Grammar of Assent. P

O'Shaughnessy, Arthur (1844): An Epic of Women. V

Reade (1814): Put Yourself in His Place [originally in Cornhill, 1869–70; dramatic version, Free Labour, performed 1870]. P

Rossetti (1828): Poems [collected: new and altered ed. 1881].

Ruskin (1819): Lectures on Art. P

Spencer (1820): Principles of Psychology [concl. 1872]. P

Stanhope, Fifth Earl (1805): History of England, comprising the Reign of Queen Anne until the Peace of Utrecht. P

Stubbs (1825): Ed. Select Charters and other Illustrations of English Constitutional History. P

Swinburne (1837): Ode on Proclamation of French Republic. V

Wallace (1823): Natural Selection. P

Whymper (1840): Scrambles among the Alps. P

Franco - Prussian War, 1870–1.
Education Act.
Thomas Sturge Moore b.
Hilaire Belloc b.
Charles Dickens d.
Benjamin Jowett Master of Balliol.
W. D. Christie, ed. Dryden's Poetical Works.
Historical MSS. Commission's Reports begin.
Brewer's 'Dictionary of Phrase and Fable'.
Dumas d.
Mérimée d.

Alcott, Louisa (1832): Little Men. P

Arnold (1822): Friendship's Garland. P

Austen (d. 1817): Lady Susan, The Watsons [in 2nd ed. of Memoir (by J. E. Austen Leigh). First ed. of Memoir in 1870]. P

Beecher, Henry Ward (1813): Life of Jesus. P

Besant and Rice: The Golden Butterfly. P

Black, William (1841): A Daughter of Heth. P

Browning (1812): Balaustion's Adventure. V Prince Hohenstiel-Schwangau. V

Burroughs, John (1837): Wake-Robin. P

Cooke, John Esten (1830): Life of Robert E. Lee. P

Darwin (1809): Descent of Man. P

Erskine, Thomas (d. 1870): The Spiritual Order. P

Freeman (1823): Historical Essays, series I [II 1873, III 1879, IV 1892]. P

Froude (1818): Short Studies on Great Subjects, series II [see 1867]. P

'George Eliot' (1819): Middlemarch [in parts]. P

Gilbert (1836): Pygmalion and Galatea [acted]. D

Hardy (1840): Desperate Remedies. P

Hare (1834): Walks in Rome. P

Hay, John (1838): Pike County Ballads. V Castilian Days. P

Howells (1837): Their Wedding Journey. P

Hutton, Richard Holt (1826): Essays. P

Jowett (1817): Trs. Dialogues of Plato. P

Kingsley (1813): At Last. P

Lear (1812): Nonsense Songs and Stories. V

'Lewis Carroll' (1832): Through the Looking Glass. P

Lewis, Leopold David (1828): The Bells [acted]. D

Longfellow (1807): The Divine Tragedy. D

Lowell (1819): My Study Windows. P

Lytton (1803): The Coming Race. P

Macdonald (1824): At the Back of the North Wind. P

Maine (1822): Village Communities. P

Marston, Philip Bourke (1850): Songtide. V

Maurice (1805): Moral and Metaphysical Philosophy [collective ed., concl. 1872]. P

Maxwell, James Clerk (1831): Theory of Heat. P

Meredith (1828): Harry Richmond. P

Miller, Joaquin (1839): Songs of the Sierras. V

Morris, Sir Lewis (1833): Songs of Two Worlds, series I [II 1874, III 1875]. V

Reade (1814): A Terrible Temptation. P

Ruskin (1819): Fors Clavigera [concl. 1887]. P

Stephen (1832): Playground of Europe. P

Swinburne (1837): Songs before Sunrise. V

Whitman (1819): Democratic Vistas. V Passage to India. V

Abolition of religious tests at Oxford, Cambridge, and Durham.

John Millington Synge b.

William Henry Davies b.

Erskine Childers b.

George Grote d.

Thomas William Robertson d.

Robert Buchanan ('Thomas Maitland') attacks Rossetti in article, 'Fleshly School of Poetry', in 'Contemporary Review', Oct. R.'s reply, 'Stealthy School of Criticism', in 'Athenaeum', 16 Dec.

Walter Skeat, 'Specimens of English from 1394 to 1597'.

F. J. Furnivall, ed. of Chaucer's Minor Poems (concl. 1879).

Bayard Taylor trs. 'Faust'.

Horace Howard Furness, 'Variorum Shakespeare' (publication begun).

W. Elwin and W. J. Courthope, ed. of Pope (concl. 1889).

Marcel Proust b.

Alcott, Amos Bronson (1799): Concord Days. P
Bagehot (1826): Physics and Politics. P
Besant and Rice: Ready-Money-Mortiboy. P
Black (1841): Strange Adventures of a Phaeton. P
Blackmore (1825): Maid of Sker. P
Browning (1812): Fifine at the Fair. V
Butler (1835): Erewhon. P
Calverley (1831): Fly Leaves. V
Cooper, Thomas (1805): Life, written by himself. P
Darwin (1809): Expression of the Emotions in Man and Animals. P.
De Morgan, Augustus (d. 1871): Budget of Paradoxes. P
Domett, Alfred (1811): Ranolf and Amohia. V
Forster (1812): Life of Dickens, vol. i [ii 1873, iii 1874]. P
Freeman (1823): English Constitution. P
Froude (1818): The English in Ireland [concl. 1874]. P
Hardy (1840): Under the Greenwood Tree. P
Hare (1834): Memorials of a Quiet Life. P
Holmes (1809): The Poet at the Breakfast-Table. P and V
Ingelow (1820): Off the Skelligs. P
Lang (1844): Ballads and Lyrics of Old France. V
Lear (1812): More Nonsense Songs. V
Liddon, Henry (1829): Some Elements of Religion. P
Longfellow (1807): Three Books of Song. V
Macdonald (1824): The Princess and the Goblin. P
'Mark Twain' (1835): Roughing It. P
Morley (1838): Voltaire. P
Morris (1834): Love is Enough: a Morality [1873]. V
Pusey (1800): University Sermons [collected].
Reade, William Winwood (1838): Martyrdom of Man. P
Ruskin (1819): Munera Pulveris. P
    Aratra Pentelici: Six Lectures on Sculpture. P
    Michael Angelo and Tintoret. P
    Eagle's Nest. P
Stanley, H. M. (1841): Finding of Livingstone. P
Swinburne (1837): Under the Microscope [reply to Buchanan's attack in 1871]. P
Tennyson (1809): Gareth and Lynette. V
    Poems, first collected, with Epilogue to the Queen [concl. 1873; cont. Idylls of the King, complete and in sequence: see 1859, 1869].

Bertrand Russell, Earl Russell b.
Max Beerbohm b.
Charles James Lever d.
Frederick Denison Maurice d.
'The Light Green', ed. Arthur Clement Hilton (two nos. only).
Eng. trs. of Taine's 'History of English Literature' (see 1863).
Richard Morris, 'Historical Outlines of English Accidence'.
William Blades, 'Shakespeare and Typography'.
James Gairdner, ed. Paston Letters, 1440–1486 (concl. 1875).
Gautier d.
Calendar of Clarendon State Papers, vol. i, ed. Ogle and Bliss [ii–iii ed. Macray 1869–76, vol. iv ed. Routledge 1932: see 1767].

Aldrich (1836): Marjorie Daw. P
Arnold (1822): Literature and Dogma. P
Bagehot (1826): Lombard Street. P
Bridges (1844): Poems. V
Brown, O. M. (1855): Gabriel Denver. P
Brown, T. E. (1830): Betsy Lee [in Macmillan's Magazine, Apr.: see 1881]. V
Browning (1812): Red Cotton Nightcap Country. V
Butler (1835): Fair Haven. P
Collins (1824): New Magdalen. P
Cooper, Thomas (1805): Paradise of Martyrs. V
Dobson (1840): Vignettes in Rhyme.
Ewing, Juliana Horatia (1841): A Flatiron for a Farthing. P
Freeman (1823): Essays, series II [see 1871]. P
Grote (d. 1871): Minor Works, ed. A. Bain.
Hardy (1840): Pair of Blue Eyes. P
Harte (1836): Mrs. Skaggs's Husbands. P
Howells (1837): Chance Acquaintance. P
Lytton (1803): Kenelm Chillingly. P
 The Parisians. P
'Mark Twain' (1835): The Gilded Age. P
Martineau, J. (1805): Hymns of Praise and Power.
Max Müller (1823): The Science of Religion. P
Maxwell, James Clark (1831): Treatise on Electricity and Magnetism. P
Mill (d. 1873): Autobiography. P
Morley (1838): Rousseau. P
Myers (d. 1851): Catholic Thoughts [see 1834]. P
Pater (1839): Studies in the Renaissance. P
Spencer (1820): Study of Sociology. P
 The English [first instalment of Descriptive Sociology. Eight instalments during S.'s lifetime 1873–81]. P
Stephen, Sir James Fitzjames (1829): Liberty, Equality, Fraternity. P
Stephen, Sir Leslie (1832): Essays on Freethinking and Plain Speaking. P
Stubbs (1825): Constitutional History of England [concl. 1878].
Thackeray, Anne Isabella (1837): Old Kensington. P
Timrod, Henry (d. 1867): Collected Poems. V
Trollope (1815): Phineas Redux. P
 The Eustace Diamonds. P
Tyndall (1820): Lectures on Light. P
Wills, William Gorman (1828): Charles the First. D
Yonge (1823): The Pillars of the House. P

Walter de la Mare b.
H. M. Tomlinson b.
John Stuart Mill d.
Edward John Bulwer-Lytton, Lord Lytton, d.
Samuel Wilberforce d.
The New Shakspere Society founded by F. J. Furnivall.
George Bannatyne MS. pub. by Hunterian Club (concl. 1902).
Henry Morley, 'First Sketch of English Literature'.
Anna Swanwick, trs. Aeschylus.

President U.S.A. Grant (2nd term).

Adams, John Quincey (d. 1848): Memoirs. P
Aldrich, Thomas Bailey (1836): Prudence Palfrey. P
Black, William (1841): A Princess of Thule. P
Blackie, John Stuart (1809): On Self-Culture. P
Cairnes, John Elliot (1823): Political Economy. P
Cox, George William (1827): History of Greece. P
Ewing, Juliana Horatia (1841): Lob lie by the Fire. P
Farrar (1831): Life of Christ. P
Fiske, John (1842): Cosmic Philosophy. P
Frere (d. 1846): Collected Works, ed. Bartle Frere.
'George Eliot' (1819): Legend of Jubal and Other Poems.
Green (1837): Short History of the English People. P
Greville (d. 1865): Greville Memoirs, series I, 1817–37 [II 1885, III 1887].
Hardy (1840): Far from the Madding Crowd. P
Jevons, William Stanley (1835): Principles of Science. P
Lewes (1817): Foundations of a Creed [Series I of Problems of Life and Mind: see 1877, 1879].
Mill (d. 1873): Three Essays on Religion. P
Morley (1838): On Compromise. P
Motley, John Lothrop (1814): The Life and Death of John of Barneveld. P
O'Shaughnessy (1844): Music and Moonlight. V
'Ouida' (1839): Two Little Wooden Shoes. P
'Owen Meredith' (1831): Fables in Song. V
Parkman, Francis (1827): The Old Régime in Canada. P
Pusey (1800): Lenten Sermons. P
Ruskin (1819): Val d'Arno. P
Sidgwick (1838): Methods of Ethics. P
Smiles, Samuel (1812): Lives of the Engineers [collected]. P
Stephen (1832): Hours in a Library, series I [II 1876; III 1879; collected and enlarg. 1907]. P
Stubbs (1825): Memorials of St. Dunstan. P
Swinburne (1837): Bothwell, a Tragedy. D
Ed. of George Chapman.
Taylor (1817): Lady Clancarty [acted]. D
Thomson (1834): City of Dreadful Night [in National Reformer, Mar.–May; separately, with other poems, 1880]. V
Wordsworth, Dorothy (d. 1855): Recollections of a Tour in Scotland (1803), ed. Shairp. P

Maurice Baring b.
Gilbert Keith Chesterton b
Somerset Maugham b.
Gordon Bottomley b.
Gertrude Stein b.
Bryan Waller Procter ('Barry Cornwall') d.
Sydney Dobell d.
Agnes Strickland d.
Oliver Madox Brown d.
'Illustrated Sporting and Dramatic News' (weekly).
'The World' (weekly).
W. M. Rossetti, ed. of Blake.
Henry Sweet, 'History of English Sounds'.
Guizot d.

Arnold (1822): God and the Bible. P
Blades, William (1824): Some Early Type Specimen Books. P
Browning (1812): Aristophanes' Apology. V
　The Inn Album. V
Burroughs, John (1837): Winter Sunshine. P
Byron (1834): Our Boys [acted]. D
Carlyle (1795): Early Kings of Norway. Essay on Portraits of John Knox. P
Dobell (d. 1874): Collected Poetical Works.
Dowden, Edward (1843): Shakespeare: his Mind and Art. P
Eddy, Mary Baker (1821): Science and Health [often revised and reprinted]. P
Emerson (1803): Letters and Social Aims. P
Harte (1836): Tales of the Argonauts. P
Howells, W. Dean (1837): A Foregone Conclusion. P
Keble (d. 1866): Sermons for the Christian Year [concl. 1880].
Lightfoot (1828): Commentary on St. Paul's Epistle to the Colossians.
Longfellow (1807): The Masque of Pandora. V
Marston, Philip Bourke (1850): All in All. V
Martin (1816) **and Aytoun** (1813): Life of the Prince Consort [concl. 1880]. P
Meynell, Alice (1847): Preludes. V
Morris (1834): Trs. Aeneid of Virgil [1876]. V
　Trs. Three Northern Love-Stories from Icelandic [with E. Magnússon]. P
Norton, Charles Eliot (1827): William Blake. P
Palgrave (1824): Children's Treasury. V
Pattison (1813): Isaac Casaubon. P
Peacock (d. 1866): Works ed. Sir Henry Cole (ed. Brett-Smith 1924–35).
Ruskin (1819): Mornings in Florence [in six separate parts, 1875–7; collected 1889]. P
　Proserpina [in ten parts, 1875–86]. P
　Deucalion [concl. 1883]. P
Scott, W. B. (1811): Poems: Ballads, Studies from Nature, Sonnets, &c.
Swinburne (1837): Essays and Studies [collected]. P
　Songs of Two Nations [reprint of Song of Italy 1867 and Ode on French Republic 1870]. V
Symonds (1840): Renaissance in Italy [concl. 1886]. P
Tennyson (1809): Queen Mary. D
Trollope (1815): The Way we live now. P
Ward, Adolphus William: History of English Dramatic Literature [new ed. 1899].
Whyte-Melville (1821): Katerfelto. P

Charles Kingsley d.
Sir Charles Lyell d.
Sir Arthur Helps d.
Connop Thirlwall d.
George Finlay d.
'*Encyclopaedia Britannica*', 9th ed. (*concl. 1889*).
The Gilbert-Sullivan opera series starts with '*Trial by Jury*' *at the Royalty.*
Swinburne's attack on Robert Buchanan, entitled '*The Devil's Due*', *in* '*The Examiner*', 28 *Dec.* (*see 1871–2*).
Charles Cowden Clarke, ed. of Shakespeare (*called Cassell's Shakespeare, 1886*).
Edward Arber, ed. of '*Stationers' Register*', 1554–1660 (*concl. 1894*).
Henry Morley, '*Library of English Literature*' (*concl. 1881*).
Sir William Smith, '*Dictionary of Christian Antiquities*' (*concl. 1880*).
J. W. Ebsworth, ed. of '*Westminster Drollery*' *and* '*Merry Drollery*'.
Max Müller's series of '*Sacred Books of the East*' *commences.*
Eng. trs. of Ranke's '*History of England, principally in the Seventeenth Century*'.
A. B. Grosart, '*Occasional Issues of Unique and very rare Books*'.

Bentham (d. 1832): Theory of Legislation [trs. Fr. of Dumont by R. Hildreth: see 1802]. P

Bradley, F. H. (1846): Ethical Studies. P

Bridges (1844): The Growth of Love [enlarged edition 1889]. V

Brooke, Stopford (1832): English Literature. P

Brown (d. 1874): Literary Remains, ed. W. M. Rossetti and F. Hueffer.

Browning, R. (1812): Pacchiarotto. V

Dobell (d. 1874): Collected Prose Works.

Ewing, Juliana Horatia (1841): Jan of the Windmill. P

Fitzgerald (1809): Trs. Aeschylus' Agamemnon. V

Forster (d. 1876): Life of Swift. P

'George Eliot' (1819): Daniel Deronda. P

Gilbert (1836): Original Plays [coll.; concl. 1911]. P

Hardy (1840): Hand of Ethelberta. P

Harte (1836): Gabriel Convoy. P

Haydon, Benjamin Robert (d. 1846): Correspondence and Table Talk, ed. his son. P

Houghton (1809): Collected Works.

James (1843): Roderick Hudson. P

Landor (d. 1864): Works, ed. Forster.

Lanier, Sidney (1842): Florida. P

'Lewis Carroll' (1832): Hunting of the Snark. V

Mahony, Francis Sylvester (d. 1866): Final Reliques of Father Prout [see 1836]. P

Melville (1819): Clarel. V

Meredith (1828): Beauchamp's Career. P

Morris (1834): Two Sides of the River. V
Sigurd the Volsung, and Fall of the Niblungs [1877]. V

Shelley (d. 1822): Daemon of the World, pt. ii, ed. H. B. Forman [pt. i pub. with Alastor, 1816]. V

Spencer (1820): Principles of Sociology, vol. i [ii 1882, iii 1896]. P

Stephen (1832): English Thought in the Eighteenth Century. P
Hours in a Library, series II [see 1874]. P

Swinburne (1837): Erechtheus, a Tragedy. V
Note on the Muscovite Crusade. P

Tennyson (1809): Harold [1877]. D

Thackeray (d. 1863): Orphan of Pimlico. P

Trevelyan (1838): Life of Macaulay. P

Trollope (1815): The Prime Minister. P

Tupper (1810): Proverbial Philosophy, series I–IV complete [see 1838]. V

Wallace (1823): Geographical Distribution of Animals. P

Wordsworth (d. 1850): Prose Works, first collected ed. A. B. Grosart [ed. W. Knight 1896].

George Macaulay Trevelyan b.
Harriet Martineau d.
Henry Kingsley d.
John Forster d.
'Mind' started.
Thomas Arnold (jnr.), ed. of 'Beowulf', with trs.
Henry Sweet, 'Anglo-Saxon Reader'.
J. W. Ebsworth, ed. of 'Bagford Ballads' (concl. 1878).
A. B. Grosart, 'Chertsey Worthies Library' (concl. 1881; reprts. of Nicholas Breton, John Davies of Hereford, Joshua Sylvester, Francis Quarles, Joseph Beaumont, Henry More, Abraham Cowley).
William Carew Hazlitt, 'Bibliographical Collections and Notes' (concl. 1904).
George Sand d.

Acton (1834): History of Freedom in Antiquity, and History of Freedom in Christianity [Bridgnorth Addresses]. P

Alcott, Amos Bronson (1799): Table-Talk. P

Aldrich, Thomas Bailey (1836): The Queen of Sheba. P

Arnold (1822): Collected Poems (revised). V
Last Essays on Church and Religion. P

Bradley (1846): Mr. Sidgwick's Hedonism. P

Browning, E. B. (d. 1861): Letters to Richard Hengist Horne, ed. Mayer. P

Browning, R. (1812): Trs. Agamemnon of Aeschylus. V

Burnett, Frances Hodgson (1849): That Lass o' Lowrie's. P

Butler (1835): Life and Habit. P

Coleridge (d. 1834): Letters to J. P. Estlin, ed. Bright [concl. 1884].

Dobson (1840): Proverbs in Porcelain. V

Finlay (d. 1875): History of Greece from its Conquest by the Romans to the Present Time [collected ed.; see 1844–51–6–61]. P

Froude (1818): Short Studies on Great Subjects, series III [see 1867]. P

Green (1837): Hist. of the English People [concl. 1880; distinct from Short Hist. '74]. P

James (1843): The American. P

Keble (d. 1866): Occasional Papers, ed. Pusey.

Lewes (1817): Physical Basis of Mind [series II of Problems of Life and Mind: see 1874, 1879]. P

Lanier (1842): Poems.

Mallock, William Hurrell: New Republic. P

Manning, Henry Edward (1808): Miscellanies [concl. 1878].

Martineau (d. 1876): Autobiography. P

Meredith (1828): Idea of Comedy [in New Quarterly Magazine; separately 1897]. P

Morris, Sir Lewis (1833): Epic of Hades. V

Patmore (1823): The Unknown Eros and Other Poems.

Procter (d. 1874): Autobiographical Fragment, ed. C[oventry] P[atmore].

Sewell, Anna (1820): Black Beauty. P

Swinburne (1837): Charlotte Brontë. P
A Year's Letters [see 1905]. P

Thomson, Sir Charles Wyville (1830): Voyage of the Challenger. P

Trollope (1815): The American Senator. P

Russo - Turkish War, 1877–8.
Walter Bagehot d.
'Truth' (weekly) started.
'Nineteenth Century' started.
Edward Arber, 'English Garner' (concl. 1896).
Sir William Smith, 'Dictionary of Christian Biography' (concl. 1887).
George Long, trs. of Epictetus.
F. J. Furnivall, ed. of Shakespeare.
Ibsen, 'Pillars of Society'.

President U.S.A. Hayes.

Acton (1834): Democracy in Europe [in Quarterly Review, Jan.]. P

Besant and Rice: By Celia's Arbour. P
Monks of Thelema. P

Black, William (1841): Macleod of Dare. P

Browning (1812): La Saisiaz, Two Poets of Croisic. V

Cowden Clarke, Charles and Mary: Recollections of Writers. P

Dixon, Richard Watson (1833): History of the Church of England 1529–1570 [concl. 1902]. P

Green, Anna Katharine (1847): The Leavenworth Case. P

Hardy (1840): Return of the Native. P

Hatton, Christopher, Viscount Hatton (d. 1706): Correspondence of the Hatton family, 1601–1704, ed. E. M. Thompson.

James (1843): Watch and Ward. P

Jefferies (1848): Gamekeeper at Home. P

Keats (d. 1821): Letters to Fanny Brawne, ed. H. B. Forman.

Lecky (1838): History of England in the Eighteenth Century [concl. 1890]. P

Longfellow (1807): Keramos. V

Martin (1816): Trs. Poems and Ballads of Heine. V

Max Müller (1823): Origin and Growth of Religion. P

Morley (1838): Diderot and the Encyclopaedists. P

Seeley (1834): Life and Times of Stein. P

Senior, William Nassau: Conversations with Thiers, Guizot, and other Persons during the Second Empire. P

Stanley (1841): Through the Dark Continent. P

Stephen (1832): Samuel Johnson [English Men of Letters Series]. P

Stevenson (1850): An Inland Voyage. P

Swinburne (1837): Poems and Ballads, series II [see 1866, 1889].

Trelawny (1792): Records of Shelley, Byron, and the Author [see 1858]. P

Trollope (1815): Is he Popenjoy? P

Wallace, Alfred Russel: Tropical Nature. P

Walpole, Sir Spencer: History of England from 1815 [concl. 1886. A Continuation, History of Twenty-five Years (1856–80), 1904–8].

John Masefield b.
Wilfrid Gibson b.
Edward Thomas b.
George Henry Lewes d.
George John Whyte-Melville d.
'*English Men of Letters*' *series started.*
Edward Arber, '*English Scholars*' *Library*' (*concl. 1884*).
Matthew Arnold's *selection* '*Six Chief Lives*' *from Johnson*'s '*Lives of the Poets*'.
Grove's '*Dictionary of Music*' (*completed 1889*).

Adams, Henry (1838): Life of Albert Gallatin. P
Anson (1843): Law of Contract. P
Arnold, Edwin (1832): Light of Asia. V
Arnold (1822): Mixed Essays. P
Bagehot (d. 1877): Literary Studies, ed. R. H. Hutton [1878]. P
Balfour (1848): A Defence of Philosophic Doubt. P
Barnes (1801): Poems of Rural Life in the Dorset Dialect [collected; separately 1844–63].
Bridges (1844): Poems. V
Browning (1812): Dramatic Idyls, series 1. V
Burroughs (1837): Locusts and Wild Honey. P
Butler (1835): Evolution, Old and New. P
Cable (1844): Old Creole Days. P
Church (1815): Spenser. P
Clifford (d. 1879): Lectures and Essays, ed. Leslie Stephen and F. Pollock. P
Fiske, John (1842): Darwinism and other Essays. P
Freeman (1823): Essays, series III [see 1871]. P
'George Eliot' (1819): Theophrastus Such. P
Gladstone (1809): Gleanings from Past Years. P
Hodgkin, Thomas (1831): Italy and her Invaders [concl. 1899]. P
Howells (1837): A Lady of the Aroostook. P
Huxley (1825): David Hume. P
James (1843): Daisy Miller. P
  The Europeans. P
  Madonna of the Future. P
  Hawthorne. P
Lang (1844) **and Butcher**: Trs. Odyssey. P
Lewes (d. 1878): Study of Psychology [series III of Problems of Life and Mind: see 1874–7]. P
Meredith (1828): The Egoist. P
Morley (1838): Edmund Burke. P
Morris, Sir Lewis (1833): Gwen. V
Pattison (1813): Milton. P
Sewall, Samuel (d. 1730): Diary. P
Sidgwick (1838): Outlines of the History of Ethics. P
Spencer (1820): Principles of Ethics [concl. 1893]. P
Stephen (1832): Hours in a Library, series III [see 1874]. P
Stevenson (1850): Travels with a Donkey in the Cevennes. P
Tennyson (1809): The Lover's Tale [privately prtd. 1833; pirated 1875]. V
Trollope (1815): Thackeray. P

Edward Morgan Forster b.
Harold Monro b.
Charles Jeremiah Wells d.
William Kingdon Clifford d.
'The Cambridge Review.'
'Boys' Own Paper' started.
Walter Skeat, 'Etymological Dictionary of the English Language' (concl. 1882).
Mr. and Mrs. Cowden Clarke, 'Shakespeare Key'.
Ibsen, 'A Doll's House'.

Adams, Henry (1838): Democracy. P

Aldrich, Thomas Bailey (1836): The Stillwater Tragedy. P

Bagehot (d. 1877): Biographical Studies and Economic Studies, ed. R. H. Hutton.

Baring-Gould, Sabine (1834): Mehalah. P

Black, William (1841): White Wings. P
Sunrise. P

Blunt (1840): Love Sonnets of Proteus. V

Bridges (1844): Poems, Third Series. V

Browning (1812): Dramatic Idyls, series II [see 1879]. V

Cable, George Washington (1844): The Grandissimes. P

Dickens (d. 1870): Speeches, ed. R. H. Shepherd. Letters, ed. G. Hogarth and M. Dickens.

Disraeli (1804): Endymion. P

Gissing (1857): Workers in the Dawn. P

Groome, Francis Hindes (1851): In Gypsy Tents. P

Hardy (1840): Trumpet Major. P

Harris, Joel Chandler (1848): Uncle Remus: his Songs and Sayings.

Lang (1844): XXII Ballades in Blue China. V
Trs. Theocritus, Bion and Moschus. P

Lanier, Sidney (1842): The Science of English Verse. P

Longfellow (1807): Ultima Thule. V

Macdonald (1824): The Diary of an Old Soul. V

'Mark Twain' (1835): A Tramp Abroad. P

Meredith (1828): The Tragic Comedians [in Fortnightly Review and separately]. P

Morris, Sir Lewis (1833): Ode of Life. V

Norton, Charles Eliot (1827): Church-building in the Middle Ages. P

Oliphant (1828): A Beleaguered City. P

'Ouida' (1839): Moths. P

Ruskin (1819): Arrows of the Chace. P
Elements of English Prosody. P

Shorthouse, Joseph Henry (1834): John Inglesant. P

Stephen (1832): Alexander Pope. P

Swinburne (1837): Studies in Song. V
Songs of the Springtides. V
Heptalogia [parodies]. V
Study of Shakespeare. P

Tennyson (1809): Ballads and Other Poems.

Trevelyan (1838): The Early History of Charles James Fox. P

Trollope (1815): The Duke's Children. P

Turner, Charles Tennyson (d. 1879): Collected Sonnets.

Wallace, Lewis (1827): Ben Hur. P

Webster, Augusta (1837): Disguises. D

John Freeman b.
Giles Lytton Strachey b.
Alfred Noyes b.
Mary Ann Cross ('George Eliot') d.
Tom Taylor d.
'The Stage' (weekly).
T. Humphry Ward, 'English Poets' (anthology: with Preface by Matthew Arnold).
A. B. Grosart, ed. of Spenser (concl. 1888).
Sir Richard Francis Burton, trs. Lusiads of Camoens (Commentary and Life of C. 1881; trs. Lyrics 1884).

Alcott, Amos Bronson (1799): New Connecticut.V
Besant and Rice: Chaplain of the Fleet. P
Bible: Revised Version of the New Testament.
  Wescott and Hort, Greek New Testament.
Brown, T. E. (1830): Fo'c'sle Yarns [Betsy Lee
  (see 1873) and three other poems].
Butler (1835): Alps and Sanctuaries of Piedmont
  and the Canton Ticino. P
Carlyle (d. 1881): Reminiscences, ed. J. A. Froude.
Conway, Moncure (1832): Thomas Carlyle. P
Cox, George William (1827): Introduction to
  Science of Comparative Mythology. P
Fitch, Sir Joshua: Lectures on Teaching. P
Halliwell-Phillipps, J. O. (1820): Outlines of Life
  of Shakespeare (enlarg. edd. 1882-3-4-7). P
Hardy (1840): A Laodicean. P
Hill, George Birkbeck (1835): Colonel Gordon in
  Central Africa. P
James (1843): Portrait of a Lady. P
Jefferies (1848): Wood Magic. P
Lang (1844): XXXII Ballades in Blue China [see
  1880]. V
'Mark Rutherford' (1831): Autobiography of
  Mark Rutherford. P
Matthews, Brander (1852): French Dramatists of
  the 19th Century. P
Morley (1838): Life of Richard Cobden. P
O'Shaughnessy (d. 1881): Songs of a Worker, ed.
  Deacon. V
Romanes, George John (1848): Animal Intelli-
  gence. P
Rossetti, C. (1830): A Pageant, and Other Poems. P
Rossetti, D. G. (1828): Ballads and Sonnets [Rose
  Mary, White Ship, King's Tragedy, Bride's
  Prelude, &c.]. V
Southey (d. 1843): Correspondence with Caroline
  Bowles, ed. Dowden. P
Stevenson (1850): Virginibus Puerisque. P
Swinburne (1837): Mary Stuart, a Tragedy. D
Trollope (1815): Dr. Wortle's School. P
  Ayala's Angel. P
Wilde (1856): Poems.

Pelham Grenville Wode-
  house b.
Lascelles Abercrombie b.
Thomas Carlyle d.
Benjamin Disraeli, Earl
  of Beaconsfield, d.
George Borrow d.
Arthur Penrhyn Stanley
  d.
Arthur O'Shaughnessy d.
'*The Evening News*'
  (*daily*).
Browning and Wiclif So-
  cieties founded by F. J.
  Furnivall.
F. J. Furnivall, ed. of
  Chaucer's 'Troilus'.
Matthew Arnold, ed. of
  Burke's Letters,
  Speeches, and Tracts
  on Irish Affairs.
A. B. Grosart, 'Huth
  Library' (concl. 1886;
  reprts. of Robert Greene,
  Thomas Nashe, Gabriel
  Harvey, Thomas Dek-
  ker's Prose Tracts,
  Samuel Daniel).
A. Beljame, 'Le public et
  les hommes de lettres en
  Angleterre au dix-
  huitième siècle'.
G. Vigfússon d.
F. York Powell's 'Corpus
  Poeticum Boreale'.
Ibsen, 'Ghosts'.
Jowett, trs. Thucydides.

President U.S.A.
  Garfield (assassi-
  nated), Arthur

Alcott, Amos Bronson (1799): Sonnets and Canzonets. V

Anstey, F. (1856): Vice Versa. P

Arnold (1822): Irish Essays and Others. P

Bancroft, George (1800): Formation of the Constitution of the United States. P

Besant, Sir Walter (1836): All Sorts and Conditions of Men. P

Caine, Hall (1853): Recollections of D. G. Rossetti. P

Carlyle (d. 1881): Reminiscences of my Irish Journey in 1849, ed. J. A. Froude. P

Last Words of Carlyle, ed. J. C. Aitken. P

Crawford, Francis Marion (1854): Mr. Isaacs. P

Creighton, Mandell (1843): History of the Papacy during the Reformation [concl. 1894]. P

Dickens (d. 1870): Plays and Poems, ed. R. H. Shepherd [suppressed; new ed. 1885].

Froude (1818): History of First Forty Years of Carlyle's Life [see 1884]. P

Green (1837): The Making of England. P

Hardy (1840): Two on a Tower. P

Howells (1837): A Modern Instance. P

Jefferies (1848): Bevis, the Story of a Boy. P

Jones (1851): The Silver King. D

Lang (1844): Helen of Troy. V

Longfellow (d. 1882): In the Harbour. V

Morris (1834): Hopes and Fears for Art. P

Mozley, Thomas (1806): Reminiscences, chiefly of Oriel and the Oxford Movement. P

'Ouida' (1839): In Maremma. P

Saintsbury (1845): A Short History of French Literature. P

Scott, W. B. (1811): A Poet's Harvest Home [enlarg. 1893]. V

Seeley (1834): Natural Religion. P

Sharp (1855): Human Inheritance, New Hope, Motherhood. V

Dante Gabriel Rossetti: a Record and a Study. P

Shaw (1856): Cashel Byron's Profession. P

Stephen (1832): Swift. P

Science of Ethics. P

Stevenson (1850): Familiar Studies of Men and Books. P

Treasure Island. P

New Arabian Nights. P

Swinburne (1837): Tristram of Lyonesse, and Other Poems.

Whitman (1819): Specimen Days in America. P

James Stephens b.

James Joyce b.

John Drinkwater b.

Martin Armstrong b.

Charles Darwin d.

Dante Gabriel Rossetti d.

Edward Bouverie Pusey d.

James Thomson d.

Anthony Trollope d.

William Stanley Jevons d.

William Harrison Ainsworth d.

Ralph Waldo Emerson d.

Henry Wadsworth Longfellow d.

Oxford Historical Society.

A. H. Bullen, 'Collection of Old English Plays' (concl. 1885; new series 1887–90).

W. Knight, ed. Wordsworth (Poetry: see 1896).

Aldrich, Thomas Bailey (1836): Mercedes. V
Bradley (1846): Principles of Logic. P
Bridges (1844): Prometheus the Firegiver. V
Browning (1812): Jocoseria. V
Burnett, Frances Hodgson (1849): Through One Administration. P
Carlyle, Jane Welsh (d. 1866): Letters and Memorials, prepared by Thomas Carlyle and ed. J. A. Froude [New Letters and Memorials, 1903]. P
Carlyle (d. 1881): Correspondence with Emerson.
Carpenter (1844): Towards Democracy. V
Crawford, F. Marion (1854): Dr. Claudius. P
Dixon (1833): Mano. V
Drummond, Henry (1851): Natural Law in the Spiritual World. P
Ewing, Juliana H. (1841): Jackanapes. P
Froude (1818): Short Studies, series IV [see'67]. P
Galton (1822): Inquiries into Human Faculty. P
Gardiner (1829): History of England from the Accession of James I [rev. ed.: see 1886, 1895]. P
Green, J. R. (d. 1883): Conquest of England. P
Green, T. H. (d. 1882): Prolegomena to Ethics. P
Harris (1848): Nights with Uncle Remus. P
Jefferies (1848): Story of my Heart. P
Lang (1844), Leaf, Myers: Trs. Iliad [see 1879]. P
Lanier, Sidney (1842): The English Novel. P
'Lewis Carroll' (1832): Rhyme? and Reason? V
Longfellow (1807): Michael Angelo. D
Lytton (d. 1873): Life, Letters, &c.
MacDonald (1824): The Princess and Curdie. P
'Mark Twain' (1835): Life on the Mississippi. P
Marston, Philip Bourke (1850): Wind Voices. V
Meredith (1828): Poems and Lyrics of the Joy of Earth. V
Myers (1843): Essays: Modern. P
Pusey (d. 1882): Parochial & Cathedral Sermons.
Schreiner, Olive (1855): The Story of an African Farm. P
Seeley (1834): Expansion of England. P
Shaw (1856): An Unsocial Socialist. P
Sidgwick (1838): Political Economy. P
Stephen, Sir James Fitzjames (1829): History of the Criminal Law of England. P
Stevenson (1850): Silverado Squatters. P
Swinburne (1837): A Century of Roundels. V
Trollope (d. 1882): Autobiography. P
Victoria, Queen (1819): More Leaves from a Journal [see 1868]. P

Edward FitzGerald d.
John Richard Green d.
'The Oxford Magazine.'
J. W. Ebsworth, ed. of Roxburghe Ballads, vols. iv–ix (concl. 1899: see 1869).
Sir Richard Jebb, ed. of Sophocles with Eng. trs. (concl. 1896).
H. B. Forman, ed. Keats's Poetical Works (enlarged 1889, 1901–2, 1906).
Henry Morley, 'Universal Library' (concl. 1888).
Dobson, 'Fielding' (English Men of Letters Series).
Wagner d.
Leopold von Ranke, 'Weltgeschichte' (concl. 1888).

Bible: Revised Version of the Old Testament.

Birrell (1850): Obiter Dicta [2nd vol. 1887]. P

Browning (1812): Ferishtah's Fancies. V

Cable, George Washington (1844): Creoles of Louisiana. P

Crawford, F. Marion (1854): Roman Singer. P

Croker, John Wilson (d. 1857): Memoirs, Diaries and Correspondence, ed. L. J. Jennings.

De Vere, A. T. (1814): Poetical Works.

Dixon (1833): Odes and Eclogues. V

Emerson (d. 1882): Lectures and Biographical Sketches. P

Ewing, Juliana H. (1841): Daddy Darwin's Dovecote. P

Froude (1818): Carlyle's Life in London [see '82]. P

'George Eliot' (d. 1880): Essays, and Leaves from a Note Book, ed. C. L. Lewes. P

　Life, as related in Letters and Journals, ed. J. W. Cross. P

Gissing (1857): The Unclassed. P

Howells, W. Dean (1837): Rise of Silas Lapham. P

James (1843): Tales of Three Cities. P

Jefferies (1848): Life of the Fields. P

Lang (1844): Custom and Myth. P

Lanier, Sidney (d. 1881): Poems. V

'Mark Twain' (1835): The Adventures of Huckleberry Finn. P

Matthews, Brander (1852): Margery's Lovers. P

Moore, George (1852): A Mummer's Wife. P

Parkman, Francis (1827): Montcalm and Wolfe. P

Rogers, J. E. Thorold (1823): Six Centuries of Work and Wages. P

Ruskin (1819): Art of England. P

　Pleasures of England. P

Sharp (1855): Earth's Voices. V

Spencer (1820): Man versus the State. P

Stevenson (1850) and Henley (1849): Beau Austin. D

　Admiral Guinea. D

Swinburne (1837): A Midsummer Holiday. Poems.

Symonds (1840): Wine, Women, and Song: trs. Medieval Latin students' songs. V

Tennyson (1809): The Cup, and The Falcon. D　Becket. D

Thomson (d. 1882): Voice from the Nile and Other Poems, with Memoir by B. Dobell. V

　Satires and Profanities. P

　The New Lucian. P

Ward (1851): Miss Bretherton. P

　Trs. Amiel's Journal Intime. P

James Elroy Flecker b.

Hugh Walpole b.

Sir John Collings Squire b.

Charles Reade d.

Richard Henry (or 'Hengist') Horne d.

Henry James Byron d.

Charles Stuart Calverley d.

Mark Pattison d.

'*Oxford English Dictionary' (ed. Sir James Murray) begins to appear (completed 1928).*

John Earle, 'Anglo-Saxon Literature'.

Fabian Society founded.

Austin, Alfred (1835): At the Gate of the Convent. V

Arnold (1822): Discourses in America. P

Beecher, Henry Ward (1813): Evolution and Religion. P

Birrell (1850): Life of Charlotte Brontë. P

Bridges (1844): Nero [Part II, 1894]. D
Eros and Psyche [rev. 1894]. V

Burton, Sir Richard Francis (1821): Trs. Arabian Nights [privately prtd.; concl. 1888; rev. 'for household reading' 1887–8]. P

Clifford, William Kingdon (d. 1879): Common Sense of the Exact Sciences, ed. K. Pearson.

Crawford, F. Marion (1854): Zoroaster. P

Disraeli (d. 1881): Home Letters, 1830–1 [new ed. by Ralph Disraeli 1887].

Dobson (1840): At the Sign of the Lyre. V

Ewing, Juliana H. (d. 1885): The Story of a Short Life. P

Fargus, Frederick ('Hugh Conway') (d. 1885): Called Back. P

Fiske, John (1842): American Political Ideas. P

Gordon, Charles George (d. 1885): Journals at Khartoum. P

Green, T. H. (d. 1882): Works, ed. Nettleship [later vols. 1886, 1888]. P

Greville (d. 1865): Memoirs, series II, 1837–52 [see 1874, 1887]. P

Haggard, Rider (1856): King Solomon's Mines. P

Holmes (1809): A Mortal Antipathy. P

Hudson (1841): The Purple Land. P

Lang (1844): Rhymes à la Mode. V

Lightfoot (1828): Apostolic Fathers, pt. ii [Ignatius and Polycarp].

'Mark Rutherford' (1831): Mark Rutherford's Deliverance. P

Martineau (1805): Types of Ethical Theory. P

'Owen Meredith' (1831): Glenaveril. V

Meredith (1828): Diana of the Crossways [originally in Fortnightly Review 1884–5]. P

Morris (1834): Pilgrims of Hope [in The Commonweal, 1885–6; separately 1886]. V

Pater (1839): Marius the Epicurean. P

Powell, Frederick York, and Tout, T. F.: History of England [concl. 1898]. P

Ruskin (1819): On the Old Road [collection of essays, pamphlets, &c., 1834–85].
Praeterita [concl. 1889]. P

Stannard, Henrietta ('John Strange Winter') (1856): Bootles' Baby. P

David Herbert Lawrence b.
Ezra Pound b.
Richard Monckton Milnes, Lord Houghton, d.
Fall of Khartoum.
'The Commonweal' (contrib. by Morris, &c.) started.
Scottish History Society founded.
Henry Sweet's 'Oldest English Texts'.
Victor Hugo d.

President U.S.A. Cleveland.

Stevenson (1850): Prince Otto. P
   Child's Garden of Verses. V
   More New Arabian Nights, The Dynamiter. P
   Macaire [with William Ernest Henley]. D
Swinburne (1837): Marino Faliero, a Tragedy. D
Tennyson (1809): Tiresias and Other Poems.
Whistler (1834): The Ten o'clock Lecture. P

1886

Alcott, Louisa (1832): Jo's Boys. P
Anson, Sir William (1843): Law and Custom of
   the Constitution [concl. 1892]. P
Burnett, Frances Hodgson (1849): Little Lord
   Fauntleroy. P
Corelli (1854): A Romance of Two Worlds. P
Disraeli (d. 1881): Correspondence with his sister,
   1832–52, ed. Ralph Disraeli.
Dobson (1840): Steele. P
Dowden, Edward (1843): Life of Shelley. P
Froude (1818): Oceana. P
Gardiner (1829): History of the Great Civil War
   [concl. 1891: see 1883, 1895]. P
Gissing (1857): Isabel Clarendon. P
   Demos. P
Hardy (1840): Mayor of Casterbridge. P
James (1843): The Bostonians. P
   Princess Casamassima. P
Kipling (1865): Departmental Ditties. V
Lawless, Emily: Hurrish. P
Maine (1822): Popular Government. P
Rossetti (d. 1882): Collected Works, ed. W. M.
   Rossetti. V and P
Stevenson (1850): Dr. Jekyll and Mr. Hyde. P
   Kidnapped. P
   The Merry Men and Other Tales. P
Stubbs (1825): Lectures on Study of History. P
Swinburne (1837): A Study of Victor Hugo. P
   Miscellanies. P
Symons, Arthur (1865): Introduction to Brown-
   ing. P
Tennyson (1809): Locksley Hall, sixty years after.
   Promise of May, and Other Poems. V
Ward, James (1843): Psychology. P

Lennox Robinson b.
Siegfried Sassoon b.
Richard Chevenix Trench
   d.
Sir Henry Taylor d.
Shelley Society.
'Scribner's   Magazine'
   started.
'Dictionary of National
   Biography', 1st vol. (ed.
   Leslie Stephen 1886–91,
   Sidney Lee 1891 ff.).
'English Historical Re-
   view' (ed. Mandell
   Creighton).
'Cassell's National Lib-
   rary' (ed. Henry Mor-
   ley; concl. 1890).
Frederic Gard Fleay,
   'Chronicle History of
   Life and Work of
   Shakespeare'.
A. H. Bullen, 'Lyrics from
   the Song Books of the
   Elizabethan Age'.

Blackmore (1825): Springhaven. P
Brown, T. E. (1830): The Doctor and Other Poems.
Browning (1812): Parleyings with Certain People. V
Butler (1835): Luck or Cunning. P
Caine (1853): The Deemster. P
Carlyle (d. 1881): Early Letters, ed. Norton. P
     Correspondence with Goethe, ed. Norton. P
Carpenter (1844): Civilisation, Its Cause and
     Cure. P
Crawford, F. Marion (1854): Marzio's Crucifix. P
     Saracinesca. P
Darwin (d. 1882): Life and Letters, with Auto-
     biography, ed. F. Darwin. P
Dixon (1833): Lyrical Poems.
Doyle, Arthur Conan (1859): A Study in Scarlet. P
Freeman, Mary Eleanor Wilkins (1852): A
     Humble Romance and Other Stories. P
Gissing (1857): Thyrza. P
Greville (d. 1865): Memoirs, series III, 1852–60
     [see 1874, 1885]. P
Haggard, Rider (1856): She. P
     Allan Quartermaine. P
Hardy (1840): The Woodlanders. P
Holmes (1809): One Hundred Days in Europe. P
Jefferies (d. 1887): Amaryllis at the Fair. P
Jessopp, Augustus (1823): Arcady, for better for
     worse. P
Lang (1844): Myth, Ritual, and Religion [rev.
     1899]. P
     Trs. Aucassin and Nicolete. P
Laughton, Sir John Knox (1830): Studies in Naval
     History. P
Lowell (1819): Democracy and other Addresses. P
'Mark Rutherford' (1831): Revolution in Tanner's
     Lane. P
Meredith (1828): Ballads and Poems of Tragic
     Life. V
Morison, James Cotter (1832): Service of Man. P
Morris (1834): Trs. Odyssey. V
Pater (1839): Imaginary Portraits. P
Saintsbury (1845): Elizabethan Literature. P
Stevenson (1850): Underwoods. V
     Memories and Portraits. P
Swinburne (1837): Locrine, a Tragedy. D
     The Question. V
     Selections from Poems, made by himself. V
Thackeray (d. 1863): Letters, 1847–55, ed. Brook-
     field. P
     Sultan Stork and other Stories and Sketches. P

Rupert Brooke b.
Edith Sitwell b.
Richard Jefferies d.
Selden Society founded.
George Birkbeck Hill, ed.
     of Boswell's 'Life of
     Johnson'.
Henry Morley, 'English
     Writers' (recast from ed.
     of 1864–7; concl. 1895).
Robert William Lowe,
     'Bibliographical Ac-
     count of English
     Theatrical Literature'.

Allingham (1824): Poetical Works [concl. 1893].

Archer (1856): Masks and Faces. P

Arnold (d. 1888): Essays in Criticism, series II [see 1865].

Barrie (1860): Auld Licht Idylls. P

Bellamy, Edward (1850): Looking Backward. P

Black (1841): Strange Adventures of a House-Boat. P

'Boldrewood, Rolf' (1826): Robbery under Arms. P

Bosanquet (1848): Logic. P

Bryce (1838): American Commonwealth. P

Butler (1835): Ex Voto. P

Dobson (1840): Goldsmith. P

Doughty (1843): Travels in Arabia Deserta. P

Garnett, Richard (1835): Twilight of the Gods and Other Tales. P

Gissing (1857): A Life's Morning. P

Hardy (1840): Wessex Tales. P

Henley (1849): A Book of Verses.
Deacon Brodie [with R. L. Stevenson; privately prtd. 1880]. D

Holmes (1809): Over the Teacups (completed 1890). P

Hume (d. 1776): Letters to Strahan. P

James (1843): The Reverberator. P
Partial Portraits. P

Kipling (1865): Soldiers Three. P
Plain Tales from the Hills. P

Lang (1844): Grass of Parnassus. V

Lowell (1819): Heartsease and Rue. V
Political Essays. P

Meredith (1828): A Reading of Earth. V

Moore (1852): Confessions of a Young Man. P

Morris (1834): Dream of John Ball. P
Signs of Change [Seven Lectures]. P

Osborne, Dorothy, Lady Temple (d. 1695): Letters, ed. E. A. Parry [complete: see 1836, ed. G. C. Moore Smith 1928].

Quiller-Couch (1863): Troy Town. P

Rogers, J. E. Thorold (1823): Economic Interpretation of History. P

Sharp (1855): Romantic Ballads and Poems of Phantasy. V

Stevenson (1850): Black Arrow. P
Wrong Box [with Lloyd Osbourne]. P
Deacon Brodie [with W. E. Henley]. D

Ward (1851): Robert Elsmere. P

Wilde (1856): Happy Prince and Other Tales. P

Wordsworth (d. 1850): The Recluse. V

Yeats (1865): Fairy and Folk Tales of the Irish Peasantry. P

Katharine Mansfield b.
Thomas Stearns Eliot b.
Matthew Arnold d.
Sir Henry Maine d.
Edward Lear d.
'The Star' started.
Accession of Kaiser Wilhelm II.

Adams, Henry (1838): History of the United States of America. P

Alexander, Samuel (1859): Moral Order and Progress. P

Bancroft, George (1800): Marten van Buren. P

Barrie (1860): A Window in Thrums. P

Booth, Charles (1840): Life and Labour of the People in London (9 vols. 1889–97). P

Bridges (1844): The Feast of Bacchus. D

Brown, T. E. (1830): Manx Witch and Other Poems.

Browning, E. B. (d. 1861): Poetical Works, ed. R. Browning [concl. 1890; ed. Kenyon 1897].

Browning, R. (d. 1889): Asolando. V

Burney (d. 1840): Early Diary, 1768–78, with Letters, ed. A. R. Ellis [see 1842].

Caird, Edward (1835): Critical Philosophy of Immanuel Kant. P

Coleridge (d. 1834): Critical Annotations, ed. from marginal notes in books, W. F. Taylor. P

Davidson (1857): Scaramouch in Naxos. D
An Unhistorical Pastoral. D
A Romantic Farce. D

Doyle (1859): The Sign of Four. P

Field, Eugene (1850): Western Verse. V
Profitable Tales. P

FitzGerald (d. 1883): Collected Works, with Letters and Literary Remains, ed. W. A. Wright [another ed. 1902].

Galton (1822): Natural Inheritance. P

Gissing (1857): The Nether World. P

Jerome, Jerome K. (1859): Idle Thoughts of an Idle Fellow. P
Three Men in a Boat. P

Kipling (1865): From Sea to Sea. P

Lear (d. 1888): Nonsense Drolleries. V

Levy, Amy (d. 1889): A London Plane Tree. V
Reuben Sachs. P

'Lewis Carroll' (1832): Sylvie and Bruno [concl. 1893]. P

Mandeville, Sir John: Travels [first Eng. version derived from the Egerton MS.; pub. by Roxburghe Club: see 1499, 1725]. P

'Mark Twain' (1835): A Connecticut Yankee in King Arthur's Court. P

Martin (1816): Song of the Bell, and other trs. from German Poets. V

Meredith (1828): Sandra Belloni [see 1864]. P

Morris (1834): House of the Wolfings. P and V

Pater (1839): Appreciations. P

Patmore (1823): Principle in Art, &c. P

Robertson (d. 1871): Principal Dramatic Works.

W. J. Turner b.
John Middleton Murry b.
Philip Guedalla b.
Robert Browning d.
Martin Tupper d.
Edward Bradley ('*Cuthbert Bede*') *d.*
Gerard Manley Hopkins d.
William Wilkie Collins d.
William Allingham d.
Parnell Commission.
British Record Society founded.
'*The Granta.*'
'*The Scots Observer*' *started by Henley.*
David Masson, ed. of De Quincey.
A. H. Bullen, ed. Works of Thomas Campion.
William Archer's trs. of '*A Doll's House*' *acted.*
Tolstoy, '*Kreutzer Sonata*'.

President U.S.A. Harrison.

Shaw (1856): Fabian Essays in Socialism [with Webb, Clarke, Olivier, Besant, & Bland]. P
Stevenson (1850): Master of Ballantrae. P
Swinburne (1837): Poems and Ballads, series III [see 1866, 1878].
   A Study of Ben Jonson. P
Tennyson (1809): Demeter and Other Poems.
Yeats (1865): The Wanderings of Oisin. V

1890

Barrie (1860): My Lady Nicotine. P
Booth, William (1829): In Darkest England. P
Bridges (1844): Shorter Poems [additional vol. 1893]. Palicio. D. Return of Ulysses. D Christian Captives. D. Achilles in Scyros. D
Caine (1853): Bondman. P
Chesterfield (d. 1773): Letters to his Godson, ed. Lord Carnarvon [see 1774, 1777]. P
Crawford, F. Marion (1854): Cigarette-maker's Romance. P
Dickinson, Emily (d. 1886): Poems [2nd series 1891, 3rd series 1896].
Dobson (1840): Horace Walpole. P
Frazer, James George (1854): The Golden Bough [2 original vols., 2nd ed, rev. and enlarged 1900, 3rd ed. 12 vols. 1907–8]. P
Gilbert (1836): Original Comic Operas [Sorcerer, H.M.S. Pinafore, Pirates of Penzance, Iolanthe, Patience, Princess Ida, Mikado, Trial by Jury]. D
   Foggerty's Fairy and Other Tales. P
   Songs of a Savoyard [from the Savoy operas]. V
Gissing (1857): The Emancipated. P
Grundy, Sidney (1848): A Pair of Spectacles. D
Hake (1809): The New Day. V
Hawker, Mary ('Lanoe Falconer'): Mdlle Ixe. P
Henley (1849): Views and Reviews: Literature. P
James, Henry (1843): The Tragic Muse. P
James, William (1842): Principles of Psychology. P
'Mark Rutherford' (1831): Miriam's Schooling. P
Martineau, J. (1805): Authority in Religion. P
Morris (1834): Roots of the Mountains. P
   News from Nowhere [in The Commonweal; sep. 1891]. P
North (d. 1734): Lives of the Norths [Francis, Dudley, and John] with Letters, and Roger North's Autobiography [see 1742, 1744]. P
Stanley, H. M. (1841): In Darkest Africa. P
Stevenson (1850): Ballads.
Watson (1858): Wordsworth's Grave. V
Whistler (1834): The Gentle Art of Making Enemies. P

Aldous Huxley b.
John Henry Newman d.
Richard William Church d.
William Bell Scott d.
John Westland Marston d.
William Morris founds the Kelmscott Press.
'Daily Graphic'.
'Review of Reviews'.
Frederick Gard Fleay, 'Chronicle History of London Stage' (see 1891).
Fall of Bismarck.
Ibsen, 'Hedda Gabler'.

Bierce, Ambrose (1842): Tales of Soldiers and Civilians. P

Barrie (1860): The Little Minister. P

Browning (d. 1889): Life and Letters, by Mrs. S. Orr.

Church (d. 1890): Oxford Movement. P

Davidson (1857): In a Music Hall and Other Poems.

Dobson (1840): William Hogarth. P

Doyle (1859): Adventures of Sherlock Holmes. P

Field, Eugene (1850): Echoes from the Sabine Farm. V

Freeman, Mary Eleanor Wilkins (1852): A New England Nun, and Other Stories. P

Garland, Hamlin (1860): Main-Travelled Roads. P

Gissing (1857): New Grub Street. P

Hardy (1840): Group of Noble Dames. P
Tess of the d'Urbervilles. P

Howells (1837): Criticism and Fiction. P

'John Oliver Hobbes' (1867): Some Emotions and a Moral. P

Jones (1851): Saints and Sinners. D

Keats (d. 1821): Letters to his Family and Friends, ed. Sidney Colvin.

Kipling (1865): Life's Handicap. P
The Light that Failed. P

Meredith (1828): One of our Conquerors. P

Moore (1852): Impressions and Opinions. P

Morris (1834): Poems by the Way.
Story of the Glittering Plain. P
The Saga Library, ed. Morris and E. Magnússon [concl. 1895].

Pinero (1855): The Times. D
Lady Bountiful. D.   The Profligate. D

Shaw (1856): Quintessence of Ibsenism. P

Sidgwick (1838): Elements of Politics. P

Stephen, James Kenneth (1859): Quo Musa Tendis. V
Lapsus Calami. V

Wilde (1856): Lord Arthur Savile's Crime, and Other Stories. P
A House of Pomegranates. P
Picture of Dorian Gray [Preface separately in Fortnightly Review, Mar.]. P
Intentions [essays collected from reviews]. P

Alexander William Kinglake d.

Edward Robert Bulwer, Earl Lytton ('Owen Meredith') d.

James Russell Lowell d.

Herman Melville d.

F. G. Fleay, 'Biographical Chronicle of English Drama' (see 1890).

'Oxford Poets' ed. of Shakespeare (1st of the series).

'Life and Times of Anthony Wood,' ed. Andrew Clark (completed 1900).

The Chace Act makes it possible for foreigners to obtain copyright in the United States on condition of printing there.

Bierce, Ambrose (1842) : Black Beetles in Amber. P
Birrell (1850) : Res Judicatae. P
Bosanquet (1848) : History of Aesthetic. P
Conway, Moncure (1832) : Life of Thomas Paine. P
Dobson (1840) : Eighteenth Century Vignettes
    [concl. 1896; other volumes of a similar
    character.] P
Du Maurier (1834) : Peter Ibbetson [1891]. P
Field, Eugène (1850) : With Trumpet and Drum. V
Freeman (d. 1892) : Essays, IV series [see 1871]. P
Gissing (1857) : Born in Exile. P
    Denzil Quarrier. P
Harris (1848) : Uncle Remus and his Friends. P
Henley (1849) : Song of the Sword and Other
    Verses [incl. London Voluntaries which be-
    came the title of the 2nd ed., enlarg., 1893].
    Views and Reviews: Art [see 1890]. P
    Lyra Heroica : Book of Verse for Boys.
Hudson (1841) : A Naturalist in La Plata. P
Kipling (1865) : Barrack-Room Ballads. V
    (with **W. Balestier**) : The Naulahka. P
Max Müller (1823) : Anthropological Religion. P
'Owen Meredith' (d. 1891) : King Poppy [privately
    prtd. 1875]. V
Pinero (1855) : Cabinet Minister. D
    Hobby Horse. D
Ritchie, Mrs. Anne (1837) : Records of Tennyson,
    Ruskin, and the Brownings. P
Romanes (1848) : Darwin and after Darwin. P
Severn, Joseph (d. 1879) : Life and Letters, ed.
    William Sharp.
Stevenson (1850) : The Wrecker [with Lloyd
    Osbourne]. P.   Across the Plains. P
Swinburne (1837) : The Sisters, a Tragedy. D
Tennyson (d. 1892) : The Foresters. D
    Death of Œnone, Akbar's Dream, and other
    poems.
Ward (1851) : History of David Grieve. P
Watson (1858) : Lachrymae Musarum. V
Whymper, Edward (1840) : Travels among the
    Great Andes of the Equator. P
Williams, Isaac (d. 1865) : Autobiography, ed.
    Sir George Prevost.
Yeats (1865) : Countess Kathleen. V
    Ed. Irish Fairy Tales.
Zangwill, Israel (1864) : Children of the Ghetto. P

Edward Shanks b.
Victoria Sackville-West b.
Richard Aldington b.
Stella Benson b.
David Garnett b.
Lord Tennyson d.
Edward Augustus Free-
    man d.
Sir Richard Owen d.
London   Bibliographical
    Society founded.
G. Birkbeck Hill, ed. of
    Johnson's Letters.
E. Dowden, ed. of Words-
    worth (poetry).
C. Plummer, ed. of 'Anglo-
    Saxon Chronicle'.
Henry Sweet, 'A New
    English Grammar'.
English trs. of 'Peer Gynt'.
Eng. trs. of Zola.
Renan d.

Benson, E. F. (1867): Dodo. P
Bierce, Ambrose (1842): Can Such Things be. P
Bradley (1846): Appearance and Reality. P
Bridges (1844): Milton's Prosody [originally two
　　essays printed '87, '89; enlarged 1901]. P
　Humours of the Court. D
Brown, T. E. (1830): Old John. V
Carman, Bliss (1861): Low Tide on Grand Pré. V
Corelli (1854): Barabbas. P
Crackanthorpe, Hubert: Wreckage. P
Davidson (1857): Fleet Street Eclogues. V
De Tabley, John, Lord (1835): Poems, Dramatic
　　and Lyrical [concl. 1895].
Doyle (1859): Memoirs of Sherlock Holmes. P
Emerson (d. 1882): Natural History of Intellect. P
Gissing (1857): The Odd Women. P
Grahame (1859): Pagan Papers. P
Grand, Sarah (1862): The Heavenly Twins. P
Hopkins (d. 1889): in Poets and Poetry of the
　　Century, ed. Bridges.
Hort (d. 1892): The Way, the Truth, and the
　　Light. P
Hudson (1841): Idle Days in Patagonia. P
Huxley (1825): Collected Essays [concl. 1894]. P
James (1843): The Private Life. P
Jones (1851): The Crusaders. D
Kipling (1865): Many Inventions. P
Liddon, Henry Parry (d. 1890): Life of Pusey.
Lowell (d. 1891): Letters. P
'Mark Rutherford' (1831): Catharine Furze. P
Matthews, Brander (1852): The Decision of the
　　Court. D
Meynell (1847): Poems. V
Pater (1839): Plato and Platonism. P
Patmore (1823): Religio Poetæ. P
Pinero (1855): Dandy Dick. D
　Sweet Lavender. D
Smith, Goldwin (1823): The United States. P
Stevenson (1850): A Footnote to History. P
　Island Nights' Entertainments. P
　Catriona [sequel to Kidnapped 1886]. P
Thompson (1859): Poems [Hound of Heaven,
　　Love in Dian's Lap, &c.].
Weyman (1855): A Gentleman of France. P
Wilde (1856): Lady Windermere's Fan. D
　Salomé [in original French in Paris: see '94]. D
Yeats (1865): Celtic Twilight. P
　Ed. Blake [with E. J. Ellis].

Robert Nichols b.
John Tyndall d.
Benjamin Jowett d.
John Addington Symonds
　d.
'*Westminster Gazette.*'
Bibliographical Society's
　'*Transactions*', *1st vol.*
Ibsen, '*The Master*
　Builder' acted in Eng-
　land.
Taine d.

President U.S.A.
Cleveland (2nd
term).

Austin (1835): The Garden that I Love. P

Blackmore (1825): Perlycross. P

Blatchford, Robert (1851): Merrie England. P

Carman, Bliss (1861): Songs from Vagabondia [2nd series 1896].

Davidson (1857): Ballads and Songs.
    Plays Collected [Bruce 1886, Smith 1888, An Unhistorical Pastoral 1889, A Romantic Farce 1889, Scaramouch in Naxos 1889].

Dickinson, Emily (d. 1886): Letters.

Du Maurier (1834): Trilby. P

Freeman, Mary Eleanor (1852): Pembroke. P

Froude (d. 1894): Life and Letters of Erasmus. P

Gissing (1857): In the Year of Jubilee. P

Grossmith, George (1847) and **Weedon** (1854): The Diary of a Nobody. P

Hake (1809): Poems, selected by Alice Meynell.

Hardy (1840): Life's Little Ironies. P

Hearn (1850): Glimpses of Unfamiliar Japan. P

'Hope, Anthony' (1863): The Prisoner of Zenda. P
    The Dolly Dialogues. P

Jones (1851): Judah. D

Kipling (1865): Jungle Book. P

Lincoln (d. 1865): Complete Works. P

'Mark Twain' (1835): The Tragedy of Pudd'n Head Wilson and the Comedy. P

Meredith (1828): Lord Ormont and his Aminta. P

Moore (1852): Esther Waters. P

More, Paul Elmer (1864): The Great Refusal. P

Morris (1834): Wood beyond the World. P

Pater (d. 1894): The Child in the House. P

Pinero (1855): The Weaker Sex. D
    The Schoolmistress. D

Raleigh (1861): The English Novel. P

Russell (Æ.; 1867): Homeward, Songs by the Way. P

Steel, Flora Annie (1847): The Potter's Thumb. P

Stevenson (d. 1894): The Ebb-Tide [with Lloyd Osbourne]. P. Collected Works, ed. Colvin [concl. 1898; ed. Gosse 1905–7].

Swinburne (1837): Astrophel and Other Poems.
    Studies in Prose and Poetry. P

Thackeray (d. 1863): Loose Sketches, An Eastern Adventure [contributions to The Britannia 1841 and Punch's Pocket Book 1847].

Ward (1851): Marcella. P

Watson (1858): Odes and Other Poems.

Weyman (1855): Under the Red Robe. P

Wilde (1856): A Woman of no Importance. D
    Salomé; Eng. trs. by Lord Alfred Douglas, and illustr. by Aubrey Beardsley [see 1893]. D
    The Sphinx. V

Yeats (1865): Land of Heart's Desire. D

Robert Louis Stevenson d.
James Anthony Froude d.
Walter Pater d.
Christina Rossetti d.
George John Romanes d.
Oliver Wendell Holmes d.
Walter Skeat ed. Complete Works of Chaucer.
Aubrey Beardsley and others, 'Yellow Book'.
John Bartlett, 'Concordance to Shakespeare's Plays and Poems'.
Israel Gollancz, 'Temple Shakespeare'.
Dreyfus Trial.
English translation of Maeterlinck.

Acton (1834): Lecture on Study of History.
Allen, Grant (1848): The Woman who did. P
Arnold (d. 1888): Letters, ed. G. W. E. Russell.
Balfour (1848): The Foundations of Belief. P
Barrie (1860): Sentimental Tommy. P
Bridges (1844): Essay on Keats. P
Carman, Bliss (1861): Behind the Arras. V
Coleridge (d. 1834): Letters, 1785–1834, ed. E. H.
    Coleridge [additional letters, ed. Turnbull
    1911; ed. Prideaux 1913]. P
    Anima Poetae, ed. E. H. Coleridge. P
Conrad (1857): Almayer's Folly. P
Corelli (1854): The Sorrows of Satan. P
Crackanthorpe, Hubert: Sentimental Studies. P
Crane (1871): The Red Badge of Courage. P
Froude (d. 1894): English Seamen in the Six-
    teenth Century. P
Gardiner (1829): History of Commonwealth and
    Protectorate [concl. 1901: see '83, '86]. P
Gissing (1857): Eve's Ransom. P
    Paying Guests. P.   Sleeping Fires. P
Grahame (1859): The Golden Age. P
Hardy (1840): Jude the Obscure. P
Harris, Frank (1856): Elder Conklin. P
Hearn (1850): Out of the East. P
Holmes (d. 1894): Complete Poetical Works.
James (1843): The Reprobate. P
Johnson (1867): Poems.
Kipling (1865): Second Jungle Book. P
Maitland (1850): History of English Law before
    Edward I [with Sir Frederick Pollock]. P
Mathews, Brander (1852): Books and Playbooks. P
    His Father's Son. P
Meredith (1828): The Amazing Marriage. P
Moore (1852): Celibates. P
Morris (1834): Child Christopher and Goldilind
    the Fair. P
    Trs. Beowulf. P
Pater (d. 1894): Greek Studies. P
    Miscellaneous Studies. P
Patmore (1823): Rod, Root, and Flower. P
Pinero (1855): The Notorious Mrs. Ebbsmith. D
    The Second Mrs. Tanqueray. D
    The Amazons. D
Rossetti (d. 1882): Family Letters, with Memoir by
    W. M. Rossetti.
Stevenson (d. 1894): Vailima Letters. P
Thompson, Francis (1859): Sister Songs.
Thomson, James (d. 1882): Poetical Works.
Ward (1851): Bessie Costrell. P
Wells (1866): Time Machine. P
Yeats (1865): Poems.

Robert Graves b.
Thomas Henry Huxley d.
Sir John Seeley d.
Thomas Gordon Hake d.
S. H. Butcher, ed. Aris-
    totle's 'Poetics' with Trs.
W. J. Courthope, 'His-
    tory of English Poetry'
    (concl. 1905).
W. R. Nicoll and T. J.
    Wise, 'Literary Anec-
    dotes of the 19th Cen-
    tury'.
John Horace Round,
    'Feudal England'.
Dumas fils d.
G. Thorn Drury, ed. of
    Keats (with Prefatory
    Essay by R. Bridges).

Barrie (1860): Margaret Ogilvie. P
Beerbohm (1872): Works of Max Beerbohm. P
Belloc (1870): A Bad Child's Book of Beasts. V
Browning (d. 1889): Collected Works, ed. Birrell
 and Kenyon [Centenary ed. 1912 ff.].
Burroughs, John (1837): Whitman, a Study. P
Coleridge, Mary (1861): Fancy's Following. V
Conrad (1857): An Outcast of the Islands. P
Corelli (1854): The Mighty Atom. P
Davidson (1857): Fleet Street Eclogues, ser. II
 [see 1893]. V
Dickinson, G. L. (1861): The Greek View of Life. P
Dolling, Robert (1851): Ten Years in a Ports-
 mouth Slum. P
'Fiona Macleod' (1855): Green Fire. P
 From the Hills of Dreams. V
Froude (d. 1894): Council of Trent. P
Hearn (1850): Gleanings in Buddha Fields. P
Housman, A. E. (1859): Shropshire Lad. V
Jacobs, W. W. (1863): Many Cargoes. P
James (1843): Embarrassments. P
 The Other House. P
Jones (1851): Michael and his Lost Angel. D
Kipling (1865): The Seven Seas. V
M'Taggart, John M'T. Ellis (1866): Studies in
 Hegelian Dialectic. P
'Mark Rutherford' (1831): Clara Hopgood. P
'Mark Twain' (1835): Personal Recollections of
 Joan of Arc. P
Meynell (1847): The Colour of Life. P
Morris (d. 1896): Well at the World's End. P
 Trs. Old French Romances. P
 Ed. Kelmscott Chaucer.
Pater (d. 1894): Gaston de Latour. P
Pinero (1855): Benefit of the Doubt. D
Romanes (d. 1894): Thoughts on Religion. P
Rossetti, C. (d. 1894): Poems, Unpublished or
 Uncollected, ed. W. M. Rossetti.
Stevenson (d. 1894): Weir of Hermiston. P
 Fables [in a new ed. of Jekyll and Hyde]. P
 Songs of Travel. V
Stout, G. F. (1860): Analytic Psychology. P
Swinburne (1837): Tale of Balen. V
Ward (1851): Sir George Tressady. P
Wells (1866): Island of Dr. Moreau. P
 Wheels of Chance. P
Wilson, Woodrow (1856): Mere Literature and
 Other Essays. P

Edmund Blunden b.
William Morris d.
Coventry Patmore d.
Thomas Hughes d.
George Du Maurier d.
Alfred Austin poet-lau-
 reate.
'Savoy' (8 numbers).
The 'Daily Mail' started.
W. Knight, ed. of Words-
 worth (Prose and
 Poetry).
J. B. Bury, ed. Gibbon's
 'Decline and Fall', com-
 pleted 1900.
'Temple Classics' started.
Legouis, 'La Jeunesse de
 William Wordsworth'.

Beerbohm (1872): The Happy Hypocrite. P
Bellamy, Edward (1850): Equality. P
Browning, E. B. (d. 1861): Letters, ed. F. G. Kenyon.
Butler (1835): The Authoress of the Odyssey. P
Caine (1853): The Christian. P
Carman, Bliss (1861): Ballads of Lost Haven. V
Coleridge, Mary (1861): King with Two Faces. P
Conrad (1857): Nigger of the Narcissus. P
Cooper, E. H. (1867): Mr. Blake of Newmarket. P
Cory (d. 1892): Letters and Journals. P
Davidson (1857): New Ballads. V
Dowson (1867): Pierrot of the Minute. D
Du Maurier (d. 1896): The Martian. P
Gissing (1857): The Whirlpool. P
Grant Duff, Sir Mountstuart Elphinstone (1829):
     Notes from a Diary [contd. 1898–1905].
Hardy (1840): The Well-Beloved. P
James, Henry (1843): What Maisie Knew. P
     The Spoils of Poynton. P
James, William (1842): The Will to Believe. P
'John Oliver Hobbes' (1867): School for Saints. P
Jones (1851): The Case of Rebellious Susan. D
Ker (1855): Epic and Romance. P
Kipling (1865): Captains Courageous. P
Meredith (1828): Essay on Comedy. P
Meynell (1847): Flower of the Mind [selections]. V
Morris (d. 1896): Water of the Wondrous Isles. P
Newbolt (1862): Admirals All. V
Raleigh (1861): Style. P
Robinson, Edward Arlington (1869): The Chil-
     dren of the Night. V
Rossetti (d. 1882): Letters to William Allingham,
     ed. G. Birkbeck Hill.
Russell ('Æ.'; 1867): Earth Breath. V
Steel, Flora Annie (1847): On the Face of the
     Waters. P
Stevenson (d. 1894): St. Ives [completed by A. T.
     Quiller Couch]. P
Tennyson, Hallam: Alfred Tennyson: a Memoir. P
Thompson (1859): New Poems.
Tyrrell, George (1861): Nova et Vetera. P
Voynich, Mrs. E. L. (1864): The Gadfly. P
Ward, Wilfrid Philip (1856): Life and Times of
     Cardinal Wiseman. P
Watts-Dunton (1832): Coming of Love. V
Wells (1866): Invisible Man. P
     Plattner Story. P
Wordsworth, Dorothy (d. 1855): Journals, ed.
     W. Knight (Life by E. de Selincourt 1934).
Yeats (1865): Secret Rose. P. Tables of the Law.
     P.   Adoration of the Magi. P

Jean Ingelow d.
Thomas Edward Brown d.
Margaret Oliphant d.
Francis Turner Palgrave
    d.
' *Country Life*' (*weekly*).
G. Birkbeck Hill, ed. of
    Johnsonian Miscella-
    nies.

President U.S.A.
    McKinley.

Bridges (1844): Poetical Works [completed in 6 vols. 1905: enlarged ed. in 7 vols. 1912].
Carman, Bliss (1861): By the Aurelian Wall. V
Churchill, Winston (1871): The Celebrity. P
Dunne, Finlay Peter (1867): Mr. Dooley in Peace and War. P
'Elizabeth': Elizabeth and her German Garden. P
Gissing (1857): Human Odds and Ends. P
    The Town Traveller. P. Charles Dickens. P
Grahame (1859): Dream Days. P
Hardy (1840): Wessex Poems.
Hewlett (1861): Forest Lovers. P
Hodgson, Shadworth Hollway (1832): Metaphysic of Experience. P
'Hope, Anthony' (1863): Rupert of Hentzau. P
Huxley (d. 1895): Scientific Memoirs, ed. Foster and Lankester [concl. 1903].
James (1843): In the Cage. P. The Two Magics. P
Jones (1851): The Rogue's Comedy. D
    The Tempter. D
Kipling (1865): The Day's Work. P
Lee, Sidney (1859): Life of Shakespeare. P
Maitland (1850): Roman Canon Law in the Church of England. P
    Township and Borough. P
Meynell (1847): The Spirit of Place. P
Morris (d. 1896): The Sundering Flood. V
Newbolt (1862): The Island Race. V
Phillips (1864): Poems.
Phillpotts, Eden (1862): The Children of the Mist. P
Saintsbury (1845): A Short History of English Literature. P
Shaw (1856): Plays Pleasant and Unpleasant [vol. i, Unpleasant: Widower's Houses, Philanderer, Mrs. Warren's Profession; vol. ii, Pleasant: Arms and the Man, Candida, Man of Destiny, You Never can Tell].
    The Perfect Wagnerite. P
Sidgwick (1838): Practical Ethics. P
Tyrrell, George (1861): Hard Sayings. P
Ward (1851): Helbeck of Bannisdale. P
Watson (1858): Collected Poems.
Watts-Dunton (1832): Aylwin. P
Wells (1866): War of the Worlds. P
Wilde (1856): Ballad of Reading Gaol. V

William Ewart Gladstone d.
Charles Lutwidge Dodgson ('Lewis Carroll') d.
William Black d.
'Harmsworth's Magazine'.
Byron's Works and Letters, ed. Coleridge and Prothero (completed 1904).
Oxford Classical Texts begun.

Bierce, Ambrose (1842): Fantastic Fables. P
Beerbohm (1872): More. P
Bosanquet (1848): Theory of the State. P
Browning, E. B. (d. 1861) and R. (d. 1889): Love-
Letters, 1845–6, ed. F. G. Kenyon.
Churchill, Winston (1871): Richard Carvel. P
Davidson (1857): The Last Ballad. V
Dunne, Finlay Peter (1867): Mr. Dooley in the
Hearts of his Countrymen. P
'Elizabeth': The Solitary Summer. P
Ellis, Havelock (1859): Studies in Psychology of
Sex, vol. i [7 more volumes at various dates].
'Fiona Macleod' (1855): Dominion of Dreams. V
Firth, Sir Charles (1857): The Protectorate. P
Gissing (1857): Crown of Life. P
Henley (1849): Hawthorn and Lavender. V
Hewlett (1861): Little Novels of Italy. P
Inge (1860): Christian Mysticism. P
James, Henry (1843): The Awkward Age. P
James, William (1842): Talks on Psychology. P
Jones (1851): The Physician. D.
Triumph of the Philistines. D.
Kipling (1865): Stalky & Co. P
Lanier, Sidney (d. 1887): Letters.
Mackail, J. W. (1859): Life of William Morris. P
Nesbit (1858): The Treasure-Seekers. P
Norris, Frank (1870): McTeague. P
Norton, Charles Eliot (1827): Rudyard Kipling. P
Oliphant, Margaret (d. 1897): Autobiography. P
Phillpotts (1862): The Human Boy. P
Pinero (1855): Trelawny of the Wells. P
Quiller-Couch (1863): The Ship of Stars. P
Rossetti, William Michael (ed.): Ruskin, Rossetti
and Pre-Raphaelitism [Papers 1854–62].
Somerville, Œ., and Ross, Martin: Some Experi-
ences of an Irish R. M. [Further Experiences
1908]. P
Stephen (1832): Studies of a Biographer, series I
[II 1902]. P
Stevenson (d. 1894): Letters, ed. S. Colvin.
Swinburne (1837): Rosamund, Queen of the Lom-
bards. D
Tyrrell, George (1861): External Religion. P
Ward, James (1843): Naturalism and Agnosti-
cism. P
Wells (1866): When the Sleeper Wakes. P
Whistler (1834): Baronet and Butterfly. P
Whiteing, Richard (1840): No. 5 John Street. P

Noel Coward b.
Beginning of S. African War.
First Hague Conference.
Bridges, 'Yattendon Hymnal'.
G. C. Macaulay, ed. Works of Gower.
John Horace Round, 'The Commune of London'.

Wilde (1856): Ideal Husband. D
  Importance of being Earnest [acted 1895]. D
Yeats (1865): The Wind among the Reeds. V
  Poems.

1900

Brown, T. E. (d. 1897): Collected Poems.
Butler (1835): Trs. Odyssey. P
Conrad (1857): Lord Jim. P
Corelli (1854): Boy. P
Dreiser (1871): Sister Carrie. P
Dunne, Finlay Peter (1867): Mr. Dooley's Philo-
  sophy. P
'Fiona Macleod' (1855): Divine Adventure. P
  House of Usna [in National Review, 1 July]. D
  Immortal Hour [in Fortnightly Review, Nov.;
    separately 1908]. D
Firth, Sir Charles (1857): Oliver Cromwell. P
Harland, Henry (1861): Cardinal's Snuff Box. P
Henley (1849): For England's Sake. V
Housman, L. (1865): An Englishwoman's Love-
  letters [anonymous]. P
Hudson (1841): Nature in Downland. P
James (1843): The Soft Side. P
'John Oliver Hobbes' (1867): Robert Orange.
Lang (1844): History of Scotland [concl. 1907]. P
Lear (d. 1888): The Jumblies. V
Maitland (1850): Political Theories of the Middle
  Ages [trs. Otto Gierke, with Introduction]. P
'Mark Rutherford' (1831): Pages from a Journal. P
'Mark Twain' (1835): The Man Who Corrupted
  Hadleyburg. P
Phillips (1866): Herod [acted]. D. Marpessa. V
Pinero (1855): Gay Lord Quex. D
Raleigh (1861): Milton. P
Rossetti, William Michael: Ed. Pre-Raphaelite
  Diaries and Letters [Papers 1835–54].
Saintsbury (1845): A History of Criticism. P
Shaw (1856): Three Plays for Puritans. D
Steel, Flora Annie (1847): Voices in the Night. P
Stephen (1832): English Utilitarians. P
Ward (1851): Eleanor. P
Wells (1866): Love and Mr. Lewisham. P
Yeats (1865): Shadowy Waters. D

Boxer Rising.
Sacheverell Sitwell b.
John Ruskin d.
Oscar Wilde d.
Henry Sidgwick d.
James Martineau d.
R. W. Dixon d.
Stephen Crane d.
Friedrich Max Müller d.
Richard Doddridge Black-
  more d.
Ernest Dowson d.
'The Daily Express'
  started.
'Oxford Book of English
  Verse', ed. Quiller-
  Couch.
George Saintsbury, 'His-
  tory of Criticism' (concl.
  1904).
Henry Sweet's 'History of
  Language'.
Tolstoy, first vols. of trs.
  by A. and L. Maude.
Freud, 'Traumdeutung'.

Belloc (1870): Robespierre. P
'Bourn, George' (George Sturt): The Bettesworth Book. P
Butler (1835): Erewhon Revisited. P
Churchill, Winston (1871): The Crisis. P
Davidson (1857): Self's the Man. D
Gissing (1857): By the Ionian Sea. P
Hardy (1840): Poems of the Past and Present. V
Hewlett (1861): New Canterbury Tales. P
'Hope, Anthony' (1863): Tristram of Blent. P
Hudson (1841): Birds and Man. P
James (1843): The Sacred Fount. P
Jones (1851): The Liars. D
Kipling (1865): Kim. P
M'Taggart (1866): Hegelian Cosmology. P
Meredith (1828): A Reading of Life. V
Meynell (1847): Later Poems. V
Moore (1852): Sister Teresa. P
Nesbit (1858): The Wouldbegoods. P
Newbolt (1862): The Sailing of the Long Ships. V
Norris, Frank (1870): The Octopus. P
Pater (d. 1894): Essays from the Guardian. P
Wells (1866): First Men in the Moon. P
Yeats (1865): Poems. V

Queen Victoria d.
Sir Walter Besant d.
F. W. H. Myers d.
William Stubbs d.
Brooke Foss Westcott d.
Charlotte Mary Yonge d.
'Cambridge Modern History', first vol. pub.
'World's Classics' begun.
Thomas Mann, 'Buddenbrooks'.
President McKinley assassinated.

President U.S.A. Theodore Roosevelt.

1902

Barrie (1860): The Little White Bird. P
Belloc (1870): The Path to Rome. P
Bosanquet (1848): Individuality and Value. P
Carpenter (1844): Love's Coming of Age. P
Chesterton (1874): Robert Browning. P
Conrad (1857): Youth. P
Dobson (1840): Samuel Richardson. P
Doyle (1859): The Hound of the Baskervilles. P
Fitzgerald (d. 1883): Letters and Literary Remains, ed. Aldis Wright.
Hudson (1841): El Ombú. P
Jacobs, W. W. (1863): The Lady of the Barge. P
James, Henry (1843): The Wings of a Dove. P
James, William (1842): The Varieties of Religious Experience. P
Kipling (1865): Just So Stories. P
Lee (1859): Life of Queen Victoria. P
Masefield (1878): Salt-Water Ballads. V

Lord Acton d.
P. J. Bailey d.
Samuel Butler d.
Lionel Johnson d.
Francis Bret Harte d.
G. Murray trs. of Euripides begun.
'Encyclopaedia Britannica,' 10th ed.
Zola d.

Mason (1865): The Four Feathers. P
Nesbit (1858): Five Children and It. P
'Ramal, Walter' (W. de la Mare, 1873): Songs of
    Childhood. V
Watson (1858): Ode on Coronation. V
Yeats (1865): Cathleen Ni Houlihan. D

1903

Adamson, Robert (d. 1902): Development of
    Modern Philosophy. P
Barrie (1860): Quality Street. D
    The Admirable Crichton. D
    Little Mary. D
Belloc (1870): Caliban's Guide to Letters. P
Butler (d. 1902): The Way of All Flesh. P
Chambers, E. K. (1866): The Mediaeval Stage. P
Childers (1870): The Riddle of the Sands. P
Conrad (1857): Typhoon. P
    [With F. M. Hueffer] Romance. P
Dickinson, G. L. (1861): Letters from John China-
    man. P
Dobson (1840): Fanny Burney. P
Gissing (d. 1903): The Private Papers of Henry
    Ryecroft. P
Hudson (1841): Hampshire Days. P
James (1843): The Ambassadors. P
    The Better Sort. P
Kipling (1865): The Five Nations. V
London, Jack (1896): The Call of the Wild. P
Morley (1838): Life of William Ewart Gladstone. P
Moore (1852): The Untilled Field. P
Moore, George Edward (1873): Principia Ethica. P
Norris, Frank (1870): The Pit. P
Raleigh (1861): Wordsworth. P
Russell (1872): Principles of Mathematics. P
Shaw (1856): Man and Superman. D
Traherne (d. 1674): Poetical Works, ed. Dobell. V
Tyrrell (1861): Lex Orandi. P
Ward (1851): Lady Rose's Daughter. P
Watson (1858): For England. V
Wells (1866): Mankind in the Making. P
Yeats (1865): Ideas of Good and Evil. P
    Where there is Nothing. D

*Frederick William Farrar
    d.
George Gissing d.
William Ernest Henley d.
George Birkbeck Hill d.
William Edward Lecky d.
Herbert Spencer d.
James Macneill Whistler
    d.
Sir John Sandys, 'His-
    tory of Classical Scholar-
    ship,' vol. i (vols. ii–iii
    1908).
'Daily Mirror' started.
Mrs. Toynbee's ed. of
    Walpole's Letters (com-
    pleted 1905: supple-
    ments by P. Toynbee
    1918, '25).*

Adams, Henry (1838): Mont-Saint-Michel and Chartres. P

Barrie (1860): Peter Pan. D

Beerbohm (1872): The Poets' Corner. P

Bradley, A. C. (1851): Shakespearian Tragedy. P

Bridges (1844): Demeter, a Mask. V

Chesterton (1874): Napoleon of Notting Hill. P

Conrad (1857): Nostromo. P

Davidson (1857): Selected Poems.

de la Mare (1873): Henry Brocken. P

Ellis, Havelock (1859): Study of British Genius. P

Gissing (d. 1903): Veranilda. P

Hardy (1840): The Dynasts, Part I [II '06, III '08]. D

Hewlett (1861): The Queen's Quair. P

Hudson (1841): Green Mansions. P

James, M. R. (1862): Ghost Stories of an Antiquary. P

Kipling (1865): Traffics and Discoveries.

London, Jack (1876): The Sea-Wolf. P

More, Paul Elmer (1864): Shelburne Essays [11 vols. 1904–21].

Munro ('Saki': 1870): Reginald. P

Nesbit (1858): The New Treasure-Seekers. P
The Phoenix and the Carpet. P

Newbolt (1862): Songs of the Sea. V

Porter, W. S. ('O. Henry') (1862): Cabbages and Kings, P

Sinclair, May (1879): The Divine Fire. P

Spencer (d. 1903): Autobiography. P

Sturgis, Howard (1855): Belchamber. P

Swinburne (1837): Channel Passage. V

Swinton, Sir Ernest (1868): The Defence of Duffer's Drift [under the pseudonym of Backsight-Forethought]. P

Wells (1866): The Food of the Gods. P

Yeats (1865): The King's Threshold. D
The Hour-Glass. D

Sir Edwin Arnold d.
Lafcadio Hearn d.
Samuel Smiles d.
Sir Leslie Stephen d.
Abbey Theatre, Dublin, founded.
T. Hutchinson, ed. Shelley's Poetical Works.
Aldis Wright, ed. Ascham's English Works.
A. R. Waller ed. Crashaw.

1905

Barrie (1860): Alice Sit-by-the-Fire. D

Belloc (1870): The Old Road. D

Birrell (1850): In the Name of the Bodleian. P

Chesterton (1874): Biography for Beginners. V
The Club of Queer Trades. P

Dickinson, G. L. (1861): A Modern Symposium. P

Dowson (d. 1900): Poems, with Memoir by A. Symons. V

Doyle (1859): The Return of Sherlock Holmes. P

Forster (1879): Where Angels Fear to Tread. P

Gissing (d. 1903): Will Warburton. P

Hudson (1841): A Little Boy Lost. P

George Macdonald d.
William Sharp d.
E. V. Lucas, 'Life of Charles Lamb'.
W. P. Courtney, 'Register of Bibliographies, 2 vols. (vol. iii 1912).
York Powell's and Vigfusson's 'Origines Islandicae'.
George Saintsbury, ed Minor Poets of Caroline Period (vol. 2 1906 vol. 3 1921).

James (1843): The Golden Bowl. P
Kipling (1865): They. P
Locke, W. J. (1863): The Morals of Marcus
    Ordeyne. P
Masefield (1878): Mainsail Haul. V
Moore (1852): The Lake. P
Orczy, Baroness: The Scarlet Pimpernel. P
Shaw (1856): Major Barbara. D
Swinburne (1837): Love's Cross-Currents [as A
    Year's Letters in 1877]. P
Synge (1871): The Shadow on the Glen. D
    Riders to the Sea. D
    The Well of the Saints. D
Vachell, H. A. (1861): The Hill. P
Vinogradoff (1854): Growth of the Manor. P
Ward (1851): The Marriage of William Ashe. P
Wells (1866): A Modern Utopia. P.   Kipps. P
Wharton, Edith (1862): The House of Mirth. P
Wilde (d. 1900): De Profundis. P

J. Sampson, ed. Blake.
A. R. Waller, ed. Samuel
    Butler.
A. R. Waller, ed. Cowley's
    '*English Writings*'.
A. Ward, ed. Crabbe's
    Poems 1905-7.
A. R. Waller, ed. Prior's
    Poems.

President U.S.A.
    Theodore Roose-
    velt (2nd term).

1906

Barrie (1860): Peter Pan in Kensington Gardens.
    P
Belloc (1870): Hills and the Sea. P
    Esto Perpetua. P
Benson, A. C. (1862): From a College Window. P
Chesterton (1874): Charles Dickens. P
Conrad (1857): Mirror of the Sea. P
De la Mare (1873): Poems. V
De Morgan (1839): Joseph Vance. P
Doughty (1843): Dawn in Britain, vols. i-ii
    [iii-iv in 1907]. V
Fowler, H. W. and F. G.: The King's English
    [developed 1926 in H. W. F.'s Modern Eng-
    lish Usage]. P
Galsworthy (1867): The Man of Property. P
Gregory, Lady (1852): Gods and Fighting Men. P
Hardy (1840): The Dynasts, Part II. D
Kipling (1865): Puck of Pook's Hill. P
Locke, W. J. (1863): The Beloved Vagabond. P
London, Jack (1876): White-Fang. P
Lucas, E. V. (1868): Listener's Lure. P
M'Taggart (1868): Some Dogmas of Religion. P
Moore (1852): Memoirs of my Dead Life. P
Nesbit (1858): The Railway Children. P
Pinero (1855): His House in Order. D
Porter, W. S. ('O. Henry') (1862): The Four
    Million. P
Saintsbury (1845): History of English Prosody,
    vol. i [vol. ii 1908, vol. iii 1910].

F. W. Maitland d.
'*John Oliver Hobbes*' *d.*
Richard Garnett d.
The English Hymnal.
'*Everyman's Library*'
    started.
Sidney and Beatrice Webb,
    '*English Local Govern-*
    ment: The Parish and
    the County'.
Ibsen d.
Brunetière d.

Santayana (1863): The Life of Reason (5 vols.
　　completed 1906). P
Sinclair, Upton (1878): The Jungle. P
Wallace, Edgar (1875): Four Just Men. P

1907

Acton (d. 1902): Historical Essays and Studies. P
　　History of Freedom and Other Essays. P
Bell (1868): The Desert and the Sown. P
Belloc (1870): Cautionary Tales for Children. V
'Bourn, George' (George Sturt): Memoirs of a
　　Surrey Labourer. P
Coleridge, Mary (d. 1907): Poems. V
Colum, Padraic (1881): Wild Earth. V
Conrad (1857): The Secret Agent. P
Davidson (1857): The Triumph of Mammon. V
De Morgan (1839): Alice-for-Short. P
Flecker (1884): The Bridge of Fire. V
Forster (1879): The Longest Journey. P
Galsworthy (1867): The Country House. P
Gibson, Wilfrid (1878): The Stonefolds. V
Gosse (1849): Father and Son. P
Hewlett (1861): The Stooping Lady. P
Hodgson, Ralph: The Last Blackbird. V
Housman, L. (1865), and Barker (1877): Prunella.
　　D
James, William (1842): Pragmatism. P
Jerome, Jerome K. (1859): The Passing of the
　　Third Floor Back and Other Stories. P
Joyce (1882): Chamber Music. V
Kipling (1865): The Brushwood Boy. P
Lucas, E. V. (1868): Character and Comedy. P
Maitland (d. 1906): Domesday Book and Beyond. P
Maugham (1874): Lady Frederick. D
Murray (1866): Rise of the Greek Epic. P
Porter, W. S. ('O. Henry') (1862): The Trimmed
　　Lamp. P
Prior (d. 1721): Dialogues of the Dead, ed. A. R.
　　Waller. P and V
Raleigh (1861): Shakespeare. P
Shaw (1856): John Bull's Other Island. D
Synge (1871): Playboy of the Western World. D
　　The Aran Islands. P
Trevelyan, G. M. (1876): Garibaldi's Defence of
　　the Roman Republic. P
Tyrrell (1861): Lex Credendi. P
Victoria, Queen (d. 1901): Letters, ed. A. C. Benson
　　and Viscount Esher, 3 vols. P

Mary Coleridge d.
Francis Thompson d.
'*Cambridge History of
　Eng. Lit.*', *1st vol.*
'*Nation*' *started.*
William Archer trs. Ibsen,
　1907–12.

Wordsworth (d. 1850): Letters of the Wordsworth Family, ed. William Knight. (Early Letters of William and Dorothy Wordsworth, ed. E. de Sélincourt 1935).
Yeats (1865): Deirdre. D

1908

Abercrombie, Lascelles (1881): Interludes and Poems. V
Barrie (1860): What Every Woman Knows. D
Belloc (1870): Mr. Clutterbuck's Election. P
Bennett (1867): Buried Alive. P
The Old Wives' Tale. P
'Birmingham, George': Spanish Gold. P
Chesterton (1874): The Man Who was Thursday. P
Davidson (1857): The Testament of John Davidson. V
Mammon and His Message. V
Davies (1871): The Autobiography of a Super-Tramp. P
De Morgan (1839): Somehow Good. P
Dickinson, G. L. (1861): Justice and Liberty. P
Doughty (1843): Adam Cast Forth. V
Wanderings in Arabia [abridgement of Arabia Deserta]. P
Forster (1879): A Room with a View. P
Galsworthy (1867): A Commentary. P
Grahame (1859): The Wind in the Willows. P
Hardy (1840): The Dynasts, Part III. D
Henley (d. 1903): Complete Works, 7 vols.
Lodge (1851): Man and the Universe. P
Lucas, E. V. (1868): Over Bemerton's. P
Maitland (d. 1906): Constitutional History of England. P
Masefield (1878): Captain Margaret. P
Stein, Gertrude (1874): Three Lives. P
Swinburne (1837): The Age of Shakespeare. P
The Duke of Gandia. D
Synge (1871): The Tinker's Wedding. D
Traherne (d. 1674): Centuries of Meditations. P
Wells (1866): The War in the Air. P
Yeats (1865): Collected Works, vols. i and ii.

Edward Caird d.
'Ouida' d.
G. Birkbeck Hill, ed. *Johnson's 'Lives'.*
Henry Sweet,'The Sounds of English'.
Sidney and Beatrice Webb, 'English Local Government: The Manor and the Borough'.
Anatole France, first Eng. trs.

Barclay, Florence (1862): The Rosary. P
Barker (1877): Marrying of Ann Leete. D
  The Voysey Inheritance. D.   Waste. D
Beerbohm (1872): Yet Again. P
Binyon (1869): England and Other Poems. V
Bottomley, Gordon (1874): Riding to Lithend. D
Bradley, A. C. (1851): Oxford Lectures on Poetry. P
Browning (d. 1889): Letters to Alfred Domett. P
Carlyle, Thomas (d. 1881) and Jane Welsh (d.
  1869): Love Letters, ed. A. Carlyle. P
Davidson (d. 1909): Fleet Street. V
De Morgan (1839): It Never Can Happen Again. P
Emerson (d. 1882): Journals.
Galsworthy (1867): Plays, vol. i: The Silver Box,
  Joy, Strife. D.   Justice. D
Gregory, Lady (1859): Seven Short Plays. D
Hardy (1840): Time's Laughingstocks. V
Harris, Frank (1856): The Man Shakespeare. P
Hewlett (1861): Open Country. P
Hudson (1841): Afoot in England. P
Jacks, L. P. (1860): Mad Shepherds.
James, William (1842): The Nature of Truth. P
Kipling (1865): Actions and Reactions. P
Lodge (1851): The Survival of Man. P
Lucas, E. V. (1868): One Day and Another. P
Masefield (1878): Multitude and Solitude. P
  The Tragedy of Nan and Other Poems. D
Meredith (d. 1909): Last Poems.
Pound, Ezra (1885): Personæ and Exultations. V
Quiller Couch (1863): True Tilda. P
Swinton, Sir Ernest (1868): The Green Curve
  [under pseudonym of Ole-Luk-Oie]. P
Synge (d. 1909): Poems and Translations. V
Thompson (d. 1907): Shelley. P
Trevelyan (1876): Garibaldi and the Thousand. P
Wells (1866): Ann Veronica. P
  Tono Bungay. P

James Millington Synge d.
Algernon Charles Swin-
  burne d.
Francis Marion Craw-
  ford d.
John Davidson d.
Sir Theodore Martin d.
George Meredith d.
P. Vivian, ed. Campion's
  Works.
J. C. Smith, ed. Spenser's
  'Faerie Queene'.
'English Review' founded.
J. H. Round, 'Feudal
  England'.
United States Copyright
  Act fixes term of copy-
  right at 28 years, renew-
  able by the author or his
  executors or next of kin
  for a second 28 years.
  See 1911. In order to
  secure copyright, books
  written in English by
  foreign authors must still
  (see 1891) be printed in
  the United States.

President U.S.A.
Taft.

Acton (d. 1902): The French Revolution. P
Angell, Norman (1874): The Great Illusion. P
Arnold (d. 1888): Essays in Criticism, III.
Baring (1874): Diminutive Dramas. D
    Dead Letters. P
Belloc (1870): Verses. V
Bennett (1867): Clayhanger. P
De la Mare (1873): The Return. P
Flecker (1884): Thirty-six Poems. V
Forster (1879): Howard's End. P
Gibson, Wilfrid: Daily Bread. V
Hewlett (1861): Rest Harrow. P
Hudson (1841): A Shepherd's Life. P
James (1843): The Finer Grain. P
Kipling (1865): Rewards and Fairies. P
'Mark Rutherford' (1831): More Pages from a
    Journal. P
Masefield (1878): Pompey the Great. D
Meredith (d. 1909): Celt and Saxon. P
Montague, C. E. (1867): A Hind let loose. P
Monypenny (1866): Life of Disraeli (completed
    1920 by J. E. Buckle).
Morris (d. 1896): Complete Works.
Munro ('Saki': 1870): Reginald in Russia. P
Newbolt (1862): Songs of the Fleet. V
Raleigh (1861): Six Essays on Johnson. P
Robinson, Edward Arlington (1869): The Town
    down the River. V
Russell (1872) and Whitehead (1861): Principia
    Mathematica, vol. i.
Sinclair, May (1879): The Creators. P
Traherne (d. 1674): Poems of Felicity. V
Wells (1866): The History of Mr. Polly. P
Yeats (1865): Poems: Second Series. V

Edward VII d.
F. J. Furnivall d.
William James d.
'Encyclopaedia Britan-
    nica', 11th ed.
J. H. Round, 'Peerage
    and Pedigree'.
Sidney and Beatrice Webb,
    'English Poor Law
    Policy'.
Spenser's 'Minor Poems',
    ed. de Sélincourt.
Tolstoy d.

Abercrombie (1881): Emblems of Love. V
Barker (1877): The Madras House. D
Beerbohm (1872): Zuleika Dobson. P
Bell (1868): Amurath to Amurath. P
Bennett (1867): Hilda Lessways. P
   The Card. P
Brooke (1887): Poems. V
Chesterton (1874): Ballad of White Horse. V
   The Innocence of Father Brown. P
Conrad (1857): Under Western Eyes. P
Davies (1870): Songs of Joy. V
De Morgan (1839): A Likely Story. P
Dolben, Digby Mackworth (d. 1867): Poems, ed.
   with a Memoir by R. Bridges.
Douglas, Norman (1868): Siren Land. P
Ervine, St. John (1883): Mixed Marriage. D
Flecker (1884): Forty-two Poems. V
Forster (1879): The Celestial Omnibus. P
Galsworthy (1867): The Patrician. P
Gosse (1849): Collected Poems. V
James, Henry (1843): The Outcry. P
James, M. R. (1862): More Ghost Stories of an
   Antiquary. P
Johnson (d. 1902): Post Liminium. P
Lawrence (1885): The White Peacock. P
Leacock, Stephen (1869): Nonsense Novels. P
Lucas, E. V. (1868): Old Lamps for New. P
Mansfield (1888): In a German Pension. P
Masefield (1878): The Everlasting Mercy. V
   Jim Davis. P.   Street of To-day. P
Maugham (1874): Loaves and Fishes. P
Montague (1867): Dramatic Values. P
Moore (1852): Hail and Farewell, vol. i. P
   The Apostle. D
Munro ('Saki': 1870): Chronicles of Clovis. P
Porter, W. S. ('O. Henry') (d. 1910): The Gift of
   the Wise Men. P
   Collected Works. P
Pound, Ezra (1885): Canzoni. V
Shaw (1856): The Doctor's Dilemma, Getting
   Married, Showing-up of Blanco Posnet. D
Synge (d. 1909): Deirdre of the Sorrows. D
Trevelyan (1876): Garibaldi and the Making of
   Italy. P
Walpole (1884): Mr. Perrin and Mr. Traill. P

Sir Charles Dilke d.
Sir Francis Galton d.
Sir W. S. Gilbert d.
J. L. and Barbara Ham-
   mond, 'The Village
   Labourer'.
Legouis, 'Geoffrey
   Chaucer'.
Copyright Act extends term
   of copyright to 50 years
   from author's death (with
   certain limitations). See
   1709, 1842, 1909.

Ward, James (1843): The Realm of Ends. P
Wells (1866): The New Machiavelli. P
Wharton, Edith (1862): Ethan Frome. P
Yeats (1865): The Celtic Twilight.

1912

Archer (1856): Play-Making. P
Beerbohm (1872): A Christmas Garland. P
Bennett (1867) and Knoblock, E.: Milestones. D
Bentley, E. C. (1875): Trent's Last Case. P
Butler (d. 1902): Note Books, ed. H. Festing Jones. P
Chesterton (1874): Manalive. P
Conrad (1857): 'Twixt Land and Sea. P
De la Mare (1873): The Listeners and Other Poems. V
Galsworthy (1867): Plays, vol. ii: The Eldest Son, The Little Dream, Justice.
Houghton, W. S. (1881): Hindle Wakes. D
Lawrence (1885): The Trespasser. P
Lucas, E. V. (1868): London Lavender. P
Macaulay, Rose: The Lee Shore. P
Mackenzie, Compton (1883): Carnival. P
Masefield (1878): The Widow in the Bye Street. V
Meredith (d. 1909): Letters [2 vols.].
Moore (1852): Hail and Farewell, vol. ii. P
Munro ('Saki': 1870): The Unbearable Bassington. P
Newbolt (1862): Poems New and Old. V
Pound, Ezra (1885): Ripostes. V
Saintsbury (1845): History of English Prose Rhythm. P
Stephens, James (1882): The Charwoman's Daughter. P.   The Crock of Gold. P
Strachey (1880): Landmarks in French Literature. D
Tomlinson, H. M. (1873): The Sea and the Jungle. P
Walpole (1884): Prelude to Adventure. P
Wells (1866): Marriage. P

Andrew Lang d.
William Walter Skeat d.
Henry Sweet d.
'Georgian Poetry, 1911–12.'
'Daily Herald' started.
Tagore's 'Gitanjali', Eng. translation.
Deloney's Works, ed. F. O. Mann.
Savile's Works, ed. Walter Raleigh.
Coleridge's Poetical Works, ed. E. H. Coleridge.
A. Feuillerat, ed. Works of Sidney (completed 1926).
Dostoievsky, trs. by L. Garnett, 1912–19.
Chekhov,'Cherry Orchard', first Eng. trs.
Thomas Mann, 'Tod in Venedig'.

Austen-Leigh, W. and R. A.: Jane Austen, her Life and Letters. P
Barrie (1860): The Twelve-Pound Look. D
Bosanquet (1848): The Value and Destiny of the Individual. P
Bridges (1844): A Tract on the Present State of English Pronunciation [first printed 1910]. P
Chesterton (1874): Magic. D
Churchill, Winston (1871): The Inside of the Cup. P
De la Mare (1873): Peacock Pie. V
Flecker (1884): The Golden Journey to Samarkand. V
Fletcher, J. G. (1886): The Dominant City. V
Frost, Robert (1875): A Boy's Will. V
Gregory, Lady (1859): New Comedies. D
Holme, Constance: Crump Folk Going Home. P
Hudson (1841): Adventures among Birds. P
Jacks, L. P. (1860): All Men are Ghosts. P
James (1843): A Small Boy and Others. P
Lawrence (1885): Love Poems. V.
  Sons and Lovers. P
Lucas, E. V. (1868): Loiterer's Harvest. P
Mackenzie, Compton (1883): Sinister Street, vol. i. P
Masefield (1878): Dauber. V
  The Daffodil Fields. V
Meynell (1847): Collected Poems. V
Montague (1867): The Morning's War. P
Moore (1852): Hail and Farewell, vol. iii. P
Squire, J. C. (1884): Three Hills and Other Poems. V
Stein, Gertrude (1874): Portrait of Mabel Dodge at Villa Caronio. P
Walpole (1884): Fortitude. P
Watson (1858): The Muse in Exile. V
Wilson, Woodrow (1856): The New Freedom. P

Alfred Austin d.
Edward Dowden d.
William Hale White d.
Robert Bridges poet-laureate.
'New Statesman' started.
Marcel Proust, 'Du Côté de chez Swann'.

President U.S.A. Wilson.

1914

Blunt (1840): Poetical Works.
Bradley (1846): Truth and Reality. P
Chesterton (1874): The Flying Inn. P and V
  The Wisdom of Father Brown. P
Conrad (1857): Chance. P
De Morgan (1839): When Ghost meets Ghost. P
Dickinson, Emily (d. 1886): The Single Hound. V
Dickinson, G. L. (1861): Appearances. P
Ervine, St. John (1883): Jane Clegg. D
  Mrs. Martin's Man. P
Flecker (1884): The King of Alsander. P
Frost, Robert (1875): North of Boston. V
Galsworthy (1867): Plays, vol. iii: The Fugitive, The Pigeon, The Mob.

Beginning of Great War (4 August).
Sir William Anson d.
Mary Braddon d.
Theodore Watts-Dunton d.

Hardy (1840): Satires of Circumstance. V
Holme, Constance: The Lonely Plough. P
James (1843): Notes on Novelists. P
   Notes of a Son and Brother. P
Joyce (1882): Dubliners. P
Lawrence (1885): The Prussian Officer. P
   The Widowing of Mrs. Holroyd. D
Lowell, Amy (1874): Sword Blades and Poppy
   Seed. V
Macaulay, Rose: The Making of a Bigot. P
   The Two Blind Countries. V
Mackenzie (1883): Sinister Street, vol. ii. P
Masefield (1878): Philip the King. V
Meynell (1847): Collected Essays. P
Munro ('Saki': 1870): Beasts and Super-Beasts. P
Russell, Bertrand (1872): Our Knowledge of the
   External World. P
Shaw (1856): Misalliance, Fanny's First Play,
   The Dark Lady of the Sonnets. D
Walpole (1884): The Wooden Horse. P
Yeats (1865): Responsibilities. P

1915

Aldington (1892): Images. V
Balfour (1848): Theism and Humanism. P
Benson, Stella (1892): I Pose. P
Binyon (1869): The Winnowing Fan. V
Brooke (d. 1915): 1914 and Other Poems. V
Buchan (1875): The Thirty-nine Steps. P
Chesterton (1874): Poems. V
Conrad (1857): Victory. P
Dreiser (1871): The Genius. P
Ervine, St. John (1883): John Ferguson. D
Flecker (d. 1915): The Old Ships. V
Fletcher, J. G. (1886): Irradiations; Sand and
   Spray. V
Galsworthy (1867): The Little Man. P
Keith, Sir Arthur (1866): Antiquity of Man. P
Lawrence (1885): The Rainbow. P
Leacock, Stephen (1869): Moonbeams from the
   Larger Lunacy. P
'Mark Rutherford' (d. 1913): Last Pages from a
   Journal. P
Masefield (1878): The Faithful. D
Masters, Edgar Lee (1869): The Spoon River
   Anthology. V
Maugham (1874): Of Human Bondage. **P**
Monro, Harold (1879): Trees. V
Moore (1852): Muslin. P
Pound, Ezra (1885): Cathay. V
Sitwell, Edith (1887): The Mother. V
Stein, Gertrude (1874): Tender Buttons. P
Wodehouse (1881): Psmith, Journalist. P
Woolf, Virginia: The Voyage Out. P

James Elroy Flecker d.
Rupert Brooke d.
Stephen Phillipps d.
'Georgian Poetry, 1913–
*   15.'*
Herrick's Poetical Works,
*   ed. F. W. Moorman.*
Vaughan's Works, ed.
*   L. C. Martin.*

Anderson, Sherwood (1876): Windy McPherson's Son. P
Barrie (1860): A Kiss for Cinderella. D
Bridges (1844): The Spirit of Man; an Anthology. P and V
Brooke (d. 1915): Letters from America. P
  Webster and the Elizabethan Drama. P
  Collected Poems. V
Buchan (1875): Greenmantle. P
Davies (1871): Collected Poems. V
Drinkwater (1882): Olton Pools. V
Flecker (d. 1915): Collected Poems. V
Fletcher, J. G. (1886): Goblins and Pagodas. V
Freeman (1880): Fifty Poems. V
  Stone Trees and Other Poems. V
Gibson, Wilfrid (1878): Battle. V
Graves, Robert (1895): Over the Brazier. V
Hankey, Donald (d. 1916): A Student in Arms. P
Hewlett (1861): The Song of the Plow. V
Holme, Constance: The Old Road from Spain. P
Lawrence (1885): Amores. V
  Twilight in Italy. P
Lodge (1851): Raymond, or Life and Death. P
Lowell, Amy (1874): Men, Women, and Ghosts. V
Masefield (1878): Sonnets and Poems. V
Mew, Charlotte (1870): The Farmer's Bride. V
Moore (1852): The Brook Kerith. P
Pound (1885): Lustra. V
Powys, J. C. (1872) **& Ll.** (1884): Confessions of Two Brothers. P
Quiller Couch (1863): The Art of Writing. P
Raleigh, Walter, and others: Shakespeare's England. P
Robinson, Edward Arlington (1869): The Man against the Sky. V
Sandburg, Carl (1878): Chicago Poems. V
Shaw (1856): Androcles and the Lion, Overruled, Pygmalion. D
Sitwell, E. (1887) **and O.** (1892): Twentieth Century Harlequinade. V
Walpole (1884): The Dark Forest. P
Webb, Mary (1881): The Golden Arrow. P
Wells (1866): Mr. Britling sees it through. P
Yeats (1865): Reveries over Childhood and Youth. P

Henry James d.
Stopford Brooke d.
Hector Munro ('Saki') d.
'Wheels, an Anthology of Verse' (later volumes 1917, 1918, 1919, 1920, 1921).
Chekhov, trs. by C. Garnett 1916–20.
Jung, 'Psychology of the Unconscious'.

Barrie (1860): Dear Brutus. D
  The Old Lady shows her Medals. D
Binyon (1869): For the Fallen and Other Poems. V
Bridges (1844): Ibant Obscuri. V
Cabell (1879): The Cream of the Jest. P
Colvin (1845): Life of John Keats. P
Dane, Clemence: Regiment of Women. P
Douglas, Norman (1868): South Wind. P
Drinkwater (1882): Poems, 1908–14. V
Dunsany, Lord (1878): Plays of Gods and Men. D
Eliot, T. S. (1888): Prufrock. V
Garland, Hamlin (1860): A Son of the Middle
  Border. P
Gibson, Wilfrid (1878): Livelihood. V
Gosse (1849): Life of Swinburne. P
Graves, Robert (1895): Fairies and Fusiliers. V
Hergesheimer (1880): Three Black Pennys. P
Hodgson, Ralph: Poems. V
Joyce (1882): A Portrait of the Artist as a Young
  Man. P
Kipling (1865): A Diversity of Creatures. P
Lawrence (1885): Look! we have come through. P
Lowell, Amy (1874): Tendencies in Modern
  American Poetry. P
'Mark Twain' (d. 1910): Letters.
Masefield (1878): Good Friday. D
  Lollingdon Downs, and Other Poems. V
Meynell (1847): A Father of Women. V
Monro, Harold (1879): Strange Meetings. V
More, Paul Elmer (1864): Platonism. P
Nichols, Robert (1893): Ardours and Endurances.
  V
Pollard, A. W. (1859): Shakespeare's Fight with
  the Pirates. P
Sackville-West, V. (1892): Poems of East and
  West. V
Sassoon (1886): The Old Huntsman. V
Squire (1884): The Lily of Malud. V
Thomas (d. 1917): Poems. V
Walpole (1884): Maradick at Forty. P
Waugh, Alec (1898): The Loom of Youth. P
Webb, Mary (1881): The Spring of Joy. P
  Gone to Earth. P
Wells (1866): God the Invisible King. P
  The Soul of a Bishop. P
Wodehouse (1881): Uneasy Money. P
Yeats (1865): The Wild Swans at Coole. V

William de Morgan d.
Edward Thomas d.
'*Georgian Poetry, 1916–*
  17.'
Lenin, 'Imperialism: The
  State and Revolution'.
J. L. and B. Hammond,
  '*The Town Labourer'.*

President U.S.A.
Wilson   (2nd
term).

Armstrong, Martin (1882): Thirty New Poems. V
Bridges (1844): The Necessity of Poetry. P
　Britannia Victrix. V
Cather, Willa (1876): My Antonia. P
De la Mare (1873): Motley and Other Poems. V
Drinkwater (1882): Abraham Lincoln. D
Fletcher, John Gould (1886): Japanese Prints.
Freeman (1880): Memories of Childhood. V
Galsworthy (1869): Five Tales. P
Gibson, Wilfrid (1878): Whin. V
Hardy (1840): Moments of Vision and Miscel-
　laneous Verse. V
Holme, Constance: Beautiful End. P
Hopkins (d. 1889): Poems, ed. Bridges [2nd ed.
　1930].
Hudson (1841): Far Away and Long Ago. P
Huxley, Aldous (1894): The Defeat of Youth, and
　Other Poems. V
Inge (1860): The Philosophy of Plotinus. P
Joyce (1882): Exiles. D
Kipling (1865): The Years Between. V
Knox, Ronald (1888): A Spiritual Æneid. P
Lawrence (1885): New Poems. V
Lowell, Amy (1874): Can Grande's Castle. P
Newton, A. Edward (1864): The Amenities of
　Book-Collecting. P
Quiller Couch (1863): Studies in Literature [2nd
　series 1922, 3rd series 1929]. P
Sassoon (1886): Counter Attack. V
Sitwell, Edith (1887): Clown's Houses. V
Sitwell, Sacheverell (1900): People's Palace. P
Smith, Logan Pearsall (1865): Trivia. P
Squire (1884): Poems, 1st series. P
Stein, Gertrude (1874): Mary, he Giggled. P
Stopes, Marie Carmichael: Married Love and
　Wise Parenthood. P
Strachey (1880): Eminent Victorians. P
Swinburne (d. 1909): Letters, ed. Gosse and Wise.
Thomas (d. 1917): Last Poems. V
Tomlinson, H. M. (1873): Old Junk. P
Torr, Cecil (1857): Small Talk at Wreyland [2nd
　series 1921, 3rd Series 1923]. P
Turner, W. J. (1889): The Dark Fire. V
Walpole (1884): The Green Mirror. P
Wells (1866): Joan and Peter. P
Yeats (1865): Per amica silentia lunae. P

End of Great War.
　(*Armistice 11 Nov.*)
*Maurois: 'Silences du
Colonel Bramble'.*

Aldington (1892): Images of Desire. V
Anderson, Sherwood (1876): Winesburg, Ohio. P
Ashford, Daisy: The Young Visiters. P
Babbitt (1865): Rousseau and Romanticism. P
Barbellion (d. 1919): The Journal of a Disappointed Man. P.   Enjoying Life. P
Beerbohm (1872): Seven Men. P
Bennett (1867): Sacred and Profane Love. D
Benson, Stella (1892): Living Alone. P
Blunt (1840): My Diaries [2nd vol. 1920]. P
Buchan (1875): Mr. Standfast. P
Cabell (1879): Beyond Life. P.   Jurgen. P
Conrad (1857): The Arrow of Gold. P
De Morgan (d. 1917): The Old Madhouse. P
Dreiser (1871): Twelve Men. P
Galsworthy (1869): Saint's Progress. P
Hardy (1840): Collected Poems. V
Hergesheimer (1880): Java Head. P
Holme, Constance: The Splendid Fairing. P
Inge (1860): Outspoken Essays. P
James, M. R. (1862): A Thin Ghost and Others. P
Jones, Henry Festing (1851): Samuel Butler: a
    Memoir. P
Keynes, J. M. (1883): The Economic Consequences of the Peace. P
Kipling (1865): The Years Between. V
Macaulay, Rose: What not: a Prophetic Comedy.
    P
Masefield (1878): Reynard the Fox. V
Maugham (1874): The Moon and Sixpence. P
Milne (1882): First Plays. D
Moffatt, James (1870): The New Testament: a
    New Translation.
Moore (1852): Avowals. P
Murry (1889): Evolution of an Intellectual. P
O'Neill, Eugene (1888): The Moon of the Caribbees
    and six other Plays. D
Sassoon (1886): War Poems. V
Shaw (1856): Heartbreak House, Great Catherine,
    &c. D
Sinclair, May (1879): Mary Olivier. P
Sitwell, Osbert (1892): Argonaut and Juggernaut. V
Squire (1884): The Birds, and Other Poems. V
Walpole (1884): Jeremy. P.   The Secret City. P
Wells (1866): Outline of History. P
Woolf: Night and Day. P
Yeats (1865): The Cutting of an Agate.
    Two Plays for Dancers. D

William Michael Rossetti d.
The Society for Pure English founded by Robert Bridges.
'*London Mercury*' *started.*
'*John o'London's Weekly*' *started.*
'*Georgian Poetry, 1918–19.*'
C. K. Scott-Moncrieff, trs. '*Song of Roland*'.
J. L. and B. Hammond, '*The Skilled Labourer*'.

Alexander (1859): Space, Time and Deity. P
Asquith, Margot (1864): Autobiography [vol. ii 1922]. P
Barbellion (d. 1919): Last Diary. P
Barrie (1860): Mary Rose. D
Beerbohm (1872): And Even Now. P
Blunden (1896): The Waggoner. V
Bottomley (1874): King Lear's Wife. D
Bridges (1844): October and Other Poems. V
Chesterton (1874): The Uses of Diversity. P
Conrad (1857): The Rescue. P
De la Mare (1873): Poems, 1901–18. V
Dickinson, G. L. (1861): The Magic Flute. P
Eliot (1888): The Sacred Wood. P
Flecker (1884): Collected Prose. P
Freeman (1880): Poems New and Old. V
Galsworthy (1869): In Chancery. P
   Awakening. P.   The Skin Game. D
Gibson, Wilfrid (1878): Neighbours. V
Graves, Robert (1895): Country Sentiment. V
Guedalla (1889): Supers and Supermen. P
Hudson (1841): Dead Man's Plack. P
Huxley, Aldous (1894): Leda. V.   Limbo. P.
James (d. 1916): Letters, ed. Lubbock. P
Kipling (1865): Letters of Travel. P
Lawrence (1885): The Lost Girl. P
   Touch and Go. D
Lewis, Sinclair (1885): Main Street. P
Macaulay, Rose: Potterism. P
Mansfield (1888): Bliss, and Other stories. P
Masefield (1878): Enslaved, and Other Poems. V
Nichols, Robert (1893): Aurelia. V
O'Neill, Eugene (1888): Beyond the Horizon. P
Owen, Wilfrid (d. 1918): Poems, with an introduction by Siegfried Sassoon. V
Pound (1885): Umbra [Collected Early Poems]. V
Quiller Couch (1863): The Art of Reading. P
Sandburg, Carl (1878): Smoke and Steel. V
Santayana (1863): Little Essays. P
Shelley (d. 1822): Philosophical View of Reform. P
Sitwell, Edith (1887): The Wooden Pegasus.
Thomas, Edward (d. 1917): Collected Poems. V
Walpole (1884): The Captives. P
Webb, Mary (1881): The House in Dormer Forest. P
Wharton, Edith (1862): The Age of Innocence. P
Wodehouse (1881): The Coming of Bill. P
Wolfe, Humbert (1885): London Sonnets. V
   Shylock reasons with Mr. Chesterton. V
Yeats (1865): Michael Robartes and the Dancer. V

A. H. Bullen d.
Mrs. Humphry Ward d.
Albert Einstein, 'Relativity', authorized translation.
Spengler, 'Decline of the West'.

Anderson, Sherwood (1876): The Triumph of the
   Egg. P
Archer (1856): The Green Goddess. P
Armstrong, Martin (1882): The Buzzards. V
Baring (1874): Poems 1914–19. V
Dane, Clemence: A Bill of Divorcement. D
   Will Shakespeare. D
De la Mare (1873): Memoirs of a Midget. P
   The Veil, and Other Poems. V
De Morgan (d. 1917): The Old Man's Youth. P
Drinkwater (1882): Mary Stuart. D
   Oliver Cromwell. D
Freeman (1880): Music, Lyrical and Dramatic
   Poems. V
Galsworthy (1869): To Let. P
Graves, Robert (1895): The Pier Glass. V
Holme, Constance: The Trumpet in the Dust. P
Housman, L. (1865): Angels and Ministers. D
Hudson (1841): A Traveller in Little Things. P
Huxley, Aldous (1894): Crome Yellow. P
Lawrence (1885): Tortoises. V
   Women in Love. P
Lubbock, Percy: The Craft of Fiction. P
Macaulay, Rose: Dangerous Ages. P
M'Taggart (1866): The Nature of Existence. P
Maugham (1874): The Circle. D
Mencken, H. L. (1880): Prejudices [further series
   1921–3–5–8]. P
Moore (1852): Heloise and Abelard. P
O'Neill, Eugene (1888): The Emperor Jones. D
Russell, Bertrand (1872): The Analysis of Mind. P
Sackville-West (1892): Orchard and Vineyard. V
Shaw (1856): Back to Methuselah. D
Sitwell, Edith (1887): Troy Park. V
Smith, Logan Pearsall (1865): More Trivia. P
Strachey (1880): Queen Victoria. P
Tomlinson, H. M. (1873): London River. P
Walpole (1884): The Young Enchanted. P
Woolf: Monday or Tuesday. P
Yeats (1865): Four Plays for Dancers. D

Austin Dobson d.
*J. C. Squire's 'Selections
  from Modern Poets' (2nd
  series 1925).*
*New Cambridge Shake-
  speare begun.*

*President U.S.A.
  Harding.*

Abercrombie (1881): Four Short Plays. D
Austen (d. 1817): Love and Freindship. P
Baring (1874): The Puppet Show of Memory. P
Barrie (1860): Shall we join the Ladies. D
Beerbohm (1872): Rossetti and his Circle. P
Bennett (1867): Mr. Prohack. P
Benson, Stella (1892): The Poor Man. P
Blunden (1896): The Shepherd and Other Poems. V
Cather, Willa (1876): One of Ours. P
Chesterton (1874): The Ballad of St. Barbara. V
Colum, Padraic (1881): Dramatic Legends. V
Davies (1870): Child Lovers, and Other Poems. V
Drinkwater (1882): Preludes. V
Eliot (1888): The Waste Land. V
Flecker (d. 1915): Hassan. D
Galsworthy (1867): The Forsyte Saga [in one vol.]. P.　　　Loyalties. D
Garnett (1892): Lady into Fox. P
Guedalla (1889): The Second Empire. P
Hardy (1840): Late Lyrics and Earlier. V
Hergesheimer (1880): The Bright Shawl. P
Housman, A. E. (1859): Last Poems. V
Housman, L. (1865): Little Plays of St. Francis. D
Hudson (d. 1922): A Hind in Richmond Park. P
Huxley, Aldous (1894): Mortal Coils. P
Inge (1860): Outspoken Essays [2nd series]. P
Joyce (1882): Ulysses [pub. in Paris]. P
Lawrence (1885): Aaron's Rod. P
Lewis, Sinclair (1885): Babbitt. P
Lubbock, Percy: Earlham. P
Mansfield (1888): The Garden Party. P
Masefield (1878): Melloney Holtspur. D
Maugham (1874): East of Suez. D
　The Land of Promise. D
　On a Chinese Screen. P
Monro, Harold (1879): Real Property. V
Montague (1867): Disenchantment. P
Moore, George Edward (1873): Philosophical Studies. P
Murry (1889): Countries of the Mind. P
　The Problem of Style. P
O'Neill, Eugene (1888): Anna Christie. D
Priestley (1894): Brief Diversions. P
Raleigh (d. 1922): The War in the Air, vol. 1. P
Sitwell, S. (1900): Hundred and One Harlequins. V
Squire (1884): Poems [second series]. V
Strachey (1880): Books and Characters. P
Turner, W. J. (1889): The Man who ate the Popomack. D
Walpole (1884): The Cathedral. P
Webb, Mary (1881): Seven for a Secret. P
Woolf: Jacob's Room. P
Yeats (1865): Later Poems. V

Sir Walter Raleigh d.
Wilfrid Scawen Blunt d.
W. H. Hudson d.
Alice Meynell d.
'Georgian Poetry, 1920–2.'
C. K. Scott-Moncrieff, trs.
　of Proust, first two
　volumes.
'Encyclopaedia Britannica', 12th ed.

Abercrombie (1881): Phoenix. D

Aldington (1892): Exile and Other Poems. V

Archer (1856): The Old Drama and the New. P

Baring (1874): A Triangle. P

Belloc (1870): On. P.   Sonnets and Verse. V

Bennett (1867): Riceyman Steps. P

Blunden (1896): To Nature. V

Cather, Willa (1876): A Lost Lady. P

Chambers, E. K. (1866): The Elizabethan Stage. P

Conrad (1857): The Rover. P

Davies (1870): Collected Poems. V

De la Mare (1873): The Riddle, & Other Stories. P

Drinkwater (1882): Collected Plays. D
    Collected Poems. V.   Robert E. Lee. D

Dunsany (1878): Plays of Near and Far. D

Forster (1879): Pharos and Pharillon. P

Frost, Robert (1875): New Hampshire. V

Guedalla (1889): Masters and Men. P

Hardy (1840): Tragedy of the Queen of Cornwall. D

Housman, L. (1865): Followers of St. Francis. D

Hudson (d. 1922): Letters, ed. Garnett. P

Huxley, Aldous (1894): Antic Hay. P
    On the Margin. P

Huxley, Julian (1887): Essays of a Biologist.

Ker (d. 1923): The Art of Poetry. P

Lawrence (1885): Birds, Beasts and Flowers. V
    Kangaroo. P.   Ladybird. P.   Love Poems. V
    Fantasia of the Unconscious. P
    Sea and Sardinia. P

Lubbock, Percy: Roman Pictures.

Macaulay, Rose: Told by an Idiot. P

Mansfield (d. 1923): The Dove's Nest, and Other
    Stories. P.   Poems. V

Masefield (1878): King Cole, and Other Poems. V
    A King's Daughter. D.   Collected Poems. V

Maugham (1874): Our Betters. D

Meynell (d. 1922): Essays. P.   Last Poems. V.

Montague (1867): Fiery Particles. P

Powys, T. F. (1875): Black Bryony. P
    The Left Leg. P

Raleigh (d. 1922): Some Authors. P
    Laughter from a Cloud. P

Santayana (1863): Scepticism & Animal Faith. P

Stein, Gertrude (1874): Geography and Plays. P

Katharine Mansfield d.
William Paton Ker d.
Maurice Hewlett d.
*William Hurrell Mallock
    d.*
Viscount Morley d.
'Cambridge Ancient History', vol. i.
*'Proposals for the Revision
    of the Book of Common
    Prayer.'*
*'English Diaries', ed. A.
    Ponsonby.*
*Jane Austen's Novels,
    ed. R. W. Chapman.*
Nonesuch Press started.
Maurois: 'Ariel'.

*President U.S.A.
    Coolidge.*

Anderson, Sherwood (1876): A Story Teller's Tale. P

Babbitt (1865): Democracy and Leadership. P

Baring (1874): 'C.' P

Bennett (1867): Elsie and the Child. P

Benson, Stella (1892): Pipers and a Dancer. P

Birrell (1850): More Obiter Dicta. P

Boswell (d. 1795): Letters, ed. C. B. Tinker. P

Clare (d. 1864): Madrigals and Chronicles, ed. E. Blunden. V

Conrad (d. 1924): Laughing Anne, and One Day More. D

Coward (1899): The Rat-trap. D.   The Vortex. D

Davies (1870): Secrets. V

De la Mare (1873): Crossings. D

Ding Dong Bell. V

Dunsany (1878): Five Plays. D

Eliot (1888): Homage to John Dryden. P

Forster (1879): A Passage to India. P

Galsworthy (1869): Old English. D

The White Monkey. P

Gibson (1878): Kestrel Edge and Other Plays. D

Housman, L. (1865): Trimblerigg. P

Huxley, Aldous (1894): The Little Mexican. P

Lawrence (1885): England, my England. P

The Boy in the Bush [with M. L. Skinner]. P

Macaulay, Rose: Orphan Island. P

Mansfield (d. 1923): Something Childish, and Other Stories. P

Masefield (1878): Sard Harker. P

Melville (d. 1891): Billy Budd. P

Montague (1867): The Right Place. P

Moore (1852): Conversations in Ebury Street. P

Shaw (1856): St. Joan. D

Sitwell, Edith (1887): The Sleeping Beauty. V

Sitwell, Osbert (1892): Triple Fugue. P

Sitwell, Sacheverell (1900): Southern Baroque Art. P.   The Thirteenth Cæsar. V

Squire (1884): Grub Street Nights. P

Tomlinson, H. M. (1873): Tidemarks. P

Turner (1889): Smaragda's Lover. D

Walpole (1884): The Old Ladies. P

Webb, Mary (1881): Precious Bane. P

Wodehouse (1881): The Inimitable Jeeves. P

Wolfe, Humbert (1885): Kensington Gardens. V

Woodforde, James (d. 1803): Diary of a Country Parson, vol. i, ed. J. Beresford [1758–1802; concl. 1931]. P

Joseph Conrad d.
Francis Herbert Bradley d.
William Archer d.
Woodrow Wilson d.
Thomas Mann, 'Zauberberg'.

Aldington (1892): A Fool i' the Forest. V
Austen (d. 1817): Sanditon. P
Baring (1874): Cat's Cradle. P
  Collected Poems. V
Belloc (1870): The Cruise of the Nona. P
Benson, Stella (1892): The Little World. P
Blunden (1896): Masks of Time. V
Bottomley (1874): Poems of Thirty Years. V
Bridges (1844): New Verse written in 1921. V
Chesterton (1874): The Everlasting Man. P
Conrad (d. 1924): Suspense. P
Coward (1899): Fallen Angels. D. Hay Fever. D
De la Mare (1873): Broomsticks & Other Tales. P
Dickinson, Emily (d. 1886): Complete Poems. V
Dreiser (1871): An American Tragedy. P
Eliot (1888): Poems, 1905–25.
Flecker (d. 1915): Don Juan. D
Fletcher, J. G. (1886): Parables. P and V
Freeman (1880): The Grove, and Other Poems. V
Galsworthy (1869): Caravan. P
Garnett (1892): The Sailor's Return. P
Gibson, Wilfrid (1878): I heard a Sailor. V
Hardy (1840): Human Shows, Far Fantasies. V
Holme, Constance: The Things which Belong. P
Huxley, Aldous (1894): Those Barren Leaves. P
  Along the Road. P
Lawrence (1885): Birds, Beasts and Flowers. V
Lewis, Sinclair (1885): Arrowsmith. P
Lowell, Amy (1874): John Keats. P
Lubbock, Percy: The Region Cloud. P
Masefield (1878): The Trial of Jesus. D
Maugham (1874): The Painted Veil. P
Murry (1889): Keats and Shakespeare. P
Powys, J. C. (1872): Ducdame. P
Powys, Ll. (1884): Black Laughter. P
Powys, T. F. (1875): Mr. Tasker's Gods. P
Priestley (1894); The English Comic Writers. P
Stein, Gertrude (1874); Making of Americans. P
Wells (1866): Christina Alberta's Father. P
Wilson, Woodrow (d. 1924): Public Papers. P
Wolfe, Humbert (1885): The Unknown Goddess. V
Woolf, Virginia: The Common Reader. P
  Mrs. Dalloway. P

A. C. Benson d.
Sir Henry Rider Haggard
  d.
C. H. Wilkinson ed.
  Poems of Lovelace.

INDEX

Celia's Arbour '78, Monks of Thelema '78, Chaplain of the Fleet '81, (alone) All Sorts and Conditions of Men '82.

BEST, GEORGE, d. 1584? Voyages of Martin Frobisher 1578.

BETHUNE, ALEXANDER, 1804–43. Tales of Scottish Peasantry 1838, Scottish Peasant's Fireside '43.

BETTERTON, THOMAS, 1635?–1710. Hist. of Eng. Stage 1741.

Beware the Cat 1561.

BEWICK, THOMAS, 1753–1828. Quadrupeds 1790, British Birds '97.

Bible: Scots New Testament 1520, *Tyndale's* '24–'30, *Coverdale's* '35, '37, *Matthew's* '37, *Cranmer's* '39, *Geneva* '60, *Bishops'* '68, *Rheims* (N.T.) '82, *Douai* (O.T.) 1609, *Authorized Version* '11, *Wiclif's*, ed. Madden 1850, *Polyglot* '54, *Revised Version* (N.T.) 1881, (O.T.) '84.

BICKERSTAFFE, ISAAC, d. 1812? Love in a Village 1763, Maid of the Mill '65, Padlock '68, Lionel and Clarissa '68 (School for Fathers '73).

BIERCE, AMBROSE, 1842–1914(?). Tales of Soldiers and Civilians 1891, Black Beetles in Amber '92, Can Such Things Be '93, Fantastic Fables '99.

BIGGES, WALTER. Sir Francis Drake's West Indian Voyage 1588.

BINGHAM, JOSEPH, 1668–1723. Origines Ecclesiasticæ 1708–22.

BINYON, LAURENCE, 1869– . England and other Poems 1909, Winnowing Fan '15, For the Fallen '17.

Biographia Britannica 1747–66.

Biographical Dictionary ed. G. Long 1842.

Biographica Dramatica 1764.

BIRCH, THOMAS, 1705–66. Ed. State Papers of John Thurloe 1742, Lives '47, '52, '54.

'BIRMINGHAM, GEORGE', *see* HANNAY, JAMES OWEN.

BIRRELL, AUGUSTINE, 1850–1933. Obiter Dicta 1884, '87, Life of Charlotte Brontë '85, Res Judicatæ '92, In the Name of the Bodleian 1905, More Obiter Dicta '23.

BLACK, WILLIAM, 1841–98. A Daughter of Heth 1871, Strange Adventures of a Phaeton '72, A Princess of Thule '74, Macleod of Dare '78, White Wings '80, Sunrise '80, Strange Adventures of a House Boat '88.

BLACKIE, JOHN STUART, 1809–1895. Trs. Æschylus 1850, Lays and Legends of Ancient Greece '56, On Self-Culture '74.

BLACKLOCK, THOMAS, 1721–91. Poems 1746.

BLACKMORE, SIR RICHARD, c. 1655–1729. Prince Arthur 1695, Satyr against Wit 1700, Eliza '05, Nature of Man '11, Creation '12, Essays '16, Poems '16, Alfred '23.

BLACKMORE, RICHARD DODDRIDGE, 1825–1900. Poems by Melanter 1853, Cradock Nowell '66, Lorna Doone '69, Maid of Sker '72, Springhaven '87, Perlycross '94.

BLACKSTONE, SIR WILLIAM, 1723–80. Commentaries on Laws of England 1765–9.

Blackwood's Magazine started 1817.

BLADES, WILLIAM, 1824–90. Early Type Specimen Books 1875.

BLAIR, HUGH, 1718–1800. Dissertation on Ossian 1763, Sermons '77–1801, Lectures on Rhetoric '83.

BLAIR, ROBERT, 1699–1746. The Grave 1743.

BLAKE, WILLIAM, 1757–1827. Poetical Sketches 1783, Songs of Innocence '89, Book of Thel '89, Marriage of Heaven and Hell '90, Song of Liberty '92, Gates of Paradise '93, Daughters of Albion '93, America '93, Songs of Experience '94, Europe '94, Book of Urizen '94, Book of Los '95, Book of Ahania '95, Song of Los '95, Jerusalem 1804, Milton '04, Descriptive Catalogue '09, Life by Gilchrist '63, Selections ed. Rossetti '63, Works ed. Ellis and Yeats '93, ed. Sampson 1905.

BLANCHARD, SAMUEL LAMAN, 1804–45. Lyric Offerings 1828, Sketches from Life '46, Corporation Characters '55.

BLATCHFORD, ROBERT, 1851– . Merrie England 1894.

BLESSINGTON, LADY, 1789–1849. Conversations with Lord Byron 1834.

BLIGH, ADM. WILLIAM, 1754–1817. Voyage in the Bounty 1792.

Bloody Banquet 1620.

BLOOMFIELD, ROBERT, 1766–1823. Farmer's Boy 1800, Rural Tales '01, Wild Flowers '06, Banks of Wye '11, Mayday with the Muses '22.

BLOUNT, CHARLES, 1654–93. Trs. Apollonius Tyaneus 1680, Great is Diana of the Ephesians '80, Miscellaneous Works '95.

BLOUNT, SIR THOMAS POPE, 1649–97. Censura Celebriorum Authorum 1690, De Re Poetica '94, Essays '92.

BLUNDEN, EDMUND, 1896– . The Waggoner 1920, The Shepherd '22, To Nature '23, Masks of Time '25.

BLUNT, WILFRID SCAWEN, 1840–1922.

BRADLEY, FRANCIS HERBERT, 1846–1924. Ethical Studies 1876, Mr. Sidgwick's Hedonism '77, Principles of Logic '83, Appearance and Reality '93, Essays on Truth and Reality 1914.

BRADSTREET, ANNE, *c.* 1612–72. The Tenth Muse 1650.

BRADY, NICHOLAS, 1659–1726. New Version of the Psalms (with Tate) 1696.

BRATHWAITE, RICHARD, 1588?–1673. Scholar's Medley 1614, Strappado for the Devil '15, The Five Senses '20, English Gentleman '30, English Gentlewoman '31, Whimzies '31, Barnabae Itinerarium '38, Honest Ghost '58.

BRETON, NICHOLAS, 1545?–1626? Small handful of fragrant flowers 1575, Works of a Young Wit '77, Floorish upon Fancie '77, Briton's Bower of Delight '91, Pilgrimage to Paradise '92, Marie Magdalen's Love '95, Arbour of Amorous Devices '97, Auspicante Jehova '97, Wits Trenchamour '97, Will of Wit '97, Solemn Passion '98, Pasquil's Fooles Cap 1600, Pasquil's Mistress 1600, Pasquil's Passe 1600, Melancholike Humours 1600, Pasquil's Mad-Cap 1600, Two Excellent Princes 1600, A Divine Poem '01, Longing of a Blessed Heart '01, Soule's Harmony '02, Old Madcap's New Gallimawfry '02, Mother's Blessing '02, True Description of Unthankfulness '02, Wonders worth the Hearing '02, Poste with a Mad Packet '02, Three Philosophers '03, A Mad World, my Masters '03, Passionate Shepherd '04, Grimello's Fortune '04, Soul's Immortal Crown '05, Honour of Valour '05, Divine Considerations of the Soul '08, Wit's Private Wealth '12, Cornucopiae, Pasquil's Nightcap '12, Characters upon Essays '15, Crossing of Proverbs '16, Court and Country '18, Strange News '22, Pasquil's Mad-Cappe '26, Fantasticks '26.

BREWER, EBENEZER COBHAM, 1810–97. Dictionary of Phrase and Fable 1870.

BREWSTER, SIR DAVID, 1781–1868. Treatise on Optics 1831.

BRIDGES, ROBERT, 1844–1930. Poems 1873, '79, '80, Growth of Love '76, '89, Prometheus '83, Nero '85, Eros and Psyche '85, Feast of Bacchus '89, Palicio '90, Return of Ulysses '90, Christian Captives '90, Achilles in Scyros '90, Shorter Poems '90, Humours of the Court '93, Milton's Prosody '93, Keats '95, Poetical Works '98, Yattendon Hymnal '99, Demeter 1904, English Pronunciation '13, Spirit of Man '16, Ibant Obscuri 1917, Necessity of Poetry '18, Britannica Victrix '18, October '20, New Verse '25, Collected Essays '27, Testament of Beauty '29, Three Friends '32.

BRIGHT, WILLIAM, 1824–1901. History of the Church 1860.

BRINKELOW, HENRY, d. 1546. Complaynt of Roderyck Mors 1548.

Britain's Idea 1628.

British Critic started 1793, new series 1814.

British Drama 1817.

British Librarian 1737.

British Magazine 1760–7.

British Magazine started 1832.

British Theatre 1776–8.

British Theatre 1823.

Briton 1762–3.

BROKE, ARTHUR, d. 1563. Romeus and Juliet 1562.

BROME, RICHARD, d. 1652? Northern Lass 1632, Antipodes '40, Sparagus Garden '40, Jovial Crew '52, Five New Plays '53, Queen's Exchange '57, Five New Plays '59.

BRONTË, ANNE, 1820–49. Poems 1846, Agnes Grey '47, Tenant of Wildfell Hall '48.

BRONTË, CHARLOTTE, 1816–55. Poems 1846, Jane Eyre '47, Shirley '49, Villette '53, The Professor '57, Life by Mrs. Gaskell '57.

BRONTË, EMILY, 1818–1848. Poems 1846, Wuthering Heights '47.

BROOKE, FRANCES, 1724–89. Lady Julia Mandeville 1763, Siege of Sinope '81, Rosina '83, Marian '88.

BROOKE, HENRY, 1703?–83. Universal Beauty 1735, Gustavus Vasa '39, Fables for the Female Sex '44, Earl of Essex '61, Fool of Quality '66, Redemption '72, Juliet Grenville '74.

BROOKE, RUPERT, 1887–1915. Poems 1911, 1914 and other Poems '15, Letters from America '16, John Webster '16, Collected Poems '16.

BROOKE, STOPFORD, 1832–1916. English Literature 1876.

BROUGHAM, HENRY, Lord Brougham, 1778–1868. Practical Observations on Education 1825.

BROWN, CHARLES BROCKDEN, 1771–1810. Wieland 1798, Ormond '99, Edgar Huntley '99, Arthur Mervyn '99, 1800, Clara Howard '01, Jane Talbot '01.

'48 (in Four Volumes '55, in Six Volumes '58), Oeconomy of Human Life (?) '50, Public Virtue '53, Theatrical Records '56, Cleone '58, Annual Register '59, Fugitive Pieces '61, Select Letters '78.

DOLBEN, DIGBY MACKWORTH, 1848–67. Poems ed. Bridges 1911.

DOLLING, ROBERT WILLIAM RAD-CLYFFE, 1851–1902. Ten Years in a Portsmouth Slum 1896.

Domestic Intelligencer started 1679.

DOMETT, ALFRED, 1811–87. Venice 1839, Ranolf and Amohia '72.

Don Quixote, first trs. (by Shelton) 1612.

DONNE, JOHN, 1576–1631. Pseudo-Martyr 1610, Anatomy of the World '11, enlarged ed. '12, Ignatius his Conclave '11, Devotions upon emergent occasions '24, Five Sermons '26, Death's Duell '32, Poems '33 (later eds. '35, '39, '49, '50, '54, '69), Juvenilia '33, Eighty Sermons, with Walton's 'Life', '40, Fifty Sermons '49, Essays in Divinity '51, Letters to Several Persons of Honour '51, Paradoxes, &c. '52, Twenty-six Sermons '60.

DORAN, JOHN, 1807–78. Their Majesties' Servants 1860.

DORRINGTON, EDWARD (?). The Hermit 1727.

DORSET, CATHARINE, 1750?–1817? The Peacock 'at Home' 1807, The Lion's Masquerade '07.

DOUCE, FRANCIS, 1757–1834. Illustrations of Shakespeare 1807.

DOUGHTY, CHARLES, 1843–1926. Travels in Arabia Deserta 1888, Dawn in Britain 1906–7, Adam Cast Forth '08, Wanderings in Arabia '08.

DOUGLAS, GAVIN, 1474?–1522. Trs. Aeneid 1553, Palace of Honour '53.

DOUGLAS, NORMAN, 1868– . Siren Land 1911, South Wind '17.

DOWDEN, EDWARD, 1843–1913. Shakespeare: his Mind and Art 1875, Life of Shelley '86.

DOWLAND, JOHN, 1563?–1626?. First Book of Songs 1597, Second Book of Songs 1600, Third Book of Songs '03, Pilgrim's Solace '12.

DOWNES, JOHN, fl. 1662–1710. Roscius Anglicanus 1708.

DOWSON, ERNEST, 1867–1900. Pierrot of the Minute 1897, Poems 1905.

DOYLE, SIR ARTHUR CONAN, 1859–1930. A Study in Scarlet 1887, The Sign of Four '89, The Adventures of Sherlock Holmes '91, Memoirs of Sherlock

Holmes '93, Hound of Baskervilles 1902, Return of Sherlock Holmes '05.

DOYLE, SIR FRANCIS, 1810–88. Return of the Guards 1866.

DRAKE, SIR FRANCIS, Jun. Sir Francis Drake Revived 1626.

DRAKE, NATHAN, 1766–1836. Literary Hours 1798, Shakespeare and his times 1817, Memorials of Shakespeare '28.

DRANT, THOMAS, d. 1578. Trs. Satires of Horace 1566, Trs. Ars Poetica, Satires and Epistles of Horace '67.

DRAYTON, MICHAEL, 1563–1631. Harmonie of the Church 1591, Idea '93, Piers Gaveston '94, Matilda '94, Ideas Mirror '94, Endimion and Phoebe '95, Robert, Duke of Normandy '96, Mortimeriados '96, England's Heroical Epistles '97, Barons' War 1603, The Owle '04, Moyses in a Map of his Miracles '04, Paean Triumphall for Goldsmiths '04, Poems (earliest collection) '05, Poems Lyrick and Pastoral '06, Legend of Great Cromwell '07, Life and Death of Lord Cromwell '09, Polyolbion Pt. I '12, Pt. II '22, Battaile of Agincourt, Nimphidia, &c. '27, Muses Elizium '30.

DREISER, THEODORE 1871– . Sister Carrie 1900, The Genius '15, Twelve Men '19, American Tragedy '25.

DRINKWATER, JOHN, 1882– . Olton Pools 1916, Poems '17, Abraham Lincoln '18, Mary Stuart '21, Oliver Cromwell '21, Preludes '22, Robert E. Lee '23, Collected Plays' 23, Collected Poems '23.

DRUMMOND, HENRY, 1851–97. Natural Law in Spiritual World 1883.

DRUMMOND, WILLIAM, 1585–1649. Tears on Death of Meliades 1613, Mausoleum (with others) '13, Poems '16, Forth Feasting '17, Flowers of Sion '23, Cypress Grove '23, History of Scotland 1423–1524, '55, Poems '56, Collected Works (cont. Conversations with Jonson) 1711, Conversations with Jonson 1842.

DRYDEN, JOHN, 1631–1700. Upon Death of Lord Hastings 1649, Upon Death of Cromwell '59, Astraea Redux '60, To His Sacred Majesty '61, To My Lord Chancellor '62, Rival Ladies '64, Indian Queen '65, Annus Mirabilis '67, Indian Emperour '67, Sir Martin Mar-All '68, Secret Love '68, Dramatick Poesie '68, Wild Gallant '69, Tempest '70, Tyrannick Love '70, Evening's Love '71, Conquest of Granada '72, Marriage à la

HUBBARD, WILLIAM, c. 1621–1704. Troubles with the Indians 1677, General History of New England 1815.

HUDDESFORD, GEORGE, 1749–1809. Collected Poems 1801.

HUDSON, WILLIAM HENRY, 1841–1922. The Purple Land 1885, Naturalist in La Plata '92, Idle Days in Patagonia '93, Nature in Downland 1900, Birds and Man '01, El Ombú '02, Hampshire Days '03, Green Mansions '04, A Little Boy Lost '05, Afoot in England '09, A Shepherd's Life '10, Adventures among Birds' 13, Far Away and Long Ago '18, Dead Man's Plack '20, A Traveller in Little Things '21, A Hind in Richmond Park '22, Letters '23.

HUGHES, JOHN, 1677–1720. Hist. of England 1706, Calypso '12, Siege of Damascus '20, Poems '35.

HUGHES, THOMAS, fl. 1587. Misfortunes of Arthur 1587.

HUGHES, THOMAS, 1822–96. Tom Brown's Schooldays 1857, Scouring of the White Horse '59, Tom Brown at Oxford '61.

HULL, THOMAS, 1728–1808. Sir William Harrington 1771, Henry II '74.

HUME, DAVID, 1711–76. Treatise of Human Nature 1739, Essays Moral and Political '41, Essays concerning Human Understanding '48, Enquiry concerning Principles of Morals '51, Political Discourses '52, History of England '54–'61, Four Dissertations '57, Suicide and Immortality '77, Own Life '77, Dialogues concerning Natural Religion '79, Life and Correspondence ed. Burton 1846, Letters to Strahan '88, Letters ed. Greig 1932.

Hundred Merry Tales 1526.

HUNNIS, WILLIAM, d. 1597. Certain Psalms 1550.

HUNT, JAMES HENRY LEIGH, 1784–1859. Juvenilia 1801, Critical Essays '07, Examiner started '08, London Theatres '08, Reflector '10, Feast of the Poets '11, '14, Descent of Liberty '15, Story of Rimini '16, Foliage '18, Literary Pocket Book '18, Hero and Leander; Bacchus and Ariadne '19, Indicator '19, Trs. Tasso's Amyntas '20, The Months '21, Liberal '22, Literary Examiner '23, Ultra-Crepidarius '23, Lord Byron and his Contemporaries '28, Companion '28, Father '30, Chat of the Week '30, Poetical Works '32, Sir Ralph Esher '32, Christianism '32, London Journal '34, Indicator and Companion '34, Captain Sword and Captain Pen '35, Monthly Repository '37, Seer '40, Legend of Florence '40, Prefaces to Moxon's eds. of dramatists '40, Chaucer Modernized '41, The Palfrey '42, Hundred Romances of Real Life '43, Collected Poems '44, Wit and Humour '46, Stories from Italian Poets '46, Jar of Honey '48, The Town '48, Readings for Railways '49, Autobiography '50, Leigh Hunt's Journal '50–'51, Table-Talk '51, Old Court Suburb '55, Stories in Verse '55, Selections from Beaumont and Fletcher '55, Poetical Works '60, Saunter through the West End '61, Correspondence '62, A Day by the Fire '70.

HURD, RICHARD, 1720–1808. Moral and Political Dialogues 1759–63, Chivalry and Romance '62, Prophecies '72, Preface to Warburton '94, Edition of Addison 1811.

HUTCHESON, FRANCIS, 1694–1746. Ideas of Beauty and Virtue 1725, Passions and Affections '28, Moral Philosophy '55.

HUTCHINSON, LUCY, b. 1620. Life of Colonel Hutchinson 1806.

HUTTON, HENRY. Folly's Anatomy 1619.

HUTTON, RICHARD HOLT, 1826–97. Essays 1871.

HUXLEY, ALDOUS, 1894– . Defeat of Youth 1918, Leda '20, Limbo '20, Crome Yellow '21, Mortal Coils '22, Antic Hay '23, On the Margin '23, Little Mexican '24, Those Barren Leaves '25.

HUXLEY, JULIAN, 1887– . Essays of a Biologist 1923.

HUXLEY, THOMAS HENRY, 1825–95. Man's Place in Nature 1863, Classification of Animals '64, Lay Sermons '70, David Hume '79, Collected Essays '93–'94, Scientific Memoirs '98–1903.

Hyckescorner 1510.

HYLTON, WALTER, d. 1396. Scala Perfectionis 1494, Devout Book '94.

Hypneromachia 1592.

Idler 1758.

Ieronimo 1605.

Illustrated London News started 1842.

Illustrated Sporting and Dramatic News started 1874.

Impatient Poverty 1560.

INCHBALD, MRS. ELIZABETH, 1753–1821. Appearance is against them 1785, I'll tell you what '86, Such things are

'88, Child of Nature '88, Simple Story
'91, Everyone has his Fault '93,
Nature and Art '96, Wives as they
were '97, Lovers' Vows '98, To many or
not to many 1805, British Theatre '06.

INGE, WILLIAM RALPH, 1860– . Christian Mysticism 1899, Philosophy of
Plotinus 1918, Outspoken Essays
'19, '22.

INGELEND, THOMAS. Disobedient Child
1547, '70.

INGELOW, JEAN, 1820–97. Poems 1863,
'76, '85, Story of Doom '67, Off the
Skelligs '72.

INGERSOLL, CHARLES JARED, 1782–
1862. Rights and Wrongs of U.S.A.
1808, Inchiquin '10.

Institution of a Gentleman 1555.

Intelligencer 1663.

Intelligencer 1728–9.

IRELAND, WILLIAM, 1777–1835. Miscellaneous Papers of Shakespeare 1795,
Vortigern '96, '99, Henry II '99.

IRVING, WASHINGTON, 1783–1859.
Salmagundi 1807–8, Knickerbocker's
History of New York '09, Sketch
Book '19–'20, Bracebridge Hall '22,
Tales of a Traveller '24, Life of
Columbus '28, Conquest of Granada
'29, Alhambra '32, Life of Washington '55–59.

Jack Drum's Entertainment 1601.

Jack Jugeler (acted) *c.* 1553, (pub.) *c.*
1562.

Jack Upland 1540.

Jack Straw 1593.

JACKS, LAWRENCE PEARSALL, 1860– .
Mad Shepherds 1909, All Men are
Ghosts '13.

Jacob and Esau 1568.

JACOB, GILES, 1686–1744. Poetical
Register 1719.

Jacobite's Journal started 1747.

JACOBS, WILLIAM WYMARK, 1863– .
Many Cargoes 1896, Lady of the
Barge 1902.

JAGO, RICHARD, 1715–81. Edge Hill
1767, Collected Poems '84.

JAMES I of Scotland, 1394–1437. The
Kingis Quair 1783.

JAMES I of England, VI of Scotland,
1566–1625. Prentice in Art of Poesie
1584, Demonologie '97, Basilikon
Doron '99, True Law of Free Monarchies 1603, Counterblast to Tobacco
'04, Works '16.

JAMES, G. P. R., 1799–1860. De l'Orme
1830, Henry Masterton '32, Collected
Novels '44–'49, Arabella Stuart '44.

JAMES, HENRY, 1843–1916. Roderick

Hudson 1876, The American '77,
Watch and Ward '78, Daisy Miller
'79, The Europeans '79, Madonna of
the Future '79, Hawthorne '79, Portrait of a Lady '81, Tales of Three
Cities '84, Bostonians '86, Princess
Casamassima '86, The Reverberator
'88, Partial Portraits '88, The Tragic
Muse '90, The Private Life '93, The
Reprobate '95, Embarrassments '96,
The Other House '96, What Maisie
Knew '97, Spoils of Poynton '97, In
the Cage '98, The Two Magics '98,
The Awkward Age '99, The Soft Side
1900, The Sacred Fount '01, Wings
of a Dove '02, Ambassadors '03, The
Better Sort '03, Golden Bowl '05,
The Finer Grain '10, Outcry '11, A
Small Boy and Others '13, Notes on
Novelists '14, Notes of a Son and
Brother '14, Letters '20.

JAMES, MONTAGUE RHODES, 1862– .
Ghost Stories of an Antiquary 1904,
More Ghost Stories of an Antiquary
'11, A Thin Ghost and Others '19.

JAMES, WILLIAM, 1842–1910. Principles of Psychology 1890, Will to
Believe '97, Talks on Psychology '99,
Varieties of Religious Experience 1902,
Pragmatism '07, Nature of Truth '09.

JAMESON, ANNA, 1794–1860. Diary of
an Ennuyée 1826, Characteristics of
Women '32, Sacred and Legendary
Art '48–'60.

JEFFERIES, RICHARD, 1848–87. Gamekeeper at Home 1878, Wood Music
'81, Bevis '82, Story of my Heart '83,
Life of the Fields '84, Amaryllis at
the Fair '87.

JEFFERSON, THOMAS, 1743–1826.
Rights of British America 1781, State
of Virginia '84–'85, Parliamentary
Practice 1801, Autobiography '29.

JEFFREY, FRANCIS, Lord Jeffrey, 1773–
1850. Contributions to Edinburgh
Review 1844, '53.

JEPHSON, ROBERT, 1736–1803. Braganza 1775, Count of Narbonne '81,
Julia '87.

JEROME, JEROME K., 1859–1927. Idle
Thoughts of an Idle Fellow 1889,
Three Men in a Boat '89, Passing of
the Third Floor Back 1907.

JERROLD, DOUGLAS, 1803–57. Blackeyed Susan 1829, Sally in our Alley
'30, Rent Day '32, Men of Character
'38, Punch's Letters to his Son '43,
Story of a Feather '44, Time Works
Wonders '45, Punch's Complete
Letter-writer '45, Mrs. Caudle's Curtain Lectures '46, Chronicles of

TAILOR, ROBERT. The Hogge hath lost his Pearl 1614.

Tait's Edinburgh Magazine started 1832.

TALFOURD, SIR THOMAS NOON, 1795–1854. Ion 1836, Letters and Life of Charles Lamb '37.

Taming of a Shrew 1594.

TANNAHILL, ROBERT, 1774–1810. Poems and Songs 1807, Collected Works '15.

TANNER, THOMAS, 1674–1735. Notitia Monastica 1695, Bibliotheca Britannico-Hibernica 1748.

TATE, NAHUM, 1652–1715. Poems 1677, Brutus of Alba '78, Loyal General 80, King Richard II '81, King Lear (adapt.) '81, Ingratitude of a Commonwealth '82, Duke and No Duke '85, Island Princess '87, New Version of Psalms (with Brady), '96, Panacea 1700.

TATHAM, JOHN, fl. 1632–64. Scots Figgaries 1652, The Rump '60.

TAVERNER, RICHARD, 1505?–75. Trs. Bible 1539, Garden of Wisdom '39, Proverbs and Adagies '39.

TAYLOR, BAYARD, 1825–78. Trans. Faust 1871.

TAYLOR, SIR HENRY, 1800–86. Isaac Comnenus 1827, Philip van Artevelde '34, Statesman '36, Edwin the Fair '42, Notes from Life '47, Eve of the Conquest '47, St. Clement's Eve '62.

TAYLOR, ISAAC, 1787–1865. Natural History of Enthusiasm 1829.

TAYLOR, JANE (1783–1824) and ANN. Original Poems 1804, Hymns for Infant Minds '10.

TAYLOR, JEREMY, 1613–1667. Sacred Order of Episcopacy 1642, Concerning Prayer '46, Liberty of Prophesying '47, Great Exemplar '49, Holy Living '50, Holy Dying '51, Of Baptism and of Prayer '53, Eniautos '53, Golden Grove '55, Discourse of Friendship '57, Polemical and Moral Discourse '57, Ductor Dubitantium '60, Worthy Communicant '60.

TAYLOR, JOHN, 1580–1653. All the Works of John Taylor the Water Poet 1630.

TAYLOR, MEADOWS, 1808–76. Confessions of a Thug 1839.

TAYLOR, TOM, 1817–80. Still Waters run Deep 1855, Lady Clancarty '74.

TAYLOR, WILLIAM, 1765–1836. Trs. Iphigenie auf Tauris 1794, Trs. Wieland's Dialogues of the Gods '95, Trs. Wieland's Fairy Tales '96, Trs.

Burger's Leonore '96, Tales of Yore 1810, Survey of German Poetry '28.

TEMPLE, SIR WILLIAM, 1628–99. United Provinces 1672, Miscellanea Pt. I '80, Pt. II '92, Introduction to History of England '95, Letters ed. Swift 1700, Miscellanea Pt. III ed. Swift '01, Memoirs ed. Swift '09, Memoirs, Correspondence &c. 1836.

Temple Shakespeare started 1894.

TENNANT, WILLIAM, 1784–1848. Anster Fair 1812, Cardinal Bethune '23.

TENNENT, SIR JAMES, 1804–1869. Natural History of Ceylon 1861.

TENNYSON, ALFRED, Lord Tennyson, 1809–92. Poems by Two Brothers 1827, Timbuctoo '29, Poems Chiefly Lyrical '30, Poems '32, Poems '42, Princess '47, In Memoriam '50, Ode on Death of Wellington '52, Charge of the Light Brigade '54, '55, Maud '55, Idylls of the Kings '59, Idylls of the Hearth '64, Holy Grail and other poems '69, Gareth and Lynette '72, Poems, first collected '72, Queen Mary '75, Harold '76, The Lover's Tale '79, Ballads and other Poems '80, The Cup ; The Falcon '84, Becket '84, Tiresias '85, Locksley Hall '86, Demeter '89, The Foresters '92, Death of Œnone '92, Memoir by Hallam Tennyson '97.

TENNYSON-TURNER, CHARLES, 1808–79. Poems by Two Brothers 1827, Collected Sonnets '80.

Terence's *Andria*, trans. 1520.

THACKERAY, WILLIAM MAKEPEACE, 1811–63. The Professor 1837, Yellowplush Papers '37, Major Gahagan '38, Catherine '39, Stubbs's Calendar '39, Bedford Row Conspiracy '40, Shabby Genteel Story '40, Paris Sketch Book '40, Essay on Cruikshank '40, Character Sketches '40, Samuel Titmarsh '41, Great Hoggarty Diamond '41, Second Funeral of Napoleon '41, Comic Tales and Sketches '41, Sultan Stork '42, Fitz-Boodle Papers '42, Irish Sketchbook '43, Men's Wives '43, Bluebeard's Ghost '43, Luck of Barry Lyndon '44, Next French Revolution '44, Legend of the Rhine '45, Diary of Jeames de la Pluche '45, Cornhill to Cairo '46, Book of Snobs '46, '48, Mrs. Perkins' Ball '46, Vanity Fair '47–'48, Punch's Prize Novelists '47, Pendennis '48–'50, Dr. Birch '49, Kickleburys on the Rhine '50, Rebecca and Rowena '50, History of Henry Esmond '52, English Humorists '53, The Newcomes '53–'55, The

PRINTED IN GREAT BRITAIN AT THE UNIVERSITY PRESS, OXFORD
BY JOHN JOHNSON, PRINTER TO THE UNIVERSITY

(86) $\dfrac{94 \quad\quad our}{46} \quad 40$